# THE YEAR OF OBAMA

## *How Barack Obama Won the White House*

Edited by

Larry J. Sabato
*University of Virginia Center for Politics*

**Longman**

New York   San Francisco   Boston
London   Toronto   Sydney   Tokyo   Singapore   Madrid
Mexico City   Munich   Paris   Cape Town   Hong Kong   Montreal

Editor-in-Chief: Eric Stano
Marketing Manager: Lindsey Prudhomme
Associate Development Editor: Donna Garnier
Project Coordination, Text Design, and Page Makeup: Grapevine Publishing
    Services, Inc.
Cover Designer: Base Art Company
Manufacturing Buyer: Roy Pickering
Printer and Binder: Courier-Westford
Cover Printer: Lehigh-Phoenix

*The Year of Obama: How Barack Obama Won the White House,* by Larry Sabato et al.

5 6 7 8 9 10–CW–12 11 10

**Longman**
is an imprint of

PEARSON

www.pearsonhighered.com

ISBN 10:     0-205-65044-9
ISBN 13: 978-0-205-65044-6

# TABLE OF CONTENTS

Preface: Larry Sabato ........................................................................................................v

Chapter One: Justin Sizemore ................................................................................1
Conventions: The Contemporary Significance of a
Great American Institution

Chapter Two: Larry Sabato ........................................................................................33
The Election of Our Lifetime

Chapter Three: Rhodes Cook ........................................................................................77
From Republican "Lock" to Republican "Lockout"?

Chapter Four: Alan Abramowitz ..................................................................................91
The 2008 Presidential Election: How Obama Won and What It Means

Chapter Five: Bruce Larson ........................................................................................115
The Congressional and Gubernatorial Contests

Chapter Six: Michael Toner ........................................................................................149
The Impact of Federal Election Laws on the 2008 Presidential Election

Chapter Seven: Diana Owen ........................................................................................167
Media in the 2008 Election: 21st Century Campaign, Same Old Story

Chapter Eight: Girish J. Gulati ..................................................................................187
No Laughing Matter: The Role of New Media in the 2008 Election

Chapter Nine: Michael Cornfield ................................................................................205
Game-Changers: New Technology and the 2008 Presidential Election

Chapter Ten: Alex Theodoridis ....................................................................................231
The Nominating Process in 2008: A Look Inside the Rube Goldberg.
Did the Rules Decide?

Conclusion: Susan MacManus ....................................................................................261
Presidential Election 2008: An Amazing Race, So What's Next?

# PREFACE

In 2008 Americans stunned the world—and themselves. Overcoming centuries of racial prejudice, they elected the first African American president.

Regardless of their ballot choice, few will ever forget where they were on the evening of November 4, 2008, when a young senator from Illinois mounted the outdoor stage in Chicago's Grant Park to accept the rare honor accorded him by tens of millions of his fellow citizens.

Something this significant doesn't just happen. A combination of political, social, and demographic trends produced the election of our lifetime. Now that Barack Obama has taken the oath of office and begun his governing journey, all of us need to fully understand the election that changed the face of the nation.

This book is a product of that necessity. Some of the most perceptive analysts and shrewdest observers of American politics have joined together to write a volume that tosses aside much of the accepted conventional wisdom about the 2008 campaign and instead offers interpretations that have been ignored in a rush to judgment. "Instant books" written by campaign aides and journalists—filled with backroom gossip from the candidates' war rooms—have their place. But more useful, we believe, is a study that goes deeper into the data.

In Chapter One, attorney and long-time political aficionado Justin Sizemore begins at the beginning, brilliantly reviewing the 2008 presidential primaries and caucuses in both parties that produced Barack Obama and John McCain. The Democratic match-up between Obama and Hillary Clinton was one of the closest ever, going right down to the wire in June. Sizemore shows us how Obama scored his narrow upset over the once-heavily favored front-runner. McCain's victory came about in a very different way, owing to the Republican Party's nominating rules and the need for the GOP to put as much distance as possible between it and the unpopular incumbent, President George W. Bush. You will see the nominating battles with fresh eyes after reading Sizemore's chapter.

From the preliminaries, we move directly into the autumn general election. This editor makes his contribution in an interpretation of the November results, focusing on raw votes, regional patterns, and exit poll data. In a "big" election such as 2008, voters pour much of themselves into their ballots. Sorting and scrubbing those votes yields a wealth of information about the how, and the why, of Obama's victory. If you enjoy peeling away the layers of the political onion, you will linger over the maps and the table of exit polling, which slice and dice the votes of 131 million Americans.

Next, Rhodes Cook, the able editor of the biennial compilation, *America Votes*, adds his discerning interpretations, concentrating on the decline of the once-dominant Republican Party. What was once a GOP "lock" in the Electoral College may be evolving into a Republican "lockout." Rhodes Cook dissects the trend, which is moving away from the GOP and towards the Democrats.

Professor of Political Science, Alan Abramowitz of Emory University, offers the third interpretation of the general election results. A prolific scholar whose early election forecast for the 2008 contest was exceedingly accurate, Abramowitz helps us to separate campaign myth from reality. The Obama-McCain race was never especially competitive from the summer onwards, nor was the key turning point the mid-September Wall Street meltdown. This conclusion may surprise you because other analysts have adopted a misleading mantra to explain 2008. Abramowitz debunks it.

A wonderful scholar of politics, Professor Bruce Larson of Gettysburg College, shifts our attention to a set of 2008 elections almost as significant as the presidential result. Democrats swept the contests for both houses of Congress, adding eight seats in the Senate and twenty-one seats in the House of Representatives. This was the second consecutive Democratic triumph for Congress, following the party's takeover of both houses in 2006. As Professor Larson demonstrates, the Democratic margins of 59-to-41 seats in the Senate and 257-to-178 in the House gives the Obama administration a considerable leg up in enacting its agenda.

No one in the nation better understands the complex campaign finance system than Michael E. Toner, the former chairman of the Federal Election Commission and the current head of the election law and government ethics group at Washington's Bryan Cave Law Firm. In his usual clear style, Toner takes readers through the maze of political money, demonstrating the highs and lows of our first billion-dollar presidential contest. "Follow the money" is still the best rule for students of politics.

In the next several chapters, we turn our attention to all forms of campaign media. Initially, one of the nation's premier scholars of the mass media, Professor Diana Owen of Georgetown University, gives a thoughtful overview of the media's role in the 2008 elections. While the media determine which issues and controversies are emphasized, it is vital to remember that media come in all shapes, sizes, and viewpoints. Professor Owen looks at the very different coverage generated by the traditional newspapers and television news divisions; the online news outlets; and the infotainment shows, such as the late-night comedians. Some observers offer glib generalizations about "the media" but in this chapter, readers will understand the distinctive parts of the whole.

Other forms of media communication have developed in recent years, and all were on display in 2008. Professor of political science Girish J. "Jeff" Gulati of Bentley University smartly takes readers on a tour of the individual campaign Web sites, the Facebook dimension of the election, and the explosive use of YouTube during both the primaries and the fall contest. These Web sites were the gateways for greater citizen participation in the just-completed election cycle. As Professor Gulati suggests, future campaigns for offices at all levels will be greatly influenced by the innovations we witnessed last year.

Another viewpoint on the "new media" topic is offered by Dr. Michael Cornfield, one of the pioneers in the field. Cornfield teaches at the Graduate School of Political Management, George Washington University, and he is also a vice president of 720 Strategies, a nonpartisan public persuasion firm. Dr. Cornfield describes the 'game-changing' impacts of how the Obama campaign used Web video, small donors, and social networks.

Following all the discussion about media, Alexander G. Theodoridis, a Ph.D. candidate in political science at the University of California-Berkeley, reminds us that the rules of the game are every bit as important as how the game is covered. Suppose the political parties had had different delegate allocation systems in the winter and spring of 2008. Would the results have been different, with Hillary Clinton defeating Barack Obama for the Democratic nomination? This is a field sometimes called "counterfactual history," and it postulates a parallel universe where the results in our real world are compared to what *might* have happened in another, slightly altered one. Theodoridis's speculation is rigorous and enjoyable, although he admits that new rules would have produced adaptive campaign strategies. We can never be certain of what would have transpired.

Our volume concludes with a thought-provoking chapter by political science professor Susan MacManus of the University of South Florida-Tampa. Professor MacManus traces the campaign from beginning to end to see where conventional wisdom was right, and where it was wrong. She identifies surprises aplenty at every stage. Her broad-gauged view of the historic election of 2008 reminds us of why we are fascinated by politics. What appears to be true one month is contradicted by a new reality the next. It will always be so.

Barack Obama's ascension to the presidency will be studied for centuries. Interpretations will evolve with time, as new facts emerge and more research is conducted. But this book will give you, the student and the citizen, a thorough, reflective read on the 2008 election—the "year of Obama."

LARRY J. SABATO
Director, Center for Politics
University of Virginia
January 2009

# ACKNOWLEDGMENTS

I was very fortunate to work with a superb team on this book. The assistants are all associated in some way with the University of Virginia's Center for Politics (www.centerforpolitics.org). The Center, celebrating its tenth year, exists to encourage civic participation and provide civic education across the United States. This volume is one fulfillment of those aims, as is its National Youth Leadership Initiative—which every two years conducts the country's largest Internet mock election among primary and secondary school students.

Book coordinator Daniel Keyserling organized and edited the authors' work with great care, keeping everyone focused on the deadline while insuring the high quality of the product. Research assistant Isaac Wood skillfully fact-checked and figure-designed his way through the volume. Other essential members of the Center staff performed tasks with their usual fine professionalism: Ken Stroupe, Michael Baudinet, and Mary Brown.

The outstanding contributors to this volume, highly respected in the field of politics, deserve much credit for the resulting book. But we should never forget that a good publisher, in this case Pearson Longman, pours itself into a book too. My able, longtime editor, Eric Stano, has come through again, and his cheerful assistant, Elizabeth Alimena, deserves thanks, too.

LARRY J. SABATO

# Chapter 1

# Political Conventions in 2008

## The Contemporary Significance of a Great American Institution

### Justin M. Sizemore[1]

**B**arack Obama officially secured the Democratic Party's nomination for president on Wednesday, August 27, 2008 when, in what the Democratic National Committee later proclaimed a "dramatic move,"[2] New York Senator Hillary Rodham Clinton, Obama's former rival, rose to interrupt the roll call of states and addressed the chair:

> With eyes firmly fixed on the future, in the spirit of unity, with the goal of victory, with faith in our party and country, let's declare together in one voice, right here and right now, that Barack Obama is our candidate and he will be our president . . . I move that Senator Barack Obama of Illinois be selected by this convention by acclamation as the nominee of the Democratic Party for president of the United States.

At the Republican National Convention a week later, Alabama, Alaska, and American Samoa began the GOP's alphabetical polling of delegations, and after Montana's delegates cast their ballots John McCain had accumulated 1,170 votes, just 21 short of the 1,191 needed to win. The chair then recognized Arizona (which had passed when called upon earlier) and the presumptive nominee's home state voted unanimously for its favorite son, providing McCain with the majority he needed to secure the nomination.

Despite the dramatic pretense, both moments were little more than political stagecraft, carefully choreographed for television audiences and reporters, and served only to validate results preordained months before.

The last year in which a convention took more than one ballot to settle on a nominee was 1952, and not since 1968 have the parties' quadrennial conclaves been truly deliberative. Conventions have evolved into made-for-television political advertisements designed to market the parties' brands and their nominees for popular consumption. In the modern era, primary voters and caucus participants nominate presidents and conventions have become coronation ceremonies.

That is not to say political conventions no longer matter. While the pageantry, oratory, and spectacle might be less consequential than the deliberative role conventions once performed, the parties and their nominees devote considerable attention (and money) to using their four days in the national spotlight to maximum advantage. Conventions are still milestones in any campaign, and they serve important functions such as cementing themes for the general election, introducing the vice-presidential nominee to the public, healing the wounds of bitter nomination battles, and showcasing party unity. Both the Democrats and Republicans did all those things in 2008, and their efforts illustrate better than any recent conventions the modern relevance of this grand tradition of American politics.

## DELIBERATIVE CONCLAVES OF THE PAST

For most of American history, elites have been responsible for choosing presidential nominees: The parties' congressional caucuses performed this function for the first decades of the Republic before nominating conventions appeared in 1832.[3] For the next 136 years, conventions were occasions for decision making, events whose results could not be guaranteed in advance and at which presidential aspirants courted party leaders to broker winning coalitions.

That process was not always easy: More than half the Democratic National Conventions held between 1832 and 1936 took two or more ballots to produce a nominee, and seven of them were decided after 10 or more ballots.[4] (The longest took place in 1924, when the Democrats nominated John W. Davis after 103 ballots held over the course of 17 days.) The GOP has seen fewer bitterly divided conventions in its history,[5] but like the Democratic Conventions, Republican Conventions of the past made decisions of consequence.

From the founding until the early 1970s, the process of nominating presidential candidates was an insiders' game dominated by players whose machinations took place largely outside public view.[6] In that environment, winning the support of party leaders was tantamount to securing the nomination: The nation's network of largely autonomous state-based party organizations collectively exercised monopoly control over candidate recruitment and the tools of electioneering. Prior to the advent of television and the concomitant proliferation of candidate-centered, media-driven direct primaries, the path to the White House wound its way through party organizations based in thousands of counties across the country, and led eventually to a quadrennial gathering where the leaders of those parties debated, compromised, and eventually decided on a nominee.

Participation in the pre-reform nominating process was limited to a class of citizens variously described as elites, party regulars,[7] or political professionals.[8] According to defenders of the pre-reform system, institutional loyalty and pragmatism distinguished party regulars from other citizens; the insiders, it is argued, were dedicated not only to certain policy positions, ideologies, or candidates, but to the long-term success of the party. Since party regulars took a longer view, they are thought to have been more likely to compromise with people who had opposing viewpoints. Party regulars were more likely to build coalitions, which "arise not out of the natural bedrock interests of people but rather out of their capacity to calculate their advantage over a protracted period, and their ability to see their best interests in light of the complexity of the political world in which they exist."[9]

At the national conventions, a relatively few party leaders controlled the decisions of a large proportion of the delegates in attendance.[10] In his seminal account of the 1960 presidential campaign, Theodore H. White described convention participants this way:

> A convention is usually made up of older, if not wiser, men than the common voters who send them there. In most states delegates are chosen by party leadership to honor long-time trusted servants of the party; or from men of eminence in culture, diplomacy or the professions, who can give the luster of their achievement and their names to the delegation; or, particularly in the organization-controlled states, very heavily from those who contribute the big money to campaign chests and now crave the honorable symbol of a national delegate badge and the sense of high participation. Most of those who come to a convention have thus earned, over many years of achievement or contribution at some level, the right to be considered important.[11]

In recent decades, the national parties (especially the Democrats) have begun exerting greater control over their state-level surrogates, but prior to the second half of the twentieth century, state party organizations were free to run their affairs as they saw fit. Prior to the early 1970s, most delegates to each party's national convention were chosen in caucuses held on the state and local levels throughout the country. The rules and customs of those gatherings varied from state to state and even from city to city, but in contrast to the open caucus process of the modern era—which one critic calls the "functional equivalent of a primary"[12]—only regular party members and elected officials participated in them.

In 1928, Democrat Franklin Delano Roosevelt was elected governor of New York while his immediate predecessor, Democrat Alfred E. Smith, lost his race for the presidency. Within weeks after the 1928 election, Roosevelt sent letters to more than 5,000 Democratic Party leaders across the country, the majority of them county chairmen.[13] Roosevelt was already considered a potential standard bearer for 1932, but he was careful not to express any interest in the nomination four years ahead of time; his stated purpose was to solicit grassroots opinion about how best to strengthen the party. Roosevelt pored over the thousands of responses sent back from the political trenches with a view to establishing himself as a party leader and (almost certainly) with thoughts of laying the groundwork for his own run at the nomination.[14]

Over the next four years, Roosevelt continued reaching out to Democratic leaders, asking for their advice and earning their allegiance. The 1932 convention featured long days of compromise and bargaining among those leaders, who finally nominated Roosevelt on the fourth ballot after he agreed to the nomination of conservative Texan John Nance Garner to be his vice president.[15] Winning the nomination had taken years of hard work and preparation, but Roosevelt secured it without competing in any of the few primaries that were then on the calendar.[16]

The direct primary is a uniquely American phenomenon: No other democracy permits broad swaths of the electorate to participate directly in a political party's nominating process.[17] Born out of the Progressive movement in response to real (as well as imagined) political corruption, the primary election was viewed as a much-needed check on the power of party organizations and as a means of expanding popular involvement in the nominating process. Of course, most of the people urging the adoption of primaries as an antidote for the excesses of politics were themselves politicians: Robert M. LaFollette became an early booster of the direct primary because he hoped it would help him displace the then-dominant faction of the Wisconsin Republican Party.[18] "The direct primary may take advantage and opportunity from one set of politicians and confer them upon another set," a contemporary of LaFollette's noted, "but politicians there will be so long as there is politics."[19]

By 1912, 12 states had instituted presidential primaries, and 20 had done so by 1920, a year that proved to be the pre-1972 high-water mark for direct primaries in presidential politics.[20] But those contests remained a relatively unimportant part of the process because they yielded so few delegates; winning primaries was neither necessary nor sufficient for earning either party's nomination until the 1970s. However, many candidates chose to contest primaries for reasons other than accumulating delegates: By doing well in a primary, a presidential hopeful could prove his electoral mettle to the party leaders who would ultimately control his fate.[21] (John F. Kennedy's victory in solidly Protestant West Virginia was a turning point in his race for the White House and helped him overcome the concerns many party leaders had about a Catholic's electability.)

## THE TRANSFORMATION

Between 1968 and 1976, the rules of the presidential nominating game underwent a period of transformation more significant than any of the previous century.[22] During those eight years, the Democratic Party initiated changes that eventually handed to voters the task of nominating both parties' presidential candidates, a role party regulars had played since the early nineteenth century. The end result was not the one the reformers had meant to create, and their efforts offer a fascinating case study in the law of unintended consequences. The Democratic Party hoped to accommodate existing structures to a society that was becoming more egalitarian, and to allow participation by groups that had been shut out for most of American history. Simply stated, the reformers wanted to ensure that "party regular" would no longer be synonymous with "white male." Despite their intentions, the reformers created a largely plebiscitary system in which primary voters have almost completely displaced party regulars, and in which national political conventions have lost their previous relevance.

The Democrats' disastrous 1968 convention and the traumatic events leading up to it, examined later in this chapter, were the most proximate cause of the subsequent period of change, but the seeds of it had been sown over the previous decades. Sweeping changes in American society after World War II strained the fragile coalition of white southerners, labor unions, and northern liberals that kept Democrats in the White House for two decades. In response, the national Democratic Party began exerting control over state parties that had traditionally been accorded near total autonomy.[23] In 1948 Harry Truman faced a bitterly divided convention after agreeing to place a civil rights plank in the Democratic platform, prompting several delegations to walk out in protest. In the subsequent general election, then-governor of South Carolina Strom Thurmond ran as a Dixiecrat and carried four southern states. In hopes of avoiding a similar schism in 1952, the Democratic Party required delegates to sign loyalty oaths promising to support the eventual nominee.

Not surprisingly, the civil rights movement of the 1960s brought the national Democratic Party into even sharper conflict with its conservative southern surrogates. African Americans accounted for 40 percent of Mississippi's population in 1964, but barely 5 percent of the state's registered voters.[24] In that year (like every year before it) black citizens were excluded from the Mississippi Democratic Party's process for selecting delegates to the national convention. During the spring and early summer of 1964, a coalition of civil rights groups established the Mississippi Freedom Democratic Party (MFDP), a political organization that conducted precinct caucuses and county conventions to choose a slate of delegates that would challenge the all-white Democratic regulars at the national convention.

The MFDP earned nationwide attention and significant support from liberal Democrats and labor leaders; it also threatened to create a display of disunity that incumbent President Lyndon Baines Johnson would have preferred to avoid.

The conflict had little to do with Mississippi: Regardless of how the Party dealt with the credentials challenge, President Johnson (who signed the Civil Rights Act just weeks before the '64 convention) was not likely to carry the Magnolia State in the general election.[25] Instead, party leaders wanted to avoid the spectacle of a floor fight and prevent other southern delegations from walking out.

Following hours of nationally televised hearings, the Credentials Committee crafted a compromise: The all-white regulars would be seated and the MFDP would be given two seats at-large. Neither Mississippi delegation accepted the offer (and both walked out, along with Alabama) but the Party had kept the matter from spilling out onto the convention floor. The Call for the 1968 Convention required each state party to "assure that voters in the state, regardless of race, color, creed or national origin, will have the opportunity to participate fully in Party affairs."[26] The Democrats also adopted a policy of imposing sanctions on states that violated the antidiscrimination policy.

Four years later, the Democratic Party faced divisions that proved much less amenable to quiet resolution. Nearly 10,000 American soldiers were killed in Vietnam during the first six months of 1968, and the growing unpopularity of the war—as well as unrest at home—threatened Lyndon Johnson's chances for reelection. Johnson won the New Hampshire primary with just under 50 percent of the vote, while antiwar challenger Eugene McCarthy garnered an impressive 42 percent. Even though Johnson had not actively campaigned in New Hampshire, the closeness of the result was seen as casting doubt on the incumbent president's chances in the fall, prompting Robert F. Kennedy to enter the race and Johnson to drop out.

After Johnson withdrew, Vice President Hubert Humphrey announced his candidacy for the nomination. Humphrey had more support among Democratic Party leaders than either Kennedy or McCarthy, but his position in the Johnson administration made him extremely unpopular with the antiwar activists who were beginning to demand more influence in Democratic nominating politics. Humphrey chose not to risk the embarrassment Johnson had suffered in New Hampshire and did not enter a single primary.

Hubert Humphrey became the Democratic Party's standard bearer in 1968, but at the price of having the most bitter and divisive nominating convention in living memory. Divisions over the war spilled out onto the streets of Chicago, where the police clashed with protesters; images of the chaos were beamed into millions of homes throughout the four-day conclave. Many of Eugene McCarthy's supporters focused their ire on the Party's delegate-selection rules, which they believed had unfairly shut them out of the process. In an attempt to appease dissidents and achieve some semblance of unity, the

Convention approved a minority report from the Rules Committee authorizing a commission to review the Party's nominating process.

The Commission on Party Structure and Delegate Selection to the Democratic National Committee (commonly known as the McGovern-Fraser Commission) issued its report, *Mandate for Reform*, in April 1970. With a goal of opening up the process, the Commission provided that "Party membership, and hence the opportunity to participate in the delegate-selection process, must be open to all persons who wish to be Democrats and who are not already members of another party." Among other procedural changes, recommendations adopted by the DNC required state parties to establish uniform, written delegate-selection plans to ensure that caucus meetings were open and accessible; abolished the unit rule (which enabled party leaders to bind the votes of entire delegations according to the majority's will); prohibited the automatic seating of elected officials as delegates; and forbade any state party from beginning the delegate selection process prior to the year of a nominating convention.[27] The Commission also recommended a policy of affirmative action to ensure "a full opportunity for all minority group members to participate in the delegate-selection process."[28] (In a footnote, the Commission emphasized its understanding that ". . . this is not to be accomplished by the mandatory imposition of quotas," but many critics of the requirement saw the new rules as doing precisely that.)

In 1976, the Democrats began requiring that delegates be "chosen in a manner which fairly reflects the division of preferences expressed by those who participate in the presidential nominating process in each state."[29] The most important implication of this new rule was that it mandated proportional representation, the requirement that a state allocate delegates among candidates in proportion to their performance in a primary or caucus. Winner-take-all primaries were prohibited,[30] and the Party mandated that candidates winning as little as 10 percent of the vote receive a share of delegates. (This threshold requirement has been adjusted periodically since then and currently stands at 15 percent.) The Democrats also added a localism requirement: The bulk of a state's delegates had to be allocated proportionally at the congressional-district level.

The Democrats also enacted a provision giving candidates the right to approve their delegates, a rule which—coupled with the fair reflection requirement—ensured the convention's demise as the determinative stage of the nomination process. State party leaders once had the power to control delegations—a practice known as slate-making—but the new rules brought the practice back by giving presidential *candidates* the right of delegate approval. This rule was meant to ensure that delegates who were apportioned on the basis of primary and caucus results actually voted for the candidate to whom they were allotted.

## THE RISE OF DIRECT PRIMARIES AND PROPORTIONAL REPRESENTATION

In little more than a decade, the Democrats' reforms had fundamentally altered the way American parties nominate their presidents. The convention was no longer a bastion of white male rule: Young people, African Americans, and other minority groups were now guaranteed a place at the table. The discriminatory policies that the Mississippi Freedom Democratic Party had formed to fight were gone forever. The liberal antiwar wing of the Party, over whose vociferous objections Hubert Humphrey had won the 1968 nomination, prevailed just four years later with the nomination of George McGovern (who lost to Richard Nixon in a historic landslide). The fair reflection and localism requirements ensured the representation of minority viewpoints: Any candidate who earned enough support to cross the viability threshold (which now stands at 15 percent) in any congressional district's primary or caucuses would earn some delegates. And thanks to the regulations providing for candidate slate-making, presidential aspirants could be sure that delegates pledged to them would support them at the convention.

Yet the new system had its flaws and attracted a legion of critics both within the Democratic Party and without. Reformers had hoped state parties would react to the new rules by adopting an open "town hall" variety of the caucus-convention system.[31] As one member of the McGovern-Fraser Commission observed:

> I well remember that the first thing we . . . agreed on—and about the only matter on which we approached unanimity—was that we did not want . . . any great increase in the number of state primaries. Indeed, we hoped to prevent any such development by reforming the delegate-selection rules so that the party's nonprimary processes would be open and fair . . . and consequently the demand for more primaries would fade away.[32]

Despite the reformers' intentions, their actions led almost immediately to the rapid (and seemingly irreversible) proliferation of presidential-preference primaries. Instead of adopting a complicated and unfamiliar mode of decision making to accommodate the new rules, most state parties chose to insulate their other functions from delegate selection and adopted primaries for that purpose.[33] In 1968—the last election of the pre-reform era—nine states held primaries, and the majority of those contests were advisory (meaning that delegates were not pledged to cast their votes according to the election's results). By 2008, delegates in 35 states were allocated among candidates according to the results of primaries.

Party leaders of virtually every ideological stripe were unhappy with the expanded use of primaries, particularly those in which voters other than registered party members are allowed to participate (so-called open primaries). The Democratic Party instituted a ban on the seating of delegates selected in open primaries, and in 1981 the Supreme Court affirmed the right of national parties to select delegates as they see fit, notwithstanding any requirement in state law to the contrary.[34] Despite having the constitutional right to trump state law, the parties have been reluctant to exercise that authority for practical political reasons. Excluding a state's delegates because that state's legislature passed laws contravening party policy can create ill will and discord (as Democrats were reminded in 2008 when they stripped Michigan and Florida of their delegates for violating party rules). The "nuclear option" of denying credentials is one of the few arrows in the national parties' quivers, and the direct-primary wave has simply overwhelmed their will to use it.

Governing a democracy as large and diverse as the United States is a constant exercise in coalition-building and compromise, and the framers built an electoral system that forces candidates to garner majoritarian support. The Electoral College (and the longstanding custom of awarding electoral votes on a winner-take-all basis) rewards candidates who build broad coalitions, and it punishes those who can only mobilize factions with narrow appeal. The outcomes never please everybody, but the system almost always produces a result that is at least acceptable to a majority of Americans.

Because a successful presidential candidate has to prevail in the Electoral College, both modern parties continue requiring nominees to earn a majority of convention delegates. But the pre-reform system for nominating presidents— despite its many serious flaws—included incentives for coalition-building that its modern counterpart lacks. Candidates who could reconcile opposing viewpoints and garner the support of a majority were usually the ones who won the nomination; those with narrow appeal simply could not compete. Proportional representation allows candidates with limited appeal to compete by mobilizing small segments of the electorate, and the bargaining and compromise that were essential to conventions past are simply not possible in modern primaries.

In a primary, rivals for the same party's nomination must fight to differentiate themselves from one another, even if they have few meaningful policy differences (as is usually the case).[35] Intra-party squabbles tend to focus on matters of character and personality, and they encourage the public to perceive more conflict within the party than actually exists.[36] It is not uncommon for three or more candidates to compete in a primary, and as the field becomes more crowded, the size of the plurality needed for victory gets smaller, permitting a winner to emerge with an ever narrower slice of the electorate. The Democrats' proportional rules exacerbate this problem by award-ing delegates to candidates who garner just 15 percent in any district, making it difficult for any candidate to win a majority. As a consequence, the primary season lasts longer and is less likely to end in a decisive victory.

## SUPERDELEGATES

In addition to creating the potential for factionalism and gridlock, the post-1968 reforms virtually eliminated the previously paramount role of party lead-ers and elected officials. By the end of the 1970s, there was widespread concern among Democratic leaders that removing public officials from the process had deprived the party of a meaningful way of conducting peer review.[37] Given the lack of policy distinctions between members of the same political party, fellow elected officials might be better than voters at assessing qualities like electability and temperament. Moreover, politicians—unlike issue activists—are accountable to a constituency and must answer to voters.

After losing the 1980 election to Ronald Reagan, the Democratic Party cre-ated yet another commission—this one headed by former North Carolina Governor James Hunt—to study the possibility of creating a new role for elites at the convention. In order to ensure the involvement of political leaders at future conventions, the Hunt Commission recommended creating a new class of dele-gates.[38] These automatic delegates (popularly known as superdelegates) were guar-anteed slots at the convention, and unlike other delegates, who are pledged to specific candidates according to the results of primaries and caucuses, they would be free to back the candidate of their choice. "We fully expected them to use their discretion," remembered Commission Chairman Hunt. "There was never any intention of making them . . . automatically follow the results in their states."[39]

The Hunt Commission initially recommended that superdelegates make up 30 percent of the 1984 Democratic National Convention, a number that was later reduced to 14 percent in a final compromise.[40] Automatic slots were set aside at the '84 Convention for 60 percent of the Democratic membership of the House and Senate and for each state's Democratic Party chair and vice chair.[41] Two hun-dred fifty additional slots were set aside for mayors and other party leaders who would be selected by their respective state committees.[42] The composition of the superdelegate contingency has changed over the years, but in 2008 there were 852 of them, accounting for 20 percent of the national convention. Under the 2008 rules, the following people were entitled to serve as superdelegates:

- All members of the Democratic National Committee
- The sitting Democratic president and vice president (if any)
- All Democratic members of the House and Senate

- All current Democratic governors
- All former Democratic presidents and vice presidents; former leaders of the Senate; former Speakers, majority leaders, and minority leaders of the House; and former chairs of the Democratic National Committee
- Add-on superdelegates (selected by state parties)

In addition to superdelegates, the Democratic Party reserved 456 delegate slots for *pledged* party leaders and elected officials (PLEOs) who do not qualify to serve as superdelegates. Pledged PLEOs are just that: They must commit to a candidate (who has the right to approve them) and they must be allocated according to the results of the primary or caucuses in their state.

While superdelegates have been the subject of debate in Democratic Party circles since they were first created, very few members of the general public had heard of them prior to 2008. But that race for the Democratic nomination was the closest in modern history, and for the first time, the "independent judgment" of superdelegates determined the nominee.

## THE REPUBLICANS AND REFORM

While the Democratic Party has continually adjusted its delegate-selection rules since 1968, the GOP has enacted fewer and less drastic changes; Republican reform efforts have focused primarily on reacting to near-constant Democratic tinkering.[43] The most important spillover effect was the proliferation of primaries; those contests are creatures of state law, and when legislatures instituted them in response to the post-1968 Democratic reforms, GOP practices were modified as well.[44]

Prior to the social upheavals of the mid-twentieth century, the Republicans asserted more national-party authority over their state organs than the Democrats did.[45] But compared to the Democrats' current system, the GOP's delegate-selection process remains remarkably decentralized, and state Republican parties retain latitude in crafting their own rules. Respect for federalism is a key element of the conservative creed, so it should come as no great surprise that the GOP gives its state-level organizations so much autonomy. But in addition to ideology, recent American history helps explain the difference: The Democrats undertook their most prolific period of reform in response to deep ideological schisms (over civil rights and the Vietnam War) that the Republicans did not experience.[46] And not coincidentally, the major commissions were formed in the wake of electoral defeat for the Democrats; since Republican candidates won seven of the ten presidential elections before 2008, the GOP could claim with some justification that its system did not need to be "fixed."

The GOP has adopted its own version of several Democratic reforms, including a prohibition on discrimination (although the GOP has not adopted the strict affirmative action requirements that are anathema to most conservatives).[47] In 1976, supporters of incumbent President Gerald Ford secured a rules change providing that votes would be recorded automatically according to the results of primaries and caucuses, although that requirement was removed four years later. Both parties had once allocated delegates among the states based strictly upon their relative strength in the Electoral College, but after 1968 the Democrats began rewarding states that backed Democratic candidates with more delegates. The GOP instituted a similar bonus system in the 1970s.[48]

## DELEGATION ALLOCATION IN 2008

On the surface, the Democrats and Republicans appear to allocate delegates in a similar manner; as Table 1 shows, both parties currently apportion the lion's share of delegates among congressional districts.

**Table 1. Delegate Allocation, 2008.**

| Type | Republicans | | Democrats | |
|---|---|---|---|---|
| Congressional district | 1,305 | 54.8% | 2,331 | 52.8% |
| At-large (includes bonus delegates) | 907 | 38.1% | 779 | 17.6% |
| Pledged party leaders | n/a | n/a | 456 | 10.3% |
| Unpledged party leaders | 168 | 7.1% | 852 | 19.3% |
| Total | 2,380 | | 4,418 | |

But there are important differences: The GOP apportions three delegates to every congressional district, while the Democrats award each between three and nine, giving more to Democratic-leaning districts and fewer to those that favor Republicans.[49] GOP rules permit all manner of winner-take-all contests; delegates apportioned by the national party to congressional districts can be allocated among candidates however individual state parties see fit. With the exception of superdelegates, Democratic Party rules require all delegates to be allocated proportionally.

Superdelegates accounted for 19.3 percent of the 2008 Democratic Convention, while the Republicans reserved fewer convention slots for unpledged party leaders (just 7.1 percent of the total). However, the GOP does not require states to pledge delegates according to the results of primaries and caucuses, and many states elect not to. There were 360 technically unpledged delegates in addition to the 168 party leaders at the 2008 Republican Convention, meaning that Republican Convention rules permitted 22.2 percent of its delegates to vote however they wished.

Primaries have come to dominate both parties' nominating process, but Democrats and Republicans translate popular support into convention delegates in strikingly different ways. Under the Democratic Party's rules, all delegates chosen through primaries and caucuses must be allocated proportionally, most of them on the congressional-district level. The Republicans' decentralized process gives state parties wide latitude in choosing how to allocate their delegates, and as Table 2 shows, the GOP system is remarkably diverse.

**Table 2. Republican Delegate-Selection Summary**

| Method (states) | Delegates | | Congressional District Delegates (three per district) | At-Large and Bonus Delegates |
|---|---|---|---|---|
| Winner-take-all by district and statewide (9) | 556 | 23% | Candidate with the most votes in a district wins all three delegates. | Candidate with the most votes statewide wins all at-large and bonus delegates. |
| Majority-vote, winner-take-all by district and statewide (2) | 189 | 8% | Candidate who wins more than 50% in a district wins all three delegates; otherwise, candidate with most votes gets two and runner-up gets one. | Candidate who wins more than 50% statewide gets all at-large delegates; otherwise, delegates allocated proportionally. |
| Winner-take-all by district/caucus-convention (2) | 81 | 3% | Candidate with the most votes in a district wins all three delegates. | At-large and bonus delegates selected through local caucuses and county and state conventions; delegates are generally not bound to any candidate. |

**Table 2 continued**

| | | | | |
|---|---|---|---|---|
| Majority-vote winner-take-all by district/ caucus-convention (2) | 79 | 3% | Candidate who wins more than 50% in a district wins all three delegates; otherwise, candidate with most votes gets two and runner-up gets one. | At-large and bonus delegates selected through local caucuses and county and state conventions; delegates are generally not bound to any candidate. |
| Winner-take-all by district/ majority-vote winner-take-all | 36 | 2% | Candidates with the most votes in a district wins all three delegates. | Candidate who wins more than 50% statewide gets all at-large delegates; otherwise, delegates allocated proportionally. |
| Winner-take-all primary (11) | 424 | 18% | Candidate with the most votes statewide wins all delegates. | |
| Proportional primary (9) | 291 | 12% | All delegates allocated proportionally according to statewide primary results. (Thresholds vary by state.) | |
| Loophole primary (2) | 131 | 5% | Voters elect convention delegates directly; results of presidential-preference primary do not bind or select delegates. | |
| Advisory primary (2) | 55 | 2% | State convention selects all delegates and is not bound by results of presidential-preference primary. | |
| Caucus-convention (17) | 324 | 14% | All delegates are selected through local caucuses and county and state conventions; delegates are generally not bound. | |
| Party leaders (all states) | 168 | 7% | Each state's national committeeman, national committeewoman, and party chair serve as unpledged delegates by right. | |

*Table compiled from data available at TheGreenPapers.com.*

Most GOP contests incorporate some winner-take-all elements, allowing a candidate who consistently comes in first to run up a substantial delegate advantage over his opponents. In the 2008 California primary (which awarded delegates on a winner-take-all basis by congressional district and statewide), John McCain beat his closest opponent, Mitt Romney, by just under 12 percentage points, but the eventual nominee earned 90 percent of that state's 173 delegates. In most caucus states (and a few primary states), Republican delegates are officially "unbound," whereas the Democrats' rules require that delegates chosen in all primaries and caucuses be committed to candidates according to the results.

## PUTTING SUPERDELEGATES TO THE TEST

Superdelegates first took part in the nomination of a presidential candidate in 1984. In that year, only 60 percent of Democratic members of Congress were permitted to serve as superdelegates; the House Democratic Caucus met before the first primary to select the 164 members who would attend the convention.[50] Not surprisingly, most of the members selected chose to back institutional favorite Walter Mondale, a former senator, vice president, and clear front-runner for the nomination. "We had the first primary and won it," remembered Mondale aide Tad Devine.[51] Mondale's opponent, Gary Hart (then U.S. Senator from Colorado), finished the season strong in June and although the former vice president had a decisive lead in pledged delegates, he had to corral superdelegates to his side in order to achieve an absolute majority prior to the convention. The party leaders rallied around Mondale and put him over the top.

The race for the presidential nomination in 2008 was the closest in modern history and featured two popular, well-financed candidates who fought the primary season nearly to a draw. With more money and name recognition than any Democrat in the field, Hillary Clinton was an early favorite to win the nomination. And like Mondale in 1984, Clinton had an early advantage in superdelegates: 223 had endorsed the New York Senator by January 1, while just 122 had declared support for Barack Obama.[52]

Hillary Clinton's campaign had been planning to overwhelm her rivals and force them from the race on Super Tuesday, February 5, when 22 states held primaries and caucuses.[53] A lopsided victory on that day would have been nearly impossible to overcome, but on the morning of Wednesday, February 6, the race for the Democratic nomination was virtually tied. With more than half the pledged delegates spoken for, Barack Obama led Hillary Clinton by about 30. After Super Tuesday, it was clear that superdelegates were going to decide the nomination: Neither candidate would be able to amass enough pledged delegates to reach a majority. Barack Obama and Hillary Clinton continued to campaign hard for the next three and a half months, but the campaign entered a new phase in which winning over elites would be more important than persuading voters.

The Obama campaign expected to widen its lead with a string of victories during the week after Super Tuesday and believed its advantage in pledged delegates—though modest—would hold up through the spring. In mid-February, Obama aides predicted that they would end the season with a pledged-delegate lead of about 100, less than 2.5 percent of the convention.[54] The Democratic Party's rules do not bestow any special advantage on a candidate who wins a majority of pledged delegates, or a plurality of all delegates. Winning the nomination requires a majority of *all* delegates. And unlike delegates chosen in primaries and caucuses, superdelegates can change their minds at any time and for any reason (or for no reason at all) right up until they vote. But on Friday, February 8—just three days after Super Tuesday— Obama began laying out the themes of his campaign's pitch to superdelegates:

> My strong belief is that if we end up with the most states and the most pledged delegates from the most voters in the country, that it would be problematic for the political insiders to overturn the judgment of the voters . . . I think it is also important for superdelegates to think about who will be in the strongest position to defeat John McCain in November and who will be in the strongest position to ensure that we are broadening the base, bringing people who historically have not gotten involved in politics into the fold.[55]

Obama's central argument was rooted in the fact that after four decades of ever-expanding public participation in primaries and caucuses, Americans have come to view presidential nominations as plebiscites. According to this understanding, delegates are not free agents who bargain, compromise, and make decisions; they are instead mere proxies for voters, just another way of tallying election results.

The Clinton campaign countered—correctly—that unpledged party leaders and elected officials were meant to exercise their "independent judgment," not rubber-stamp the results of primaries and caucuses. After all, there would be little point in having superdelegates if they simply ratified the results of primaries. Clinton's principal counter-argument centered on electability: Citing exit poll data from the primaries, Clinton aides pointed out that the New York senator was doing much better than her rival in rural areas and among women, seniors, Latinos, and blue-collar whites.[56] The campaign also argued that Clinton had won more votes than Obama, although this required counting the results of primaries held in two states whose delegations had been stripped for violating party rules: Florida (in which neither candidate campaigned) and Michigan (in which Obama did not appear on the ballot).

Lying just beneath the surface of both arguments was the uncomfortable matter of race. Barack Obama was the first African American candidate with a realistic shot at winning the White House, and black voters were supporting him by a margin of more than nine to one. In his first public statement on superdelegates, Obama alluded to the prospect of party elites denying the nomination to the candidate who attracted the support of "people who historically have not gotten involved in politics." That working-class white voters had not warmed to Obama was the centerpiece of Clinton's electability argument, but her campaign had to be extremely careful not to suggest that Obama's skin color was a general-election liability.

Stuck in the middle were the superdelegates, whom both campaigns courted intensively. "This is the most stressful thing I've been through in my whole life," said Jennifer L. McClellan of Virginia, a superdelegate who endorsed Clinton early on but wound up changing her allegiance to Barack Obama. "It was never supposed to be like this."[57] In addition to the candidates' arguments and personal appeals, superdelegates had to weigh their own self-interests. Members of Congress whose districts voted overwhelmingly for one of the contenders would be hard pressed to throw their weight behind the other. "They won't want to jeopardize their local political support," Representative Artur Davis, an Obama backer, said of colleagues facing this dilemma.[58] Many unaffiliated superdelegates spent the spring hoping they would not be forced to make a decision.

As the season progressed, Barack Obama began closing the two-to-one lead in superdelegate endorsements that Clinton had enjoyed at the beginning of the year. Undecided party leaders did not break for Obama en masse until the tail end of the primary season, but the Illinois senator made steady progress throughout the spring. By April 22, the day of the Pennsylvania primary, Obama had 237 superdelegate endorsements, just 37 shy of Hillary Clinton's 274. By the second week of May, Obama had completely erased Clinton's onetime superdelegate firewall. In the last weeks of the season, most of the undecided (or undeclared, more likely) were from states Barack Obama had either won or was expected to win, and few observers could imagine them breaking decisively for Hillary Clinton unless Obama's candidacy imploded.

The Obama campaign hoped to secure enough superdelegate endorsements by the end of the primary season to claim a majority. Of course, from the perspective of the rules, it made no difference, but claiming victory on a night when votes were being counted would help avoid the perception that Obama owed his nomination to a backroom deal. Thanks to a carefully choreographed rollout of endorsements, Obama earned enough delegates on the last day of voting to claim the mantle of presumptive nominee.

On the night Barack Obama all but declared victory, Hillary Clinton declined to concede. After being introduced as the "next president of the United States," Clinton insisted she would be making no decisions that night. Prominent superdelegates—particularly congressional leaders—were becoming impatient. John McCain had secured the Republican nomination months before, and Democratic Party leaders felt that extending the fight would hurt the eventual nominee's chances in November. The next day, DNC Chairman Howard Dean, House Speaker Nancy Pelosi, and Senate Majority Leader Harry Reid issued a joint statement urging undecided superdelegates to make their decision by the end of the week.[59] "The voters have spoken," said the Democratic leaders, who stopped short of endorsing Obama.

The nominating season ended in a virtual tie, but Barack Obama maintained his slim pledged-delegate lead. In the end, superdelegates wound up ratifying the results of primaries and caucuses; conventional wisdom seemed to hold that overturning the "popular will" was unthinkable. Which begs the question: Why bother having superdelegates? Although unpledged delegates refused to reverse the voters in 2008, they might well have done so under different circumstances. Hillary Clinton's electability argument was far from ironclad—her high unfavorable ratings had always been a concern, and many superdelegates believed that Obama would be the stronger nominee. If Clinton had clearly been the more electable candidate, then the result might have been different.

Even if superdelegates do not perform meaningful peer review, 2008 showed an alternative justification for keeping them: Avoiding the gridlock that proportional representation would otherwise create. The Republican nominating process has the beauty of being decisive. With so many winner-take-all contests, the GOP calendar turns relatively narrow popular-vote margins into overwhelming delegate leads. But as 2008 illustrated, two viable, well-financed candidates can fight the Democratic nominating season to a draw. Without superdelegates, the fight could have carried on into the summer or even into the convention. The Clinton camp had been threatening to take the dispute over Florida and Michigan to the floor of the convention, and if the candidates had been separated by just a few dozen delegates, that might have happened. The Democratic Party is unlikely to eliminate the fair-reflection rule or proportional allocation any time soon, and as long as the system has such potential to create gridlock, the party needs a way to break it.

## THE FUNCTION OF MODERN CONVENTIONS

While political conventions are no longer deliberative bodies, they have taken on even greater significance as public spectacles.[60] In the modern era, they are ideal platforms from which to launch a fall campaign, and the parties use their quadrennial gatherings for four important objectives: to celebrate past glories; heal the wounds of a divisive primary season and achieve party unity (or at least showcase it for television audiences); introduce the vice-presidential nominee; and cement themes for the fall campaign.

## THE DEMOCRATIC NATIONAL CONVENTION: HISTORY IN DENVER

In the pre-reform era, a nomination fight as closely contested as the Democrats' in 2008 would have been resolved on the convention floor. But by the time delegates arrived in Denver for the 2008 Democratic National Convention, the outcome of that gathering was a foregone conclusion. After months of careful planning, Barack Obama would use the next four days of nationally televised pageantry to put his best foot forward in the general election.

### *Reintroducing the Nominee and Celebrating the Party's Past*

The son of a black student from Kenya and a white woman from Kansas, Barack Obama had grown up in Hawaii and Indonesia, had a foreign-sounding name, and had been falsely rumored to be a Muslim. On the first night of the Democratic National Convention, Obama's wife Michelle presented her husband's story as quintessentially American. A President Obama, she told the delegates, would govern by "bringing us together and reminding us how much we share and how alike we really are . . . He knows that thread that connects us . . . is strong enough to hold us together as one nation even when we disagree."

Every political convention pays homage to its heroes, and the Democrats' in 2008 was no exception. At the end of January, when Barack Obama's eventual nomination was still far from certain, Senator Edward Kennedy had endorsed the Illinois senator.[61] Kennedy is the patriarch of one of America's most revered political dynasties, and his endorsement was widely seen as a boost for Obama's campaign. Later in the spring, Kennedy was diagnosed with brain cancer but told friends he was determined to speak at "Obama's convention." The Senator suffered a debilitating bout of kidney stones shortly before the convention, but was taken from a hospital bed in Denver to give a ten-minute speech (half the length of an earlier draft).

### *Party Unity: Healing Wounds After a Long Battle*

A political party that goes into a fall campaign divided often does not fare well, as most Democrats are well aware. Both 1968 and 1972 featured bruising nomination fights and bitter conventions, and both ended in Democratic defeat. In 1980, Senator Ted Kennedy challenged incumbent President Jimmy Carter for renomination, and took his fight all the way to the convention. Carter won renomination, but not reelection.

## The Democrats in Denver: Themes and Featured Speakers

**Monday, August 25: Party Unity and Nostalgia Night**
Caroline Bouvier Kennedy, Author and Daughter of John F. Kennedy
Edward M. Kennedy, Senior U.S. Senator, Massachusetts
Michelle Obama, Attorney and Wife of Barack Obama
Nancy Pelosi, California, Speaker of the U.S. House of Representatives, Convention Chair

**Tuesday, August 26: Domestic Policy Night**
Hillary Rodham Clinton, U.S. Senator, New York, Candidate for the 2008 Nomination
Mark Warner, Keynote Speaker, former Virginia Governor and Senate Candidate

**Wednesday, August 27: Foreign Policy / National Security Night**
Joe Biden, U.S. Senator, Delaware and Vice-Presidential Nominee
Bill Clinton, former Arkansas Governor, former U.S. President.

**Thursday, August 28: Change, change, change.**
Al Gore, former Vice President
Barack Obama, U.S. Senator, Illinois, 2008 Democratic Nominee

The 2008 battle for the Democratic nomination was the longest, closest, and most expensive in American history. Hillary Clinton fought hard until the last primary, and many of her supporters were angry over the outcome. Democratic leaders were eager to end the fighting in June and nudge Clinton out of the race, but they recognized the need to heal the wounds in advance of the fall campaign. While intraparty reconciliation was an important goal for the Democrats, the dire comparisons to infamously divided conventions of the past overlooked several critical differences between 2008 and those years. In both 1968 and 1980, Democrats were facing a general election with an unpopular member of their own party occupying the White House. And in both of those years, they were internally divided over matters of substantive policy.

The 2008 general election presented the Democrats with the most favorable electoral environment they had seen since the 1930s. The Party's base was more energized than it had been in a generation, and the slowing economy, George W. Bush's record unpopularity, and widespread frustration over the Iraq War made the 2008 election the Democrats' to lose.

Hillary Clinton had fought valiantly; as the first woman to mount a serious run for a major party's nomination, she had won 18 million votes and had come as close to the nomination as any unsuccessful candidate in modern history. Clinton had said her supporters needed "catharsis" at the Convention in order to be enthusiastic for the fall.[62] In addition to granting Clinton a primetime speaking slot on the second night of the convention (and her husband, former President Bill Clinton one on the third night) the Obama camp agreed to have Hillary Clinton's name formally entered into nomination, giving her supporters the chance to vote for her during the roll call of states. Both Clintons offered impassioned endorsements of Obama, providing a poignant bookend for the historic battle.

### Introducing Joe Biden

In 2004, few people outside Chicago had ever heard of Barack Obama, then a state legislator who had been tapped to offer the keynote address at that year's convention. With not quite four years in the United States Senate under his belt, Obama had a thinner résumé than Hillary Clinton or John McCain. Obama's lack of experience was seen as his greatest potential vulnerability in a general-election matchup: Polls consistently showed the public believed the Arizona senator was more experienced than his rival.

Joe Biden was first elected to the Senate in 1973, when he was 29 years old and Barack Obama was 11. During a long, distinguished career, Biden had served as chairman of the powerful Judiciary and Foreign Relations committees. Obama selected Biden for some of the same reasons George W. Bush tapped Dick Cheney to be his vice president: Both were seasoned Washington hands whose experience would lend gravitas to the ticket. In July, John McCain had launched an effective advertising campaign that depicted Obama as a vacuous celebrity; one television spot juxtaposed images of Paris Hilton and Britney Spears with footage of the Illinois senator being greeted by 200,000 adoring Berliners. The tagline: "Not Ready to Lead." Over the summer, it appeared to most observers—including those inside the Obama campaign—that the general election would offer voters a choice of change versus experience in much the same way the primary season had.

The Obama campaign decided that the vice-presidential nominee should bring an experienced, reassuring presence to the ticket, but Joe Biden's inside-the-beltway image had its downsides. Picking such an experienced running mate could highlight Obama's comparative lack of experience, and running with the consummate insider could undercut Obama's credibility as an agent of change.[63] The convention was the Obama campaign's chance to introduce Biden to the country on its own terms. The convention emphasized Biden's everyman background instead of his Washington, D.C. résumé. Viewers learned about his working-class Catholic roots in Scranton, Pennsylvania, and his experience as a single father after the tragic loss of his wife and daughter in a car accident. In order to depict Biden as someone who had been "in Washington but not of Washington," Americans were reminded several times that Biden rarely stays the night in the capital, opting instead to take the train home to Wilmington.

### Cementing Themes for the Fall: the Acceptance Speech

Barack Obama accepted the Democratic Party's nomination for president on the final night of the convention, Thursday, August 28, 45 years to the day after Martin Luther King delivered his historic "I Have a Dream" speech on the steps of the Lincoln Memorial. The significance of the timing was lost on no one, particularly the five delegates who attended both the 1963 March on Washington and Obama's acceptance speech.[64]

In early July—before Obama's trip to Europe and the rollout of the GOP's "celebrity" ads—the Democrats had decided to move the last night of the convention to Invesco Field (formerly known as Mile High Stadium), where Obama would accept the nomination before a crowd of 75,000 people. During the summer, the celebrity attacks seemed to be working: Obama's position in the polls was less favorable than many observers thought it should have been, and some Democrats were uneasy about putting on what might look like a grandiose spectacle. Pictures emerged of the stage's design, which featured federal-style columns, and the McCain campaign quickly dubbed the set "the Temple of Obama."[65]

Publicly, aides dismissed the criticisms: "I know that Senator McCain and his people are shooting barbs on the opulence of our convention from the mountaintop in Sedona from the McCain estate," quipped Obama strategist David Axelrod. "I don't think it warrants a response."[66] But behind the scenes, convention planners worked hard to make sure the multi-million dollar event looked more "intimate" on television than a typical political rally. And when Obama made his guest appearance at the convention on Wednesday night, he explained the move as one that would ". . . open up this convention" and "make sure that everybody that wants to come can join in the party and join in the effort to take America back."

Barack Obama's 42-minute speech at Invesco Field gave the nominee his best chance to lay out the central theme of the fall campaign: change. "America, we are better than these last eight years," Obama said. "We are a better country than this." Obama laid the blame for the nation's problems on "a broken politics in Washington and the failed policies of George W. Bush." Citing John McCain's service to his country, Obama reminded the audience that "we owe him our gratitude and our respect." Obama spent the greater part of his speech tying McCain to the Bush administration, and attacking the Arizona Senator for being out of touch. "It's not because John McCain doesn't care, it's because John McCain doesn't get it."

For exactly one week, Obama's acceptance had the distinction of being the most watched in American history: 28.9 percent of American households tuned in, and 29 percent watched John McCain accept his party's nod one week later.

## THE REPUBLICANS' UNCONVENTIONAL CONVENTION

While Barack Obama was delivering his acceptance speech in Denver, Hurricane Gustav was moving toward the Gulf of Mexico. The storm was projected to make landfall somewhere on the Gulf Coast on Monday, September 1, the opening day of the 2008 Republican National Convention. The federal government's response to Hurricane Katrina in 2005 was one of the low points of George W. Bush's presidency, and another Gulf storm was an unwelcome reminder. "The Republicans can't seem to get a break when it comes to August and when it comes to the weather," observed Bush strategist Karl Rove.

But the theme of the GOP Convention was "country first," and the storm gave John McCain an opportunity to portray himself as a different kind of politician. McCain flew to Mississippi to assist with relief efforts over the weekend, and Monday's festivities were scaled back. The major speeches that had been planned for that night were either scrubbed or postponed. Instead, Gulf State governors addressed the delegates by teleconference, updating them on government responses to the storm, while Cindy McCain and Laura Bush took the stage to urge viewers to contribute to relief efforts. "Gustav is making this a very different, even unique, convention," remarked one GOP official. "It calls for something appropriate in this situation."[67]

Gustav wound up causing little damage, and its impact on the Convention was soon forgotten. But the Republicans still had to contend with the gathering political storm of 2008. George W. Bush had record-low approval ratings and 80 percent of Americans believed the country was on the wrong track. One Republican said of his party's brand in 2008, "If we were a dog food, they would take us off the shelf."[68] The Democrats were more enthusiastic than they had been in decades, and Barack Obama's decision to opt out of public financing meant McCain would almost certainly be outspent. The maverick streak that had endeared John McCain to independents earned him the ire of most Evangelicals (whose leaders McCain had once called "agents of intolerance"). The Republican base was more dispirited than it had been in any recent election; polls consistently showed that fewer McCain voters were enthusiastic about their choice than Obama voters were.

Like Hurricane Gustav, the uniquely challenging political environment of 2008 required a different kind of convention.

### The Palin Bombshell

In picking his vice-presidential nominee, John McCain had to consider two conflicting goals: He needed to reach beyond the shrinking GOP base while managing to hold the allegiance of conservative Republicans.[69] McCain was leaning toward Joe Lieberman, the Democrat-turned-independent from Connecticut who was the Democratic vice-presidential nominee in 2000.[70] Social conservatives were already suspicious of McCain, and Republicans advised the presumptive nominee that picking Lieberman (or any other pro-choice running mate) would provoke a floor fight.[71] Late summer speculation centered on two popular GOP governors: Tim Pawlenty of Minnesota and Mitt Romney of Massachusetts. Sarah Palin of Alaska did not appear on any political observer's shortlist, and every indication is that she was not under serious consideration until late in the summer.[72] From a branding standpoint, McCain's advisors did not see either Romney or Pawlenty bringing much to the ticket.[73]

In Palin, the McCain camp saw the possibility of accomplishing both of their seemingly irreconcilable goals: A committed pro-life mother of five children (the youngest with Down Syndrome) would delight social conservatives, while her record as a reformer in notoriously corrupt Alaska would attract independents. And she is a woman—electing the first female vice president would let Republican voters make history, and her presence on the ticket might help McCain win over former supporters of Hillary Clinton who would otherwise vote Democratic. Picking someone so unexpected would make news: Announcing Palin would allow John McCain to reclaim control of the news cycle.

But Palin had obvious risks, her lack of experience being the most serious. She had been governor of Alaska for less than two years and before that served as mayor of Wasilla, population 9,800. Over the summer of 2008, the campaign felt it was making inroads by portraying McCain as a tested leader and Barack Obama as the "biggest celebrity in the world" who was "not ready to lead." That argument would be tougher to make credibly if the same could be said of McCain's running mate. And regardless of Palin's qualifications to serve as vice president, there was the nearer term question of whether she was ready to run for national office. Whatever Palin's accomplishments in Juneau, Alaska, she had never been subjected to the media scrutiny of a national campaign. Even if Palin performed brilliantly, she might draw so much attention that she could overshadow McCain.

On the morning after Barack Obama accepted the Democratic nomination, John McCain flew to Dayton, Ohio where he introduced Sarah Palin to a stunned political world. "She's not from these parts, and she's not from Washington," McCain told the cheering crowd, "but when you get to know her, you're going to be as impressed as I am."[74] In Palin's first appearance on the national stage, she praised the candidacy of Hillary Clinton, adding:

"Hillary left 18 million cracks in the highest, hardest glass ceiling in America, but it turns out the women of America aren't finished yet, and we can shatter that glass ceiling once and for all."[75]

Sarah Palin was a little-known quantity when John McCain selected her, which was both a blessing and a curse for the Republicans. The convention gave the GOP a chance to ensure that the American public's first impression of their vice-presidential nominee would be a favorable one. Unfortunately, Palin's personal life—and her family's—became fodder for the media from the moment McCain selected her. On the opening day of the convention, the McCain campaign issued a statement confirming that Palin's 17-year-old daughter was five months pregnant and that she and her child's father were to be married. GOP delegates warmly embraced the extended Palin clan, but the news about Palin's daughter was an unneeded distraction during what was planned to be a carefully choreographed rollout.

### Country First

The second night of the convention was dedicated to highlighting John McCain's courage and service, and the star attraction of the evening was Democrat-turned-independent Joe Lieberman, McCain's close Senate friend and supporter who was risking the wrath of his own party to back McCain's candidacy. Lieberman touted his friend's bipartisan instincts, a message intended to go over better with television viewers than with delegates, who gave Lieberman a polite but unenthusiastic reception. President George W. Bush—whose scheduled appearance on Monday night had been scuttled by Gustav—appeared via satellite, making Bush the first sitting president not to attend his own party's convention since Lyndon Johnson skipped the Democrats' Chicago gathering in 1968.[76]

---

**The Republicans in St. Paul: Themes and Featured Speakers**

**Monday, September 1: Service**
Laura Bush, First Lady of the United States
Cindy McCain, Wife of Senator and Presidential Nominee John McCain
Gulf State Republican Governors Charlie Crist (Fla.), Bob Riley (Ala.), Haley Barbour (Miss.), Bobby Jindal (La.) and Rick Perry (TX) via satellite

**Tuesday, September 2: Reform**
George W. Bush, President of the United States
Joe Lieberman, Independent Democrat, Connecticut
Fred Thompson, former Senator, Tennessee
Norm Coleman, U.S. Senator, Minnesota
John Boehner, House Minority Leader, Ohio

---

**Wednesday, September 3: Prosperity**
Rudy Giuliani, former Mayor of New York
Sarah Palin, Governor of Alaska and Nominee for Vice President
Mike Huckabee, former Governor of Arkansas.
Mitt Romney, former Governor of Massachusetts
Meg Whitman, former President and CEO of eBay
Carly Fiorina, former Chairman and CEO of Hewlett-Packard
Bobby Jindal, Governor of Louisiana

**Thursday, September 4: Peace**
Tim Pawlenty, Governor of Minnesota
Charlie Crist, Governor of Florida
Sam Brownback, U.S. Senator, Kansas
Lindsey Graham, U.S. Senator, South Carolina
Tom Ridge, former Governor of Pennsylvania
John McCain, U.S. Senator, Arizona and Republican Nominee

---

Wednesday night's theme was "Washington is broken and the original Maverick will fix it." The evening was notable for the fact that not a single speaker uttered the name of the Republican Party's current president.[77] It was also a night for red meat—former New York Mayor Rudy Giuliani told his audience that "the choice in this election comes down to substance over style," between "a man who has dedicated his life to the service of his country" and another who "has never led anything. Nothing. Nada."

The headliner, though, was Sarah Palin. Her selection had energized social conservatives and she was met with roaring approval from the delegates. "I'm not a member of the permanent political establishment," Palin confessed:

> And I've learned quickly, these past few days, that if you're not a member in good standing of the Washington elite, then some in the media consider a candidate unqualified for that reason alone. But here's a little news flash for all those reporters and commentators: I'm not going to Washington to seek their good opinion; I'm going to Washington to serve the people of this country.

As is customarily expected of vice-presidential candidates, Palin delivered some well placed jabs at the Democratic ticket, explaining to delegates that a "small-town mayor is sort of like a 'community organizer,' except that you have actual responsibilities." While the speech was undoubtedly meant to thrill the base—and it did—it also gave Palin the chance to lay out her reformer credentials. Since Palin had become governor of Alaska by beating a scandal-plagued incumbent of her own party, Republicans hoped her reformer image would have appeal beyond the GOP base.

John McCain accepted his party's nomination on Thursday, September 4, the final night of the convention. Emphasizing country first, the Republican nominee urged his party and the nation to move beyond partisan rancor and narrow self interest. The conciliatory tone represented a marked departure from speeches offered the previous evening and, for that matter, from Barack Obama's acceptance address, in which the Democratic nominee leveled some blistering attacks at McCain.

McCain set out to seize the "change" theme and make it his own, arguing that he and fellow maverick Sarah Palin could shake up Washington and achieve results. The most poignant moments were McCain's reflections on the meaning of the time he spent as a prisoner of war:

> I fell in love with my country when I was a prisoner in someone else's. I loved it not just for the many comforts of life here. I loved it for its decency; for its faith in the wisdom, justice and goodness of its people. I loved it because it was not just a place, but an idea, a cause worth fighting for. I was never the same again. I wasn't my own man anymore. I was my country's.
>
> I'm not running for president because I think I'm blessed with such personal greatness that history has anointed me to save our country in its hour of need. My country saved me. My country saved me, and I cannot forget it. And I will fight for her for as long as I draw breath, so help me God.

## DID THE CONVENTIONS MATTER?

In 2008, the race for the Democratic nomination was closer and more competitive than the Republican contest, but ironically, the Democrats had the less interesting of the two parties' conventions. In the pre-reform era, a vigorously contested nomination battle would have been resolved at the convention, but in 2008, party rules all but ensure that nomination fights are settled well ahead of time. The Democrats' 2008 contest illustrated the potential of that party's system to produce hopeless gridlock: Proportional rules make it difficult for any candidate to accumulate a decisive majority. If the Democratic field had been more crowded, the task of assembling a majority of delegates would have become even more difficult. In 2008, superdelegates broke the tie and wound up saving the Democrats from what otherwise could have been a deadlocked convention.

Modern political conventions are marketing events aimed at the November electorate, and in 2008 both parties tried to gain maximum advantage from their gatherings. The Democrats' was the more typical of the two: Barack Obama worked toward intraparty unity, introduced his vice-presidential nominee, and drove home a general election theme—change—that his campaign had been developing for months.

John McCain, on the other hand, tried to use the Republican Convention to reboot his campaign and fundamentally change its direction. After months of attacking Obama for his thin résumé, the McCain campaign used the convention to shift the debate and compete with Obama for the mantle of "change" candidate.

As we now know, John McCain's gambit did not work. Sarah Palin had limited appeal beyond the Republican base, and her lack of experience proved to be a serious liability. More fundamentally, the party in power found it difficult to run on a "change" platform. John McCain faced a perfect storm—an electoral environment so daunting that even a perfectly choreographed, brilliantly executed convention probably could not have changed the result.

## NOTES

[1] The author wishes to thank Dr. Larry Sabato for his encouragement, mentorship, and editorial advice; Daniel Keyserling of the Center for Politics for his professionalism and assistance throughout the writing and editing of this chapter; and Bill and Mary K. Sizemore, who taught the author to love writing and whose constructive criticism the author could not do without.

[2] "2008 Democratic National Convention Roll Call Results," Democratic National Committee Press Release, September 2, 2008, available at http://www.demconvention.com/roll-call-results/.

[3] Rhodes Cook, *The Presidential Nominating Process: A Place for Us?* (Lanham: Rowman & Littlefield, 2004), p. 15.

[4] Ibid., p. 16.

[5] Since its founding, the GOP has nominated candidates based on a simple majority vote of convention delegates. But until 1936, a two-thirds majority was required to secure the Democratic Party's nomination. See Rhodes Cook, *The Presidential Nominating Process: A Place for Us?* (Lanham: Rowman & Littlefield, 2004), p. 16.

[6] Elaine Ciulla Kamarck and Kenneth M. Goldstein, "The Rules Do Matter: Post-Reform Presidential Nominating Politics," in L. Sandy Maisel, ed., *The Parties Respond* (Boulder, Colo.: Westview, 1994), p. 170.

[7] Austin Ranney, "Changing the Rules of the Nominating Game," in James D. Barber, ed., *Choosing the President* (Englewood Cliffs, N.J.: Prentice Hall, 1974), p. 73.

[8] James Ceaser, *Presidential Selection* (Princeton, N.J.: Princeton University Press, 1979), p. 266.

[9] Nelson Polsby, *Consequences of Party Reform* (New York: Oxford University Press, 1983), p. 65.

[10] Nelson W. Polsby, "Decision-Making at the National Conventions," *Western Political Quarterly* 13 (Sept. 1960), p. 612.

[11] Theodore H. White, *The Making of the President 1960* (New York: Antheum, 1961), p. 154.

[12] Kamarck and Goldstein, "The Rules Do Matter: Post-Reform Presidential Nominating Politics," p. 174.

[13] Earland I. Carlson, "Franklin D. Roosevelt's Post-Mortem of the 1928 Election," *Midwest Journal of Political Science* 8 (Aug. 1964), p. 301.

[14] Earland I. Carlson, "Franklin D. Roosevelt's Post-Mortem of the 1928 Election," p. 301.

[15] Gerald M. Pomper, "The Decline of the Party in American Elections," *Political Science Quarterly* 92 (Spring 1977), pp. 24–25.

[16] Rhodes Cook, *The Presidential Nominating Process: A Place for Us*, p. 29.

[17] Ibid., p. 115.

[18]David B. Truman, "Party Reform, Party Atrophy, and Constitutional Change: Some Reflections," *Political Science Quarterly* 99 (Winter, 1984–1985), p. 648.

[19]Quoted in Truman, "Party Reform, Party Atrophy, and Constitutional Change," p. 648.

[20]Rhodes Cook, *The Presidential Nominating Process*, p. 49.

[21]See Polsby, *Consequences of Party Reform*, pp. 11–15.

[22]Ranney, "Changing the Rules of the Nominating Game," p. 73.

[23]Jeffrey S. Walz and John Comer, "State Responses to National Democratic Party Reform," *Political Research Quarterly* 52 (March 1999), p. 192.

[24]Frank R. Parker, *Black Votes Count* (Chapel Hill: University of North Carolina Press,1990), p. 31.

[25]Gerald Pomper, "The Nomination of Hubert Humphrey for Vice-President," *Journal of Politics* 28 (Aug. 1966), p. 653.

[26]Judith A. Center, "1972 Democratic Convention Reforms and Party Democracy," *Political Science Quarterly* 89, no. 2 (June 1974), p. 327.

[27]Cook, *The Presidential Nominating Process: A Place for Us*, p. 44.

[28]Commission on Party Structure and Delegate Selection, George S. McGovern, Chair, *Mandate For Reform* (Washington, DC: Democratic National Committee, 1970), p. 34.

[29]See Also Democratic National Committee, Commission on Delegate Selection and Party Structure, *Democrats All* (Washington, 1973).

[30]Prior to 1992, the Democratic Party allowed primaries in which delegates (rather than candidates) appeared on the ballot. Since they tended to produce results similar to winner-take-all contests, they were dubbed "loophole primaries" by their critics and have since been prohibited. See David E. Price, *Bringing Back the Parties* (Washington, DC: CQ Press, 1984), p. 151.

[31]Cook, *The Presidential Nominating Process*, p. 44.

[32]Ranney, "Changing the Rules of the Nominating System," p. 73.

[33]Ibid., p. 87.

[34]*Democratic Party v. Wisconsin ex rel. La Follette*, 450 U.S. 107 (1981).

[35]Polsby, *Consequences of Party Reform*, pp. 148–149.

[36]Martin P. Wattenberg, "Participants in the Nominating Process: The Role of the Parties," in George Grassmuck, ed., *Before Nomination: Our Primary Problems* (Washington, DC: American Enterprise Institute,1985), p. 53.

[37]See David E. Price, *Bringing Back the Parties* (Washington, DC: CQ Press,1984), pp. 201–205.

[38]Ibid.

[39]David Nather, "Leaping Voters in a Single Bound," *CQ Weekly* (February 25, 2008), pp. 482–484.

[40]Ibid., p. 483.

[41]James A. Barnes and Peter H. Stone, "The Art of Wooing," *National Journal* 40, no. 8 (Feb. 22, 2008), p. 12.

[42]Ibid.

[43]See Robert J. Huckshorn and John F. Bilby, "National Party Rules and Delegate Selection in the Republican Party," *PS* 16, no. 4 (Autumn 1983), pp. 656–666.

[44]Polsby, *Consequences of Party Reform*, p. 54.

[45]Price, *Bringing Back the Parties*, p. 156.

[46]Cornelius P. Cotter and John F. Bibby, "Institutional Development of Parties and the Thesis of Party Decline," *Political Science Quarterly* 95, no. 1 (Spring 1980), p. 17.

[47]Price, *Bringing Back the Parties*, pp. 156–57.

[48]Ibid., p. 158.

[49]DNC Delegate Selection Rule 8(a).

[50]James A. Barnes et al., "The Art of Wooing," p. 12.

[51]Ibid.

[52]Data on superdelegate endorsements were compiled by the author from several sources, including thegreenpapers.com and demconwatch.blogspot.com.

[53]Clinton campaign memorandum from Harold Ickes, dated March 29, 2007, available at http://www.theatlantic.com/a/green-ickes-3-29-07.mhtml.

[54]Adam Nagourney, "Obama's Lead in Delegates Shifts Focus of Campaign," *New York Times*, February 14, 2008, p. A1.

[55]Adam Nagourney and Carl Huse, "Neck and Neck, Democrats Woo Superdelegates," *New York Times*, February 10, 2008, p. A1.

[56]Clinton campaign memorandum from Mark Penn, dated June 3, 2008, available at http://www.theatlantic.com/a/green-final-pitch-6-3-08.mhtml.

[57]Tim Craig, John Wagner, and Nikita Stewart, "In D.C. Area, a Superdelegate Tug of War," *Washington Post*, May 3, 2008, p. A1.

[58]James A. Barnes et al., "The Art of Wooing," p. 12.

[59]Adam Nagourney and Jeff Zeleny, "Clinton Ready to End Bid and Endorse Obama," *New York Times*, June 5, 2008, p. A1.

[60]See Byron E. Shafer, *Bifurcated Politics* (Cambridge, Mass.: Harvard University Press, 1988).

[61]Jeff Zeleny and Carl Huse, "Kennedy Chooses Obama, Spurning Plea by Clintons," *New York Times*, January 28, 2008, p. A1.

[62]Peter Nicholas, "Clinton to Get Moment in the Convention Sun," *Los Angeles Times*, August 15, 2008, p. A1.

[63]See Dan Fournier, "Analysis: Biden Pick Shows Lack of Confidence," Associated Press, August 23, 2008, available at http://www.breitbart.com/print.php?id=D92NQMA00&show_article=

[64]Michael Powell, "Witnesses to Dream Speech See a New Hope," *New York Times*, August 27, 2008.

[65]Jim Rutenberg and Jeff Zeleny, "Democrats Try to Minimize Stadium's Political Risks," *New York Times*, August 29, 2008, p. A1.

[66]Ibid.

[67]Dan Balz, "The Hurricane In Question Is Still Called Katrina," *Washington Post*, September 1, 2008, p. A1.

[68]Peter Baker, "Tom Davis Gives Up," *New York Times Magazine*, October 3, 2008.

[69]David Frum, "A Shrewd Pick, but a Responsible One?" *National Post*, August 30, 2008.

[70]Jane Mayer, "The Insiders: How John McCain Came to Pick Sarah Palin," *New Yorker*, October 27, 2008.

[71]Ibid.

[72]Ibid.

[73]Robert Draper, "The Making (and Remaking) of John McCain," *New York Times Magazine*, October 26, 2008.

[74]Michael Cooper and Elisabeth Bumiller, "Alaskan Is McCain's Choice; First Woman on G.O.P. Ticket," *New York Times*, August 29, 2008, p. A1.

[75]Ibid.

[76]Cheryl Gay Stolberg, "Bush and Lieberman Hail McCain as a Leader," *New York Times*, September 3, 2008, p. A1.

[77]Elisabeth Bumiller and Michael Cooper, "Palin Assails Critics and Electrifies Party," *New York Times*, September 4, 2008, p. A1.

# Chapter 2

# The Election of our Lifetime

## Larry J. Sabato

Political experts and journalists remember the details of every election. It is our game of Trivial Pursuit. Only a few elections remain fixed in the public imagination over time, however. There is simply no question that 2008 will be one of those. Americans surprised themselves by electing an African American president. They also seriously considered women candidates for national office in both parties. The economic crisis and international dramas playing out in the forefront of the election year were equally unforgettable.

The marathon election of 2008—one of the nation's longest from candidacy announcements to general Election Day[1]—is imprinted on the minds of most voters. Arguably, the 2008 presidential contest became the most watched around the world in many decades. Certainly, this analyst has never before witnessed the intensity of interest from journalists in almost every country. E-mails from everyday people, requesting information and offering opinions, poured in from every corner of the globe to shops like mine, specializing in American politics.

Centuries from now, books will still be written about the 2008 extravaganza. Yet already, the outlines of Barack Obama's stunning ascension to power are clear. In this chapter we will examine the demographics and essentials of Obama's triumph.

## THE BIG PICTURE PAINTED BY THE VOTERS

We are so inundated by public opinion polls prior to Election Day, and exit polls taken at the balloting locations on Election Day itself, that we can easily forget a cardinal rule of politics: Only real votes cast by real people actually matter. In a presidential contest, of course, those real votes by real people make a difference *state by state, not nationally.* The Electoral College is built on the constitutional principle of federalism—that states are the fundamental building blocks of national politics. Thus, there are 51 separate contests for president, in the 50 states plus the District of Columbia, with electoral votes assigned based on the number of members of the House of Representatives allotted to each state, and two additional electoral votes for the two United States senators given each state. The District of Columbia gets three electoral votes under a formula contained in the Twenty-Third Amendment to the U.S. Constitution, ratified in 1961. The overall popular vote in the country as a whole, while a curiosity, does not matter a whit in the actual election of the president and vice president. As a consequence, the national popular vote winners in 1824, 1876, 1888, and 2000 (in order, Andrew Jackson, Samuel Tilden, Grover Cleveland, and Al Gore, all Democrats) were denied the White House in those years.

This is an indirect system of democracy, by which qualified voters in each state choose among slates of electors pledged to the presidential nominees of major and minor presidential tickets. The electors of the winning party in each state meet in the state capital in early December to cast their ballots for the party's candidates for president and vice president. These electoral tallies are then forwarded to Congress, and read aloud in the U.S. Senate chamber in early January by the presiding officer (usually the incumbent vice president).[2]

Indirect or not, the popular will prevails in most cases. A handful of electors in American history have disregarded the vote of the people of their states and cast blank ballots or voted for someone else; they have been termed "faithless electors." There was none of this in 2008, a testament perhaps to the care with which the political parties now choose their electors in each state. A faithless elector in the extremely close election of 2000—a Gore delegate from the District of Columbia who cast a blank ballot—reminded everyone of the central importance of electors.[3]

Take a close look at the state-by-state vote tallies in Table 1, and the resulting electoral map in Figure 1. This macroscopic view of the election— both popular votes and electoral votes—can give us the broad picture of the

**Figure 1. Electoral College Results 2004**

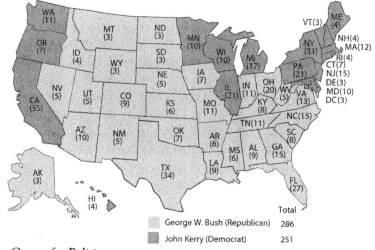

Source: Center for Politics

2008 election. The electoral map from the 2004 presidential election between incumbent George W. Bush (R) and challenger John F. Kerry (D) is also presented in Figure 2 for comparative purposes. Let's think about the numbers and maps in some detail.

**Figure 2. Electoral College Results 2008**

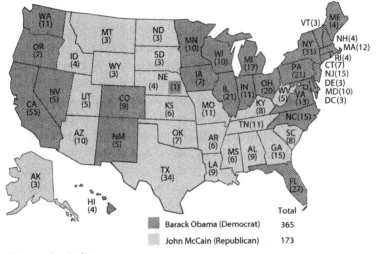

Source: Center for Politics

*Obama and the Electoral Map:* Democrats managed a remarkable transformation in the 2004 Republican Red versus Democratic Blue electoral map. Barack Obama won nine states captured by George Bush in 2004: Colorado, Florida, Indiana, Iowa, Nevada, New Mexico, North Carolina, Ohio, and Virginia. Bush was victorious in 31 states worth 286 electoral votes in 2004. Obama won just 28 states but many were grand prizes in the Electoral College, and he vastly outstripped what Bush had amassed in the Electoral College. Fully 365 electoral votes fell into Obama's column, including an unusual electoral vote from Nebraska's Second Congressional District (Omaha). Nebraska and Maine are the only states to split their electoral votes, one per congressional district with the two senatorial electoral votes going to the statewide popular vote winner. Obama won all of Maine's electoral votes, and John McCain won all of Nebraska's electoral votes, save the one. Never before had either Maine or Nebraska split its Electoral College tally.[4]

Obama kept every single one of the nineteen states won by John Kerry in 2004. Some of Obama's additional states were unsurprising, such as Iowa and New Mexico, both of which had voted for Democrat Al Gore in 2000. Others were hard won but might be expected to vote Democratic in a good year for the party such as 2008. Ohio would be in this category. After all, Ohio was closely divided in 2004, and a swing of just 60,000 votes from Bush to Kerry would have given Kerry both the Buckeye State and the presidency. Colorado and Nevada had been fairly reliably Republican, though not by landslide margins in recent elections. In 2000, Florida had proven how competitive it could be, and as a national microcosm in some ways, Obama's triumph was not stunning. On the other hand, Bush had carried the Sunshine State comfortably in 2004.

The real shockers were two Southern and one Midwestern state. North Carolina had last voted for a Democrat in 1976 (southerner Jimmy Carter), while Indiana and Virginia had stayed consistently Republican in presidential elections since Democrat Lyndon Johnson's landslide sweep in 1964. Indiana's difficult economic times clearly helped Obama, as did its next-door neighbor status to Obama's Illinois. Indiana voters were more familiar with Obama than most, due to the reach of Chicago television. As for Virginia, demographic transformation of its northern region (one-third of the statewide vote) and the Hampton Roads area (another 20 percent) had changed the Old Dominion from the northernmost Southern state into the southernmost Northern state—or at least, a Mid-Atlantic state. Transplants and diverse racial minorities shared little of the native conservatism of the traditional Richmond and rural areas. Obama was the new arrivals' cup of tea, and the once reliably red state has become permanently competitive—if not Democratic blue, then a bright purple.

Notice especially that Obama managed to win some states in every region of the nation, which offered him the electoral beginnings of a true national coalition. Whereas Al Gore and John Kerry had been mainly restricted to the deeply blue Northeast, some of the industrial Midwest, and the West Coast, Obama captured three interior West states and three large Southern states, in addition to expanding the Democratic reach in the industrial heartland.

*McCain's Limited Electoral Draw:* The South remains the Republican Party's modern base, and any Republican who cannot hold all of the South (such as Gerald Ford in 1976, George H.W. Bush in 1992, and Bob Dole in 1996) is very likely to lose. John McCain's failure to retain Florida, North Carolina, and Virginia guaranteed his defeat, even if he had done reasonably well in the other regions. McCain's campaign was especially disappointed that the Arizonan was unable to build a bulwark in his own region, losing three of Arizona's neighbors, Colorado, New Mexico, and Nevada. Had McCain not been from Arizona, it is entirely possible that Obama could have carried it, too, given the growing power of the Hispanic vote there. Obama will almost certainly target Arizona heavily in his expected reelection campaign in 2012. Bill Clinton narrowly won Arizona in 1992, the first Democrat to do so since Harry Truman in 1948, but independent Ross Perot's drain on Bob Dole's GOP voters explained Clinton's plurality win of 46.9 percent to 44.1 percent for Dole. But the Arizona of 2012 will look very different from the state of 1996.

By the way, McCain's 173 electoral vote total was only marginally better than Bob Dole's 159 votes in 1996. These two GOP candidates were similar in some ways—both war heroes in their seventies who appeared to echo old coalitions and ideas not in sync with the demands of the election year.[5]

*The Popular Vote:* As noted earlier, the popular vote—the accumulation of all votes cast by Americans in the 50 states plus D.C.—has no legal meaning. But symbolically, the total can be a powerful component of a new president's mandate. Every president wants a mandate; in effect, an order from the people to back the new chief executive and his programs, but only presidents who have won comfortable majorities actually get one. For a nonincumbent, Barack Obama fared quite well in the popular vote.

Obama secured the largest majority for a modern Democratic nominee (52.9 percent) except for Lyndon Johnson in 1964 (61.1 percent). Obama's proportion easily bested Harry Truman's 49.5 percent in 1948, John F. Kennedy's 49.7 percent in 1960, Jimmy Carter's 50.2 percent in 1976, and Bill Clinton's 43.0 percent in 1992 and 49.2 percent in 1996. Obama also exceeded the percentages won by nonincumbent Republicans Richard Nixon in 1968 (43.4 percent), Ronald Reagan in 1980 (51.0 percent), and George W. Bush in 2000 (47.9 percent). At the same time, Obama did not equal the percentages of two other non-incumbents—Dwight Eisenhower's 55.1 percent in 1952 or George H. W. Bush's 53.4 percent in 1988. Yet Obama's 52.9 percent appeared especially impressive because he exceeded George W. Bush's *reelection* edge in 2004 (50.7 percent) by a wide margin. Obama also achieved a large enough popular vote majority to reach the "tipping point" in many close states such as North Carolina and Florida, thereby adding to his imposing Electoral College total.

The final national totals gave Obama 69,459,909 votes to John McCain's 59,930,608, for an eye-popping Obama plurality of 9,529,301. McCain secured 45.7 percent of the total vote, with 1.4 percent garnered by independents and third-party candidates. Independent Ralph Nader headed the list with 737,505 votes (0.6 percent) and Libertarian Bob Barr was second, attracting 523,432 votes (0.4 percent).

This spread of over seven points between Obama and McCain erased any doubts about the sweep of the Democrat's triumph. Republicans noted that, given President Bush's unpopularity, the economic debacle, and the Iraq

War's bitter aftertaste, it was a miracle that McCain fared as well as he did. Other observers insisted this argument was a stretch. Since the Civil War, precisely two Democrats (Franklin D. Roosevelt and Lyndon B. Johnson) enjoyed landslide victories. The other six Democrats (Grover Cleveland, Woodrow Wilson, Truman, Kennedy, Carter, and Clinton) won with less than 51 percent in each of their successful elections.[6] Remarkably, then, Barack Obama ranks *third* among Democrats in the last century and a half in the size of his popular-vote victory, trailing only FDR and LBJ. Counting all 38 presidential elections since 1860, Obama secured the sixth highest proportion for a Democratic nominee, after FDR's four wins and LBJ's one.

*Voter Turnout:* The participation rate of voters was up in 2008, but not as much as most observers had expected it to be. About 61.6 percent of the 213 million Americans aged 18 and over cast early ballots or showed up at the polls on Election Day, just fractionally more than the 60.1 percent that voted in 2004.[7] The 131,235,440 voters in 2008 represented about a 7 percent increase from 2004, or a gain of about 9 million votes. This surge is less impressive when compared to the previous presidential cycle. The voter participation boost from 2000 to 2004 was even larger, up 16 percent and 17 million votes. It may be that we have reached the upper end of "normal" voter participation—about the same rates as in the three elections of the 1960s—after a long period of apathy and lower turnout from 1972 to 2000. (See Figure 3: Voter Turnout, 1960–2008.)

**Figure 3. Voter Turnout, 1960–2008**

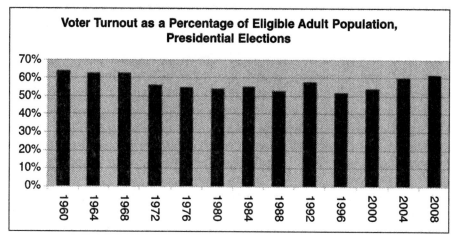

Source: Michael McDonald, George Mason University

Given the extraordinary excitement experienced in 2008 and the tapping of new technologies and techniques of contacting voters (such as text messaging, social networking Web sites, and so on), one might have expected a larger turnout.

Could it be that fears of long lines at the polls—widely discussed in the media leading up to Election Day—kept some voters home? Perhaps it will be far more difficult to motivate the remaining nonvoters even in stellar years, especially the young (where the absolute number of voters grew substantially but the overall proportion of the vote provided by those 18 to 29 did not increase greatly from 2004).

Also, there is considerable evidence that Republicans were disillusioned and did not turn out at their usual rate. The larger turnout among Democrats was balanced in part by the diminished turnout among GOP identifiers. In any event, this discussion is a kind of Rorschach test for optimism and pessimism. The glass, or ballot booth, can be seen as half-empty or half-full. It is reasonable to say that expectations for turnout were inflated, but the turnout was the highest since 1968—and surely, that is something to celebrate.

Overall, turnout was up in 33 states and the District of Columbia. North Carolina registered the biggest increase, from 57.8 percent in 2004 to 65.8 percent in 2008. It is no accident that North Carolina demonstrated one of the largest partisan shifts from election to election. George W. Bush carried the Tar Heel State by 13.4 percent; Obama won it by 0.4 percent, a swing of nearly 14 percent to the Democrats. The average swing in the nation between 2004 and 2008 was 9.6 percent. North Carolina, like most of the South, traditionally posts lower turnout percentages than much of the rest of the nation. Political culture and history always play a large role, and a culture of nonparticipation was very much a part of the South's history.[8]

Other parts of the country have had precisely the opposite culture. For instance, the Midwest usually scores highest in voter turnout. In 2008 Minnesota led the nation, with a turnout of 77.8 percent. Wisconsin, Maine, New Hampshire, and Iowa were also at the high end of the scale. Notice that Obama carried all five of the historically highest-turnout states. On the low end were West Virginia and Hawaii, with a mere 50.6 percent of the voters showing up at the polls. Arkansas, Utah, and Texas trailed in turnout just behind West Virginia and Hawaii. McCain won all but Hawaii, suggesting again the lack of enthusiasm among Republicans in 2008. Why was Hawaii so low, especially given Obama's birth ties to the Aloha State? Being halfway across the Pacific explains it. On November 4, the election was called for Obama long before the polls closed in Hawaii; his victory there was also certain in advance of the election, and he received his highest percentage in the nation (71.8 percent), except for D.C.

*The State-By-State Picture:* If you ever doubt America is a federal country, then just examine the election returns. The 51 separate components comprising the Electoral College each have their separate complexion in a presidential contest. As you look down the state-by-state vote totals in Table 1, it becomes immediately apparent that Barack Obama swept ten states with more than 60 percent of the vote: California (61 percent), Connecticut (60.7 percent), Delaware (61.9 percent), Hawaii (71.8 percent), Illinois (61.9 percent), Maryland (61.9 percent), Massachusetts (61.8 percent), New York (62.8 percent), Rhode Island (63.1 percent), and Vermont (67.5 percent), plus the District of Columbia (92.5 percent). Gargantuan California meant the most, of course—55 electoral votes and a 14-percent margin over McCain.

All of the Obama landslide states are traditionally Democratic and therefore not much of a surprise. It was elsewhere that eyebrows were raised. The Democrat scored a 9-percent victory in usually Republican Colorado; a 2.8-percent win in critical swing state Florida; a 1-percent shocker in consistently Republican Indiana; solid 16.4-percent and 10.4-percent margins in supposedly competitive Michigan and Pennsylvania; a 12.4-percent triumph in normally Republican Nevada; a 0.3-percent squeaker in heavily Republican North Carolina; and a 6.3-percent upset in Virginia. Indiana's returns caught everyone's attention, since the state had given George Bush a 20-percent landslide in 2004.

Of the swing states, only Ohio proved moderately resistant to Obama. The Buckeye State, which had produced George Bush's second term in 2004 by a narrow margin, switched to Obama, but by the comparatively unimpressive margin of 4.6 percent. Ohio had strongly backed Hillary Clinton in its March 2008 Democratic primary. Unlike Florida, Michigan, and Pennsylvania—which also supported Clinton strongly—Ohio marched near the end of the Obama parade. On the other hand, Obama's almost 259,000-vote plurality in Ohio was more than double George Bush's 119,000-vote margin in 2004.

John McCain ran well in a handful of smaller, overwhelmingly Republican states, such as Alabama (60.3 percent); Alaska, home of his running-mate Sarah Palin (59.4 percent); Idaho (61.5 percent); Oklahoma, his best state (65.6 percent); Utah (62.6 percent); and Wyoming (64.8 percent). Yet he was far below George Bush's pace even in most of these areas of strength. For example, Bush secured 71.5 percent in Utah in 2004. Even in Arizona, which he represents in the U.S. Senate, McCain could muster only 53.6 percent, and he was forced to campaign at home as the campaign ended. McCain's winning showings in states such as Georgia (52.2 percent), Missouri (a 49.4-percent squeaker), Montana (49.5 percent, just 2.2 percent more than Obama), and North Dakota (53.3 percent) were subpar. For instance, Bush captured Montana by over 20 percent and North Dakota by 27 percent in 2004. McCain ran as well or better than Bush in only three states: Louisiana, Oklahoma, and Tennessee. Obama exceeded John Kerry's 2004 percentages in the other 47 states and D.C. Even more impressively, Obama improved upon Kerry's vote proportion in 78 percent of the nation's counties. The 22 percent of counties where Obama fared worse were concentrated almost entirely in seven states of the South: Alabama, Arkansas, Kentucky, Louisiana, Oklahoma, Tennessee, and Texas.

Almost all of Obama's 9.5 million popular-vote majority was amassed in just eight states: California, Illinois, Maryland, Massachusetts, Michigan, New Jersey, New York, and Pennsylvania. These Democratic "exceptional eight" comprise the core of the national party's reliable vote. The only megastate left in the Republican column, Texas, produced a handsome plurality of just under a million votes for McCain.

*Regional Patterns:* Just as individual states have discernible political inclinations, so too do the great American regional groupings of states. Table 2 rearranges the 2008 vote by geographic sections. Barack Obama swept the Northeast with 59.5 percent of the votes in the dozen states (plus D.C.) in that region. Similarly, he achieved 60.3 percent of the votes in the four states of the Pacific West. In the industrial Midwest, Obama garnered a somewhat lower 55 percent, even though he carried seven of the eight states, missing the eighth (Missouri) by a whisker.

The three other grand regions were McCain's. The South remains a GOP bastion, though a fractured one after 2008; McCain secured 53.3 percent in these thirteen states. The nine Mountain West states, including McCain's Arizona, yielded a tiny 50.9 percent majority for the Republican ticket. Finally, the four traditionally GOP Plains States gave McCain a solid 55.7 percent of the votes.

## THE POLITICAL MAP OF AMERICA

Eight years ago in my book, *Overtime: The Election 2000 Thriller,*[9] I introduced the concept of the "political map of America," ably executed by Joshua J. Scott of the University of Virginia Center for Politics. As noted there, this exercise in cartography is based on the essential notion that "people vote, not trees or rocks or acres." The Electoral College has a certain small-state bias, for sure, driven by the two senatorial bonus votes added to every state, whether a lightly populated state such as Wyoming or a behemoth such as California. Yet, the electoral vote result is driven by the *popular vote* in each state; the candidate who wins one more popular vote than the other in each state gets all the electoral votes that state has to offer (except in Maine and Nebraska, as earlier explained).

Therefore, the political map, based on the population figures in the 2000 Census, is "what politicians, their staffs, and political consultants actually see when they look at our nation." The Northeast has lost millions of residents in recent decades, but notice how large the geographically compact region still looms politically (see Figure 4). The Northeast is more than matched by the South, whose volume on this map has *doubled* since the 1950s, led by Florida and Texas. California is the ultimate megastate, more than twice its geographical size in the political map. The large, swing Midwestern states are, like the Northeast, considerably reduced in size from what they were just a half-century ago, but their importance is clear on the political map. Finally, many of our readers will be distressed to see their states shrunk to a volume so small that a postage stamp could cover most of them. These are the states that should be very grateful for the Electoral College, and those bonus votes! As consolation, it should be stressed that many of these states in the West are growing by leaps and bounds, and the next political map of America, to be drawn in 2011, will show progress. In any event, when it comes to the political map, as in so many other areas of life, size matters, and there is just no getting around that. Poor Alaska: It is a massive piece of territory, but on the political map, it is smaller than Rhode Island!

### Figure 4. The Political Map of the United States

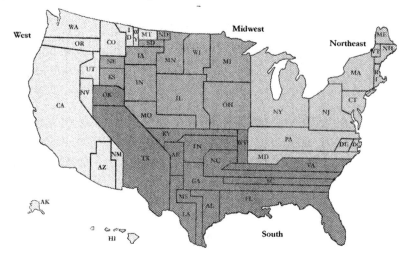

Source: Center for Politics

**Figure 5. The Political Map of the United States, 2004: Bush vs. Kerry**

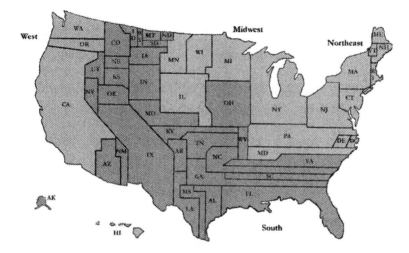

Source: Center for Politics

**Figure 6. The Political Map of the United States, 2008: Obama vs. McCain**

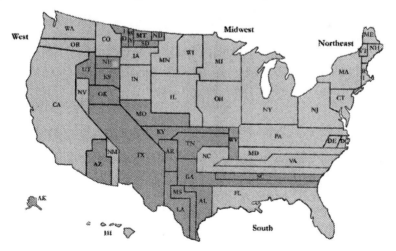

Source: Center for Politics

So what does the 2008 political map add to our understanding of the presidential election? Just compare it to the 2004 Bush-Kerry map, which shows the close division of that election, with Republican and Democratic territory fairly even and regionally polarized—with Ohio as the standout, decisive

state. By contrast, in 2008, a blue Obama ocean has flooded much of the red
GOP terrain. McCain's ground is restricted to part of the Southern/Rocky
Mountain part of the continent, with islands of backing in Arizona and the
Plains States. Certainly, Republicans running for lower offices in 2008 felt the
Democratic trend as though it was a flood, overrunning even their usually
reliable high ground.

It is possible to construct the American political map in a manner far more
favorable to Republicans. The Associated Press did just this in their revealing
popular-vote map that breaks down the results county by county across the
United States. (See Figure 7: President, 2008, All Counties in the U.S.)

**Figure 7. President, 2008, All Counties in the U.S.**

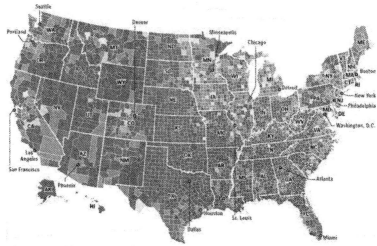

Source: Associated Press

*Note:* Unofficial results shown with some precincts not reporting. Alaska
results are statewide only.

A visitor from Mars without access to the news media would assume that
John McCain had won the election, so vast is the mass of red from coast to
coast. This map reflects the GOP's remaining demographic strength among
rural voters. The lower the density of population, in general, the better
Republicans seem to do politically. Most territory is still sparsely settled in
much of the United States, so a relative handful of voters casting GOP ballots can turn the nation red. Yet the blue dots on the map contain a large
majority of the country's voters. These central cities, suburbs, and gradually
urbanizing "exurbs" powered Obama to victory. Also, the rural counties that

have turned blue on the map are primarily majority-minority, that is, African Americans and/or Hispanics and other minorities constitute the majorities. These voters (in the South, Southwest, California, and so on) were part of Obama's base and delivered massive backing for his candidacy.

## THE ELECTION-DAY EXIT POLL: SLICING AND DICING HOW AMERICA VOTED

The history of exit polling has been a controversial one.[10] The system of interviewing voters as they leave the polls in order to project election winners and break down the electorate into its constituent parts (gender, race, age, etc.) sputtered in the miscalled presidential election of 2000, and then completely collapsed in the midterm elections of 2002. The pollsters have added better techniques and adopted significant reforms since then, including the surveying of the large number of voters who cast early and absentee ballots. All of this has helped to improve the process. Flaws remain, not the least of which is the disproportionate refusal rates (declining to participate) of certain segments of the population, including Republicans and some Independents who are suspicious of polling and/or the news media.

Nonetheless, the final exit poll results—once all the adjusting and weighting has been done—give us invaluable clues into the voting behavior of Americans. Any student of politics will want to study Table 3 at length. Fully 17,836 voters were interviewed at 300 polling places scattered across the U.S. for this profile of the electorate, a far larger sample than even the best public opinion polls provide prior to Election Day. On many national news Web sites (the TV networks, cable channels, the Associated Press, etc.) you can also find state-by-state analyzed exit poll data. For our purposes here, however, all the results are national (unless noted otherwise)—the mosaic created by citizens who cast a ballot in all jurisdictions combined. Let's review some of the highlights and see what they can tell us about ourselves in 2008.

### Gender Wars De-escalated but Racial Divisions Intact

There has been a "gender gap" in every presidential election from 1980 to the present, with women much more likely to vote Democratic than men. The reverse is also true: Men are much more likely to vote Republican. Women tend to be more liberal, and men more conservative on a wide range of issues, with the most important being war and peace. On the whole, women are a larger voter bloc than men. In 2008, for instance, women comprised 53 percent of the electorate, so winning them over is more politically potent.

The gender gap usually ranges from 5 to 10 points. In the 2000 Bush-Gore contest, for instance, it was 10 points: Bush received 53 percent of the male vote but only 43 percent of the female vote. The gender gap narrowed a bit to 7 percent in 2004, with Bush garnering 55 percent of the male vote and 48 percent of the female vote. John Kerry garnered just 44 percent of men but won women with 51 percent.

In 2008 Barack Obama managed to perform a very difficult feat by carrying both men and women. Granted, he won men by just a single percentage point—49 percent to John McCain's 48 percent (with 3 percent cast for other candidates). Obama won women handily, 56 percent to 43 percent. Even though Bill Clinton defeated Bob Dole by a wider overall margin (9 percent) in 1996 than Obama was able to defeat McCain (7 percent), Clinton still lost men by one percentage point. Clinton won women by a massive 16 percent.

Even greater polarization could be seen in the racial breakdown. Whites (both men and women, taken together) constituted almost three-quarters of the entire electorate, and they chose McCain by 55 percent, compared to 43 percent for Obama. Still, it is a welcome measure of racial liberalization that 43 percent of whites could vote for an African American candidate. That percentage probably would have been far smaller in earlier decades. In addition, whites identify disproportionately with the Republican Party, and have done so for many elections. Thus, they are inclined to deliver a majority to most GOP candidates for president. It is wrong to view the voting decisions in purely racial terms; that would be a simplistic, one-dimensional analysis.

Again, there is quite a difference between the votes of men and women. White men favored McCain by a whopping 16 percent, but white women chose McCain by 7 percent. And these national averages can be deceptive. Barack Obama won a majority of the white vote in 18 states, including eight Northeastern states (Connecticut, Delaware, Maine, Massachusetts, New Hampshire, New York, Rhode Island, and Vermont), five states in the Midwest (Illinois, Iowa, Michigan, Minnesota, and Wisconsin), one in the Southwest (Colorado), and the four Pacific states of California, Hawaii, Oregon, and Washington. On the other hand, his white percentage fell into the 10s and 20s in some Deep South states and Border South states. Alabama (10 percent), Mississippi (11percent), and Louisiana (14 percent) were Obama's worst states among whites, with Georgia (23 percent), South Carolina (26 percent), Texas (26 percent), Oklahoma (29 percent) and Arkansas (30 percent) on the next-lowest rung.

By contrast, there was virtually no distinction among African American men and women. Both genders chose Barack Obama overwhelmingly, approaching unanimity (95–96 percent). Normally, Democratic presidential nominees receive the votes of 88–90 percent of black Americans. Not surprisingly, pride in the possibility that someone of their racial identity could reach the White House for the first time produced a monolithic vote. African American turnout was higher, too, jumping about 18 percent from 2004. Blacks comprised 13 percent of the overall electorate in 2008, while whites fell from 77 percent of the total in 2004 to 74 percent in 2008.

Two-thirds of Latinos and Hispanics also favored Obama, with just 31 percent choosing McCain—a dramatic change from the approximately 40 percent who voted Republican in 2004. McCain's residence in Arizona, a state with a relatively large Hispanic population, and his identification with pro-immigration reform policies did nothing to assist him. Latinos also increased their proportion of the overall turnout from four years earlier, moving from 8 percent to 9 percent of the electorate. Latino women were slightly more likely to favor Obama than Latino men.

Incidentally, in the Democratic primaries, Hispanics and Latinos had favored Hillary Clinton over Barack Obama by a margin of about two to one. Their quick switch to Obama in the fall is a measure of their association with the Democratic Party, and the degree of sensitivity that this lower-income group has to bad economic times. The 2 percent of the voters who called themselves Asian Americans picked Obama by 62 percent to 35 percent, and the 3 percent who self-identified as belonging to some other race (such as Native American, Pacific Islander, or multiracial) were pro-Obama by 66 percent to 31 percent.

*Notice that Republicans are winning a majority only of the white vote—and not an overwhelming majority at that. In a diverse culture where, by 2042, whites will be a minority of the U.S. electorate, Republicans will have to broaden their appeal to nonwhites in order to win presidential contests.*

### The Youth Vote Awakens

One of the most exciting developments in 2008 was the awakening of the youth vote, especially on college campuses across America. Perhaps it is more accurate to say "re-awakening," since young people had driven American politics in the tumultuous late 1960s and early 1970s, as they embraced various causes from civil rights to opposition to the Vietnam War. It is no accident that the passage of the Twenty-Sixth Amendment to the Constitution, lowering the voting age from 21 to 18, occurred in July 1971. Unfortunately, after a burst of youth activity during the 1972 election, voter turnout among the young drifted much lower over the next several decades.

As we noted four years ago, a ray of hope for the Democrats was observed even in the midst of John Kerry's defeat in 2004. The Massachusetts Democrat won voters aged 18 to 29, 54 percent to 45 percent; it was the only age group he captured, in fact. The war in Iraq already appeared unpopular among young voters, and their views on social issues such as abortion and gay rights were far more closely aligned with the Democrats than the Republicans.

In 2008 the political dam burst among the young. Attracted by Obama's style and multiracial background, as well as his positions on the economy, Iraq, environmentalism, and social issues, 18- to 29-year-old voters delivered an overwhelming landslide to the Democrat: 66 percent, compared to 32 percent for McCain. Their turnout was up slightly over 2004, about 6 percent by the best estimates. *This is another ominous development for Republicans, in part because the young often keep their first party label for most or all of their life, especially when the party I.D. was acquired in a memorable, intense election like that of 2008.*

Obama did far less well with other age groups. He won those in their 30s by 10 points (54 percent to 44 percent), and tied McCain among those aged 40 to 64. John McCain's only clear support in the age cohorts came among his fellow senior citizens. Those Americans aged 65 and older picked McCain by 53 percent to 45 percent. Naturally, they probably identified more with someone closer to their own generation, who had experiences much like their own. Older voters would be especially inclined to view Obama as inexperienced, too young, and not ready for the demands of the presidency. It also has to be said that racial prejudice is likely greater among some of those who are older. Many senior citizens grew up in a segregated society, and the changes that have rapidly taken place in America since the 1960s have not sat well with all seniors.

Combining the variables of race and age produces some fascinating results. Barack Obama did win over one group of white voters; those aged 18 to 29 gave him a handsome 10-percent victory. Young Latinos were also more inclined than their elders to back Obama. The Democrat gathered an astounding 76 percent of 18- to 29-year-olds in this racial group. Once again, there was no generation gap among African Americans. About 95 of 100 blacks in every age group supported Obama.

### The Effect of Income and Education on the Vote

To a certain degree, at least politically, you are what you earn. Barack Obama won a massive 73 percent among those who make less than $15,000 a year in income, 60 percent among those with incomes between $15,000–$30,000, and 55 percent of those making $30,000–$50,000. Many minorities fall into the lower income brackets, so in that sense the Obama proportions are not surprising. These three income groups comprise 38 percent of the entire electorate.

Obama and McCain essentially split evenly the votes of those with incomes ranging from $50,000 to $250,000—although this means McCain did relatively better with these Americans than with the electorate as a whole. A solid majority (56 percent) of Americans falls into this broad income distribution. Interestingly, despite Obama's call for higher taxes on the 6 percent of citizens making $200,000 or more, he won this income group handily, 52 percent to 46 percent.

The last statistic connects directly to education. In earlier generations, Republican support tended to go up the income and education scale—the more years of formal education you had and the more you earned, the more likely it was that you would vote for the GOP candidate. This has changed rather dramatically at the top of the scale in recent times. Those with the most education (postgraduate training or degrees) tilt strongly Democratic. In 2008 Obama captured 58 percent of the votes of the 17 percent of Americans in the postgraduate category. Four years earlier, John Kerry had won 55 percent of postgraduates.

By contrast, Obama only narrowly won those who had had some college or a B.A./B.S. degree, and Kerry lost both categories. About 31 percent of Americans have had the privilege of attending college without a degree, and another 28 percent have gone on to get the degree (without moving into postgraduate studies). Traditionally, again because minorities are concentrated among those with the lowest average education, Democrats have fared well with Americans who never went beyond high school, or didn't even get as far as a high school degree. Obama won the former with 52 percent and the latter with 63 percent.

Why have postgraduates been moving so strongly to the Democrats? There are many explanations, but Republican association with the religious right and conservative GOP positions on lifestyle issues such as abortion and gay rights appear to be especially relevant factors.

### The Power of Party

Political party affiliation still makes a big difference, and the 2008 results prove it. 89 percent of Democrats voted for Obama and 90 percent of Republicans cast a ballot for McCain. Only about a tenth of those identifying with one of the two major parties defected to the other side. This is the norm in most elections.

So what was the difference for Obama in 2008? First, he won the 29 percent of Americans who call themselves Independents by 52 percent to 44 percent over McCain. Even more vital was the proportion of Democrats showing up at the polls. Of the entire 2008 electorate, Democrats comprised 39 percent, Republicans only 32 percent. Four years earlier, Democrats and Republicans each contributed 37 percent to the electorate. So Democrats were more excited by their ticket and Republicans less so in 2008. In addition, fewer people were identifying with the GOP by 2008—due to the "Bush effect"—and naturally, this carried over into Election Day. A remarkably large 17 percent of the voters who cast a ballot for Bush in 2004 reported switching to Obama, while just 9 percent of the Kerry backers picked McCain this go-round.

By the way, all the pre election talk about how white Democrats might say they were for Obama but vote for McCain in the privacy of the ballot booth appeared overblown. Just 14 percent of white Democrats defected to McCain, not much more than the 8 percent of white Republicans who abandoned McCain to vote for Obama. Certainly, the white Democratic defections were higher in Deep South and Border States, but Obama's ability to draw massive support among minority groups and young people more than compensated for the lost votes elsewhere. And what of those Democrats who said they favored Hillary Clinton in the party primaries? Obama won them over, 83 percent to 16 percent—though in a tight election, the Clinton defectors could have made the difference. Perhaps Obama should have announced his Secretary of State choice before the election.

Americans are bound not just by party, but also by ideology. Most people are willing to classify themselves as liberal (22 percent of the electorate), moderate (a large 44 percent), or conservative (34 percent). As expected, Obama swept liberals with 89 percent while McCain did well with conservatives (78 percent). It was the 60 percent among moderates and centrists that guaranteed Obama's election as president. Some may be surprised that Obama was able to secure 20 percent of the vote among conservatives; surely, this was a "time for a change" phenomenon.

### The Effect of the Campaign

About 11 percent of the voters cast their first ballot in 2008. Most of them were young, but not all. Obama garnered 69 percent among first-time voters to McCain's 30 percent. Among experienced voters, this was a tight race: Obama 50 percent and McCain 48 percent.

Six out of ten voters knew *before September* (and the financial meltdown that month) for whom they were going to vote, and Obama already had a 52 percent to 47 percent lead. It is not unreasonable to suggest that the meltdown added a point to Obama and subtracted one from McCain, but was not the determining factor in the election. The cake was in the oven well in advance of the general election's events, including the debates.

All campaigns make extensive, expensive efforts to contact voters and identify supporters, but there is no question which campaign was more successful in 2008. 26 percent of the voters (representing 34 million people) said they had been personally contacted by the Obama campaign, compared to just 18 percent (24 million) by the McCain campaign. It is worth noting that among those contacted by only one campaign and not the other, eight in ten voted for the candidate that had reached out to them. Campaigns go hunting where the ducks are, and much of the effort is spent on voters already known to be leaning a candidate's way.

### Old Time and New Style Religion

Election watchers have learned that Catholics are the religious denomination to follow—a key swing group of more than a quarter of the national electorate that usually ends up in the winner's circle. George W. Bush won them by a few percentage points in 2004. Barack Obama did even better, attracting 54 percent of Catholics. Protestants stayed with McCain by the same proportion—but that was a decline of 5 percent from 2004 for the GOP.

As usual, the Democrat also won the Jewish vote with 78 percent. Concerns among some that Obama was not perceived as pro-Israel enough had no impact, and he actually did 4 percent better than John Kerry among Jews. The 6 percent of Americans who identified with a religion other than Protestant, Catholic, and Jewish went overwhelmingly for Obama (73 percent), as did the 12 percent who said they had no religion (75 percent).

When race and religion are combined, we see that McCain won white Protestants two-to-one, and narrowly carried white Catholics with 52 percent.

The frequency of church attendance is also a telltale indicator of partisan allegiances in recent elections. Those who attend religious services once a week or more gave McCain 55 percent; the less-frequent attendees were heavily for Obama. One of the few sectors of the electorate that showed only slight Republican leakage from Bush to McCain was white evangelical/born-again Christians. McCain secured 74 percent, down 4 percent from 2004. No doubt vice-presidential candidate Sarah Palin assisted McCain in this category.

### Love and Marriage

Republicans usually fare better with voters who are married, and 2008 was no exception. McCain garnered 52 percent among the two-thirds of Americans who said they were married, whereas Obama won the normal Democratic landslide among the one-third that aren't married (65 percent).

Among the 4 percent of all voters who said they were gay, lesbian, or bisexual, Obama won 70 percent. In 2004, 77 percent of these voters cast a Kerry ballot. Perhaps there was greater tolerance among gays for John McCain than for George Bush, or concern among gays about the degree of Obama's commitment to gay rights. Considering the small number of gays interviewed, however, it is more likely a question of sampling error.

### More Exit Polling Gems

The exit poll can be mined for many a precious stone. Here are a few more as we wind up our excavation.

- *Veterans.* McCain was a Vietnam prisoner of war and has long been closely identified with the military, while Obama never served in the military. So the surprise is not that veterans preferred McCain, but that he won this select group (15 percent of the population) by such a spare margin—54 percent to 44 percent.
- *Union Members and Gun Owners.* Other categories contain no shocks. The 12 percent of Americans who are union members chose Obama by 60 percent to 37 percent, while those belonging to households with one or more guns picked McCain by 62 percent to 37 percent.
- *Changing Demographics.* For much of the 1970s through the 1990s, Republicans were in a strong political position because they were the preferred party of the suburbs, the counties surrounding central cities. While Democrats could count on large majorities in urban centers (about 30 percent of the population), the GOP had the allegiance of most suburban localities—about half the population—as well as the fifth of the nation still considered rural. This alignment has shifted considerably, as the 2008 vote underlines. Obama won the expected 63 percent in urban America, but he also drew half of the vote in suburbia to McCain's 48 percent. The Republican nominee was left only with "Ruritania," and just 53 percent of that.
- *The Running Mates.* When asked whether the vice-presidential candidates were qualified to be president, 66 percent answered yes for Joe Biden and only 38 percent for Sarah Palin. But there is precious little evidence either in preelection surveys or the exit poll that Biden or Palin made much of a difference in the election results. At the time they are announced, running mates generate extensive conversation and excitement, yet in the end they affect a relative handful of votes. Biden may have comforted and reassured some voters that an experienced Washington hand was nearby for freshman Senator Obama, but Biden also made more than his share of campaign gaffes (as is his consistent career tendency). Palin stirred the conservative GOP base and moved some fundamentalist Christians to action, but she also proved to be uninformed in many news media interviews and turned off moderates in droves. This yin-and-yang effect, somewhat self-cancelling, is typical of vice-presidential candidates. In the end, the vast majority of Americans want to designate the occupant of the White House, not the Naval

Observatory (the vice president's residence). Obama could have chosen a wide variety of Democratic officials and still won, and McCain could have selected many other GOP personalities and still lost.

## THE 2008 ELECTION IN PERSPECTIVE: JUST WHAT WE WOULD HAVE EXPECTED

Elections are often overanalyzed, and perhaps we have just committed that venial sin here. The welter of data and circumstance can overwhelm students of history, when the simple, straightforward explanations are often the most compelling.

The truth is this: Any mainstream Democratic candidate was destined to win in 2008, when the age-old slogan, "It's Time for a Change," had powerful new meaning. The electoral conditions—the fundamentals I often call "the North Stars of politics"—could not have been more clear or bright in the sky. The North Stars that applied to the 2008 contest are presidential popularity, economic conditions, and war and peace.[11]

It is undeniable that George W. Bush has been an unpopular president for longer than any of his other predecessors, at least since the dawn of the age of polling in 1936. Bush was below 50-percent job approval in the Gallup Poll for almost all of his second term, and for almost three years he was below 40 percent.[12] In the election year of 2008, he bounced between the low-20s and the mid-30s, ending up in the mid-20s right before Election Day—an unprecedented level of unpopularity at just the wrong time. Americans were unhappy with his performance in a wide variety of areas, from the Iraq War to the economy to the inadequate response after Hurricane Katrina. Just 27 percent of the actual voters on November 4 approved of President Bush's performance in office, and John McCain received 89 percent of their votes. Of the 71 percent who disapproved of Bush, Barack Obama secured 67 percent.

Of all the potential Republican nominees for president, none was better positioned than McCain to separate himself from Bush; after all, Bush and McCain had run against each other for the White House in 2000 and for years they were bitter enemies. That is what enabled McCain to draw 31 percent of the votes of those who disapproved of Bush. Any other GOP nominee likely would have lost by an even wider margin than McCain did in 2008. There is almost no imaginable way for a party to get a third consecutive term in the White House with an incumbent president as roundly disliked as Bush was in the fall.

Then there was Iraq. After President Bush's deft handling of the post-September 11 national security restructuring and his successful war in Afghanistan against the Taliban, Americans were inclined to believe him when he insisted that the United States had to invade Iraq to rid that nation of its weapons of mass destruction (WMDs). Still, many had their doubts (including a young Illinois state senator named Barack Obama), and the decision to go to war was very controversial from the beginning. The post-invasion revelation that there were no WMDs to be found was devastating, as was the internal insurrection and religious infighting that brought Iraq to the brink of civil war in 2005 and 2006.

Even the successful "surge" of additional U.S. troops that restored Iraqi stability by early 2008 could not erase Americans' belief that the war had been waged unnecessarily and at enormous cost in blood (over 4,000 troops' lives) and treasure ($600 billion by the time of the general election and sure to climb far above $1 trillion before eventual disengagement). McCain had backed Bush, and while he had criticized certain aspects of the war's prosecution, he could not escape the blame, if only by "inheritance" as the GOP nominee to succeed Bush. By contrast, Obama could say he opposed the war from the start, which gave him his winning edge over Senator Hillary Clinton, who had voted to authorize the war, as well as McCain. By Election Day, 63 percent of the voters disapproved of the war in Iraq, and Obama received 76 percent of those ballots. Just 36 percent approved of the war, and McCain gathered 86 percent of that minority.

The economy eclipsed everything else, however. Fully 63 percent of the voters said it was "the most important issue in the election" in the exit poll, a proportion that dwarfed every other topic. Traditionally, voters blame the party in power for bad times, and decide to take a chance on change even if they have some doubts about the change agent (the nominee of the other party). This is precisely what happened in 2008. There are many ways to measure the impact of the economy on a person's vote, but none is better than asking whether his or her family's financial position was getting better (24 percent), growing worse (42 percent), or staying the same (34 percent). McCain handily won those who said "better" (60 percent) and "the same" (53 percent), but the large plurality that sensed financial hard times voted overwhelmingly for Obama (71 percent).

Some analysts have tried to suggest that the election's key event was the mid-September financial meltdown, that somehow had this never happened McCain might have been able to win or at least keep the election very close. This is poppycock. Except for a brief honeymoon period for McCain after the GOP convention, Obama consistently led the polls from early summer onwards. The evidence of severe economic slowdown was everywhere from the spring to the fall, and Americans already believed that we were in a serious recession. Actually, the average person proved more prescient that the economists, who couldn't make up their minds about the state of the economy.[13]

For decades, pollsters have relied upon a simple question as a kind of summary statistic on politics: "Do you think things in this country are generally going in the right direction or are they seriously off on the wrong track?" As usual, the voters' answer to this query told us in which direction the political winds were blowing. Three-quarters picked "wrong track," and Obama was the choice of 62 percent of them. Just 20 percent said "right direction," and McCain secured 71 percent of this small group of Americans. This gale force overwhelmed worries about Obama's race or political inexperience, and it was far more critical to John McCain's defeat than his much-discussed age of 72 or controversial choice of running mate.

* * *

Every election is a discrete event. Most do not signal a durable change in voter alignments. A few do, and these are called realigning elections. It is impossible to know yet into which category Obama's victory will fall. There are some positive signs for Democrats that encourage them to think of realignment, not least the activation of young voters and their dramatic movement toward the party of Obama.

And goodness knows, Congress has undergone an enormous power shift toward the Democrats after two successive elections that ended GOP rule on Capitol Hill for now, and may have put Congress out of reach for the Republicans for a while. Take a look at Figures 7 and 8. After the GOP swept to power in 1994, ending 40 consecutive years of Democratic control of the U.S. House of Representatives, Republicans controlled a majority of the delegations in 25 states, and Democrats ruled the roost in 19. (Five states were tied, and Vermont had an Independent congressman as its sole representative.) Before the election of 2006, Republicans had expanded their House majorities to 30 states; Democrats were left with a mere 16. But the combination of Democratic tides in the 2006 and 2008 elections have produced 33 states with a majority of Democrats, and Republicans have been reduced to control of only 16.

As rosy as the picture seems to be for Democrats, real events and actual performance in office will determine the future. Will President Barack Obama be successful in helping to restore a vibrant economy? Can he keep his pledge to withdraw combat troops from Iraq while maintaining stability in that fragile nation? Can he win the fight in Afghanistan and keep the United States safe from domestic terrorist activity? How about healthcare, the environment, education, and a hundred other issues that will demand urgent attention from the White House and Congress?

Campaigns are grueling, but they are actually the easy part. Governing is the ultimate test for any president, legislature, and party coalition. The voters will be watching, and they will render their next national judgment in the midterm contests of 2010.

### Figure 8. United States House Strength After 1994

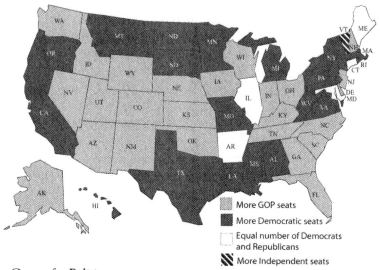

Source: Center for Politics

### Figure 9. United States House Strength After 2008

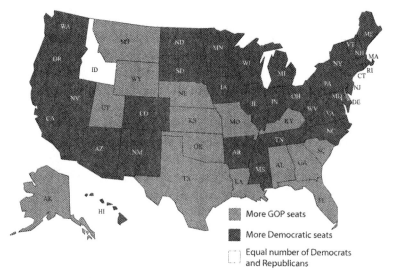

Source: Center for Politics

# APPENDIX

Table 1. 2008 Presidential Vote

| | Electoral Vote Dem. | Electoral Vote Rep. | Total Vote | Obama (Dem.) | McCain (Rep.) | Other | Rep.-Dem. Plurality | | Percentage of Total Vote Obama (Dem.) | McCain (Rep.) | Other |
|---|---|---|---|---|---|---|---|---|---|---|---|
| Alabama | | 9 | 2,099,819 | 813,479 | 1,266,546 | 19,794 | 453,067 | R | 38.7% | 60.3% | 0.9% |
| Alaska | | 3 | 326,197 | 123,594 | 193,841 | 8,762 | 70,247 | R | 37.9% | 59.4% | 2.7% |
| Arizona | | 10 | 2,293,475 | 1,034,707 | 1,230,111 | 28,657 | 195,404 | R | 45.1% | 53.6% | 1.2% |
| Arkansas | | 6 | 1,086,617 | 422,310 | 638,017 | 26,290 | 215,707 | R | 38.9% | 58.7% | 2.4% |
| California | 55 | | 13,561,900 | 8,274,473 | 5,011,781 | 275,646 | 3,262,692 | D | 61.0% | 37.0% | 2.0% |
| Colorado | 9 | | 2,401,349 | 1,288,568 | 1,073,584 | 39,197 | 214,984 | D | 53.7% | 44.7% | 1.6% |
| Connecticut | 7 | | 1,648,560 | 1,000,994 | 628,873 | 18,693 | 372,121 | D | 60.7% | 38.1% | 1.1% |
| Delaware | 3 | | 412,412 | 255,459 | 152,374 | 4,579 | 103,085 | D | 61.9% | 36.9% | 1.1% |
| Florida | 27 | | 8,390,744 | 4,282,074 | 4,045,624 | 63,046 | 236,450 | D | 51.0% | 48.2% | 0.8% |
| Georgia | | 15 | 3,924,440 | 1,844,137 | 2,048,744 | 31,559 | 204,607 | R | 47.0% | 52.2% | 0.8% |
| Hawaii | 4 | | 453,568 | 325,871 | 120,566 | 7,131 | 205,305 | D | 71.8% | 26.6% | 1.6% |
| Idaho | | 4 | 655,032 | 236,440 | 403,012 | 15,580 | 166,572 | R | 36.1% | 61.5% | 2.4% |
| Illinois | 21 | | 5,523,051 | 3,419,673 | 2,031,527 | 71,851 | 1,388,146 | D | 61.9% | 36.8% | 1.3% |
| Indiana | 11 | | 2,751,054 | 1,374,039 | 1,345,648 | 31,367 | 28,391 | D | 49.9% | 48.9% | 1.1% |
| Iowa | 7 | | 1,537,123 | 828,940 | 682,379 | 25,804 | 146,561 | D | 53.9% | 44.4% | 1.7% |
| Kansas | | 6 | 1,235,872 | 514,765 | 699,655 | 21,452 | 184,890 | R | 41.7% | 56.6% | 1.7% |
| Kentucky | | 8 | 1,826,508 | 751,985 | 1,048,462 | 26,061 | 296,477 | R | 41.2% | 57.4% | 1.4% |
| Louisiana | | 9 | 1,960,761 | 782,989 | 1,148,275 | 29,497 | 365,286 | R | 39.9% | 58.6% | 1.5% |
| Maine | 4 | | 731,163 | 421,923 | 295,273 | 13,967 | 126,650 | D | 57.7% | 40.4% | 1.9% |
| Maryland | 10 | | 2,630,947 | 1,628,995 | 959,694 | 42,258 | 669,301 | D | 61.9% | 36.5% | 1.6% |

Table 1 continued

| | Electoral Vote Dem. | Rep. | Total Vote | Obama (Dem.) | McCain (Rep.) | Other | Rep.-Dem. Plurality | | Percentage of Total Vote Obama (Dem.) | McCain (Rep.) | Other |
|---|---|---|---|---|---|---|---|---|---|---|---|
| Massachusetts | 12 | | 3,080,985 | 1,904,097 | 1,108,854 | 68,034 | 795,243 | D | 61.8% | 36.0% | 2.2% |
| Michigan | 17 | | 5,001,766 | 2,872,579 | 2,048,639 | 80,548 | 823,940 | D | 57.4% | 41.0% | 1.6% |
| Minnesota | 10 | | 2,910,369 | 1,573,354 | 1,275,409 | 61,606 | 297,945 | D | 54.1% | 43.8% | 2.1% |
| Mississippi | | 6 | 1,289,865 | 554,662 | 724,597 | 10,606 | 169,935 | R | 43.0% | 56.2% | 0.8% |
| Missouri | | 11 | 2,925,205 | 1,441,911 | 1,445,814 | 37,480 | 3,903 | R | 49.3% | 49.4% | 1.3% |
| Montana | | 3 | 490,109 | 231,667 | 242,763 | 15,679 | 11,096 | R | 47.3% | 49.5% | 3.2% |
| Nebraska | 1 | 4 | 801,281 | 333,319 | 452,979 | 14,983 | 119,660 | R | 41.6% | 56.5% | 1.9% |
| Nevada | 5 | | 967,848 | 533,736 | 412,827 | 21,285 | 120,909 | D | 55.1% | 42.7% | 2.2% |
| New Hampshire | 4 | | 710,970 | 384,826 | 316,534 | 9,610 | 68,292 | D | 54.1% | 44.5% | 1.4% |
| New Jersey | 15 | | 3,868,237 | 2,215,422 | 1,613,207 | 39,608 | 602,215 | D | 57.3% | 41.7% | 1.0% |
| New Mexico | 5 | | 830,158 | 472,422 | 346,832 | 10,904 | 125,590 | D | 56.9% | 41.8% | 1.3% |
| New York | 31 | | 7,594,813 | 4,769,700 | 2,742,298 | 82,815 | 2,027,402 | D | 62.8% | 36.1% | 1.1% |
| North Carolina | 15 | | 4,310,789 | 2,142,651 | 2,128,474 | 39,664 | 14,177 | D | 49.7% | 49.4% | 0.9% |
| North Dakota | | 3 | 316,621 | 141,278 | 168,601 | 6,742 | 27,323 | R | 44.6% | 53.3% | 2.1% |
| Ohio | 20 | | 5,698,260 | 2,933,388 | 2,674,491 | 90,381 | 258,897 | D | 51.5% | 46.9% | 1.6% |
| Oklahoma | | 7 | 1,462,661 | 502,496 | 960,165 | | 457,669 | R | 34.4% | 65.6% | |
| Oregon | 7 | | 1,827,864 | 1,037,291 | 738,475 | 52,098 | 298,816 | D | 56.7% | 40.4% | 2.9% |
| Pennsylvania | 21 | | 5,991,064 | 3,276,363 | 2,651,812 | 62,889 | 624,551 | D | 54.7% | 44.3% | 1.0% |
| Rhode Island | 4 | | 469,767 | 296,571 | 165,391 | 7,805 | 131,180 | D | 63.1% | 35.2% | 1.7% |
| South Carolina | | 8 | 1,920,969 | 862,449 | 1,034,896 | 23,624 | 172,447 | R | 44.9% | 53.9% | 1.2% |

Table 1 continued

| | Electoral Vote Dem. | Rep. | Total Vote | Obama (Dem.) | McCain (Rep.) | Other | Rep.-Dem. Plurality | | Percentage of Total Vote Obama (Dem.) | McCain (Rep.) | Other |
|---|---|---|---|---|---|---|---|---|---|---|---|
| South Dakota | | 3 | 381,975 | 170,924 | 203,054 | 7,997 | 32,130 | R | 44.7% | 53.2% | 2.1% |
| Tennessee | | 11 | 2,599,749 | 1,087,437 | 1,479,178 | 33,134 | 391,741 | R | 41.8% | 56.9% | 1.3% |
| Texas | | 34 | 8,077,795 | 3,528,633 | 4,479,328 | 69,834 | 950,695 | R | 43.7% | 55.5% | 0.9% |
| Utah | | 5 | 952,370 | 327,670 | 596,030 | 28,670 | 268,360 | R | 34.4% | 62.6% | 3.0% |
| Vermont | 3 | | 325,046 | 219,262 | 98,974 | 6,810 | 120,288 | D | 67.5% | 30.4% | 2.1% |
| Virginia | 13 | | 3,723,260 | 1,959,532 | 1,725,005 | 38,723 | 234,527 | D | 52.6% | 46.3% | 1.0% |
| Washington | 11 | | 3,036,878 | 1,750,848 | 1,229,216 | 56,814 | 521,632 | D | 57.7% | 40.5% | 1.9% |
| West Virginia | | 5 | 714,246 | 304,127 | 398,061 | 12,058 | 93,934 | R | 42.6% | 55.7% | 1.7% |
| Wisconsin | 10 | | 2,983,417 | 1,677,211 | 1,262,393 | 43,813 | 414,818 | D | 56.2% | 42.3% | 1.5% |
| Wyoming | | 3 | 254,658 | 82,868 | 164,958 | 6,832 | 82,090 | R | 32.5% | 64.8% | 2.7% |
| Dist. of Col. | 3 | | 265,853 | 245,800 | 17,367 | 2,686 | 228,433 | D | 92.5% | 6.5% | 1.0% |
| TOTAL | 365 | 173 | 131,235,440 | 69,459,909 | 59,930,608 | 1,844,923 | 9,529,301 | D | 52.9% | 45.7% | 1.4% |

*Note:* Results are based on official returns posted on the election Web sites of states and the District of Columbia. They are subject to minor changes.

Source: "The Rhodes Cook Letter," December 2008.

Table 2. 2008 Presidential Vote—By Region

| | Electoral Vote Dem. | Rep. | Total Vote | Obama (Dem.) | McCain (Rep.) | Other | Rep.-Dem. Plurality | | Obama (Dem.) | McCain (Rep.) | Other |
|---|---|---|---|---|---|---|---|---|---|---|---|
| **SOUTH** | | | | | | | | | | | |
| Alabama | | 9 | 2,099,819 | 813,479 | 1,266,546 | 19,794 | 453,067 | R | 38.7% | 60.3% | 0.9% |
| Arkansas | | 6 | 1,086,617 | 422,310 | 638,017 | 26,290 | 215,707 | R | 38.9% | 58.7% | 2.4% |
| Florida | 27 | | 8,390,744 | 4,282,074 | 4,045,624 | 63,046 | 236,450 | D | 51.0% | 48.2% | 0.8% |
| Georgia | | 15 | 3,924,440 | 1,844,137 | 2,048,744 | 31,559 | 204,607 | R | 47.0% | 52.2% | 0.8% |
| Kentucky | | 8 | 1,826,508 | 751,985 | 1,048,462 | 26,061 | 296,477 | R | 41.2% | 57.4% | 1.4% |
| Louisiana | | 9 | 1,960,761 | 782,989 | 1,148,275 | 29,497 | 365,286 | R | 39.9% | 58.6% | 1.5% |
| Mississippi | | 6 | 1,289,865 | 554,662 | 724,597 | 10,606 | 169,935 | R | 43.0% | 56.2% | 0.8% |
| North Carolina | 15 | | 4,310,789 | 2,142,651 | 2,128,474 | 39,664 | 14,177 | D | 49.7% | 49.4% | 0.9% |
| Oklahoma | | 7 | 1,462,661 | 502,496 | 960,165 | | 457,669 | R | 34.4% | 65.6% | |
| South Carolina | | 8 | 1,920,969 | 862,449 | 1,034,896 | 23,624 | 172,447 | R | 44.9% | 53.9% | 1.2% |
| Tennessee | | 11 | 2,599,749 | 1,087,437 | 1,479,178 | 33,134 | 391,741 | R | 41.8% | 56.9% | 1.3% |
| Texas | | 34 | 8,077,795 | 3,528,633 | 4,479,328 | 69,834 | 950,695 | R | 43.7% | 55.5% | 0.9% |
| Virginia | 13 | | 3,723,260 | 1,959,532 | 1,725,005 | 38,723 | 234,527 | D | 52.6% | 46.3% | 1.0% |
| Total | 55 | 113 | 42,673,977 | 19,534,834 | 22,727,311 | 411,832 | 3,192,477 | R | 45.8% | 53.3% | 1.0% |
| **MOUNTAIN WEST** | | | | | | | | | | | |
| Alaska | | 3 | 326,197 | 123,594 | 193,841 | 8,762 | 70,247 | R | 37.9% | 59.4% | 2.7% |
| Arizona | | 10 | 2,293,475 | 1,034,707 | 1,230,111 | 28,657 | 195,404 | R | 45.1% | 53.6% | 1.2% |
| Colorado | 9 | | 2,401,349 | 1,288,568 | 1,073,584 | 39,197 | 214,984 | D | 53.7% | 44.7% | 1.6% |
| Idaho | | 4 | 655,032 | 236,440 | 403,012 | 15,580 | 166,572 | R | 36.1% | 61.5% | 2.4% |

Table 2 continued

| | Electoral Vote Dem. | Rep. | Total Vote | Obama (Dem.) | McCain (Rep.) | Other | Rep.-Dem. Plurality | | Percentage of Total Vote Obama (Dem.) | McCain (Rep.) | Other |
|---|---|---|---|---|---|---|---|---|---|---|---|
| Montana | | 3 | 490,109 | 231,667 | 242,763 | 15,679 | 11,096 | R | 47.3% | 49.5% | 3.2% |
| Nevada | 5 | | 967,848 | 533,736 | 412,827 | 21,285 | 120,909 | D | 55.1% | 42.7% | 2.2% |
| New Mexico | 5 | | 830,158 | 472,422 | 346,832 | 10,904 | 125,590 | D | 56.9% | 41.8% | 1.3% |
| Utah | | 5 | 952,370 | 327,670 | 596,030 | 28,670 | 268,360 | R | 34.4% | 62.6% | 3.0% |
| Wyoming | | 3 | 254,658 | 82,868 | 164,958 | 6,832 | 82,090 | R | 32.5% | 64.8% | 2.7% |
| Total | 19 | 28 | 9,171,196 | 4,331,672 | 4,663,958 | 175,566 | 332,286 | R | 47.2% | 50.9% | 1.9% |
| **PLAINS STATES** | | | | | | | | | | | |
| Kansas | | 6 | 1,235,872 | 514,765 | 699,655 | 21,452 | 184,890 | R | 41.7% | 56.6% | 1.7% |
| Nebraska | 1 | 4 | 801,281 | 333,319 | 452,979 | 14,983 | 119,660 | R | 41.6% | 56.5% | 1.9% |
| North Dakota | | 3 | 316,621 | 141,278 | 168,601 | 6,742 | 27,323 | R | 44.6% | 53.3% | 2.1% |
| South Dakota | | 3 | 381,975 | 170,924 | 203,054 | 7,997 | 32,130 | R | 44.7% | 53.2% | 2.1% |
| Total | 1 | 16 | 2,735,749 | 1,160,286 | 1,524,289 | 51,174 | 364,003 | R | 42.4% | 55.7% | 1.9% |
| **REPUBLICAN 'L'** | 75 | 157 | 54,580,922 | 25,026,792 | 28,915,558 | 638,572 | 3,888,766 | R | 45.9% | 53.0% | 1.2% |
| **NORTHEAST** | | | | | | | | | | | |
| Connecticut | 7 | | 1,648,560 | 1,000,994 | 628,873 | 18,693 | 372,121 | D | 60.7% | 38.1% | 1.1% |
| Delaware | 3 | | 412,412 | 255,459 | 152,374 | 4,579 | 103,085 | D | 61.9% | 36.9% | 1.1% |
| Maine | 4 | | 731,163 | 421,923 | 295,273 | 13,967 | 126,650 | D | 57.7% | 40.4% | 1.9% |

Table 2 continued

| | Electoral Vote Dem. | Electoral Vote Rep. | Total Vote | Obama (Dem.) | McCain (Rep.) | Other | Rep.-Dem. Plurality | | Percentage of Total Vote Obama (Dem.) | McCain (Rep.) | Other |
|---|---|---|---|---|---|---|---|---|---|---|---|
| Maryland | 10 | | 2,630,947 | 1,628,995 | 959,694 | 42,258 | 669,301 | D | 61.9% | 36.5% | 1.6% |
| Massachusetts | 12 | | 3,080,985 | 1,904,097 | 1,108,854 | 68,034 | 795,243 | D | 61.8% | 36.0% | 2.2% |
| New Hampshire | 4 | | 710,970 | 384,826 | 316,534 | 9,610 | 68,292 | D | 54.1% | 44.5% | 1.4% |
| New Jersey | 15 | | 3,868,237 | 2,215,422 | 1,613,207 | 39,608 | 602,215 | D | 57.3% | 41.7% | 1.0% |
| New York | 31 | | 7,594,813 | 4,769,700 | 2,742,298 | 82,815 | 2,027,402 | D | 62.8% | 36.1% | 1.1% |
| Pennsylvania | 21 | | 5,991,064 | 3,276,363 | 2,651,812 | 62,889 | 624,551 | D | 54.7% | 44.3% | 1.0% |
| Rhode Island | 4 | | 469,767 | 296,571 | 165,391 | 7,805 | 131,180 | D | 63.1% | 35.2% | 1.7% |
| Vermont | 3 | | 325,046 | 219,262 | 98,974 | 6,810 | 120,288 | D | 67.5% | 30.4% | 2.1% |
| West Virginia | | 5 | 714,246 | 304,127 | 398,061 | 12,058 | 93,934 | R | 42.6% | 55.7% | 1.7% |
| Dist. of Col. | 3 | | 265,853 | 245,800 | 17,367 | 2,686 | 228,433 | D | 92.5% | 6.5% | 1.0% |
| Total | 117 | 5 | 28,444,063 | 16,923,539 | 11,148,712 | 371,812 | 5,774,827 | D | 59.5% | 39.2% | 1.3% |
| **PACIFIC WEST** | | | | | | | | | | | |
| California | 55 | | 13,561,900 | 8,274,473 | 5,011,781 | 275,646 | 3,262,692 | D | 61.0% | 37.0% | 2.0% |
| Hawaii | 4 | | 453,568 | 325,871 | 120,566 | 7,131 | 205,305 | D | 71.8% | 26.6% | 1.6% |
| Oregon | 7 | | 1,827,864 | 1,037,291 | 738,475 | 52,098 | 298,816 | D | 56.7% | 40.4% | 2.9% |
| Washington | 11 | | 3,036,878 | 1,750,848 | 1,229,216 | 56,814 | 521,632 | D | 57.7% | 40.5% | 1.9% |
| Total | 77 | 0 | 18,880,210 | 11,388,483 | 7,100,038 | 391,689 | 4,288,445 | D | 60.3% | 37.6% | 2.1% |
| **DEMOCRATIC COASTS** | 194 | 5 | 47,324,273 | 28,312,022 | 18,248,750 | 763,501 | 10,063,272 | D | 59.8% | 38.6% | 1.6% |

Table 2 continued

| | Electoral Vote Dem. | Electoral Vote Rep. | Total Vote | Obama (Dem.) | McCain (Rep.) | Other | Rep.-Dem. Plurality | | Percentage of Total Vote Obama (Dem.) | McCain (Rep.) | Other |
|---|---|---|---|---|---|---|---|---|---|---|---|
| **INDUSTRIAL MIDWEST** | | | | | | | | | | | |
| Illinois | 21 | | 5,523,051 | 3,419,673 | 2,031,527 | 71,851 | 1,388,146 | D | 61.9% | 36.8% | 1.3% |
| Indiana | 11 | | 2,751,054 | 1,374,039 | 1,345,648 | 31,367 | 28,391 | D | 49.9% | 48.9% | 1.1% |
| Iowa | 7 | | 1,537,123 | 828,940 | 682,379 | 25,804 | 146,561 | D | 53.9% | 44.4% | 1.7% |
| Michigan | 17 | | 5,001,766 | 2,872,579 | 2,048,639 | 80,548 | 823,940 | D | 57.4% | 41.0% | 1.6% |
| Minnesota | 10 | | 2,910,369 | 1,573,354 | 1,275,409 | 61,606 | 297,945 | D | 54.1% | 43.8% | 2.1% |
| Missouri | | 11 | 2,925,205 | 1,441,911 | 1,445,814 | 37,480 | 3,903 | R | 49.3% | 49.4% | 1.3% |
| Ohio | 20 | | 5,698,260 | 2,933,388 | 2,674,491 | 90,381 | 258,897 | D | 51.5% | 46.9% | 1.6% |
| Wisconsin | 10 | | 2,983,417 | 1,677,211 | 1,262,393 | 43,813 | 414,818 | D | 56.2% | 42.3% | 1.5% |
| Total | 96 | 11 | 29,330,245 | 16,121,095 | 12,766,300 | 442,850 | 3,354,795 | D | 55.0% | 43.5% | 1.5% |
| **NATIONAL TOTAL** | 365 | 173 | 131,235,440 | 69,459,909 | 59,930,608 | 1,844,923 | 9,529,301 | D | 52.9% | 45.7% | 1.4% |

Note: Results are based on official returns posted on the election Web sites of states and the District of Columbia. They are subject to minor changes.

Source: "The Rhodes Cook Letter," December 2008.

Table 3. The 2004 and 2008 Presidential Votes

| State | 2-Party Vote Percentage–2004 Kerry | | 2-Party Vote Percentage–2004 Bush | | 2-Party Vote Percentage–2008 Obama | | 2-Party Vote Percentage–2008 McCain | | Obama change from Kerry |
| --- | --- | --- | --- | --- | --- | --- | --- | --- | --- |
| | Votes | Percent | Votes | Percent | Votes | Percent | Votes | Percent | |
| Alabama | 693,933 | 37.1% | 1,176,394 | 62.9% | 813,479 | 39.1% | 1,266,546 | 60.9% | 2.0% |
| Alaska | 111,025 | 36.8% | 190,889 | 63.2% | 123,594 | 38.9% | 193,841 | 61.1% | 2.2% |
| Arizona | 893,524 | 44.7% | 1,104,294 | 55.3% | 1,034,707 | 45.7% | 1,230,111 | 54.3% | 1.0% |
| Arkansas | 468,631 | 45.0% | 572,770 | 55.0% | 422,310 | 39.8% | 638,017 | 60.2% | −5.2% |
| California | 6,745,485 | 55.0% | 5,509,826 | 45.0% | 8,274,473 | 62.3% | 5,011,781 | 37.7% | 7.2% |
| Colorado | 1,001,732 | 47.6% | 1,101,255 | 52.4% | 1,288,568 | 54.6% | 1,073,584 | 45.4% | 6.9% |
| Connecticut | 857,488 | 55.3% | 693,826 | 44.7% | 1,000,994 | 61.4% | 628,873 | 38.6% | 6.1% |
| Delaware | 200,152 | 53.8% | 171,660 | 46.2% | 255,459 | 62.6% | 152,374 | 37.4% | 8.8% |
| Florida | 3,583,544 | 47.5% | 3,964,522 | 52.5% | 4,282,074 | 51.4% | 4,045,624 | 48.6% | 3.9% |
| Georgia | 1,366,149 | 41.6% | 1,914,254 | 58.4% | 1,844,137 | 47.4% | 2,048,744 | 52.6% | 5.7% |
| Hawaii | 231,708 | 54.4% | 194,191 | 45.6% | 325,871 | 73.0% | 120,566 | 27.0% | 18.6% |
| Idaho | 181,098 | 30.7% | 409,235 | 69.3% | 236,440 | 37.0% | 403,012 | 63.0% | 6.3% |
| Illinois | 2,891,989 | 55.2% | 2,346,608 | 44.8% | 3,419,673 | 62.7% | 2,031,527 | 37.3% | 7.5% |
| Indiana | 969,011 | 39.6% | 1,479,438 | 60.4% | 1,374,039 | 50.5% | 1,345,648 | 49.5% | 10.9% |
| Iowa | 741,898 | 49.7% | 751,957 | 50.3% | 828,940 | 54.8% | 682,379 | 45.2% | 5.2% |
| Kansas | 434,993 | 37.1% | 736,456 | 62.9% | 514,765 | 42.4% | 699,655 | 57.6% | 5.3% |
| Kentucky | 712,733 | 40.0% | 1,069,439 | 60.0% | 751,985 | 41.8% | 1,048,462 | 58.2% | 1.8% |
| Louisiana | 820,299 | 42.7% | 1,102,169 | 57.3% | 782,989 | 40.5% | 1,148,275 | 59.5% | −2.1% |
| Maine | 396,842 | 54.6% | 330,201 | 45.4% | 421,923 | 58.8% | 295,273 | 41.2% | 4.2% |
| Maryland | 1,334,493 | 56.6% | 1,024,703 | 43.4% | 1,628,995 | 62.9% | 959,694 | 37.1% | 6.4% |
| Massachusetts | 1,803,800 | 62.7% | 1,071,109 | 37.3% | 1,904,097 | 63.2% | 1,108,854 | 36.8% | 0.5% |
| Michigan | 2,479,183 | 51.7% | 2,313,746 | 48.3% | 2,872,579 | 58.4% | 2,048,639 | 41.6% | 6.6% |

Table 3 continued

| State | 2-Party Vote %—2004 | | | | 2-Party Vote %—2008 | | | | Obama change from Kerry |
|---|---|---|---|---|---|---|---|---|---|
| | Kerry Votes | Kerry Percent | Bush Votes | Bush Percent | Obama Votes | Obama Percent | McCain Votes | McCain Percent | |
| Minnesota | 1,445,014 | 51.8% | 1,346,695 | 48.2% | 1,573,354 | 55.2% | 1,275,409 | 44.8% | 3.5% |
| Mississippi | 457,766 | 40.5% | 672,660 | 59.5% | 554,662 | 43.4% | 724,597 | 56.6% | 2.9% |
| Missouri | 1,259,171 | 46.4% | 1,455,713 | 53.6% | 1,441,911 | 49.9% | 1,445,814 | 50.1% | 3.6% |
| Montana | 173,710 | 39.5% | 266,063 | 60.5% | 231,667 | 48.8% | 242,763 | 51.2% | 9.3% |
| Nebraska | 254,328 | 33.2% | 512,814 | 66.8% | 333,319 | 42.4% | 452,979 | 57.6% | 9.2% |
| Nevada | 397,190 | 48.7% | 418,690 | 51.3% | 533,736 | 56.4% | 412,827 | 43.6% | 7.7% |
| New Hampshire | 340,511 | 50.7% | 331,237 | 49.3% | 384,826 | 54.9% | 316,534 | 45.1% | 4.2% |
| New Jersey | 1,911,430 | 53.4% | 1,668,003 | 46.6% | 2,215,422 | 57.9% | 1,613,207 | 42.1% | 4.5% |
| New Mexico | 370,942 | 49.6% | 376,930 | 50.4% | 472,422 | 57.7% | 346,832 | 42.3% | 8.1% |
| New York | 4,314,280 | 59.3% | 2,962,567 | 40.7% | 4,769,700 | 63.5% | 2,742,298 | 36.5% | 4.2% |
| North Carolina | 1,525,849 | 43.8% | 1,961,166 | 56.2% | 2,142,651 | 50.2% | 2,128,474 | 49.8% | 6.4% |
| North Dakota | 111,052 | 36.1% | 196,651 | 63.9% | 141,278 | 45.6% | 168,601 | 54.4% | 9.5% |
| Ohio | 2,739,952 | 48.9% | 2,858,727 | 51.1% | 2,933,388 | 52.3% | 2,674,491 | 47.7% | 3.4% |
| Oklahoma | 503,966 | 34.4% | 959,792 | 65.6% | 502,496 | 34.4% | 960,165 | 65.6% | -0.1% |
| Oregon | 943,163 | 52.1% | 866,831 | 47.9% | 1,037,291 | 58.4% | 738,475 | 41.6% | 6.3% |
| Pennsylvania | 2,938,095 | 51.3% | 2,793,847 | 48.7% | 3,276,363 | 55.3% | 2,651,812 | 44.7% | 4.0% |
| Rhode Island | 259,760 | 60.6% | 169,046 | 39.4% | 296,571 | 64.2% | 165,391 | 35.8% | 3.6% |
| South Carolina | 661,699 | 41.4% | 937,974 | 58.6% | 862,449 | 45.5% | 1,034,896 | 54.5% | 4.1% |
| South Dakota | 149,244 | 39.1% | 232,584 | 60.9% | 170,924 | 45.7% | 203,054 | 54.3% | 6.6% |
| Tennessee | 1,036,477 | 42.8% | 1,384,375 | 57.2% | 1,087,437 | 42.4% | 1,479,178 | 57.6% | -0.4% |
| Texas | 2,832,704 | 38.5% | 4,526,917 | 61.5% | 3,528,633 | 44.1% | 4,479,328 | 55.9% | 5.6% |
| Utah | 241,199 | 26.7% | 663,742 | 73.3% | 327,670 | 35.5% | 596,030 | 64.5% | 8.8% |
| Vermont | 184,067 | 60.3% | 121,180 | 39.7% | 219,262 | 68.9% | 98,974 | 31.1% | 8.6% |

Table 3 continued

| State | 2-Party Vote %–2004 Kerry | | Bush | State | 2-Party Vote %–2008 Obama | | McCain | | Obama change from Kerry |
|---|---|---|---|---|---|---|---|---|---|
| | Votes | Percent | Percent | | Votes | Percent | Votes | Percent | |
| Virginia | 1,454,742 | 45.9% | 54.1% | Virginia | 1,959,532 | 53.2% | 1,725,005 | 46.8% | 7.3% |
| Washington | 1,510,201 | 53.6% | 46.4% | Washington | 1,750,848 | 58.8% | 1,229,216 | 41.2% | 5.1% |
| West Virginia | 326,541 | 43.5% | 56.5% | West Virginia | 304,127 | 43.3% | 398,061 | 56.7% | -0.2% |
| Wisconsin | 1,489,504 | 50.2% | 49.8% | Wisconsin | 1,677,211 | 57.1% | 1,262,393 | 42.9% | 6.9% |
| Wyoming | 70,776 | 29.7% | 70.3% | Wyoming | 82,868 | 33.4% | 164,958 | 66.6% | 3.8% |
| Dist. Of Col. | 202,970 | 90.5% | 9.5% | Dist. Of Col. | 245,800 | 93.4% | 17,367 | 6.6% | 2.9% |
| Total | 59,026,013 | 48.8% | 51.2% | Total | 69,459,909 | 53.7% | 59,930,608 | 46.3% | 4.9% |
| Votes | 62,025,554 | | | | | | | | |

Sources: 2004 figures adapted from Larry Sabato, *Divided States of America: The Slash and Burn Politics of the 2004 Presidential Election.* New York: Pearson Longman, 2005

2008 figures adapted from "The Rhodes Cook Letter," December 2008.

## Table 4. U.S. President Election Results—National Exit Poll

### Vote by Gender

| | Obama | | McCain |
|---|---|---|---|
| Total | 2008 | Change from Kerry (2004) | 2008 |
| Male (47%) | 49% | +5% | 48% |
| Female (53%) | 56% | +5% | 43% |

### Vote by Race and Gender

| | Obama | | McCain |
|---|---|---|---|
| Total | 2008 | Change from Kerry (2004) | 2008 |
| White Men (36%) | 41% | +4% | 57% |
| White Women (39%) | 46% | +2% | 53% |
| Black Men (5%) | 95% | n/a | 5% |
| Black Women (7%) | 96% | n/a | 3% |
| Latino Men (4%) | 64% | n/a | 33% |
| Latino Women (5%) | 68% | n/a | 30% |
| All Other Races (5%) | 64% | n/a | 32% |

### Vote by Race

| | Obama | | McCain |
|---|---|---|---|
| Total | 2008 | Change from Kerry (2004) | 2008 |
| White (74%) | 43% | +2% | 55% |
| African-American (13%) | 95% | +7% | 4% |
| Latino (9%) | 67% | +14% | 31% |
| Asian (2%) | 62% | +6% | 35% |
| Other (3%) | 66% | +12% | 31% |

### Vote by Age

| | Obama | | McCain |
|---|---|---|---|
| Total | 2008 | Change from Kerry (2004) | 2008 |
| 18–29 (17%) | 66% | +12% | 32% |
| 30–44 (29%) | 52% | +6% | 46% |
| 45–59 (30%) | 50% | +2% | 49% |
| 60 and Older (24%) | 45% | –1% | 53% |

Table 4 continued

**Vote by Age and Race**

| Total | Obama 2008 | Change from Kerry (2004) | McCain 2008 |
|---|---|---|---|
| White 18–29 (11%) | 54% | n/a | 44% |
| White 30–44 (20%) | 41% | n/a | 57% |
| White 45–64 (30%) | 42% | n/a | 56% |
| White 65 and Older (13%) | 40% | n/a | 58% |
| Black 18–29 (3%) | 95% | n/a | 4% |
| Black 30–44 (4%) | 96% | n/a | 4% |
| Black 45–64 (4%) | 96% | n/a | 3% |
| Black 65 and Older (1%) | 94% | n/a | 6% |
| Latino 18–29 (3%) | 76% | n/a | 19% |
| Latino 30–44 (3%) | 63% | n/a | 36% |
| Latino 45–64 (2%) | 58% | n/a | 40% |
| Latino 65 and Older (1%) | 68% | n/a | 30% |
| All Others (5%) | 64% | n/a | 33% |

**Vote by Income**

| Total | Obama 2008 | Change from Kerry (2004) | McCain 2008 |
|---|---|---|---|
| Under $15,000 (6%) | 73% | +10% | 25% |
| $15–30,000 (12%) | 60% | +3% | 37% |
| $30–50,000 (19%) | 55% | –5% | 43% |
| $50–75,000 (21%) | 48% | +5% | 49% |
| $75–100,000 (15%) | 51% | +6% | 48% |
| $100–150,000 (14%) | 48% | +6% | 51% |
| $150–200,000 (6%) | 48% | +6% | 50% |
| $200,000 or More (6%) | 52% | +17% | 46% |

**Vote by Income**

| Total | Obama 2008 | Change from Kerry (2004) | McCain 2008 |
|---|---|---|---|
| Less than $50,000 (38%) | 60% | +5% | 38% |
| $50,000 or More (62%) | 49% | +6% | 49% |

**Vote by Income**

| Total | Obama 2008 | Change from Kerry (2004) | McCain 2008 |
|---|---|---|---|
| Less than $100,000 (74%) | 55% | +5% | 43% |
| $100,000 or More (26%) | 49% | +8% | 49% |

Table 4 continued

### Are you a union member?

| Total | Obama 2008 | Change from Kerry (2004) | McCain 2008 |
|---|---|---|---|
| Yes (12%) | 60% | n/a | 37% |
| No (88%) | 52% | n/a | 46% |

### Do you work full-time?

| Total | Obama 2008 | Change from Kerry (2004) | McCain 2008 |
|---|---|---|---|
| Yes (65%) | 55% | +10% | 44% |
| No (35%) | 50% | +1% | 48% |

### Vote by Education

| Total | Obama 2008 | Change from Kerry (2004) | McCain 2008 |
|---|---|---|---|
| No High School (4%) | 63% | +13% | 35% |
| H.S. Graduate (20%) | 52% | +5% | 46% |
| Some College (31%) | 51% | +5% | 47% |
| College Graduate (28%) | 50% | +4% | 48% |
| Postgraduate (17%) | 58% | +3% | 40% |

### Vote by Party ID

| Total | Obama 2008 | Change from Kerry (2004) | McCain 2008 |
|---|---|---|---|
| Democrat (39%) | 89% | 0 | 10% |
| Republican (32%) | 9% | +3% | 90% |
| Independent (29%) | 52% | +3% | 44% |

### Vote by Race and Party ID

| Total | Obama 2008 | Change from Kerry (2004) | McCain 2008 |
|---|---|---|---|
| White Democrats (23%) | 85% | n/a | 14% |
| White Independents (23%) | 47% | n/a | 49% |
| White Republicans (29%) | 8% | n/a | 91% |
| All Others (26%) | 80% | n/a | 18% |

Table 4 continued

### Vote by Ideology

| | Obama | | McCain |
|---|---|---|---|
| Total | 2008 | Change from Kerry (2004) | 2008 |
| Liberal (22%) | 89% | +4% | 10% |
| Moderate (44%) | 60% | +6% | 39% |
| Conservative (34%) | 20% | +5% | 78% |

### Have you ever voted before?

| | Obama | | McCain |
|---|---|---|---|
| Total | 2008 | Change from Kerry (2004) | 2008 |
| No (11%) | 69% | +16% | 30% |
| Yes (89%) | 50% | +2% | 48% |

### Vote by Religion

| | Obama | | McCain |
|---|---|---|---|
| Total | 2008 | Change from Kerry (2004) | 2008 |
| Protestant (54%) | 45% | +5% | 54% |
| Catholic (27%) | 54% | +7% | 45% |
| Jewish (2%) | 78% | +4% | 21% |
| Other (6%) | 73% | −1% | 22% |
| None (12%) | 75% | +8% | 23% |

### Vote by Religion Among Whites

| | Obama | | McCain |
|---|---|---|---|
| Total | 2008 | Change from Kerry (2004) | 2008 |
| White Protestant (42%) | 34% | n/a | 65% |
| White Catholic (19%) | 47% | n/a | 52% |
| White Jewish (2%) | 83% | n/a | 16% |
| White—Other Religion (3%) | 67% | n/a | 28% |
| White—No Religion (8%) | 71% | n/a | 26% |
| Non-whites (26%) | 79% | n/a | 18% |

### White Evangelical/Born-Again

| | Obama | | McCain |
|---|---|---|---|
| Total | 2008 | Change from Kerry (2004) | 2008 |
| Yes (26%) | 24% | +3% | 74% |
| No (74%) | 62% | +6% | 36% |

Table 4 continued

**Vote by Church Attendance**

| Total | Obama | | McCain |
| --- | --- | --- | --- |
| | 2008 | Change from Kerry (2004) | 2008 |
| More Than Weekly (12%) | 43% | +8% | 55% |
| Weekly (27%) | 43% | +2% | 55% |
| Monthly (15%) | 53% | +4% | 46% |
| A Few Times a Year (28%) | 59% | +10% | 39% |
| Never (16%) | 67% | +5% | 30% |

**Have you ever served in the military?**

| Total | Obama | | McCain |
| --- | --- | --- | --- |
| | 2008 | Change from Kerry (2004) | 2008 |
| Yes (15%) | 44% | +3% | 54% |
| No (85%) | 54% | +4% | 44% |

**Vote by Marital Status**

| Total | Obama | | McCain |
| --- | --- | --- | --- |
| | 2008 | Change from Kerry (2004) | 2008 |
| Married (66%) | 47% | +5% | 52% |
| Unmarried (34%) | 65% | +7% | 33% |

**Are you gay, lesbian, or bisexual?**

| Total | Obama | | McCain |
| --- | --- | --- | --- |
| | 2008 | Change from Kerry (2004) | 2008 |
| Total | 2008 | Kerry (2004) | 2008 |
| Yes (4%) | 70% | −7% | 27% |
| No (96%) | 53% | +7% | 45% |

**Gun owner in household?**

| Total | Obama | | McCain |
| --- | --- | --- | --- |
| | 2008 | Change from Kerry (2004) | 2008 |
| Yes (42%) | 37% | +1% | 62% |
| No (58%) | 65% | +8% | 33% |

Table 4 continued

**When did you decide who to vote for?**

| | Obama | | McCain |
|---|---|---|---|
| Total | 2008 | Change from Kerry (2004) | 2008 |
| Within Last Week (7%) | 49% | n/a | 48% |
| Earlier in October (18%) | 53% | n/a | 44% |
| Sometime in September (14%) | 54% | n/a | 45% |
| Earlier Than That (60%) | 52% | n/a | 47% |

**Most Important Issue**

| | Obama | | McCain |
|---|---|---|---|
| Total | 2008 | Change from Kerry (2004) | 2008 |
| Energy Policy (7%) | 50% | n/a | 46% |
| Iraq (10%) | 59% | n/a | 39% |
| Economy (63%) | 53% | n/a | 44% |
| Terrorism (9%) | 13% | n/a | 86% |
| Health Care (9%) | 73% | n/a | 26% |

**How Bush is Handling His Job**

| | Obama | | McCain |
|---|---|---|---|
| Total | 2008 | Change from Kerry (2004) | 2008 |
| Approve (27%) | 10% | +1% | 89% |
| Disapprove (71%) | 67% | −26% | 31% |

**Most Important Quality**

| | Obama | | McCain |
|---|---|---|---|
| Total | 2008 | Change from Kerry (2004) | 2008 |
| Shares My Values (30%) | 32% | n/a | 65% |
| Can Bring Change (34%) | 89% | n/a | 9% |
| Experience (20%) | 7% | n/a | 93% |
| Cares About People (12%) | 74% | n/a | 24% |

**U.S. War in Iraq**

| | Obama | | McCain |
|---|---|---|---|
| Total | 2008 | Change from Kerry (2004) | 2008 |
| Approve (36%) | 13% | n/a | 86% |
| Disapprove (63%) | 76% | n/a | 22% |

Table 4 continued

**Family's Financial Situation**

| Total | Obama | | McCain |
|---|---|---|---|
| | 2008 | Change from Kerry (2004) | 2008 |
| Better (24%) | 37% | +18% | 60% |
| Worse (42%) | 71% | –8% | 28% |
| Same (34%) | 45% | –5% | 53% |

**Were you contacted by Obama campaign?**

| Total | Obama | | McCain |
|---|---|---|---|
| | 2008 | Change from Kerry (2004) | 2008 |
| Yes (26%) | 64% | n/a | 34% |
| No (72%) | 48% | n/a | 50% |

**Were you contacted by McCain campaign?**

| Total | Obama | | McCain |
|---|---|---|---|
| | 2008 | Change from Kerry (2004) | 2008 |
| Yes (18%) | 38% | n/a | 60% |
| No (79%) | 55% | n/a | 43% |

**Did any campaign contact you personally?**

| Total | Obama | | McCain |
|---|---|---|---|
| | 2008 | Change from Kerry (2004) | 2008 |
| Yes, Only Obama (13%) | 80% | n/a | 19% |
| Yes, Only McCain (6%) | 17% | n/a | 82% |
| Yes, Both (13%) | 47% | n/a | 51% |
| No Contact (66%) | 50% | n/a | 48% |

**Presidential Vote in 2004**

| Total | Obama | | McCain |
|---|---|---|---|
| | 2008 | Change from Kerry (2004) | 2008 |
| Kerry (37%) | 89% | n/a | 9% |
| Bush (46%) | 17% | n/a | 82% |
| Someone Else (4%) | 66% | n/a | 24% |
| Did Not Vote (13%) | 71% | n/a | 27% |

Table 4 continued

## Country is Going In . . .

| Total | Obama 2008 | Change from Kerry (2004) | McCain 2008 |
|---|---|---|---|
| Right Direction (20%) | 27% | +17% | 71% |
| Wrong Track (75%) | 62% | –24% | 36% |

### Vote by Size of Place

| Total | Obama 2008 | Change from Kerry (2004) | McCain 2008 |
|---|---|---|---|
| Urban (30%) | 63% | +9% | 35% |
| Suburban (49%) | 50% | +3% | 48% |
| Rural (21%) | 45% | +3% | 53% |

### Who did you want to win the Democratic nomination?

| Total | Obama 2008 | Change from Kerry (2004) | McCain 2008 |
|---|---|---|---|
| Clinton Democrats (14%) | 83% | n/a | 16% |
| Obama Democrats (20%) | 98% | n/a | 2% |
| Dems for Other Candidates (2%) | 63% | n/a | 35% |
| Dems with No Preference (2%) | 75% | n/a | 25% |
| Independents/Republicans (59%) | 31% | n/a | 67% |

### Is Biden qualified to be President?

| Total | Obama 2008 | Change from Kerry (2004) | McCain 2008 |
|---|---|---|---|
| Yes (66%) | 71% | n/a | 28% |
| No (32%) | 17% | n/a | 80% |

### Is Palin qualified to be President?

| Total | Obama 2008 | Change from Kerry (2004) | McCain 2008 |
|---|---|---|---|
| Yes (38%) | 8% | n/a | 91% |
| No (60%) | 82% | n/a | 16% |

Source: CNN, http://www.cnn.com/ELECTION/2008/results/polls/#USP00p1

# NOTES

[1]There have actually been longer campaigns. When Andrew Jackson was defeated by John Quincy Adams in the disputed election of 1824, Jackson was bitter about the so-called "corrupt bargain" between Adams and another presidential candidate, Henry Clay. Clay threw his support to Adams, and President Adams in turn made Clay his secretary of state, at that time the position widely viewed as the best preparation for the presidency. Jackson had led both the popular and Electoral College votes in 1824, so the Adams-Clay alliance deposed the frontrunning Jackson when the House of Representatives broke the deadlock and selected the president. The furious Jackson launched his second, eventually successful attempt at the White House in the spring of 1825, shortly after Adams took the oath of office. In 1888, when President Grover Cleveland won the popular vote for a second term but lost the Electoral College majority, he told everyone from the Congress to the White House staff that he would be back in 1892, and indeed he was. Cleveland waged a four-year-long campaign against the president, Benjamin Harrison, whose single term (1889–1893) bracketed Cleveland's nonconsecutive terms.

[2]This can produce an awkward situation, as when Vice Presidents Richard Nixon in 1960 and Albert Gore in 2000 announced their own defeats at the hands of, respectively, John F. Kennedy and George W. Bush. Both Nixon and Gore handled the matter with grace.

[3]Apparently, this was a protest of the fact that the District has no voting members in either house of Congress. But the somewhat pointless act deprived Democrat Al Gore of an elector that could have mattered under other circumstances. Bush defeated Gore by 271 to 266 electoral votes, with the faithless elector's vote not counted. In 2004 there was yet another faithless elector, in Minnesota, where a vote was cast for Democratic vice-presidential nominee John Edwards instead of presidential nominee John Kerry. However, we should stress that faithless electors are rare, and there have been only six out of 5,380 since 1968. See Larry J. Sabato, A More Perfect Constitution (New York: Walker, 2007), Chapter Four.

[4]Maine's split system went into effect with the 1972 presidential election, and Nebraska's with the 1992 presidential election. Obama received 50.0 percent to McCain's 48.8 percent in Nebraska's Second District—a close margin of about 3,300 votes out of approximately 278,000 cast.

[5]See Larry J. Sabato, ed., TOWARD THE MILLENNIUM: The Elections of 1996 (Boston: Allyn and Bacon, 1997).

[6]Democrat Samuel J. Tilden received a shade under 51 percent in the hotly disputed presidential election of 1876, but Republican Rutherford B. Hayes won the White House with the narrowest possible, and arguably fraudulent, Electoral College majority.

[7]These estimates are based on the voting-eligible population (VEP), as constructed by Michael McDonald of George Mason University. The VEP is the number of American residents over the age of 18, excluding noncitizens and ineligible felons, per state law. For more on the VEP, visit http://elections.gmu.edu or see Michael McDonald, "The Return of the Voter: Voter Turnout in the 2008 Presidential Election," The Forum, forthcoming.

[8]See V.O. Key, Southern Politics in State and Nation (New York, Alfred A. Knopf, 1949).

[9]New York: Longman Publishers, 2002. pp. 103–105.

[10]See Larry J. Sabato, OVERTIME! The Election 2000 Thriller (New York: Pearson, 2002), pp. 111–117; Sabato, Midterm Madness: The Elections of 2002 (Lanham, Mass.: Rowman & Littlefield, 2003), pp. 10–11, 32; and Sabato, Divided States of America: The Slash and Burn Politics of the 2004 Presidential Election (New York: Pearson Longman, 2005), pp. 65–69.

[11]Other "North Stars" include the scandal factor and cutting cultural and social issues, but neither had much impact in 2008, so overwhelming were the three "Stars" cited in the text.

[12]Gallup, "Presidential Job Approval in Depth," http://www.gallup.com/poll/1723/Presidential-Job-Approval-Depth.aspx.

[13]Alan Abramowitz, Thomas Mann, and Larry J. Sabato, "The Myth of a Toss-up Election," *Larry Sabato's Crystal Ball* (July 24, 2008). http://www.centerforpolitics.org/crystalball/article.php?id=AIA2008072401

# Chapter 3

# From Republican "Lock" to Republican "Lockout"?

### Rhodes Cook

The presidential election of 2008 was long and historic. And at the end, the Democratic victor, Barack Obama, established himself as the most impressive vote-getter of the new millennium.

His electoral vote total of 365 was the highest for any presidential winner since Bill Clinton's reelection in 1996.

His 53-percent share of the total popular vote was the largest since George H.W. Bush won a comparable proportion in 1988.

His popular vote margin of more than 9 million votes was the widest since Ronald Reagan's landslide reelection victory over Walter Mondale in 1984.

And Obama's popular vote total of more than 69 million was by far the most ever received by a presidential candidate in the nation's history. It easily surpassed the previous record of 62 million cast for George W. Bush in 2004.[1]

It is hard to imagine that barely 20 years ago, it was fashionable to talk of a Republican "lock"—a GOP dominance of the electoral map so strong that it appeared to guarantee the party possession of the White House for years to come.

But, as is often said: That was then and this is now. Then, the Republicans had the "three S's" on their side—the South, the suburbs and small-town America. Now, many of the suburbs have defected to the Democrats, the South is no longer an exclusively GOP preserve, and small-town America does not have the votes to keep the Republicans consistently competitive in national politics.

In their presidential heyday of the 1970s and 1980s, the GOP swept 40 or more states in four separate elections with three different presidential candidates—Richard Nixon, Reagan (twice) and Bush the elder.[2] In the aggregate tally for these two decades, Republicans won nearly 50 million more popular votes than the Democrats and the GOP averaged 440 electoral votes per election.[3]

But since then, Democrats have won three of the last five presidential elections (four, if their popular vote victory in 2000 is counted), and surpassed 350 electoral votes in 1992, 1996 and 2008. The George W. Bush interlude produced modest Republican victories of 271 and 286 electoral votes respectively.[4]

---

**Figure 1. 2008 Popular Vote for President**

More votes were cast for president in 2008 than any previous election in the nation's history. And more votes were cast for Barack Obama than any previous presidential candidate. Candidates listed here drew at least 100,000 votes in the 2008 presidential election.

| Candidate (Party) | Vote | Percentage | Best State | |
|---|---|---|---|---|
| Barack Obama (Democrat) | 69,459,909 | 52.93% | Hawaii | (71.8%) |
| John McCain (Republican) | 59,930,608 | 45.67% | Oklahoma | (65.6%) |
| Ralph Nader (Independent) | 737,505 | 0.56% | Maine | (1.5%) |
| Bob Barr (Libertarian) | 523,432 | 0.40% | Indiana | (1.1%) |
| Chuck Baldwin (Constitution) | 197,453 | 0.15% | Utah | (1.3%) |
| Cynthia McKinney (Green) | 161,313 | 0.12% | Louisiana | (0.5%) |
| Others | 225,220 | 0.17% | — | |
| TOTAL VOTE | 131,235,440 | | | |
| *Obama Plurality* | *9,529,301* | | | |

Note: The popular vote for president in 2008 is based on official returns from the election Web sites of the states and the District of Columbia, subject to minor amendment. The percentages are based on each candidate's share of the total votes cast for presidential candidates. No blank ballots are included in this tally. Best State refers to the state in which each candidate received their highest percentage of the total vote. Although Hawaii was Obama's best state, he drew 92.5% of the vote in the District of Columbia.

Source: The Rhodes Cook Letter, December 2008 issue.

---

After two close elections in 2000 and 2004, the Democrats show signs of launching a new era in presidential politics where it might be difficult for the Republicans to compete. As for the latter, what has gone wrong?

First of all, both Bush presidencies were undermined at the end by sour economies, which smoothed the road for Democratic comebacks in 1992 and 2008.

Second, the Republican "brand" itself was in tatters by 2008—undercut by the lingering war in Iraq, big budget deficits, and the worst economic crisis in decades—all of which were personalized in the unpopular presidency of George W. Bush.

Third, Republicans responded more often than not by nominating aging war heroes—George H.W. Bush (68 years old in 1992), Bob Dole (age 73 in 1996), and John McCain, (72 in 2008). Their nominations painted the picture of a party rooted in the past, as glorious and honorable as that past may have been. Meanwhile, by fielding articulate, 40-something nominees such as Clinton and Obama—the latter the first African American nominated by a major party in the nation's history—the Democrats offered candidates who could be readily identified with the present and the future.[5]

Yet it is far too soon to be talking of a Democratic "lock" with any sense of conviction. New political eras take several elections to validate.

In the meantime, the electorate is in the midst of significant change demographically, as the nation's minority population continues to grow.

More and more voters are finding the ranks of the Independents the place to be.

And for the first time since the early 1990s, Democrats will control both ends of Pennsylvania Avenue in 2009—reaping any blame that is likely to accrue for their governance in these difficult times.

In short, the Republicans could be back on top in a few years just by keeping their distance from any catastrophes that might develop on the Democrats' watch.

But it would also be wise for the Republicans to take a look at how far they have fallen in the past two decades. In 1988, the last presidential election when pundits could point to the possibility of a Republican "lock," the elder Bush swept the majority of states in every region of the country. And with the lone exception of New York, he won all of the big ones that year: Pennsylvania and New Jersey in the Northeast; Illinois, Michigan and Ohio in the Midwest; Florida and Texas in the South; and California in the West.[6]

This year, the picture was reversed. Obama carried all of these large electoral vote prizes, except Texas. And most of them he won by eye-popping margins. The Illinois senator swept California by roughly 3.2 million votes, New York by 2 million, Illinois by nearly 1.4 million, Michigan by more than 800,000, and New Jersey and Pennsylvania by more than 600,000 votes. Of these big electoral vote states, only the high-profile battlegrounds of Florida and Ohio were comparatively close, although Obama won each by a clear-cut margin of more than 200,000 votes.[7]

And for good measure, he also pulled Indiana and Virginia into the Democratic column for the first time since 1964, North Carolina for the first time since 1976, Colorado, Florida, Nevada and Ohio for the first time since the Clinton years, and Iowa and New Mexico for the first time since 2000. Altogether, Obama picked off nine states that had voted for Bush in 2004, as well as holding the 19 states (and the District of Columbia) that had voted Democratic last time.[8]

Part of Obama's sweeping success was due to the unusual amount of energy and enthusiasm he was able to generate around his historic candidacy, the record sums of campaign money he was able to attract, and the successful voter registration drives the Democrats conducted, which helped to expand their base in state after state, particularly among youth and minorities.

In each of these areas, the Democrats far outperformed the Republicans, enabling the Obama campaign to act both aggressively and expansively when looking at the electoral map.

Ominously for the GOP, the Democrats not only competed in a number of states that had been conceded to the Republicans for years, but they also won several of them. The result was a reversal of fortune from 20 years ago. Rather than the hope of a Republican "lock" at the presidential level, the GOP now faces the prospect of a Republican "lockout" for years to come if they do not move quickly to get their act together.

---

**Figure 2.**

**Presidential Voting:**
**Largest States Shifting from Republican to Democrat**

A quarter century or so ago, the Republicans regularly won the White House by dominating presidential voting in the nation's most populous states. But that is no longer the case. In 2008, Democrat Barack Obama scored a decisive electoral vote victory by carrying seven of the eight states with more than 15 electoral votes. Obama won most of them by double-digit margins percentagewise, including California, New York, Pennsylvania, Michigan and his home state of Illinois. Texas was the only state with more than 15 electoral votes to give its tally to Republican John McCain.

| | | Number of Times Voted Democratic | | |
|---|---|---|---|---|
| | '08 Electoral Vote | 1972–1988 (5 elections) | 1992–2008 (5 elections) | 2008 Result |
| California | 55 | 0 | 5 | Obama by 24% |
| Texas | 34 | 1 | 0 | McCain by 12% |
| New York | 31 | 2 | 5 | Obama by 27% |
| Florida | 27 | 1 | 2 | Obama by 3% |
| Illinois | 21 | 0 | 5 | Obama by 25% |
| Pennsylvania | 21 | 1 | 5 | Obama by 10% |
| Ohio | 20 | 1 | 3 | Obama by 4% |
| Michigan | 17 | 0 | 5 | Obama by 16% |

Source: Larry J. Sabato's Crystal Ball, Nov. 13, 2008.

## BUSH, REPUBLICANS AND THE SECOND-TERM BLUES

A part of the GOP's electoral problems have been due to guilt by association—or more specifically, the abysmally low job approval rating for President Bush during his second term. It clouded the electoral prospects for the entire Republican Party in 2008. And it made it hard to remember that as recently as 2004, Republicans were celebrating Bush's reelection coupled with the largest GOP majorities in the House and Senate in more than a half century.

After 2008, Republicans controlled neither end of Pennsylvania Avenue, and their numbers in each chamber of Congress were the lowest since a decade or two back in the last millennium.

To be sure, a president's second term is often filled with angst, whether it was the impeachment of Bill Clinton in the late 1990s, the forced resignation of Richard Nixon in 1974 over the Watergate crisis, or the increasing violence at home and abroad during Lyndon Johnson's one full term in the White House in the mid-1960s.

Yet regardless of the president's popularity, his second term often finds his party shedding congressional seats capped by the loss of the White House itself.

The 2008 election marked the sixth time since Dwight Eisenhower's election in 1952 that one party had held the presidency for two consecutive terms. Yet only once had voters given the president's party a four-year extension in the Oval Office—that, in 1988, when Republican George H.W. Bush won what many observers described as Ronald Reagan's "third term."[9]

Similarly, only once in the last half century has the president's party avoided second term losses in Congress. That came a decade ago when Democrats actually gained a few Senate and House seats during Democrat Bill Clinton's second term.[10]

Yet Republican losses during President George W. Bush's second term were more than the usual election cycles in action. They were steeper than that.

During Eisenhower's recession-plagued second term, the number of Republican senators plunged by 11. During LBJ's embattled term in office following the assassination of John Kennedy, the Democrats dropped ten seats in the Senate and 52 in the House. In turn, Richard Nixon's Watergate-clouded second term, which culminated with Gerald Ford's interregnum, resulted in a Republican loss of nearly 50 House seats.[11]

Pending the outcome of the Minnesota Senate race, Republicans lost 14 Senate seats and about 54 House seats during George W. Bush's second term. And it did not come in the form of a one-time rejection. Rather, the GOP suffered a series of stinging rebukes. It began with the loss of six Senate and 30 House seats in the midterm election of 2006, continued with the loss of

## Figure 3.

## Presidential Approval Ratings:
## Often a Preview of the Election to Come

There is a close, if not inviolable, correlation between a president's preelection job approval rating and his party's success, or lack thereof, in the presidential election that follows. The Gallup Poll began measuring presidential approval in advance of the 1940 election. Since then, the president's party has captured the White House in all but two elections when the incumbent's last preelection rating was above 50%. On the other hand, the president's party has lost all but two elections when the incumbent's final preelection approval score has fallen below 50%, and all of them when the rating has fallen below 40%. With a presidential approval rating of 25% on the eve of the 2008 election, George W. Bush registered the lowest preelection job approval rating ever. That survey was taken Oct. 31–Nov. 2, 2008.

### Presidents Since 1940

| President | Election | President's Status | Last Preelection Approval Rating | Presidential Election Outcome for President's Party |
|---|---|---|---|---|
| Lyndon Johnson (D) | 1964 | On Ballot | 74% | Won by 23% |
| Dwight Eisenhower (R) | 1956 | On Ballot | 68% | Won by 15% |
| Franklin Roosevelt (D) | 1944 | On Ballot | 66% | Won by 7% |
| Franklin Roosevelt (D) | 1940 | On Ballot | 64% | Won by 10% |
| Dwight Eisenhower (R) | 1960 | Open | 58% | Lost by 0.2% |
| Ronald Reagan (R) | 1984 | On Ballot | 58% | Won by 18% |
| Bill Clinton (D) | 2000 | Open | 57% | Won by 0.5%* |
| Richard Nixon (R) | 1972 | On Ballot | 56% | Won by 23% |
| Bill Clinton (D) | 1996 | On Ballot | 54% | Won by 9% |
| Ronald Reagan (R) | 1988 | Open | 51% | Won by 8% |
| George W. Bush (R) | 2004 | On Ballot | 48% | Won by 2% |
| Gerald Ford (R) | 1976 | On Ballot | 45% | Lost by 2% |
| Lyndon Johnson (D) | 1968 | Open | 42% | Lost by 0.7% |
| Harry Truman (D) | 1948 | On Ballot | 40% | Won by 4% |
| Jimmy Carter (D) | 1980 | On Ballot | 37% | Lost by 10% |
| George H.W. Bush (R) | 1992 | On Ballot | 33% | Lost by 6% |
| Harry Truman (D) | 1952 | Open | 32% | Lost by 11% |
| George W. Bush (R) | 2008 | Open | 25% | Lost by 7% |

Note: An asterisk (*) indicates that Democrat Al Gore won the popular vote in 2000, but that Republican George W. Bush won the all-important electoral vote.

Source: Based on Gallup Polls originally published in The Rhodes Cook Letter, October 2008.

three special House elections in early 2008, and culminated that fall with the loss of eight more Senate and more than 20 additional House seats.[12]

What this says loudly and succinctly was that the Republicans lost control of an electoral map that was once their oyster. Simply take a look at the recent House strength of each party to see what has happened geographically. When the GOP captured control of the "people's chamber" in 1994, they did so by winning a majority of seats in three of the four regions—all but the Northeast.

As the years went by, House Republicans also lost their advantage in the West, but maintained control of the body by consolidating their base in the South (the cornerstone of the modern GOP) and the Midwest (the birthplace of the party of Lincoln). Republicans came out of the 2004 election with 40 more House seats than the Democrats in the South and 20 more in the Midwest.[13]

But even that "follow the base" route to a congressional majority was lost during Bush's second term. With the lingering war in Iraq, the worst economic crisis in decades, and the president's job approval numbers in the pits, the Republican "brand" was worth about as much as Confederate money in the months leading up to the 2008 election.

The GOP came out of the election possessing a majority of House seats in just one region—the South. The Democrats held ten more seats than Republicans in the Midwest, nearly 30 more in the West, and almost 60 more in the Northeast. If anyone controls the electoral map these days, it is the Democrats.[14]

## CITIES AND SUBURBS: A WINNING COMBINATION FOR DEMOCRATS

It is not hard to tell where the Republican Party has come a cropper: It's in the nation's suburbs.

Urban America has been a cornerstone of the Democratic Party since Franklin Roosevelt's New Deal. The rural heartland, by and large, has been a Republican mainstay since the party's inception on the eve of the Civil War. But when it comes to winning presidential elections, it is what lies in between that matters most. And Barack Obama's advantage in this often independent, fast-growing terrain—the vote-rich suburbs—ensured his election as the nation's forty-fourth president.

Suburbia helped Republicans control the White House through most of the 1970s and 1980s, backed Democrat Bill Clinton in the 1990s, then Republican George W. Bush as the calendar flipped to the new millennium. In 2008, suburban voters put their faith in Obama—although their level of support resembled a hearty handshake more than a full-scale embrace of the Democratic victor.

According to Election Day exit polls, cities cast 30 percent of all ballots and favored Obama by a margin of nearly 30 percentage points. Small towns and rural areas cast roughly 20 percent of the vote and backed Republican John McCain by nearly 10 points. Meanwhile, the nation's suburbs, which supplied nearly half of all the votes, preferred Obama by a margin of 2 points.[15]

The close nature of the overall suburban vote in part reflects its diversity. Geographically, McCain ran well among suburban voters across the southern tier of the country, from the outskirts of Atlanta to Southern California's Orange County, the latter a bastion of Sun Belt conservatism since the days of Barry Goldwater. But his support there did not help McCain win states that had not already been firmly in the Republican column.

Meanwhile, Obama dominated in Frost Belt suburbs from the tip of Long Island to the San Francisco Bay area, helping him win such key states as Colorado, Michigan, and Pennsylvania.

In Colorado, he won the three suburban counties that ring Denver—Adams, Arapahoe, and Jefferson—becoming the first Democratic presidential nominee to carry the trio since Lyndon Johnson in 1964.

In Michigan, Obama carried both working-class Macomb and more affluent Oakland counties outside Detroit. Macomb, the fabled home of blue-collar "Reagan Democrats" had supported Bush in 2004.

And in Pennsylvania, Obama swept all four suburban counties outside Philadelphia (Bucks, Chester, Delaware, and Montgomery), again, the first Democrat to do so since LBJ.[16]

But probably nowhere was the suburban vote more critical to the Illinois senator than in Virginia, where his strength in the bustling array of communities across the Potomac River from the nation's capital helped a Democrat carry the Old Dominion for the first time since 1964. Altogether, Obama swept the Northern Virginia suburbs by roughly 235,000 votes, almost identical to his victory margin statewide.[17]

The distribution of Obama's vote in Northern Virginia illustrated an important aspect of suburban political archaeology: Democratic strength is often greatest in the inner suburbs adjoining a city and steadily declines as one moves out toward the countryside.

Case in point: The cities of Arlington and Alexandria, which are barely a stone's throw from Washington, D.C., are both inner suburbs. Demographically diverse and liberal in their politics, they each gave Obama more than 70 percent of their vote.

Directly to the west, the middle-class, Republican-oriented Fairfax County of a quarter century ago has been replaced by a more diverse version with a high-tech economy and growing minority population. Fairfax County, the most populous jurisdiction in Virginia, gave Obama 60 percent of the vote.

Meanwhile, the outer suburban counties of Loudoun and Prince William are no longer so Republican as they age and fill in with voters of all stripes. Both counties went for Obama with roughly 55 percent of the vote.[18]

The bad news for Republicans is that it was not so long ago that all of these suburban jurisdictions were voting Republican. Loudoun and Prince William counties both backed Bush in 2004. Fairfax County was in the Democratic presidential column in 2004, but had supported Bush in 2000. Arlington and Alexandria voted for Ronald Reagan in 1980 and for GOP nominees in several elections before that.[19]

The problem for Republicans is that their suburban decline is not just a Virginia problem, but one that is being replicated in other parts of the country. To capture the White House again, the GOP will need to build a coalition that includes rural America and suburbia, just as the Democrats built their own winning coalition in 2008 that featured the cities and the suburbs.

## VOTER TURNOUT: GOOD, BUT NOT GREAT

More than 130 million Americans cast ballots in 2008, the largest turnout for a presidential election in the nation's history.[20]

Yet with the historic nature of this campaign, the intense voter interest in it, and the unusually long lines to cast ballots (both early and on Election Day), many political observers expected a much larger jump in voter turnout than the 8-million vote increase that was recorded.

What happened?

For starters, this was not an election such as 2004, which included a controversial president, a polarized electorate, and two parties that were effectively able to turn out their base vote. The result in 2004 was a turnout spike of nearly 17 million votes from 2000, with both parties turning out millions of voters who had not participated four years earlier.[21]

This year, energy and enthusiasm was disproportionately with one party—the Democrats. Republicans were weighed down by the second-term unpopularity of President Bush, a dispiriting factor that was only partially offset by the addition to the ticket of Alaska's vibrant governor, Sarah Palin, as McCain's running mate.

Meanwhile, the Democrats offered an intriguing (even exciting) candidate in Obama, who ran one of the most audaciously effective presidential campaigns in American history. In the end, the Democratic presidential vote was up more than 10 million from 2004, while the Republican tally was down more than 2 million.[22]

Clearly, there were many stay-at-home Republicans in 2008. In every region of the country except the South, GOP nominee John McCain won fewer ballots than President Bush did four years ago. The Republican downturn was particularly severe in the Democratic strongholds of the Pacific West and the Northeast (off by a combined total of roughly 1.5 million votes). But McCain also ran significantly behind Bush in the battleground states of the Midwest (the swath that extends from Ohio west to Iowa, Minnesota, and Missouri). There, the falloff in the Republican presidential vote was more than 1 million.

In contrast to McCain, Obama increased the Democratic presidential vote from 2004 in every region of the country, with his most notable gains in the Republican heartland of the South, the Plains states and the Mountain West. There, Obama not only picked off six states that Bush had carried last time (Florida, North Carolina, and Virginia in the South, plus Colorado, Nevada, and New Mexico in the Mountain West), but he also drew roughly 4.5 million more votes in this GOP bastion than Democrat John Kerry had last time.

For good measure, Obama also showed himself to be a formidable vote-getter on more favorable terrain. He drew more than 3.5 million more votes than Kerry on the Democratic coasts, and nearly 2 million more in the Midwestern battleground states (where he pulled a trio of states that Bush had carried in 2004 into the Democratic column—Indiana, Iowa, and Ohio).[23]

As demonstration of his broad acceptability, Obama triumphed in four populous states where he had earlier lost primaries decisively to Senator Hillary Clinton—California, New York, Pennsylvania, and Ohio. His combined margin of victory in these four states was in the vicinity of 6 million votes.

The breadth of the Obama victory was a validation of his 50-state strategy, which he executed successfully not once, but twice. The first time came during the Democratic nominating process, when he outlasted Senator Clinton with the help of strong showings in Republican-leaning primary and caucus states. The second time came in the summer and fall. With ground organizations already in place across the country, Obama was able to go on the offensive and mount effective voter registration and get-out-the-vote drives in both traditional battleground and GOP-leaning states.

The high-octane Democratic effort went largely unmatched on the Republican side, with the outcome a significant rise in the presidential vote for the Democrats and a decline for the Republicans. The result: an overall voter turnout that set a record in total numbers, but did not generate the really big surge at the ballot box that many had anticipated.

**Figure 4. Turnout Firsts for Presidential Elections**

Like the nation itself, voter turnout for presidential elections has grown steadily since the early years of the Republic. Less than 400,000 votes were cast in the presidential election of 1824, the first in which there was the semblance of a nationwide popular vote tally.

Turnout exceeded 1 million for the first time for the election of Andrew Jackson in 1828. Forty years later, in the wake of the Civil War, it reached 5 million, and it surpassed the 10-million vote mark in the 1880s. But it was not until women were given the franchise in 1920 that the number of voters reached 25 million.

The 50-million vote mark was not exceeded until after World War II. But turnout has grown quickly since then, surpassing 100 million for the first time in 1992 and 125 million in 2008.

| First Time Election Turnout Exceeded: | Year | Turnout | Winner |
|---|---|---|---|
| 1 million votes | 1828 | 1,148,018 | Andrew Jackson (D-R) |
| 5 million votes | 1868 | 5,722,440 | Ulysses S. Grant (R) |
| 10 million votes | 1884 | 10,058,373 | Grover Cleveland (D) |
| 25 million votes | 1920 | 26,768,613 | Warren Harding (R) |
| 50 million votes | 1952 | 61,550,918 | Dwight Eisenhower (R) |
| 75 million votes | 1972 | 77,718,554 | Richard Nixon (R) |
| 100 million votes | 1992 | 104,425,014 | Bill Clinton (D) |
| 125 million votes | 2008 | 131,235,440 | Barack Obama (D) |

Note: The 2008 turnout figure is based on official returns from the election Web sites of the states and the District of Columbia. The results are subject to minor amendment.

Sources: *Guide to U.S. Elections* (CQ Press); *America at the Polls* (CQ Press).

# THE 2008 ELECTION: A FITTING OUTCOME

In many respects the 2008 election was a fitting conclusion to what was arguably the longest campaign in American history. Obama and the Democrats scored a decisive victory, but not one of landslide proportions. Obama's triumph, by a margin of 7 percentage points in the popular vote tally, lay almost equidistant between a nail-biter and a double-digit romp.

Meanwhile, Democrats gained seats on both sides of Capitol Hill. Yet on the Senate side, they finished short of the 60-seat supermajority that would have enabled them to run the Senate with an iron fist. And in the House, the Democratic pickup fell short of the number that many were projecting they would gain.

In its scope, the 2008 results more closely resembled the Democrats' 1992 win with Bill Clinton atop the ticket than the party's 1964 landslide triumph with Lyndon Johnson at the helm. In short, it had the earmarks of another, "It's the economy, stupid," election, with Democrats greatly benefiting in '08, as they did 16 years earlier, from an economy that had turned sour during a Bush presidency.[24]

As for the Republicans, they were defeated but not annihilated, as some in the party had feared. They emerged from the election with their base in the American heartland penetrated but largely intact. And for the eleventh straight presidential contest since 1964, the GOP nominee won at least 159 electoral votes, a total the Democrats have fallen below a half dozen times in the post-World War II years.[25]

In its contours, the 2008 election was positively "Bubbaesque": "Bubba" Clinton won by 6 percentage points in 1992; Obama won by 7. Clinton won 370 electoral votes; Obama had 365. Clinton was joined by 57 Senate and 258 House Democrats when he was first inaugurated. The '08 voting produced nearly identical Democratic totals.

Where Clinton and Obama dramatically differed was in their share of the popular vote. In 1992, Clinton took 43 percent in a three-way race that included independent Ross Perot. This time, Obama won 53 percent, the largest share for any Democrat since Johnson in 1964. As such, Obama could claim more of a mandate than George W. Bush famously did after his reelection in 2004, when he drew 50.7 percent of the popular vote and 286 electoral votes.[26]

Yet even if he were so inclined, there would not appear to be the votes on Capitol Hill for Obama to fashion an expansive liberal agenda along the lines of LBJ's "Great Society." Moreover, it is doubtful that Obama would want to reprise the aggressively partisan approach that Clinton practiced in the early stages of his presidency, which culminated with the Republican takeover of Congress in 1994.

# Figure 5. Presidential Elections Since 1948: Pendulum Swings to the Democrats

Republicans have won a majority of presidential elections since World War II (9 of 16). But Democrats have had the upper hand of late, taking 3 of the last 5, not counting their popular vote victory in 2000. With Democrats emerging from the 2008 election controlling both ends of Pennsylvania Avenue, what was termed a 50–50 nation at the beginning of the millennium now clearly leans Democratic.

| Election | Candidates | Turnout | Percentage of Total Vote | | | | Plurality (in votes) | Electoral Votes | | |
| --- | --- | --- | --- | --- | --- | --- | --- | --- | --- | --- |
| | | | Dems. | Reps. | Others | | | Dems. | Reps. | Others |
| 1948 | TRUMAN (D)*–Dewey (R) | 48,793,826 | 50% | 45% | 5% | D | 2,188,054 | 303 | 189 | 39 |
| 1952 | EISENHOWER (R)*–Stevenson (D) | 61,550,918 | 44% | 55% | – | R | 6,621,242 | 89 | 442 | – |
| 1956 | EISENHOWER (R)*–Stevenson (D) | 62,026,908 | 42% | 57% | 1% | R | 9,567,720 | 73 | 457 | 1 |
| 1960 | KENNEDY (D)*–Nixon (R) | 68,838,219 | 49.7% | 49.5% | 1% | D | 118,574 | 303 | 219 | 15 |
| 1964 | JOHNSON (D)*–Goldwater (R) | 70,644,592 | 61% | 38% | – | D | 15,951,378 | 486 | 52 | – |
| 1968 | NIXON (R)*–Humphrey (D)–Wallace (AI) | 73,211,875 | 42.7% | 43.4% | 14% | R | 510,314 | 191 | 301 | 46 |
| 1972 | NIXON (R)*–McGovern (D) | 77,718,554 | 38% | 61% | 2% | R | 17,999,528 | 17 | 520 | 1 |
| 1976 | CARTER (D)–Ford (R)* | 81,555,889 | 50% | 48% | 2% | D | 1,682,970 | 297 | 240 | 1 |
| 1980 | REAGAN (R)–Carter (D)*–Anderson (Ind.) | 86,515,221 | 41% | 51% | 8% | R | 8,420,270 | 49 | 489 | – |
| 1984 | REAGAN (R)*–Mondale (D) | 92,652,842 | 41% | 59% | 1% | R | 16,877,890 | 13 | 525 | – |
| 1988 | BUSH (R)–Dukakis (D) | 91,594,809 | 46% | 53% | 1% | R | 7,077,023 | 111 | 426 | 1 |
| 1992 | CLINTON (D)–Bush (R)*–Perot (Ind.) | 104,425,014 | 43% | 37% | 20% | D | 5,805,444 | 370 | 168 | – |
| 1996 | CLINTON (D)*–Dole (R)–Perot (Reform) | 96,277,872 | 49% | 41% | 10% | D | 8,203,602 | 379 | 159 | – |
| 2000 | G.W. BUSH (R)–Gore (D) | 105,396,627 | 48.4% | 47.9% | 4% | D | 537,179 | 266 | 271 | 1 |
| 2004 | G.W. BUSH (R)*–Kerry (D) | 122,295,345 | 48% | 51% | 1% | R | 3,012,171 | 251 | 286 | 1 |
| 2008 | OBAMA (D)–McCain (R) | 131,235,440 | 53% | 46% | 1% | D | 9,529,301 | 365 | 173 | 1 |

Note: Winning presidential candidates are listed first in each election and their names are capitalized. An asterisk (*) denotes an incumbent president. Independent or third-party candidates who received at least 5% of the popular vote are listed. The Democratic and Republican vote percentages are presented in tenths of a percentage point for races that were decided by less than 1 point. A dash (–) indicates that the combined vote share for Others was less than 0.5%. Percentages do not always add to 100 due to rounding. In 2000, Democrat Al Gore won the popular vote, but Republican George W. Bush won the all-important electoral vote. The 2008 voter turnout figure is based on official results posted on the election Web sites of the states and the District of Columbia, and may be subject to minor revisions.

Source: America Votes 26 (CQ Press).

Rather, the Democratic presidential and congressional majorities—strong but not overwhelming—are likely to encourage Obama to follow what appear to be his natural instincts for pragmatism and bipartisan cooperation. That penchant for caution may be even more pronounced as Obama gets set to govern under the cloud of economic crisis and the burden of two wars to manage in Iraq and Afghanistan.

In any event, this election was a fitting outcome for both parties. With the Republicans saddled with an unpopular two-term president, a huge budget deficit, the greatest economic meltdown in decades, and lingering wars in the Middle East, any defeat short of a landslide was about the best they could hope for. As for the Democrats, they now control both ends of Pennsylvania Avenue for the first time since the early 1990s, with strengthened majorities on both sides of Capitol Hill. It gives them room to govern, but not unilaterally. And in these troubled times, that is probably all to the good.

*Note:* This chapter is based on columns by the author that appeared in "Larry J. Sabato's *Crystal Ball*" at http://www.centerforpolitics.org/crystalball/ and the online edition of the *Wall Street Journal.*

## NOTES

[1]Richard M. Scammon, Alice V. McGillivray, and Rhodes Cook, *America Votes 26* (Washington, DC: CQ Press, 2005), p.11. All of the comparative comments in the opening paragraphs of the text on Obama's 2008 presidential showing are based on information found in the two historical charts on page 11 of *America Votes* on the popular vote for president, 1920 to 2004, and the electoral vote for president, 1920 to 2004.

[2]*Mapping the Political Landscape 2005* (Washington, DC Pew Research Center, 2005), p. 120.

[3]Compiled by the author using the charts in *America Votes 26*, p. 11.

[4]*Ibid.*

[5]Michael Beschloss, *American Heritage: The Presidents* (New York, Simon & Schuster, Inc.), p. 477, p. 487, for the ages of George H.W. Bush and Bill Clinton. See Michael Barone with Richard E. Cohen, *The Almanac of American Politics 1996 and 2008* (Washington, DC: National Journal Group, 2008) for the ages of other presidential candidates mentioned with a congressional background.

[6]Alice V. McGillivray, Richard M. Scammon and Rhodes Cook, *America at the Polls 1960–2004* (Washington, DC: CQ Press, 2005), p.11.

[7]Compiled by the author based on official results of the 2008 presidential vote as posted on state election Web sites in November and December 2008.

[8]*Guide to U.S. Elections, Fifth Edition, Volume II* (Washington, DC: CQ Press, 2005), pp. 1620–21.

[9]*America Votes 26*, p. 11.

[10]Harold W. Stanley and Richard Niemi, *Vital Statistics on American Politics 2007–2008* (Washington, DC: CQ Press, 2007), pp. 40–41.

[11]*Ibid.* Computed by the author using the chart, "House and Senate Election Results, by Congress, 1788–2006."

[12]*The Rhodes Cook Letter*, December 2008, 3. The Republican loss of eight Senate seats in 2008 is pending the outcome of the recount in the Minnesota Senate race. If it is won by Republican incumbent Norm Coleman, then the GOP Senate loss in 2008 would stand at seven seats.

[13]*America Votes 26*, ix. The regions are defined as follows: Northeast (12 states plus the District of Columbia): Connecticut, Delaware, Maine, Maryland, Massachusetts, New Hampshire, New Jersey, New York, Pennsylvania, Rhode Island, Vermont, and West Virginia; Midwest (12 states): Illinois, Indiana, Iowa, Kansas, Michigan, Minnesota, Missouri, Nebraska, North Dakota, Ohio, South Dakota, and Wisconsin; South (13 states): Alabama, Arkansas, Florida, Georgia, Kentucky, Louisiana, Mississippi, North Carolina, Oklahoma, South Carolina, Tennessee, Texas, and Virginia; West (13 states): Alaska, Arizona, California, Colorado, Hawaii, Idaho, Montana, Nevada, New Mexico, Oregon, Utah, Washington, and Wyoming.

[14]Rhodes Cook, "Republicans Are Latest to Suffer the Second-Term Blues," *The Wall Street Journal Online*, posted Nov. 20, 2008. This piece can be accessed at http://blogs.wsj.com/politicalperceptions/2008/11/20/republicans-are-latest-to-suffer-the-second-term-blues/. Last accessed March 23, 2009.

[15]Based on the results of a national exit poll of 17,836 respondents that can be accessed at the Cable News Network (CNN) Web site: http://www.cnn.com/ELECTION/2008/results/polls/ in a table titled "Vote by Size of Place." Last accessed March 23, 2009.

[16]Based on a review of county-by-county presidential vote tables for Colorado, Michigan, and Pennsylvania in *America at the Polls 1960–2004*.

[17]The 2008 official presidential election returns for Virginia counties and cities can be accessed at the Web site of the Virginia State Board of Elections: http:www.voterinfo.sbe.virginia.gov/election/DATA/2008/

[18]*Ibid.*

[19]Based on a review of county-by-county presidential vote tables for Virginia in *America at the Polls 1960–2004*.

[20]*America Votes 26*, p.11.

[21]*Mapping the Political Landscape 2005*, p.119. The Republican presidential vote grew by 11.6 million from 2000 to 2004, while the Democratic presidential vote increased by 8 million. Meanwhile, the presidential vote for Ralph Nader dropped by 2.4 million from 2000 to 2004. Nader was the Green Party presidential nominee in 2000 but ran as an independent four years later.

[22]Compiled by the author based on official results of the 2008 presidential vote as posted on state election Web sites in November and December 2008.

[23]In this version of the national political map, the Democratic coasts combine the states of the Northeast (as defined in footnote 13) and the Pacific West (California, Hawaii, Oregon, and Washington). The Republican "L" encompasses the South (again as defined in footnote 13), the Plains States (Kansas, Nebraska, and North and South Dakota) and the Mountain West (Alaska, Arizona, Colorado, Idaho, Montana, Nevada, New Mexico, Utah, and Wyoming). The Midwestern battleground states include Illinois, Indiana, Iowa, Michigan, Minnesota, Missouri, Ohio, and Wisconsin.

[24]In 1964, President Lyndon B. Johnson won 61 percent of the popular vote, and the Democrats emerged with 68 Senate and 295 House seats—producing majorities greater than two to one in both the House and Senate. *Vital Statistics on American Politics 2007–2008*, p. 40.

[25]*America Votes 26*, 11.

[26]*Ibid.*

# Chapter 4

# How Obama Won and What It Means

### Alan I. Abramowitz

It was one of the most remarkable elections in American history. On November 4, 2008, Barack Obama, the son of a white mother from Kansas and a black father from Kenya, was elected to the nation's highest office. On his way to becoming the country's first African American president, the first-term senator from Illinois had to overcome not just racial prejudice, but also persistent rumors that he was a Muslim and concerns about his lack of experience on the national stage. Before that, to win his party's nomination he had to overcome the enormous financial and organizational resources of the early favorite for the Democratic nomination, New York Senator and former First Lady Hillary Clinton, herself a pathbreaking candidate. But he did overcome all of these obstacles, and in so doing, made history. In addition to being the first African American president, the 47-year-old Obama was the first non-southern Democrat to win the White House since John F. Kennedy in 1960 and the youngest candidate to win the presidency since Kennedy. Obama's victory was accompanied by major Democratic gains in the congressional elections. Democrats picked up at least seven seats in the Senate and 20 seats in the House of Representatives, giving them their largest majorities in both chambers since 1995.

2008 was the first presidential election in over 50 years without an incumbent president or vice president on the ballot and the first in over 30 years without a candidate named Clinton or Bush on the ballot. On the Republican side, Arizona Senator John McCain, a party gadfly whose campaign appeared to be dead in the water a year before the election, overcame a field of high profile challengers and the opposition of many conservatives within his own party to secure the GOP nomination. McCain, who turned 72 shortly before

Election Day, was the oldest major party candidate in American history. The gap of 25 years in age between the two major party nominees was also a record.

The 2008 presidential election sparked the interest of the American people like no other in the past 40 years—from the first caucuses and primaries in January all the way until Election Day. Over 131 million Americans cast ballots in the presidential election, an increase of more than 8 million from the 2004 figure of 123 million. The estimated turnout of 62 percent of eligible voters was one of the highest since World War II and the highest since the vote was extended to 18- to 20-year-olds in 1972.[1] African American turnout shattered all previous records. And Americans not only voted in record numbers in 2008, they also volunteered, displayed yard signs and bumper stickers, and donated money to the parties and candidates in record numbers.

It was a campaign full of twists and turns—from Barack Obama's surprise victory in the Iowa caucuses to former New York mayor and early Republican front-runner Rudolph Giuliani's decision to skip the early caucuses and primaries and concentrate on Florida; Hillary Clinton's comeback victory in the New Hampshire primary; revelations of incendiary comments by Obama's former pastor, Jeremiah Wright; Bill Clinton's attacks on Obama in South Carolina; Obama's strong showing in the Super Tuesday primaries and his subsequent victories in a series of primaries and caucuses that gave him a commanding lead in delegates; John McCain's decisive victory over former Massachusetts Governor Mitt Romney in Florida and his subsequent domination of Romney and former Arkansas governor and Baptist minister Mike Huckabee on Super Tuesday; a prolonged dispute between the Obama and Clinton campaigns over the seating of delegates from Florida and Michigan; McCain's selection of little-known Alaska governor Sarah Palin as his running-mate; and a major financial crisis that forced both campaigns to react on the fly to a proposed $700 billion federal bailout of some of the nation's largest banks. Through all of these twists and turns, however, the campaign was shaped by two dominant features of the political environment in 2008—a deteriorating economy and a deeply discontented but divided electorate.

## THE POLITICAL ENVIRONMENT IN 2008

As the 2008 campaign progressed, it became increasingly clear that the United States was experiencing its most serious economic crisis in decades.[2] While it was a financial meltdown on Wall Street that brought the crisis to a head in mid-September, millions of ordinary Americans had been experiencing severe economic stress for months: Unemployment had been rising and the real incomes of most Americans had been falling for well over a year. Underlying the crisis on Wall Street was the reality of falling home values and growing numbers of families facing foreclosure because they were unable to make their mortgage payments. The financial crisis served to reinforce the public's already overwhelmingly negative perceptions of economic conditions. According to a Gallup Poll, for example, between September 14 and September 24, the proportion of Americans rating economic conditions as "excellent" or "good" fell from 22 percent to 12 percent while the proportion rating economic conditions as "poor" rose from 40 percent to 55 percent.[3]

Complicating the challenge posed by the increasingly dire condition of the economy was the fact that the man responsible for dealing with the crisis was one of the most unpopular presidents of the modern era. Even before September's financial meltdown, George W. Bush's approval ratings had been mired in the upper-20s to low-30s for many months. The president was so unpopular, in fact, that his own party took pains to ensure that neither he nor his equally unpopular vice president appeared in person at the Republican National Convention. Of course, that did not stop Democrats from continually attempting to tie the Republican nominee to the man in the White House.

George Bush's low approval ratings were not the only sign of a deeply discontented electorate in 2008. Congress, too, was receiving record-low approval ratings and overwhelming majorities of Americans were telling pollsters that the country was on the wrong track. The high level of discontent among the electorate was affecting the congressional elections as well, contributing to the decisions of 29 Republican House incumbents and five GOP Senate incumbents to retire rather than face potentially tough reelection battles with little prospect of their party regaining majority status. By retiring, these Republican incumbents increased the likelihood that their open seats would be taken over by Democrats. In contrast, only six Democratic House incumbents and one Democratic Senate incumbent chose to voluntarily give up their seats. And the toxic political environment for Republicans was also contributing to a large Democratic advantage in fund-raising in House and Senate elections. Not only were Democratic challengers and open-seat candidates raising considerably more money than Republican challengers and open-seat candidates, but the Democratic House and Senate campaign committees were also raising far more money than their Republican counterparts. As a result, the Democratic committees were able to provide much more assistance to their party's candidates in competitive races than the Republican committees.[4]

But while there was growing sentiment that the country was in serious trouble and that major changes were needed, there was much less agreement about either the causes of the nation's problems or the types of changes that were needed. Americans remained deeply divided over foreign and domestic policy issues, with Democrats and Republicans disagreeing sharply about what to do in Iraq and Afghanistan, how to deal with Iran, how to reform healthcare, whether to extend the Bush tax cuts, how to respond to global warming, whether to allow gays and lesbians to marry, and whether to restrict or expand women's access to abortion.

These disagreements were nothing new, of course. Partisan polarization had been growing in the United States since at least the 1980s. The conservative Democrats and liberal Republicans who exercised considerable influence in the U.S. Senate and House of Representatives during the 1950s and 1960s had become endangered species by the beginning of the twenty-first century. Almost all of them had died, retired, or switched parties. As a result, the parties in Congress were more ideologically distinctive and more internally unified than at any time since the New Deal Era. And it wasn't just party leaders and office-holders that were moving apart. Partisan polarization was increasing among the public as well. Ordinary Democrats and Republicans were as divided in 2008 as at any time in recent history.[5]

One of the most important consequences of growing partisan polarization over the past 30 years has been a significant increase in party loyalty and a marked decline in ticket splitting among voters. In recent presidential and congressional elections, Democratic and Republican identifiers, including independents leaning toward each party, have voted overwhelmingly for their own party's presidential and congressional candidates. As a result, the strongest predictor of the outcome of an election is the proportion of voters who identify with each party in a given constituency.

Given these trends, one of the most important developments in American politics between the 2004 and 2008 elections was an increasing Democratic advantage in party identification. According to annual data compiled by the Gallup Poll, between 2004 and 2008 the percentage of Democratic identifiers in the U.S. electorate increased from 34 percent to 36 percent while the percentage of Republican identifiers decreased from 34 percent to 28 percent. With leaning independents included, the shift was even larger: the percentage of Democrats increased from 48 percent to 52 percent while the percentage of Republicans decreased from 45 percent to 40 percent.[6] Other polling organizations found very similar trends in party identification during this time period.

Gains in party identification were a major factor contributing to the Democratic takeover of the House and Senate in the 2006 midterm elections. According to the national exit polls, between 2004 and 2006 the balance of party identification among voters shifted from a 1-point Republican advantage to a 3-point Democratic advantage. The exit poll questionnaires did not include a question asking independents which party if any they leaned toward. However, the fact that 59 percent of independents in the 2006 national exit poll indicated that they had voted for a Democratic House candidate suggests that Democratic gains in party identification would have been even larger if leaning independents could have been included in the party totals.

The growing Democratic advantage in party identification meant that Barack Obama had a much easier task than John McCain in 2008. In order to win the election, Obama merely had to unify and energize the Democratic base. McCain, in contrast, had to not only unify and energize the Republican base, he also had to cut into Obama's support among weak and independent Democrats. Although he had overcome long odds merely to win his party's nomination, in the end the combination of a deepening economic crisis and a shrinking party base would prove an impossible burden for McCain to overcome.

## THE GENERAL ELECTION CAMPAIGN: THE MONEY GAME

Republicans had reason to feel optimistic in the immediate aftermath of their party's national convention in early September. Presidential candidates typically receive a bounce in the polls right after their party's convention, but John McCain's bounce was larger than most and larger than the bounce Barack Obama had received following the Democratic Convention—large enough to give him a small lead in a number of post-convention polls. Tempering the Republican's optimism, though, were two crucial facts: The national political environment remained extremely difficult for the GOP and, for the first time ever, the Democratic presidential candidate had a significant financial advantage over his Republican opponent.

Barack Obama's decision in June to turn down public financing for his general election campaign received widespread criticism from pundits and political commentators. Obama was the first presidential candidate to turn down public financing of his general election campaign since the current system was created following the Watergate scandal in the 1970s. Some commentators thought that it was risky to turn down $84 million in public funds in the hope that the campaign would be able to raise more money in private contributions. Others thought that the decision would damage Obama's image as a reformer and allow the McCain campaign to paint him as an opportunistic "flip-flopper" since he had earlier agreed to accept public financing.[7] As it turned out, though, the critics were badly mistaken. While the McCain campaign tried to turn Obama's rejection of public financing into a campaign issue, these criticisms never seemed to resonate with the electorate. Public opinion polls found that voters in 2008 were much more concerned about issues that directly affected their lives, such as jobs, taxes, and healthcare, than they were about an "inside baseball" issue like campaign finance. And by turning down public financing, the Obama campaign was able to use the sophisticated fundraising apparatus that it had constructed for the primaries to financially overwhelm the McCain campaign.

By accepting public financing, John McCain received an infusion of $84.1 million into his campaign immediately following the Republican Convention. But it also meant that he could not raise additional campaign funds from private donors, and in the month of September alone, Barack Obama raised over $150 million. As a result, even with substantial assistance from the Republican National Committee, the McCain campaign found itself being badly outspent during the fall campaign.

According to data compiled by the Campaign Finance Institute, between September 1 and October 14, the Obama campaign and the Democratic National Committee outspent the McCain campaign and the Republican National Committee by $266 million to $176 million. Moreover, the McCain campaign was much more financially dependent on the RNC than the Obama campaign was on the DNC. Almost two-thirds of the spending on the Republican side, $111 million out of $176 million, came from the Republican National Committee. In contrast, less than a quarter of the spending on the Democratic side, $64 million out of $266 million, came from the Democratic National Committee.[8] This meant that the Obama campaign had much more control over how money was spent, including the content of political advertising, than did the McCain campaign.

Because of its huge fundraising advantage, the Obama campaign was able to outspend the McCain campaign on television advertising by a wide margin in almost every battleground state. In Florida, Virginia, Ohio, and Colorado, voters saw two or three times as many Obama ads as McCain ads during the final weeks of the campaign. And in the final week of the campaign, the Obama campaign was so flush with cash that it was able to purchase air time on several major networks to broadcast a 30-minute infomercial during prime time, an infomercial that was viewed by more than 30 million households across the United States.

**Table 1. Campaign Ad Buys during September, October and November**

|                    | Obama   | McCain  |
|--------------------|---------|---------|
| Cable TV-Units     | 2,092   | 1,518   |
| Network TV-Units   | 432     | 345     |
| Syndicated TV-Units| 31      | 0       |
| Spot TV-Units      | 299,207 | 164,556 |

Source: The Nielsen Company

The data summarized in Table 1 clearly show that as Election Day approached the Obama campaign's messages were being viewed by more voters more frequently than the McCain campaign's messages. While the McCain campaign was able to almost match the Obama campaign's ad buys on cable and network TV, the Obama campaign was able to run far more spot ads on local television. From the beginning of September through Election Day, the Obama campaign enjoyed nearly a 2-to-1 advantage in local spot advertising, almost all of it focused on the battleground states.

## THE CAMPAIGN MESSAGES

Given the political environment in which the 2008 election took place, it is not surprising that both campaigns emphasized messages of change during their conventions and in their subsequent political advertising. As the out-party, it was natural for the Democrats to focus their message heavily on criticism of the performance of the incumbent Republican administration. At every opportunity, Barack Obama and Joe Biden sought to tie John McCain to President Bush, emphasizing the Republican standard-bearer's support for the president's policies at home and abroad, and especially his support for the administration's economic policies. McCain and Palin, on the other hand, sought to put as much distance between themselves and the unpopular occupant of the Oval Office as possible. They frequently referred to themselves as "mavericks" who had challenged the Republican establishment during their political careers, and promised to bring reform to Washington if elected. Neither President Bush nor his equally unpopular vice president, Dick Cheney, ever appeared on the campaign trail with John McCain or Sarah Palin. Nor did they appear in any political ads sponsored by the McCain campaign or the Republican Party. The president and vice president were featured prominently, however, in ads sponsored by the Obama campaign and the Democratic Party.

Beyond a common emphasis on the need for change, however, there were marked differences between the advertising strategies and messages of the Obama and McCain campaigns. While both campaigns ran a wide variety of ads, and the Obama campaign ran far more ads than the McCain campaign, according to data compiled by the Wisconsin Advertising Project, the proportion of negative ads was much higher on the Republican side than on the Democratic side.[9] During the final weeks of the campaign, the large majority of ads sponsored by the Republican Party and the McCain campaign consisted of attacks on Barack Obama's character and record. These ads sought to portray Obama as inexperienced in national affairs, naïve in his approach to foreign policy, and an extreme liberal on domestic issues.

In addition to portraying Obama as an extreme liberal who would raise taxes on the middle class and surrender in Iraq, Republican ads and speeches by John McCain and Sarah Palin on the campaign trail repeatedly sought to suggest that Obama had a hidden radical past by linking him with William Ayers, a one-time member of a radical anti-Vietnam War organization called the Weather Underground, which had carried out a series of bombings during the 1960s and 1970s. Years later, Ayers had become a distinguished professor in the Department of Education at the University of Illinois campus in Chicago where he served on several local community boards, regularly consulted with prominent political leaders, and came to know Barack Obama. But while Obama and Ayers were acquainted, and Ayers had hosted a fundraiser for Obama during his first campaign for the Illinois State Senate, the two were never personal friends and Obama had strongly criticized Ayers's actions as a member of the Weather Underground—actions that took place when Obama was still in grade school.

The use of fear tactics has a long history in American political campaigns and they have sometimes been successful. In 2002, for example, Republican ads in the aftermath of the September 11 attacks suggested that several incumbent Democratic senators, including Vietnam War veteran and triple-amputee Max Cleland of Georgia, were soft on terrorism because they had opposed provisions of the USA PATRIOT ACT that would have reduced the job protections of federal employees. The ads juxtaposed images of the Democratic senators with an image of Osama bin Laden. Several of the Democratic incumbents, including Cleland, lost their seats. In 2008, however, the McCain campaign's attempt to link Barack Obama to Bill Ayers and the Weather Underground appeared to fall flat. Polls conducted during the final weeks of the campaign indicated that voters found the ads unpersuasive, and they disliked the negative tone of the McCain campaign.

Whether any political message is effective depends on both the plausibility of the message and the mood of the public.[10] In the fall of 2002, barely a year after the September 11 attacks, with American troops at war in Afghanistan and George W. Bush enjoying an approval rating of over 60 percent, many voters were receptive to a message suggesting that Democratic senators who opposed the president on a national security issue were soft on terrorism. In 2008, however, with the economy in crisis and President Bush's approval rating below 30 percent, far fewer voters were receptive to the McCain campaign's message that Barack Obama was an extreme liberal who enjoyed, in the words of Sarah Palin, "palling around with" domestic terrorists.

## THE FINANCIAL CRISIS

At the beginning of the fall campaign the mood of the American public was already extremely sour. Real incomes had been falling and home foreclosures and unemployment had been rising for months. Most Americans believed that the country was already in a recession, even though official government statistics had not yet confirmed that fact. And the public's mood turned even more negative after September 14, 2008. On that date it was announced that Lehman Brothers, one of Wall Street's largest and most prestigious investment banks, was declaring bankruptcy due to massive losses on its mortgage-related securities. That same day, the sale of Merrill Lynch, another Wall Street icon, to Bank of America was announced. Again, the explanation was huge losses on the firm's mortgage-related investments. Although warning signs of an impending financial crisis had been evident for months, it was the beginning of the Wall Street meltdown of 2008.[11]

On Monday, September 15, the Dow Jones Industrial Average lost more than 500 points, or more than 4 percent of its value. Over the next several days, the stock market remained volatile but generally continued to spiral downward. More importantly, national and international credit markets began to seize up out of fear that other large financial institutions might fail. On September 17, AIG, one of the nation's largest insurance companies, suffered a liquidity crisis due to the declining value of its investments in the credit default swaps market. To stave off a bankruptcy that could have had disastrous consequences for the credit markets as well as for many individuals, businesses, and government agencies insured by AIG, the Federal Reserve announced a plan to provide the insurance giant with 85 billion dollars in additional credit in exchange for an ownership share in the company. It was an unprecedented move, and was especially shocking in coming from a conservative, pro-business administration. But it was only a hint of even more massive government intervention in the credit markets to come.

With little apparent improvement in the credit markets and more financial institutions teetering on the brink of bankruptcy, on Friday, September 19, Treasury Secretary Henry Paulson proposed a dramatic plan to save the nation's faltering financial institutions—a $77 billion bailout plan that would have the federal government purchase toxic assets from endangered banks in order to infuse capital into the nation's financial system. It was a plan so enormous and so unprecedented that it forced an immediate reaction not only from Wall Street but from leaders in Congress and the presidential candidates.

Despite the strong endorsement of President Bush, initial reactions to the proposed bailout plan from Democratic and Republican leaders on Capitol

Hill were decidedly mixed. While recognizing the severity of the crisis and the need for action, many Democrats were suspicious of any plan proposed by the Bush administration and wanted major changes to provide stronger guarantees to taxpayers and direct assistance to homeowners threatened by foreclosure before they were willing to sign on. At the same time, many Republicans found the idea of a massive federal bailout of private sector institutions antithetical to their conservative, free-market ideology. The bailout plan was clearly going to be a hard sell on Capitol Hill.

Initially both presidential candidates adopted a wait-and-see attitude toward the proposed bailout. But then the McCain campaign made a startling announcement. On Wednesday, September 24, John McCain announced that he was suspending his campaign to go back to Washington and participate in the negotiations in Congress on the bailout legislation. He also asked that the first presidential debate, which was scheduled to take place two days later in Oxford, Mississippi, be postponed until an agreement could be reached on the bailout plan.

McCain's announcement was greeted with a mixture of surprise and skepticism by most media commentators. Since the negotiations over the bailout package were already well underway in Congress, it was not clear what role, if any, Senator McCain could play in that process. In fact, even after his return to Washington there was little evidence that he was deeply involved in the discussions. Meanwhile, both the debate organizers and the Obama campaign announced that they were opposed to postponing the first presidential debate. Although no agreement had been reached on a bailout package, on Friday morning the McCain campaign announced that the Arizona Senator would take part in the debate because sufficient progress toward a compromise had been made. However, when the bailout legislation came to a vote in the House of Representatives on Monday, September 29, it went down to defeat because a large majority of Republicans voted against the bill despite Senator McCain's endorsement. It was not until ten days later, after a major decline in stock market prices and frenzied negotiations between Secretary Paulson and congressional leaders, that the Senate, and then the House, passed a revised bailout bill. Both John McCain and Barack Obama voted in favor of the revised bill in the Senate.

Passage of the bailout plan did not end the financial crisis. Over the next several weeks credit markets remained tight and stock prices continued to plummet, with key indices falling to their lowest levels in many years. Meanwhile, other economic indicators were turning even more negative than earlier in the year. In October, the Commerce Department announced that the nation's gross domestic product, the total output of goods and services, had fallen by an estimated 0.3 percent during the third quarter of 2008. It was the worst GDP report in more than a decade and was widely seen as signaling that the nation was already in a recession. Then in early November, the Labor Department announced that the U.S. economy had shed more than 200,000 jobs during the month of October and that the official unemployment rate had risen to 6.5 percent, its highest level in 14 years.

The worsening condition of the nation's economy during the fall was clearly a major problem for the McCain campaign. Making the situation even worse, though, was Senator McCain's erratic behavior in the aftermath of the financial crisis and his statement in early September, before the collapse of the stock market, that the nation's economy was "fundamentally sound." The Obama campaign was quick to exploit the opening that Senator McCain provided, featuring the "fundamentally sound" comment in many of its campaign speeches and advertisements and using the financial crisis to link John McCain to the failed economic policies of the Bush administration. Meanwhile, Senator Obama himself, by remaining above the fray during the negotiations over the bailout package and then endorsing the final product, was able to appear calm and "presidential" in contrast to Senator McCain, who appeared to adopt a new strategy every 24 hours.[12] By mid-September, the lead that John McCain had briefly enjoyed in the polls following the Republican Convention had evaporated, and by the end of the month Barack Obama had established a clear advantage in the national polls and in most of the battleground states. It was an advantage he would never relinquish. Between September 26 and Election Day, John McCain never led Barack Obama in a single national poll.

## THE PRESIDENTIAL AND VICE-PRESIDENTIAL DEBATES

Although the first televised debate between presidential candidates took place in 1960 between Richard Nixon and John F. Kennedy, debates have only been a regular feature of these contests since 1976, with the first vice-presidential debate taking place in 1984 between George H. W. Bush and Geraldine Ferraro.[13] Every presidential campaign since 1992 has included three presidential debates and a single vice-presidential debate. While these events are often eagerly anticipated by the media, and the presidential and vice-presidential candidates devote a great deal of time and effort to preparing for them, their effects on the presidential race are typically fairly small[14] since, by the time the debates take place, most voters already have made up their minds and those supporting a candidate rarely change their opinion as a result of watching a debate. In addition, presidential and vice-presidential candidates are generally skilled at answering the questions they want to answer during a debate, regardless of what questions they are asked. As a result, major gaffes are rare.

The 2008 presidential and vice-presidential debates were no exception to these rules. Although the formats of the debates and the subjects discussed varied, the results were similar. Polls taken immediately after all three presidential debates and the single vice-presidential debate found that the Democratic candidates, Barack Obama and Joe Biden, had bested the Republican candidates, John McCain and Sarah Palin. One interesting sidelight to these debates, though, was that for the first time the audience for the vice-presidential debate was larger than the audience for any of the presidential debates. Apparently many members of the public were eager to see how Sarah Palin would do in the vice-presidential debate in the aftermath of her widely criticized interview with CBS news anchor Katie Couric. Most media commentators felt that Palin performed well in the debate, avoiding any mistakes and displaying the folksy charm that she had used so effectively in her acceptance speech at the Republican convention. Nevertheless, according to the polls, most viewers of the debate rated Joe Biden as the winner.

The third presidential debate was also notable for John McCain's repeated references to an Ohio plumber named Joe Wurzelbacher to illustrate his criticisms of Barack Obama's tax proposals. McCain claimed that "Joe the Plumber" was upset about Obama's plan to "redistribute the wealth" by raising taxes on Americans earning more than $250,000 a year. Obama countered that far more Americans would benefit from his proposal to cut taxes on low-to-moderate income taxpayers than from McCain's proposal to continue the Bush tax cuts. The debate may not have changed many voters' minds, but "Joe the Plumber" quickly became a fixture in campaign speeches by John McCain and Sarah Palin, and Wurzelbacher himself actually appeared at several McCain campaign events.

While the debates produced no major shifts in the polls, they may have helped to cement support for Barack Obama among some swing voters. The debates allowed Obama to go head-to-head with the much more experienced McCain on a wide range of issues, including foreign policy and national security. By simply holding his own on national security and foreign policy issues, Obama may have helped to ease some voters' concerns about his lack of experience and reduced McCain's advantage on these issues. At the same time, the debates may have reinforced Obama's advantage on domestic issues and especially on the economy. After the debates, polls generally found that his advantage over McCain on these issues was somewhat larger than before the debates.[15]

## THE GROUND GAME

Modern political campaigns are not just about media and message. They are also about mobilization, and in this area as well, the Obama campaign had a decided advantage over the McCain campaign. In 2004, both parties poured resources into registering and turning out voters in the swing states and the result was a dramatic increase in turnout. But, in the end, it was the Republicans who triumphed in the key battlegrounds of Florida and Ohio by putting into effect the 72-hour program that had been developed by Karl Rove. This involved using individuals identified as Bush supporters to turn out their friends and neighbors through the most effective form of voter mobilization, personal contact. The result was that while Democratic turnout increased, Republican turnout increased even more. In 2008, the Obama campaign was determined not to let that happen again.

The Obama campaign had two crucial advantages over the McCain campaign when it came to voter mobilization: money and enthusiasm. It put both of these advantages to good use. Because of the enormous success of its fundraising operation, the Obama campaign was able to open dozens of field offices and send hundreds of paid organizers into every one of the major battleground states including Florida, Ohio, Pennsylvania, Virginia, Indiana, and North Carolina. The size of the Obama field operation was unprecedented in the history of modern political campaigns. In most of the battleground states the number of Obama field offices greatly exceeded the number of McCain field offices. According to a count by Nate Silver of fivethirtyeight.com, as of August 9 the Obama campaign had opened 336 field offices in battleground states compared with 101 for the McCain campaign, and unlike the Obama offices, many of the McCain field offices were actually being staffed by local Republican Party organizations. Obama field offices outnumbered McCain field offices by 33-to-9 in Ohio, 28-to-6 in Virginia, 27-to-7 in Missouri, and 14-to-3 in New Hampshire. In fact, Florida was the only state where McCain field offices (35) outnumbered Obama field offices (25).[16]

The other major advantage that the Obama campaign enjoyed when it came to voter mobilization was the much greater level of enthusiasm among Obama's supporters. This allowed the campaign to leverage its investment in campaign offices and paid staffers into an army of volunteers who could conduct voter registration and get-out-the-vote drives. Preliminary evidence indicates that this advantage in manpower allowed the Obama campaign to contact a larger proportion of the electorate than the McCain campaign in many of the key battleground states. According to data from state exit polls compiled by Nate Silver, the percentage of voters reporting contact by the

Obama campaign exceeded the proportion reporting contact by the McCain campaign in 11 of 12 battleground states. The largest gap was in Nevada, where 50 percent of voters reported contact by the Obama campaign versus 29 percent who reported contact by the McCain campaign. There were also double-digit contact gaps in favor of Obama in Colorado, Indiana, Virginia, Pennsylvania, and Iowa and smaller gaps in favor of Obama in Florida, North Carolina, Missouri, Ohio, and Wisconsin. The only state where more voters reported contact by the McCain campaign was West Virginia, where there was a 2-point gap in favor of the Republican candidate. But most political observers never considered West Virginia to be a battleground state in 2008.[17]

## THE RACE TO THE FINISH LINE

During the last frantic days of the campaign, as the presidential and vice-presidential candidates crisscrossed the country in search of votes, it was apparent to most observers that the Democratic ticket was in a much stronger position than the Republican ticket when it came to securing the 270 votes needed to win a majority in the Electoral College. Not only did the Obama-Biden ticket lead the McCain-Palin ticket by an average margin of between 6 and 8 points in the national polls, but they also held clear leads in all 19 states that John Kerry had carried in 2004, and at least five states that George Bush had carried in that election: Iowa, New Mexico, Colorado, Virginia, and Ohio. Several other Bush states, including Florida, North Carolina, Missouri, Nevada, and Indiana were also clearly in play. Starting with a secure base of 252 electoral votes that John Kerry had won in 2004, all the Obama campaign needed to do was add one large state such as Ohio or Florida, or two medium-sized states such as Virginia and North Carolina, to get to 270.

With polls indicating that Virginia, Colorado, and Ohio were tilting toward Obama, the McCain campaign decided that their only hope of winning the election was to turn around at least one large state that had supported John Kerry in 2004 and hope that one or more of the Bush states that were leaning toward Obama would return to the Republican fold in the end. Based on their internal polling, and despite numerous published polls showing Barack Obama with a comfortable lead, the blue state where the McCain campaign chose to make its last stand was Pennsylvania. And so, in the final week of the campaign, both John McCain and Sarah Palin devoted several days to campaigning in Pennsylvania, despite polls showing a narrower Obama margin in several other large states including Florida and Ohio. It was a decision that puzzled many outside observers. On Election Day, Barack Obama carried Pennsylvania by more than 10 percentage points.

## THE RESULTS

At precisely 11:00 p.m. Eastern Standard Time on November 4, just as the polls closed in California, Oregon, and Washington, all of the major networks declared Barack Obama to be the winner of the 2008 presidential election. After more than a year of campaigning it took only a few hours of vote counting to determine that Obama would have the 270 electoral votes that he needed to become the forty-fourth president of the United States. In fact, he would eventually receive 365 electoral votes, the largest total since Bill Clinton in 1996.

Obama's margin of more than 9 million votes was the largest for any presidential candidate since Ronald Reagan in 1984. More than 69 million Americans cast their ballots for Barack Obama, while almost 60 million voted for John McCain and almost 2 million for minor party candidates. The Democratic ticket won approximately 53 percent of the vote to approximately 46 percent for the Republican ticket and just over 1 percent for minor party candidates. By the standards of postwar presidential elections it was a decisive win but certainly not a landslide. The total number of votes cast for the Obama-Biden ticket was a record, however. Obama was the first Democratic presidential candidate since Jimmy Carter to win a majority of the popular vote, and Obama's 53-percent share of the popular vote was the largest for any presidential candidate since George H. W. Bush in 1988, and the largest for any Democratic candidate since Lyndon Johnson in 1964.

Democrats scored major gains in the congressional elections as well, picking up at least seven seats in the Senate and at least 20 seats in the House of Representatives. It marked the second consecutive election in which Democrats made significant gains in the House and Senate. In the 2006 midterm elections they had picked up six Senate seats and 30 House seats. When the new Congress convened in January of 2009, Democrats would hold at least 56 seats in the Senate, even without counting Joe Lieberman, and at least 256 seats in the House, both the largest Democratic totals since the 1994 midterm election.

A glance at the 2008 electoral map demonstrates the breadth of the Democratic sweep across the nation. The Obama-Biden ticket carried 28 states and the District of Columbia, including all 19 states won by John Kerry in 2004 and nine states won by George W. Bush in that election. The nine Bush states that switched to Obama were Florida, Ohio, Virginia, North Carolina, Indiana, Iowa, New Mexico, Colorado, and Nevada. Obama and Biden carried seven of the eight most populous states: California, New York, Florida, Illinois, Pennsylvania, Ohio, and Michigan. Among the most populous states, only President Bush's home state of Texas voted for John McCain. Obama's 365 electoral votes came to just over two-thirds of the total number of 538 and included one electoral vote from the state of Nebraska. Nebraska is one of only two states, along with Maine, that awards its electoral votes based on congressional district results. Since the Obama-Biden ticket carried one of the state's three House districts, the one that includes the city of Omaha, it received one of the state's five electoral votes. The McCain-Palin ticket received the other four electoral votes from Nebraska—two for carrying the state and one for each of the two remaining House districts.

While Barack Obama's margin in the national popular vote would not be considered a landslide, the Democratic ticket did carry many individual states by landslide or near-landslide margins, including several of the most populous states. For example, Obama carried California by 24 points, New York by 26 points, Illinois by 25 points, Michigan by 16 points, and Pennsylvania by 10 points. Of the 28 states carried by the Democratic ticket, the margin was greater than 10 points in 22 states and less than 5 points in only four states. And despite the decisive Democratic victory, many individual states that voted for the Republican ticket also did so by landslide or near-landslide margins. Of the 22 states carried by John McCain, the margin was greater than 10 points in 15 states and less than 5 points in only two states. And while the nation as a whole was moving in a Democratic direction between 2004 and 2008, the Republicans managed to increase their margin of victory in five states: Oklahoma, Arkansas, Louisiana, West Virginia, and Tennessee.

A similar pattern was evident in the election results at the county level. According to an analysis by the *New York Times*, between 2004 and 2008 the Democratic share of the vote increased in 2,437 of the nation's 3,141 counties; at the same time, however, the Republican share of the vote increased in 678 counties. The Democratic share of the vote increased by more than 10 points in 1,173 counties; however, the Republican share of the vote increased by more than 10 points in 225 counties. Counties with the largest increases in the Democratic share of the vote were generally found in large metropolitan areas with relatively high levels of education and large concentrations of Hispanic and African American voters. Counties with the largest increases in the Republican share of the vote were generally found in small towns and rural areas with relatively low levels of education, small minority populations and high concentrations of Southern Baptists. Many of these Republican-tilting counties were located in the Appalachian region.[18]

The overall picture that emerges from an examination of the 2008 electoral map is one of a country that had moved rather dramatically in a

Democratic direction since 2004 but that remained deeply divided. Across all 50 states and the District of Columbia, the average margin of victory for the winning party increased from 15.8 points in 2004 to 17.4 points in 2008. There were more landslide and near-landslide states and fewer closely contested states. The number of states in which the winning candidate's margin of victory was greater than 10 points increased from 30 to 37, while the number in which the winning candidate's margin of victory was less than 5 points decreased from 11 to 6. Of the seven most populous states, only Florida and Ohio were decided by less than 5 points while New York, California, and Illinois were decided by more than 20 points.

Although Barack Obama won a decisive victory in 2008, there was wide divergence in his support across states and regions of the country. While he made inroads into the Republican Party's southern base by carrying Virginia, North Carolina, and Florida, John McCain carried the other eight states of the old Confederacy, along with the border states of Kentucky, West Virginia, and Oklahoma, winning most of them by double-digit margins. Altogether, McCain won 54 percent of the vote in the southern and border states while Obama won 57 percent of the vote in the rest of the country.

The high level of geographical polarization in 2008 is consistent with the pattern evident in other recent presidential elections, including the 2004 election, but it represents a dramatic change from the more homogeneous voting patterns that existed during the 1960s and 1970s. In the closely contested 1960 and 1976 elections, for example, there were far more closely contested states and far fewer landslide states than in recent presidential elections. And in both of those elections every one of the most populous states was closely contested, including California, New York, Illinois, and Texas. The divisions between red states and blue states are far deeper today than they were 30 or 40 years ago and the 2008 election did nothing to change that reality.

Further evidence of shifting voting patterns can be seen in the results of the 2004 and 2008 national exit polls. No Democratic presidential candidate since Lyndon Johnson has won a majority of the white vote, so the fact that Barack Obama lost the white vote was hardly surprising. In fact, Obama's 12-point deficit among white voters was identical to that of Al Gore in 2000. However, the fact that white voters favored the Republican presidential candidate by a double-digit margin in 2008 despite the poor condition of the economy and the extraordinary unpopularity of the incumbent Republican president suggests that racial prejudice did have an impact on the level of white support for the Democratic candidate.

Table 2. Democratic Presidential Vote by Age and Race in 2004 and 2008

| Group | 2004 | 2008 | Change |
|---|---|---|---|
| 18–29 | 54% | 66% | + 12% |
| 30–44 | 46% | 52% | + 6% |
| 45–64 | 48% | 50% | + 2% |
| 65 + | 46% | 45% | – 1% |
| White | 41% | 43% | + 2% |
| African American | 88% | 95% | + 7% |
| Hispanic | 53% | 67% | + 14% |
| Other Races | 55% | 64% | + 9% |

Source: 2004 and 2008 National Exit Polls

Further evidence of the effects of race can be seen in state exit poll results. White support for Barack Obama varied dramatically across regions and states, ranging from a low of around 10 percent in the Deep South to close to 60 percent in parts of the Northeast and West. In many states outside the South, Obama did substantially better than Kerry among white voters. Between 2004 and 2008 the Democratic share of the white vote increased by 5 points in California and Washington, 7 points in Michigan and Wisconsin, 8 points in Colorado, and 9 points in Oregon. In many southern and border states, however, Obama did no better, and often worse, than Kerry among white voters. Between 2004 and 2008 the Democratic share of the white vote fell by 4 points in Mississippi, 6 points in Arkansas, 9 points in Alabama, and 10 points in Louisiana. Based on these results, it is hard to avoid the conclusion that racial prejudice was a factor in limiting support for Barack Obama among white voters in the southern and border states. But this was not enough to cost Obama the election because his losses among these groups of white voters were offset by gains among white voters in other parts of the country, especially among younger white voters, and by increased turnout and support among African American and Hispanic voters.

It is impossible to know whether a white candidate like Hillary Clinton would have won the election by a bigger margin than Obama. Clinton might have run somewhat stronger than Obama among older, less-educated white voters and she probably would have won a larger share of the vote in southern and border states such as Arkansas, Kentucky, and West Virginia; but Clinton might not have run as strongly as Obama among younger and better-educated white voters, and she almost certainly would not have generated the level of turnout and support among African American voters that Obama did—turnout and support that was crucial in producing Democratic victories in states such as Virginia and North Carolina.

## EXPLAINING OBAMA'S VICTORY

The decisive Democratic victory in the 2008 presidential election can best be understood as a product of three distinct sets of factors: changes in the composition of the American electorate, some of which had been developing for decades and some of which were more recent in origin; short-term forces at work in 2008, including the unpopularity of President Bush and the dire condition of the U.S. economy; and the campaigns conducted by the Democratic and Republican candidates. Economic conditions and the actions of the presidential and vice-presidential candidates received extensive coverage in the media during the campaign, but far less attention was paid to shifts in the composition of the electorate. However, Barack Obama's election would not have been possible without these changes.

Perhaps the most important long-term trend in the composition of the American electorate has been a gradual increase in the proportion of non-white voters. This trend has been occurring for at least 50 years and it is likely to continue for the foreseeable future based on Census Bureau projections of the racial and ethnic makeup of the American population between now and 2050. It has been a result of increased immigration from Asia, Africa, and Latin America, higher birth rates among minority groups, and increased registration and turnout among African Americans, Hispanics, and other non-white citizens.

Figure 1 displays data from the American National Election Studies on the changing racial composition of the U.S. electorate over the past six decades. According to these data, between the 1950s and the first decade of the twenty-first century the nonwhite share of the U.S. electorate increased dramatically, going from less than one in twenty voters in 1956 to close to one in four voters in 2004. This trend continued in 2008, helped in part by an aggressive Democratic registration and get-out-the-vote campaign in African American and Hispanic communities. National exit poll data show that the nonwhite share of the electorate increased from 23 percent in 2004 to 26 percent in 2008 with African Americans going from 11 percent of the electorate in 2004 to 13 percent in 2008 and Hispanics going from 8 percent to 9 percent.

Figure 1. Racial Composition of U.S. Electorate by Decade

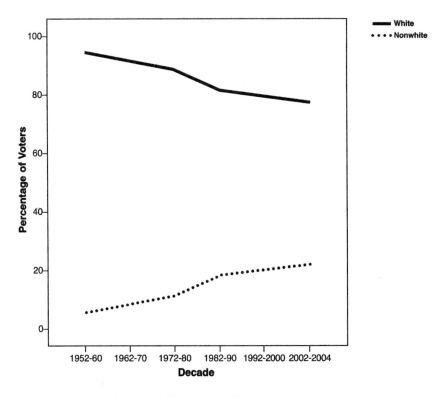

Source: American National Election Studies

Since the 1970s the composition of the nonwhite electorate has itself been changing, with Hispanics (who are included here in the nonwhite population although they can be of any race) and Asian Americans comprising a growing share of nonwhite voters. Both of these groups continue to be underrepresented in the electorate relative to their numbers in the voting-age population due to high rates of non-citizenship and relatively low registration and turnout rates. However, both groups are growing rapidly. Hispanics are now the largest minority group in the U.S. population and their share of the electorate has been rising steadily.

The growth of the nonwhite electorate, beginning with African Americans in the 1960s and 1970s and continuing with Hispanics and Asian Americans since the 1980s, has had profound consequences for the party system and the electoral process in the United States. African American and Hispanic voters now comprise a large proportion of the electoral base of the Democratic Party in much of the country. The expansion of the African

American electorate made Barack Obama's nomination possible, as they provided him with a large proportion of his support in many of the Democratic primaries, especially in the South. In addition, the growth of the nonwhite electorate as a whole made his election possible, as African American and other nonwhite voters provided him with a large enough margin to offset a substantial deficit among white voters.

Short-term political factors were another key element in Obama's victory. Democratic gains in party identification as well as the Democratic victories in the 2008 presidential and congressional elections all reflected the dramatic changes in the political climate in the United States since the 2004 presidential election. Those changes can be clearly seen in the results of the national exit polls. Between 2004 and 2008, the proportion of voters approving of President Bush's job performance fell from 53 percent to 27 percent, while the proportion disapproving of his performance rose from 46 percent to 71 percent; the proportion of voters describing their family's financial situation as better than a year earlier fell from 32 percent to 24 percent, while the proportion describing it as worse rose from 28 percent to 42 percent; and the proportion of voters rating the national economy as "excellent" or "good" fell from 47 percent to 7 percent, while the proportion rating it as "not so good" or "poor" rose from 52 percent to 93 percent.

Such a toxic political environment would have been very difficult for any candidate from the incumbent party to overcome, even with a perfect campaign. As it was, the McCain campaign, in addition to finding itself out-organized and outspent, had great difficulty coming up with an appealing message. With a collapsing economy and a president with one of the lowest approval ratings of any chief executive in the past half century, John McCain clearly could not run on the record of the Bush administration. But despite his history of challenging the Republican establishment, McCain's attempt to position himself as a candidate of change had only limited success. In the national exit poll, half of voters thought that McCain would continue President Bush's policies, while half thought he would take the country in a different direction. Among voters who thought that he would continue Bush's policies, McCain lost to Obama by a margin of 90 percent to 8 percent. Many voters also found the tone of the McCain campaign to be overly negative. McCain's and Palin's frequent references to Obama's relationship with former Weather Underground member Bill Ayers and their attempts to suggest that Obama was concealing a radical past were ineffective. In the national exit poll, 64 percent of voters indicated that the McCain campaign had attacked Barack Obama unfairly, while only 49 percent indicated that the Obama campaign had attacked John McCain unfairly.

One final problem for John McCain was that after the initially positive response of voters to his choice of Sarah Palin as his running mate, opinions about the Alaska governor had turned increasingly negative in response to her performance in the Katie Couric interview, controversies over large expenditures on her makeup and wardrobe, and an ongoing investigation into the role she and her husband had played in the firing of a state trooper who had been involved in a messy divorce with Palin's sister. While she remained wildly popular among GOP activists and religious conservatives and continued to draw large and enthusiastic crowds on the campaign trail, by Election Day, according to the national exit poll, only 38 percent of voters viewed her as qualified to serve as president, compared with 66 percent who viewed Joe Biden as qualified. By picking Palin as his running mate John McCain may have energized the Republican base but he may have also alienated many independent and moderate voters whose support he desperately needed.

## TOWARD THE FUTURE

In the aftermath of the 2008 election the Democratic Party finds itself in its strongest position in government since the early 1990s. In 2009 Democrats will control the White House and both houses of Congress and their majorities in the Senate and House of Representatives will be the largest for either party since the 1994 midterm election. But President Obama and the Democratic leadership of the House and Senate will be presiding over a nation facing immense challenges at home and overseas, including a failing domestic economy, a global financial crisis, and two wars with no end in sight. And with their expanded majorities in Congress, the Democrats will have to deal with greater regional and ideological diversity in their ranks. Many of the Democrats elected to the House and Senate in 2006 and 2008 are moderates who represent districts and states with a history, until recently, of supporting Republican presidential candidates. Keeping their expanded majorities united behind President Obama's legislative program will be a difficult assignment for Speaker Pelosi and Majority Leader Reed. And in the Senate, lacking 60 votes to cut off debate, Democrats will still face the threat of Republican filibusters unless they can win over a few of the handful of remaining Republican moderates.

The Republican Party today faces the opposite problem from the Democrats. With their numbers greatly reduced by the results of the 2006 and 2008 elections, Republicans in Congress are left with a shrunken and overwhelmingly conservative party. The large majority of those who remain represent safe Republican districts and states, many in the South. There are almost no moderate Republicans left in either chamber, and the party has been decimated in the Northeast, where it now holds only a handful of House seats and only three of 22 Senate seats.

The GOP's electoral base has also been shrinking. Its voters are overwhelmingly white, socially conservative, middle-aged or older, and located in small towns and rural areas. In a country that is becoming increasingly urban, nonwhite and socially tolerant, that is not a good position to be in. The party's weakness among younger Americans, who not only voted for Barack Obama over John McCain by a 2-to-1 margin but who also increasingly identify with the Democratic Party, should be especially concerning to Republican strategists since research shows that once young adults form an attachment to a political party they frequently maintain that attachment for many years.[19] In order to revive their fortunes, Republicans will need to find a way to reach beyond their current base—to appeal to nonwhites, young people, and an increasingly educated and socially moderate electorate.

None of this should be taken to mean that 2008 was a realigning election and that the Democratic Party will now dominate American politics for many years to come. History teaches us that winning a decisive election victory is no guarantee of future success for a political party. In 1964 the Democratic Party won an even bigger victory in the presidential and congressional elections—a victory that allowed President Lyndon Johnson to push an ambitious legislative program through Congress, including civil rights legislation, federal aid to education, the war on poverty, and Medicare. Stories in the media about the demise of the Republican Party were rampant. But two years later, with the country deeply divided over the Vietnam War, racial unrest, and a growing youth culture, Democrats suffered major setbacks in the midterm elections, and in 1968 Richard Nixon defeated Hubert Humphrey to reclaim the White House for the Republicans. Whether the Democrats will be able to consolidate the gains they have made since 2006 is very much an open question. The answer to that question depends largely on how they govern over the next two to four years and how the American people view their results.

## NOTES

[1]For up-to-date and accurate information on voter turnout in the 2008 election and in previous presidential elections, see Michael McDonald's "United States Elections Project" Web site: http://elections.gmu.edu/voter_turnout.htm.

[2]Four weeks after the election, the National Bureau of Economic Research officially announced that the U.S. economy had been in a recession since December, 2007. See Neil Irwin, "Economic Signs Point to Longer, Deeper Recession; Decline Began a year Ago, Experts Declare, Wall Street Reacts with Huge Sell-Off," *Washington Post*, December 2, 2008, p. A-1.

[3]The Gallup Poll Web site provides a vast amount of information on the economic outlook of the American public during the months leading up to the 2008 election. See: http://www.gallup.com/poll/107827/Gallup-Daily-Consumer-Confidence.aspx.

[4]Information about fundraising by individual candidates and party committees can be found on the Web site of the Federal Election Commission: www.fec.gov. In addition, excellent reports on campaign finance in 2008 and in previous elections can be found on the Web site of the Campaign Finance institute: http://www.cfinst.org.

[5]For evidence concerning growing polarization in American politics see Alan I. Abramowitz and Kyle L. Saunders, "Is Polarization a Myth?" *Journal of Politics*, 70 (April, 2008), pp. 542-555. Competing viewpoints on the extent of polarization can be found in Pietro S. Nivolo and David W. Brady, eds., *Red and Blue Nation? Characteristics and Causes of America's Polarized Politics* (Washington, DC: Brookings Institution Press, 2006). See also Jeffrey M. Stonecash, Mark D. Brewer, and Mack D. Mariani, *Diverging Parties: Social Change, Realignment, and Party Polarization* (Boulder, CO: Westview Press, 2003).

[6]Gallup's party identification data through 2007 is summarized in Jeffrey M. Jones, "GOP Identification in 2007 Lowest in Last Two Decades," Gallup Poll: http://www.gallup.com/poll/103732/GOP-Identification-2007-Lowest-Last-Two-Decades.aspx. Data for 2004 through 2008 can be found at: http://www.gallup.com/poll/15370/Party-Affiliation.aspx.

[7]See for example Kenneth P. Vogel, "Obama: Change Agent Goes Conventional," *Politico*, June 26, 2008: http://www.politico.com/news/stories/0608/11384.html.

[8]This information was compiled from Federal Election Commission data by the Campaign Finance Institute. See: http://www.cfinst.org/president/pdf/Pres08_12G_Table1.pdf.

[9]Dennis Chaptman, "Wisconsin Advertising Project Analyzes Tone of Ads in White House Race," University of Wisconsin-Madison: http://www.news.wisc.edu/15800.

[10]There is an ongoing debate in political science literature on the effectiveness of political advertising in general and negative political advertising in particular. For a review of this debate and an extensive analysis of data on the effects of political advertising, see Michael M. Franz, Paul B. Freedman, Kenneth M. Goldstein, and Travis N. Ridout, *Campaign Advertising and American Democracy* (Philadelphia: Temple University Press, 2008). See also John G. Geer, *In Defense of Negativity: Attack Ads in Presidential Campaigns* (Chicago: University of Chicago Press, 2006).

[11]For an account of the impact of the financial crisis on the presidential campaign, see Dan Balz and Robert Barnes, "Economy Becomes New Proving Ground for McCain, Obama," *Washington Post*, September 16, 2008, p. A-1.

[12]See "The Candidates Intervene; The Politics of the Bail-Out," *The Economist*, U.S. edition, September 27, 2008.

[13]See Alan Schroeder, *Presidential Debates: Fifty Years of High-Risk TV* (New York: Columbia University Press, 2008).

[14]For a summary of evidence on the effects of presidential debates, see Lydia Saad, "Presidential Debates Rarely Game Changers," Gallup Poll: http://www.gallup.com/poll/110674/Presidential-Debates-Rarely-GameChangers.aspx.

[15]For an overview of the effects of the 2008 debates, see Jeffrey M. Jones, "Obama Viewed as Winner of Third Debate," Gallup Poll: http://www.gallup.com/poll/111256/Obama-Viewed-Winner-Third-Debate.aspx.

[16]See Nate Silver, "Obama Leads Better than 3:1 in Field Offices," August 9, 2008: http://www.fivethirtyeight.com/2008/08/obama-leads-better-than-31-in-field.html.

[17]Nate Silver, "The Contact Gap: Proof of the Importance of the Ground Game?" http://www.fivethirtyeight.com/2008/11/contact-gap-proof-of-importance-of.html.

[18]The county level results can be viewed as part of an interactive map on the *New York Times* Web site: http://elections.nytimes.com/2008/results/president/map.html.

[19]See M. Kent Jennings and Richard G. Niemi, *Generations and Politics: A Panel Study of Young Adults and their Parents* (Princeton, NJ: Princeton University Press, 1981).

# Chapter 5

# The 2008 Congressional and Gubernatorial Contests[1]

## Bruce Larson

## INTRODUCTION

The historic nature of the 2008 presidential contest understandably over-shadowed contests for non-presidential races across the United States. But the separation of powers and federalist features of the United States govern-ment make the outcomes of congressional and gubernatorial contests enor-mously important. Indeed, the U.S. House's failure to enact President Bush's financial bailout package on September 29 (which precipitated a nearly 800-point drop in the Dow Jones Industrial Average and shook world markets), as well Congress's eventual approval of a bailout plan on October 3, demonstrat-ed just how little the president can do when Congress wants to put up road-blocks.[2] In the United States' system of shared powers, congressional and gubernatorial races determine who will share power with the chief executive.

This chapter analyzes the 2008 U.S. House and Senate contests, as well as the 11 gubernatorial races that took place around the nation in 2008. The U.S. House and Senate contests were characterized by a continuation of par-tisan change that began two years ago. Democrats added significantly to the majorities they began building in 2006, netting 21 seats in the U.S. House and seven in the U.S. Senate.[3] By contrast, the 2008 gubernatorial contests were characterized mostly by continuity, with only one race (in Missouri) yielding a change in party control of the governor's mansion. Taken together, the outcomes of the U.S. House, Senate, and gubernatorial contests make for a considerably "bluer" America—though perhaps not quite as blue as one would have predicted given the powerful headwinds buffeting Republicans.

## THE POLITICAL SETTING:
## NATIONAL FORCES AND THE DEMOCRATIC ADVANTAGE

A party that gains a significant number of seats in a congressional election rarely makes significant gains in the next election as well. Figure 1, which graphs the net shift in House seats held by Democrats from 1946 to 2008, makes this clear. Most "tide" elections are followed by something of a correction, in which the party that made big gains in the tide election loses seats in the next election, ceding back seats that more naturally belong to the other party.[4] In fact, in the 30 congressional elections held between 1946 and 2006, the lone exceptions were 1950 and 1952, in which Republicans won 28 and 22 seats, respectively, and 1978 and 1980, in which the GOP won 15 and 33 seats, respectively.

**Figure 1. Democratic Net Seat Gain/Loss, 1946–2008**

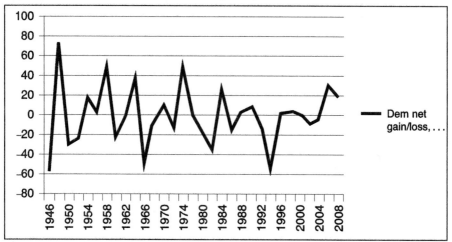

Data source: 2008, author's calculations; 1956–2006, Norman J. Ornstein, Thomas E. Mann, and Michael Malbin, *Vital Statistics on Congress*, 2008 (Washington, DC: Brookings, 2008)

We can now add Democrats in 2006 and 2008 to the list of exceptions. While frustration with President Bush and the Iraq War led voters to cast ballots against Republicans in the 2006 midterm elections, continuing frustration with Bush as well as substantial voter anxiety about the economy left voters seeking more change in 2008. Fairly or not, the subprime mortgage crisis and the sharp economic downturn further tarnished the GOP brand name, putting Republicans in significant danger again.

For Republicans looking for signs that the electorate was finished punishing their party, the outcomes of three special elections held early in 2008 didn't bode well. The first defeat, in March 2008, occurred in Illinois's 14th District, the Republican-leaning district left vacant by former GOP Speaker Dennis Hastert's retirement. Touting his campaign as a referendum on the Bush administration, millionaire scientist and political novice Bill Forster defeated GOP candidate Jim Oberweis, 53 to 47 percent.[5] Then in May 2008, conservative Democrat Don Cazayoux won a special election in Louisiana's vacant 6th District, a seat that had been held by Republicans for three decades. (The loss of the Louisiana's 6th likely dampened the GOP's joy at holding on to Louisiana's 1st District in another special election on the same day.[6]) Ten days later, Democrat Travis Childers added to the Republicans' woes by winning a special election in Mississippi's 1st District. The Republican-leaning district, which gave Bush 62 percent of the vote in 2004, had been held by GOP incumbent Roger Wicker for12 years. (Wicker was appointed to the U.S. Senate to complete the term of Trent Lott, who resigned in 2007.) The spring special-election defeats generated angst in the GOP as they looked toward November. Indeed, former National Republican Congressional Committee (NRCC) Chair Tom Davis III (R-VA) sent a memo to House Republicans claiming that "the political atmosphere facing House Republicans this November is the worst since Watergate and is far more toxic than the fall of 2006, when we lost 30 seats."[7]

The national political mood in 2008 favored Democrats across the nation, though the economy surpassed Iraq as the primary issue on voters' minds.[8] And with good reason. As the housing bubble burst, the nation's home prices collapsed, diminishing Americans' net worth and constraining their ability to secure credit through home equity loans.[9] Mortgage defaults began to pile up across the nation.[10] In a foreboding sign of what was to come, the U.S. government bailed out Bear Stearns, a powerhouse American investment bank that found itself deeply over-invested in bad subprime mortgage debt.[11] Adding to Americans' worries, gas prices soared during the summer, peaking at an average of $4.11 per gallon on July 14.[12] High fuel prices cut into Americans' already tight budgets, and the near collapse of the big SUV market made it nearly impossible for Americans to unload their gas guzzling behemoths for more fuel efficient vehicles. In August, Republicans gained a momentary political advantage from the spike in gas prices, as GOP House members issued a barrage of speeches from the House floor protesting Speaker Nancy Pelosi's unwillingness to call lawmakers back to Washington to vote on legislation that would allow more drilling for oil and gas.[13] Yet as problems go, the summer's skyrocketing gas prices paled in comparison to the global financial meltdown to come.

The scope of the financial crisis became apparent in mid-September, when overexposure to the subprime mortgage market drove Lehman Brothers, a major American investment bank, into bankruptcy and prompted an emergency government rescue of several other major American firms and investment banks. As the ripple effects shook world markets, economists worried publicly that the meltdown could be the worst financial crisis since the Great Depression. Americans' confidence in the economy fell as precipitously as stock prices did.

House members and senators worried, too. For incumbents, few things could be less desirable than casting a public vote on a controversial piece of legislation proposed by a highly unpopular president a month before an election. And yet, that is precisely what House and Senate incumbents were forced to do in considering President Bush's $700 billion bailout package at the end of September. The politics weren't pretty, especially in the House. Although both parties' leaders backed the package, neither party's leadership put strong pressure on their members to support it. Indeed, many Americans viewed Bush's proposal as an over-priced bailout of Wall Street high rollers, and neither party wanted to be the object of voter scorn so close to an election. Challengers, for their part, were ready and willing to exploit the crisis for political gain. In Pennsylvania's 4th Congressional District, for example, Republican challenger Melissa Hart (a former House member who had been defeated in 2006) said she would attack freshman Democratic incumbent Jason Altmire *whichever* position he took on the legislation.[14]

House members convened to vote on the bailout measure (HR 3997) on Monday, September 29. Remarkably, the bill went down to defeat by a vote of 228 to 205, with 95 Democrats joining 133 Republicans in opposition.[15] Stock markets reacted swiftly and sharply, with the Dow Jones Industrial Average falling by nearly 800 points and markets around the globe registering similarly sharp declines. Almost immediately, House members began hearing a different tune coming from constituents.[16] Just two days later, the Senate, surveying the damage and "proceeding with more coolness" (to quote Madison in the *Federalist Papers*), passed a somewhat revised bailout package by a bipartisan vote of 74 to 25. Nine Democrats and 15 Republicans opposed the measure, with senators up for reelection in 2008 somewhat less likely to vote yes than senators not standing for reelection.[17] Speculation was rampant on whether the House would pass the measure.[18] It did, by a vote of 263 to 171, with 35 Democrats and 32 Republicans reversing their prior no votes.[19] President Bush immediately signed the bill into law, which temporarily calmed the stock markets. But the political environment remained roiled, as incumbents, only a month out from the election, frantically rushed home to explain their votes to voters.

Voter pessimism, as well as continuing frustration with President Bush (and by extension the GOP), was reflected in autumn poll results. The standard "right-direction-wrong-track" question asked by pollsters consistently indicated unprecedented gloom in the electorate about the nation's well being. An NBC News/*Wall Street Journal* poll conducted from October 17 to October 20, 2008, for example, found that 78 percent of Americans sampled believed the United States was on the wrong track.[20] President Bush's grades fared no better. In the nine Gallup Polls measuring voter approval of President Bush from July 20 to October 19, 2008, the president's average approval rating was a mere 29.4 percent. This was only one percentage point higher than former President Nixon's average approval rating in polls conducted by Gallup between October 20, 1973, and January 19, 1974.[21] Congressional Republicans were not immune from the fallout. Throughout the summer and fall, the generic congressional ballot question asked by survey researchers consistently favored Democrats by substantial margins.[22]

Not surprisingly, the strong headwinds buffeting the GOP led to a slew of Republican retirements in the House and Senate. Facing a grueling campaign and—if they were fortunate enough to win—another stint in the minority party, 23 GOP House members and five GOP senators decided to call it quits. By contrast, and reflecting the more favorable national mood for Democrats, only three Democratic House members and no Democratic senators retired. (The numbers for the House don't include three Democratic incumbents who left the House to seek U.S. Senate seats.) The open seats produced by the Republican retirements created substantial opportunities for Democrats to pick up seats, many of which (as we will see below) the party capitalized on.

Scandal also remained a constant on the Hill, with ethical problems and indictments causing at least some of the retirements mentioned above. Indeed, the Capitol Hill newspaper *Roll Call* tallied 17 congressional incumbents embroiled in some type of serious scandal or other. A sampling of the cases includes a House member indicted on 35 counts of corruption (Rick Renzi, R-AZ), another indicted on 16 counts of corruption (William Jefferson, D-LA), a House member arrested for drunk driving while traveling to visit his mistress and their child in Northern Virginia (Vito Fossella, R-NY), a House member who neglected to report rental income from property he owns in Dominican Republic (Charles Rangel, D-NY), a senator arrested for allegedly soliciting sex in a Minneapolis airport restroom (Larry Craig, R-ID), and a senator convicted on seven counts of violating federal ethics laws (Ted Stevens, R-AK). (The congressional scandals, of course, were accompanied by the high profile non-congressional scandals involving New York Governor Elliot Spitzer and former senator and Democratic presidential candidate John Edwards.) While the scandals no doubt contributed to Congress's ever-declining approval ratings, they seemed to register less than usual with the public—perhaps a measure of just how bad voters perceived other problems in the nation to be.[23]

## THE U.S. HOUSE RACES

Economic uncertainty, continuing anti-Bush sentiment, GOP incumbent retirements, and effective Democratic recruitment all produced fewer safe Republican House seats in 2008 than in prior years. As Figure 2 shows, the percentage of GOP seats rated safe by *Congressional Quarterly* (CQ) took a significant downturn from 2006 (and 2006 saw a big dip from 2004), with only about 60 percent of Republican seats rated as completely safe in 2008.

**Figure 2. Percentage of Safe U.S. House Seats, 1992–2008**

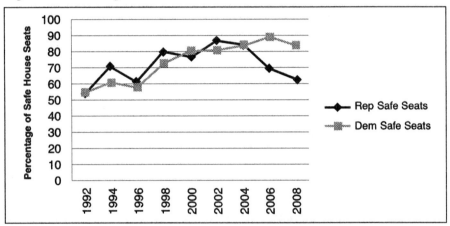

The figure is based on *Congressional Quarterly's* ratings for each year.

The unfavorable climate facing the GOP was reflected in the November election outcomes, which produced a net gain of 21 seats for House Democrats (following the party's net gain of 30 seats in 2006). Table 1 provides an overview of the House results by party for both incumbent-challenger and open-seat contests. Looking first at the figures for House incumbent-challenger contests, we can see that the incumbent reelection rate was significantly higher for Democratic incumbents (98 percent) than for Republican incumbents (90 percent).

**Table 1. Summary of 2008 U.S. House Races**

|  | Democrats | Republican |
|---|---|---|
| Incumbents reelected | 224 (98%) | 156 (90%) |
| Challenger victories | 14 | 5 |
| Open seats successfully defended | 7 (of 7) | 17 (of 29) |
| Open seats captured from opposition | 12 | 0 |
| Total seats | 257 | 178 |
| Net gain/loss from 110th Congress | +21 | –21 |

All told, Democratic challengers ousted 14 House Republican incumbents. The losses were mostly unsurprising. Of the 14 GOP incumbents defeated, all but two had won in 2006 with less than 55 percent of the vote, and six were from districts won by Bush in 2004 with less than 55 percent of the vote. One (Chris Shays, CT-4) represented a district won by Kerry in 2004.[24] Finally, with an average of 4.5 terms under their belts, the ousted GOP incumbents tended to be neither newcomers nor veterans.

Especially in the more competitive districts, the ousted GOP incumbents likely fell at least partly because of their vulnerability to Democratic claims that they were too close to President Bush. But a variety of other factors likely also explain some of the defeats. Republican Steve Chabot's Ohio district, for example, is more than 25 percent black, and enthusiasm for Democratic presidential candidate Barack Obama may well have increased African American turnout, helping to sink Chabot in the process.[25] In Florida's 24th District, Tom Feeney was almost surely done in by his involvement with convicted lobbyist Jack Abramoff.[26] Some GOP incumbents, moreover, seemed to go out of their way to undermine their reelections. Although Representative Robin Hayes's North Carolina district can't be characterized as liberal, Hayes, who had nearly been defeated in 2006, probably didn't do much to advance his election prospects by publicly claiming that "liberals hate real Americans that work and accomplish and achieve and believe in God."[27] The uproar generated by the statement was a major distraction in the final weeks of the campaign for Hayes, who was already highly unpopular with many textile industry workers in his district for a series of votes he cast on trade deals in Congress.[28]

The defeat of Representative Chris Shays (R-CT) represents the completion (at least in the House) of the GOP's demise in New England. Shays, who since 1987 had represented Connecticut's increasingly Democratic 4th District (the most southern in New England), held off two strong challenges in 2004 and 2006. But it seemed nearly impossible for him to prevail a third time against a powerful blue tide sweeping New England. To make matters worse, Democratic challenger Jim Himes—a former New York investment banker turned nonprofit leader—seemed a perfect fit for Connecticut's 4th (which includes Greenwich, an affluent bedroom community for Manhattan's financial sector).[29] Predictably, the contest was one of the most expensive House races, with the two candidates spending a total of more than $6.5 million. Following the 2006 midterm elections, Shays was the sole New England House Republican left standing; his defeat in 2008 means that New England won't include a single House Republican for the first time since the GOP's founding in 1854.[30]

Even for House GOP incumbents who survived, it was not an easy election. Whereas 86 percent of winning House Democratic incumbents garnered 60 percent or more of the vote, only 64 percent of winning GOP incumbents did so.[31]

Yet, as battered as GOP incumbents were in 2008, they are fortunate not to have fared worse. Indeed, 10 GOP incumbents squeaked by with only 52 percent or less of the vote, and 23 won with 55 percent or less. So a larger number of GOP incumbent defeats was not beyond the realm of possibilities. Several of the GOP incumbents who squeaked by, such as Don Young (AK-AL) and Dave Reichert (WA-8), were in fiercely contested races from the outset that were rated as toss-ups by the various rating publications. Young, who was under federal investigation in 2008, was ranked *the* most endangered incumbent on *Roll Call's* election-year list of the top ten most vulnerable House incumbents.[32] Others, such as Michele Bachmann (MN-6), started the campaign season in a reasonably strong position but lost support later in the game. Bachmann, who won with only 46.4 percent of the vote, caused massive trouble for herself by stating on MSNBC's *Hardball with Chris Matthews* that Barack Obama, as well as some members of Congress, may hold anti-American views.[33] Her comments prompted scores of offended Democrats and Obama supporters to pour roughly $800,000 dollars into the campaign of her opponent, Elwyn Tinklenberg.[34] Still other GOP incumbents, such as Ken Calvert (CA-44), had unexpectedly close calls. Either way, it is possible that better fundraising and/or more effective campaigns by Democratic challengers in these districts could have made 2008 an even worse year than it was for Republican incumbents.

In most tide elections, at least one incumbent unexpectedly goes down to defeat. In 2008, this distinction surely belongs to Virginia Republican Virgil Goode (VA-5). As of this writing, Virginia had certified Democratic challenger and nonprofit leader Tom Perriello as the winner against Goode by 745 votes. While Goode requested a recount, there was little reason to expect the final outcome to change.[35] No congressional election raters predicted Goode to be in trouble in 2008, and for good reason. A sixth-term member who has been a Democrat, an Independent, and a Republican during his 12 years in Congress, Goode had garnered an average of 68 percent of the vote in his six elections. Caught by surprise by Goode's sudden weakness, the NRCC didn't run ads in his district until October 30, though the DCCC had run ads earlier.[36] Goode has not exactly steered clear of controversy. In 2005, he was associated with a scandal involving a defense contractor, and in 2006 he claimed that Muslims who live in the U.S. threaten "the values and beliefs traditional to the U.S." Goode also objected to Representative Keith Ellison's (D-MN) use of the Koran (instead of the Bible) at his swearing in.[37] (Ellison is the House's only Muslim member.) Nevertheless, Goode was not thought to be vulnerable in 2008.

In contrast to 2006—in which House Democrats lost no seats—Democrats did not come away entirely unscathed in 2008. Republicans defeated five House Democratic incumbents: Nancy Boyda (KS-2), Don Cazayoux (LA-6), William Jefferson (LA-2), Nick Lampson (TX-22), and Tim Mahoney (FL-16). Most of these outcomes were unsurprising. All except Jefferson were freshmen lawmakers elected in (or since) 2006 in solid or Republican-leaning districts. Cazayoux, for example, won a special election victory in a May 2008 in a district that, prior to his election, had been held by Republicans for three decades. Lampson, from the district of former GOP majority leader Tom DeLay, won in 2006 when DeLay's resignation left the GOP with no candidate on the ballot. Boyda was a freshman who pulled off a razor-thin (50.6 percent) upset victory in 2006 in a district in which President Bush won 59 percent of the vote in 2004. And Democrat Tim Mahoney, elected in 2006 by ousting sex-scandal plagued GOP incumbent Mark Foley, had his own sex scandal.[38] The average vote received by these defeated freshmen lawmakers in their prior elections was 50.3 percent; the average 2004 Bush vote in their districts was 59.25 percent.

Democrat William Jefferson's defeat in Louisiana's 2nd District was a major surprise. Indicted on federal corruption charges in June 2007, Jefferson was nevertheless favored to win reelection simply because of the political composition of his district. (The 2nd is 64 percent African American and gave Kerry 75 percent of the vote in 2004). Instead, voters opted for Republican political novice Anh Cao—a Vietnamese American lawyer who highlighted ethics in his campaign.[39] But it will likely be difficult for Cao to hold the heavily Democratic district in 2010.

Nearly all of the Democrats who captured Republican seats in 2006 won reelection in 2008. In fact, House Democrats in the class of 2006 garnered a median-vote share of 57 percent in 2008, a 3.7 percentage point increase over their 2006 showing. This should concern the GOP, since these districts will likely become more difficult for Republicans to win back as Democratic incumbents solidify their hold on them.

To be sure, a few Democratic incumbents barely squeaked by. In fact, three Democratic incumbents—two freshmen and scandal-plagued veteran Paul Kanjorski (PA-11)—won by less than 52 percent of the vote or less, and 10 Democratic incumbents won by 55 percent of the vote or less. Republicans also had a potential late-breaking opportunity in Pennsylvania's 11th District, after veteran Democratic incumbent John Murtha publically pronounced western Pennsylvania (where his district is located) "a racist area."[40] However, with a tight budget allocated mainly to defending Republican incumbents, the NRCC lacked the necessary resources to capitalize on potential opportunities in these contests. Even Murtha won his seat back with 58 percent of the vote, down only 3 percentage points from 2006.

Open-seat outcomes also contributed to the Democratic tide. As Table 1 shows, Democrats won all seven of the open seats they were defending, with Democratic candidates amassing a median-vote share of 56.5. Of the seven contests, the slimmest Democratic victories were, not surprisingly, in the two districts carried by George W. Bush in 2004. By contrast, Republicans won only 17 of the 29 open seats they were defending, with 12 GOP open seats captured by Democrats. Republicans ran well in the 17 open seats they retained, winning more than 55 percent of the vote in 10 of the 17 contests and more than 60 percent in four of the 17. But the 12 GOP open seats captured by Democrats is a stinging defeat for Republicans, and the sting is surely made worse by the fact that 10 of the 12 Democratic pick ups occurred in districts won by George W. Bush in 2004.

Until 2006, at least some political observers believed that the GOP tilt of the congressional district map would make it nearly impossible for Democrats to win a majority in the House for the rest of the decade.[41] But the 2008 (and 2006) House elections show that, as political scientist Gary Jacobson has noted, a sufficiently big partisan tide can overcome even difficult structural disadvantages in the electoral map.[42]

## THE U.S. SENATE RACES

In Senate contests, of course, the fortunes of each party depend not only on national tides and candidate effectiveness, but on which seats are up in the first place. While the U.S. Constitution stipulates that one-third of U.S. Senate's seats are to be up for election every two years, 2008 saw 35 U.S. Senate contests in 33 states. The unusual number reflects additional contests in Mississippi and Wyoming in which incumbents Roger Wicker (R-MS) and John Barrasso (R-WY) were running to complete the terms of senators they were appointed to replace.[43] Since the other incumbent Republican senators of Mississippi (Thad Cochran) and Wyoming (Mike Enzi) were also up for reelection in 2008, these states each had two U.S. Senate contests on the ballot.

One difficulty for Senate Republicans was that they were defending 23 of the 35 seats up for election. To compound the GOP's problems, five of the 23 seats they were defending were open seats, thanks to the retirements of Republican incumbents Wayne Allard (CO), Larry Craig (ID), Chuck Hagel (NE), Pete Domenici (NM), and John Warner (VA). By contrast, no Democratic incumbent senators were retiring, leaving Democrats with no open seats to defend. Finally, four of the states in which Republicans were defending seats (Colorado, North Carolina, New Mexico, and Virginia) went from supporting Bush in 2004 to supporting Obama in 2008, no doubt providing added wind at Democrats' backs.

As with the results for House races, Senate outcomes reflected the unfavorable political climate facing Republicans. All told, Democrats gained seven seats, defeating GOP incumbents in Alaska, North Carolina, New Hampshire, and Oregon and capturing GOP-held open seats in Colorado, New Mexico, and Virginia. (These results exclude the contest in Minnesota, which as of this writing remains undecided.[44]) Of the total votes cast in the 35 Senate contests, 52 percent went to Democrats, nearing Obama's national popular vote percentage. If we examine Senate elections since the 1980, Democrats' seven-seat gain in the Senate is a strong showing, trailing only the GOP's 12-seat gain in 1980, Democrats' own nine-seat gain in 1986, and the eight-seat Republican gain in 1994.

Table 2 provides an overview of the Senate outcomes by party and type of contest. As with the House, the incumbent reelection rate was higher for Democratic incumbents (100 percent) than for Republican incumbents (76 percent).[45] Democratic challengers ousted four Republican incumbents: Ted Stevens (AK), Elizabeth Dole (NC), John Sununu (NH), and Gordon Smith (OR). By contrast, no Democratic incumbents were defeated, with Louisiana's Mary Landrieu—the only vulnerable Democrat incumbent—winning her race against Louisiana State Treasurer John Kennedy by a margin of 52 to 46 percent. Of the incumbent senators who won, most were reelected handily, though Democratic incumbents no doubt had an easier time than did Republican incumbents. Of the 12 Democratic incumbent senators reelected, ten (83 percent) garnered 60 percent or more of the vote, while only seven (54 percent) of the 13 GOP incumbent senators reelected amassed 60 percent of the vote or more. The median-vote share won by Democratic incumbent victors (63.4) was also somewhat higher than the median-vote share won by GOP incumbent victors (60.8).

**Table 2. Summary of U.S. Senate Race Outcomes**

| | Democrats | Republican |
|---|---|---|
| Seats not up | 39 | 26 |
| Incumbents reelected | 12 (100%) | 13 (76%)[a] |
| Challenger victories | 4 (AK, NH, NC, OR) | 0 |
| Open seats successfully defended | 0 (of 0) | 2 (of 5) (ID, NE) |
| Open seats captured from opposition | 3 (CO, NM, VA) | 0 |
| **Total seats** | 58 | 41 |
| **Net gain/loss from 110th Congress** | +7 | –7 |

[a]18 GOP incumbent senators ran for reelection. As of this writing, the Senate contest in Minnesota between Republican incumbent Norm Coleman and Democratic challenger Al Franken remains undecided. A statewide recount will decide the contest. The reelection rate for GOP incumbents does not include this contest in either the numerator or denominator.

In addition to handily winning in states carried by Obama, Democratic incumbent senators ran well in four states won by McCain. These include Arkansas (Mark Pryor, 79.4 percent), Montana (Max Baucus, 72.9 percent), South Dakota (Tim Johnson, 62.5 percent), and West Virginia (Jay Rockefeller, 63.7 percent). Democratic incumbent Mary Landrieu also won in a McCain state (Louisiana), though by the smaller margin of 52 percent. Susan Collins (R-ME) was the only GOP Senate incumbent to win in a state carried by Obama (although a Coleman victory in Minnesota, a race still undecided as of this writing, would bring the total to two).

The four GOP incumbent losses were not particularly surprising. In Alaska, longtime Senate incumbent Ted Stevens won the GOP primary with 63 percent of the vote despite being indicted on federal charges for failing to report gifts valued at more than $250,000. Found guilty of seven counts just one week before the election, Stevens still managed to poll 46.6 percent against Anchorage Mayor Mark Begich.[46] Stevens' loss, which wasn't certain until two weeks after the election, saved his Senate colleagues the trouble and heartache of expelling him from the Senate, which they would likely have done had Stevens won the contest.[47]

In New Hampshire, a formidable Democratic challenger (popular former New Hampshire Governor Jeanne Shaheen), the deepening blue tide flooding New England, and incumbent John Sununu's close ties to George W. Bush created a near-perfect storm against Sununu. For Shaheen, linking Sununu with Bush and his policies was clearly the central strategy. "The policies of George Bush and John Sununu," she hammered away, "have been out of step from where the voters of New Hampshire are."[48] Recent partisan trends in New Hampshire surely didn't help Sununu. In 2006, the Granite State elected two Democratic House members (both reelected in 2008), and 2008 Democratic presidential candidate Barack Obama improved on John Kerry's 2004 showing in the state by more than 4 percentage points. What's more, New Hampshire Governor John Lynch, a Democrat, has been elected with 70 percent or more in his last two elections.

Instructively, fellow GOP New Englander Susan Collins (ME) did not suffer Sununu's fate. Her decisive 61.4 percent win against former Democratic House member Tom Allen was surely aided by her moderate record, which stands in stark contrast to Sununu's. While Sununu voted with Senate Republicans on 91 percent of roll call votes in 2006, Collins sided with her Senate GOP colleagues only 66 percent of the time during that year.[49] Collins represents the increasingly rare breed of Republican that can still win in New England.

Ties to George W. Bush surely hurt GOP incumbent Gordon Smith in the Democratic-trending state of Oregon as well. With Obama improving on

Kerry's 2004 performance in Oregon by 6 percentage points, even a solid, politically moderate reputation wasn't enough to save Gordon Smith from a successful challenge by Oregon State Legislature Speaker Jeff Merkley. During the contest, Smith did more than merely tout his political independence; he ran ads linking his policy preferences with those of Obama and liberal icon Ted Kennedy (D-MA).[50] But to no avail. In a state in which registration numbers have increasingly favored Democrats, Smith was likely harmed most by the "R" next to his name on the ballot.[51]

In North Carolina, GOP incumbent Senator Elizabeth Dole's campaign for a second term was undermined by a combination of a well-funded and energetic, if relatively unknown, challenger (State Senator Kay Hagan) and Barack Obama's important victory in the state. With more seasoned Democrats Mike Easley and Erskine Bowles (who lost to Dole in 2002 and to Richard Burr in 2004) opting out of the race,[52] Democratic Senatorial Campaign Committee (DSCC) Chair Chuck Schumer (D-NY) recruited the 55-year old Hagan to run what turned out to be a referendum on the 72-year-old Dole. Democrats attacked hard from the start, running ads that purposely left voters confused about Dole's age (insinuating she was in her early 90s), pointing voters to a nonpartisan Web site (Congress.org) that listed Dole as only the ninety-third most effective senator in the 110th Congress, and releasing figures implying that Dole had spent only 30 days in North Carolina in all of 2005 and 2006.[53] The DSCC helped finance these efforts, spending more than $11.5 million in the race.[54] Trailing in the polls, Dole may have sealed her fate by releasing an October ad that called into question Hagan's religious faith. The ad, which highlighted Hagan's attendance at a fundraiser sponsored by a political committee called the Godless Americans Political Action Committee (which was committed to separation of church and state), ended with a picture of Hagan and a female voice overlay uttering the words "There is no God."[55] Several state newspapers decried the ad as offensive, and Hagan herself sued the Dole campaign for defamation (though she withdrew the lawsuit after winning the election).[56] Finally, Obama's narrow win in North Carolina—he improved on John Kerry's 2004 showing by 6 percentage points—likely helped to boost Hagan's vote share.[57]

Well-funded Democrats made solid attempts at defeating Republican incumbents in Minnesota, Kentucky, and Georgia. Democrats were unsuccessful in Kentucky and Georgia, while the Minnesota contest remained locked in a legal battle over a statewide recount as this book went to press. The Minnesota race, which featured scores of attack ads, may well rival the North Carolina Senate contest as the nastiest race of the 2008 season. For much of the fall, GOP incumbent Norm Coleman repeatedly attacked opponent Al Franken for incorrect tax returns and a multitude of vulgar utterances Franken had made as a comedian and radio-show host, while Franken counterattacked Coleman for "rubber stamping the Bush agenda" and for allegedly receiving campaign contributions from a Texas donor funneled through Coleman's wife's business.[58] In the second week of October, Coleman announced that he would pull all negative ads until Election Day, but the harsh tenor of the contest had already been set. Complicating matters for both candidates, the race featured an independent (and antiwar) candidate, Dean Barkley, an ally of former Governor Jesse Ventura, who polled 15 percent of the statewide vote and possibly helped Coleman by providing anti-Coleman voters with an alternative to Franken. To be sure, statewide trends favoring Democrats very likely cut into the vote totals of Coleman. As a measure of Minnesota's recent affinity for Democrats, Senator Amy Klobuchar (D) won 58 percent of the vote in her first election in 2006, and Obama added roughly 3 percentage points to Kerry's 51 percent showing in the state in 2004. As of this writing, the Coleman-Franken contest remains undecided, with Coleman filing a legal challenge to the state-certified recount that put Franken ahead by a mere 225 votes.[59] Franken's comedic past provided an easy target for Coleman, and it seems plausible that a Democratic challenger with a more traditional biography might have given Democrats an easier time in Minnesota.

In Georgia, a state law requiring victors to win 50 percent plus 1 of the vote forced GOP incumbent Saxby Chambliss (who amassed 49.8 percent of the vote) into a December 2 runoff with former State Representative Jim Martin. Key to Chambliss's difficulties was his vote in favor of the October financial bailout package.[60] After the vote, the Martin campaign ran an ad lambasting Chambliss, saying, "$700 billion for Wall Street, while Georgia families get nothing."[61] With the runoff (along with the Minnesota contest) pivotal in determining whether Senate Democrats would achieve a filibuster-proof (60-seat) majority, party and interest group money poured into the race.[62] In the November 6 contest, Martin was likely advantaged by Libertarian candidate Allen Buckley, who garnered 3.4 percent of the vote and probably siphoned more support from Chambliss than from Martin. With Buckley excluded, and without Obama on the ballot to boost turnout among Democrats (particularly African American voters), Chambliss easily won the runoff, 57.5 to 42.5 percent, over Martin.[63] The GOP victory dashed Democrats' hopes for a filibuster-proof majority in the Senate.

Democrats also fell short in Kentucky and Mississippi. In Kentucky, Democrats were hopeful that wealthy businessman Bruce Lunsford could unseat Senate Republican Leader Mitch McConnell as payback for the GOP's defeat of Democratic Leader Tom Daschle in 2004. Most polls toward the end of October showed McConnell with a small but consistent lead.[64] In the end, big spending by DSCC, as well as by Lunsford himself, helped Democrats shave nearly 12 points from McConnell's 2002 vote share. But McConnell still won, 53 to 47 percent. In his victory speech, a relieved McConnell noted that "Winston Churchill one said that the most exhilarating feelings is to be shot at—and missed. And after the last few months," added McConnell, "I think what he meant to say is that there's nothing more exhausting."[65]

In Mississippi, Democrats had high hopes of defeating GOP incumbent Roger Wicker, who, appointed by Governor Haley Barbour when GOP Senator Trent Lott resigned in 2008, was running to complete Lott's term. Running against Wicker was former Mississippi governor Ronnie Musgrove, a candidate defeated by Barbour in 2003 but with obvious name recognition in the state. Many political observers expected the Mississippi race to be close; indeed, CQ rated it as a toss-up. Both parties thought it would be close as well: The DSCC spent at least $8.3 million in the race, while the NRSC spent roughly $4.4 million. But Wicker ended up with a solid win, amassing 55.3 percent to Musgrove's 44.7 percent, and likely helped by McCain's 56.4 percent win in Mississippi.

Yet in Louisiana, McCain's even stronger showing (nearly 59 percent) couldn't help Republicans unseat Democratic incumbent Mary Landrieu, who won 52.1 percent against Democrat-turned-Republican State Treasurer John Kennedy. Landrieu outspent Kennedy by more than two to one, and the NRSC seemed to jump in and out of the contest.[66] This was a closely watched race, especially given the departure of many New Orleans African Americans (an important part of Democrats' coalition) following Hurricane Katrina in 2005.[67] But ultimately, Louisiana voters opted to stay with the incumbent.

As Table 3 shows, the five Senate open seats were surprisingly uncompetitive, especially given that three (CO, NM, and VA) involved a shift in party control from Republican to Democrat. In a battle of New Mexico congressmen, Democratic House member Steve Udall beat Republican House member Steve Pearce, 61.2 to 38.8 percent, to capture the Senate seat of retiring GOP veteran Pete Domenici. Many observers attribute Pearce's defeat to his hard-core conservatism in a year in which voters were seeking centrists.[68] Obama's 6-point improvement over Kerry's 2004 showing in New Mexico no doubt helped Udall as well.

Table 3. Summary of Outcomes in 2008 Open-Seat U.S. Senate Races

| State | Retiring Incumbent | Democrat | Dem Vote | Republican | Rep Vote |
|-------|--------------------|----------|----------|------------|----------|
| CO | Wayne Allard (R) | Mark Udall | 52.3 | Bob Schaffer | 43.0 |
| ID | Larry Craig (R) | Larry LaRocco | 34.1 | Jim Risch | 57.6 |
| NE | Chuck Hagel (R) | Scott Kleeb | 39.9 | Mike Johanns | 57.7 |
| NM | Pete Domenici (R) | Steve Udall | 61.2 | Steve Pearce | 38.8 |
| VA | John Warner (R) | Mark Warner | 64.7 | Jim Gilmore | 34.1 |

Two former governors competed in Virginia, with Mark Warner easily defeating Jim Gilmore, 64.7 to 34.1 percent, to capture the seat of retiring GOP incumbent John Warner. With Northern Virginia's large and diverse population driving a shift toward Democrats in the Old Dominion—the party has won two gubernatorial races and a U.S. Senate contest since 2001— Gilmore never seemed to have a chance in this race.[69] Gilmore's problems were compounded his severe lack of resources and, of course, by Obama's important victory in Virginia.

Democrats also captured a Republican open seat in Colorado, another state trending toward Democrats in recent years. In the Colorado race, Democratic House member Mark Udall defeated former House member Bob Schaffer by nearly 10 points, 52.3 to 43 percent, to win retiring GOP incumbent Wayne Allard's seat. As with Mark's cousin Steve Udall, whose U.S. Senate victory in New Mexico was aided by Obama's strong showing in that state, Mark Udall's win was surely helped along by Obama's 53.5 percent victory in Colorado (which reflected a 6.5 point increase over Kerry's 2004 performance in the state).

In two other open-seat contests, Republicans easily held on to seats in Nebraska, with former U.S. Agriculture Secretary Mike Johanns (57.7 percent) besting college professor Scott Kleeb (39.9 percent), and in Idaho, with Lieutenant Governor Jim Risch handily beating former House member Larry LaRocco (57.6 to 34.1 percent).

## CONGRESSIONAL CAMPAIGN FINANCE

As political scientist Gary Jacobson notes, a strong national tide favoring a party is not by itself sufficient to produce party victories. Well-funded candidates with the ability to capitalize on the tide are also necessary.[70] 2008 campaign finance data demonstrate the substantial role of money in helping Democrats exploit GOP weaknesses. In the House, Democratic challengers who defeated GOP incumbents raised an impressive average of $1.67 million—80 percent of the average amount ($2.1 million) raised by defeated GOP incumbents. Political scientists have long known that challengers need not out-raise incumbents in order to defeat them, as long as they can amass sums sufficient to mount an effective campaign. Victorious Democratic challengers were clearly able to raise the sums they needed.

Amassing sufficient funds is not always easy, though, and it is possible that more robust challenger fundraising could have produced additional victories for House Democrats. In fact, there were several contests in which the House Republican incumbent survived with 55 percent or less of the vote. But in many of these contests, the Democratic challenger raised significantly less than the sums raised by Democratic challengers who toppled GOP incumbents. Better fundraising and/or more effective challengers might have yielded additional Democratic victories in some of these districts.[71]

Not surprisingly, money and outcomes were associated in open-seat House contests. According to the Campaign Finance Institute's November 6 report, winning open-seat House candidates raised an average of $1.6 million, whereas open-seat losers raised an average of only $954,286. Democrats, though, had a sizable fundraising advantage among open-seat winners, with Democratic open-seat winners ($1.9 million) raising an average of $600,000 more than Republican open-seat winners ($1.3 million).[72]

Senate contests, especially the competitive races, were characteristically expensive. The average amount raised by winning Senate incumbents was $8.1 million, while losing Senate incumbents spent an average of $11 million.[73] The average amount raised by winning Senate challengers was $5.7 million, while losing Senate challengers raised an average of only $1.6 million.[74] Thus, as with successful House challengers, victorious Senate challengers, while typically unable to out-raise their incumbent opponents, were able to raise sufficient funds to mount effective campaigns (and were typically supplemented by sizable party expenditures). In contests such as Oregon, where GOP incumbent Gordon Smith significantly out-raised Democratic challenger Jeff Merkeley by a margin of two to one, the DSCC came through with $12 million of independent spending—more than double the sum spent by the NRSC in the race. In the five open-seat Senate contests, money was associated with victory, with winning candidates out-raising losing candidates by an average of $7.4 to $3.4 million. The open-seat Senate contest in Virginia saw particularly lopsided fundraising, with shoo-in Democrat Mark Warner raking in nearly $13 million to GOP candidate Jim Gilmore's $2.6 million.

Prohibited by the Bipartisan Campaign Finance Reform Act (BCRA) from raising soft money, political parties nevertheless continue to play an influential fundraising role in House and Senate contests. Importantly, in 2008, Democratic Party organizations held a sizable fundraising advantage over Republican Party organizations, with Republicans forced to make difficult decisions about where to spend money.[75] On the House side, the DCCC outspent the NRCC by more than $50 million ($75.3 million to $22.8 million) in independent expenditures. Indeed, DCCC independent expenditures totaled $1 million or more in fully 38 House contests, whereas the NRCC could afford this level of independent spending in only four House contests. In a few instances, DCCC independent spending reflected the party's attempt to expand the playing field; a luxury afforded by its vast resource advantage over the NRCC. For example, the DCCC spent more than $2 million in Arizona's 3rd District, a fairly safe Republican district held by GOP incumbent John Shadegg. Shadegg garnered 59 percent of the district vote in 2006, and George W. Bush carried the district with 58 percent in 2004. But DCCC spending and a credible campaign run by Democratic challenger Robert Lord held Shadegg to his lowest percentage ever (54 percent) in 2008.

On the Senate side, the DSCC spent almost twice as much ($70.1 million) in Senate contests as did the NRSC ($36.1 million). Not surprisingly, the same five contests showed up, albeit in different order, on each party committee's top-five list of heaviest independent expenditures: Minnesota, Mississippi, New Hampshire, North Carolina, and Oregon. For Democrats, these five contests consumed roughly 73 percent of the DSCC's total independent expenditures; for the NRSC, the figure was 78 percent. But in all five contests, the DSCC outspent the NRSC, and it did so by at least two to one in the North Carolina and Oregon contests. Only in Mississippi did Republicans win.

As has become the new norm in congressional contests, members of Congress themselves also did their part by contributing substantial sums of campaign money to candidates in tight contests and to the party congressional campaign committees.[76] By June 30, House Democrats had already collectively transferred nearly $30 million to the DCCC, while GOP incumbents, embattled though they were, still managed to give $13 million to the NRCC. Not surprisingly, congressional party leaders played a leading role in these efforts, but rank-and-file members (especially in the House Democratic caucus) gave at record rates as well.[77] In fact, on the Democratic side, even some nonincumbent candidates kicked into the DCCC's coffers.[78] Senate incumbents tend to engage in member contribution activity at lower levels than do House members, and 2008 was no different.[79] By June 30, Democratic senators had given $4,964,000 to the DSCC, while GOP Senate incumbents had turned over a scant $1,121,172 to the NRSC.[80] Publicly critical of his colleagues' insufficient generosity, NRSC Chair John Ensign (R-NV) said he would be forced to scale back the NRSC's independent expenditure budget.[81] Meanwhile, DSCC Chair Chuck Schumer promised outside donors that Senate incumbents would triple every contribution made to the committee on the day before the election.[82]

Incumbents also supplemented their contributions to the party committees with contributions directly to candidates from their leadership political action committees (PACs) and principal campaign committees. For example, in addition to the $885,000 that House Ways and Means Chair Charles Rangel (D-NY) gave to the DCCC from his principal campaign committee, he contributed $836,292 to Democratic congressional candidates from his leadership PAC and another $373,900 from his principal reelection account.[83] For House Republicans, Eric Cantor (R-VA)—elected by his House GOP colleagues to the top House Republican whip post for the 111th Congress—was one of the most generous member donors. Cantor gave $964,500 to candidates from his leadership PAC, another $54,000 to candidates from his principal campaign committee, and an additional $103,157 from his reelection account to the NRCC. By supplementing the efforts of their party's campaign committees, incumbent donations can provide essential support for their party's competitive candidates. It is no surprise, then, that over the past decade, congressional party leaders have increasingly leaned on incumbents to share their campaign wealth with the party and its candidates. Indeed, members who neglect to give to the party can forget about advancing in party and committee hierarchies.[84]

Interest groups were also heavily involved in the financing of congressional elections. At the time of this writing, the Federal Election Commission (FEC) had not yet released final contribution data on the 4,000-plus PACs registered at the federal level in 2008. But preliminary data released by the FEC on November 21 show that of the $273 million in PAC contributions given to House candidates through October 15, 2008, Democratic candidates received $169.1 million (62 percent), while GOP candidates took in $103.9 million (38 percent). The substantial increase in PAC contributions collected by House Democrats compared to the 2005–2006 cycle—when Democrats were still the House minority party—reflect the party's increased numbers in the chamber and the PAC fundraising advantages typically enjoyed by majority party members (especially with corporate and trade PACs).[85] In contests for the U.S. Senate, on the other hand, Republican candidates had an edge over Democrats in PAC contributions, raising $38.8 million to Democrats' $30 million.[86] The GOP PAC contribution advantage in the 2008 U.S. Senate contests reflects two facts: that six more Republican than Democratic incumbents were up for reelection in 2008, and that GOP incumbents raised, on average, slightly more from PACs than did Democratic incumbents.

In addition to federal PACs, many 527 and 501(c) groups spent substantial sums of unregulated money on voter mobilization efforts and issue ads—ads that praise or criticize a candidate's record without expressly advocating his or her election or defeat.[87] The disclosure requirements for 527s and, especially, 501(c) groups are less stringent than those for federal PACs, making expenditure data more difficult to assemble. But an October 2008 report by the Campaign Finance Institute (CFI) estimates that 527s and 501(c) groups would spend more than $400 million by the end of the 2008 election, with much of the money spent in the most competitive House and Senate contests. Among the CFI report's other important findings are that 527 groups favoring Democrats had a sizable financial advantage over 527s favoring Republicans, that many 527 committees are associated with interest groups that also organize hard money PACs, and that campaign activity by 501(c) groups—which are even less tightly regulated than 527 committees—increased substantially in the 2007–2008 election cycle. Clearly, and despite various regulatory attempts, unregulated group money has become a permanent feature of congressional campaigns.

## THE 2008 GUBERNATORIAL CONTESTS

There were also 11 governorships, as well as hundreds of state legislative seats, up for grabs in 2008. In the six states where Democrats were defending governorships, four featured incumbents (Montana, New Hampshire, Washington, Wyoming) and two were open-seat contests (Delaware and North Carolina). Of the five governorships Republicans were defending, four were held by incumbents (Indiana, North Dakota, Utah, and Vermont) and one was an open-seat race (Missouri). The three open-seat races (Delaware, North Carolina, and Missouri) were produced by a combination of forced and voluntary retirements. In Delaware and North Carolina, Democratic incumbent governors Ruth Ann Miner and Mike Easley were term-limited. In Missouri, Republican incumbent Matt Blunt, beleaguered by low public approval ratings and facing a grueling and expensive contest against four-term Missouri Attorney General Jay Nixon, decided to step down after just one term.

As Table 4 shows, voters opted for continuity in electing governors in 2008. Of the eight incumbent governors running for reelection, all were reelected—most by strikingly high vote margins. Indeed, the median incumbent vote share for the eight incumbent governors was nearly 68 percent, and GOP incumbents John Hoeven of North Dakota and Jon Huntsman of Utah each dispatched with their Democratic challengers by winning considerably more than 70 percent of the vote. A few Democratic governors racked up impressive vote margins as well. In New Hampshire, highly popular Governor John Lynch beat GOP State Senator Joe Kenney by 70.2 to 27.6 percent, though Lynch's showing was actually 3.8 percentage points *lower* than his 2006 showing. Similarly, in West Virginia, Governor Joe Manchin defeated former Republican state senator Russ Weeks by 69.8 to 25.8 percent. Clearly, Manchin seemed unharmed by a scandal in which his daughter, who worked for one of Manchin's corporate contributors, was awarded an MBA degree by West Virginia University without ever completing the degree requirements.[88]

**Table 4. Summary of Outcomes in
2008 Incumbent-Challenger Gubernatorial Races**

| State | Incumbent | Inc vote | Challenger | Chall vote | Incumbent vote change from last election |
|---|---|---|---|---|---|
| IN | Mitch Daniels-R | 61.9 | Jill Long Thompson-D | 35.9 | +8.7 |
| MT | Brian Schweitzer-D | 65.4 | Ray Brown-R | 32.6 | +15.0 |
| ND | John Hoeven-R | 74.4 | Tim Mathern-D | 23.5 | +3.1 |
| NH | John Lynch-D | 70.2 | Joe Kenney-R | 27.6 | –3.8 |
| UT | Jon Huntsman-R | 77.7 | Bob Springmeyer-D | 19.7 | +20.0 |
| VT | Jim Douglas-R | 54.6 | Anthony Polina-I | 21.3 | |
| | | | Gaye Symington-D | 21.1 | –1.8 |
| WA | Christine Gregoire-D | 53.9 | Dino Rossi-R | 46.1 | +5.0 |
| WV | Joe Manchin-D | 69.8 | Russ Weeks-R | 25.8 | +6.3 |
| **Median incumbent vote** | | **67.6** | **Median challenger vote** | **30.1** | **Median incumbent change   +5.7** |

Of the gubernatorial contests featuring incumbents, only the Washington rematch between Democrat Christine Gregoire and Republican Dino Rossi even neared a close outcome. Gregoire, who in 2004 beat Rossi by a mere 129 votes following two recounts and multiple court rulings, defeated Rossi this time with a decisive 54 percent of the vote. The 2008 race saw a reprise of the partisan vitriol that characterized the 2004 race.[89] But the advantages of incumbency, the strong national Democratic tide, and Democratic presidential candidate Barack Obama's strong showing (57.4 percent) in the state of Washington, all surely helped propel Gregoire to a more convincing victory in 2008. Vermont's GOP incumbent Governor Jim Douglas, who garnered 54.6 percent of the vote, may have had a more challenging reelection if Independent Anthony Polina and Democrat Gaye Symington had spent less time attacking each other in their quests for Vermont's liberal vote.[90]

As Table 5 shows, even two of the three open-seat contests produced relatively lopsided outcomes. In Delaware, Democrat and State Treasurer Jack Markell handily defeated Republican retired state Judge William Lee by 35 percentage points, replacing term-limited Democratic Governor Ruth Ann Miner. Similarly, in Missouri, Democrat Jay Nixon defeated former GOP House member Kenny Hulshof by nearly 20 percentage points. A strong candidate with significant statewide experience as Missouri attorney general, Nixon was likely aided by Obama's competitive showing in Missouri—a 3-percentage-point improvement over John Kerry's 2004 vote total in the state.[91]

**Table 5. Summary of Outcomes in 2008 Open-Seat Gubernatorial Races**

| State | Retiring Incumbent | Democrat | Dem Vote | Republican | Rep Vote |
|-------|--------------------|----------|----------|------------|----------|
| DE | Ruth Ann Miner-D (term limited) | Jack Markell | 67.5 | William Lee | 32.0 |
| MO | Matt Blunt-R (retired) | Jay Nixon | 58.4 | Kenny Hulshof | 39.5 |
| NC | Mike Easley-D (term limited) | Beverly Perdue | 50.2 | Pat McCrory | 46.9 |

Of 2008's gubernatorial contests, the North Carolina open-seat contest yielded the closest outcome, with Democratic Lieutenant Governor Beverly Perdue defeating GOP Charlotte Mayor Pat McCrory by roughly 3 percentage points (50.2 to 46.9 percent) to become North Carolina's first female governor. Throughout the fall, the North Carolina gubernatorial contest swung back and forth in the polls, remaining closer than the U.S. Senate contest between Dole and Hagan.[92] GOP candidate McCrory pushed something akin to Obama's central message of change, highlighting ethical problems in the North Carolina's Democratically controlled state legislature.[93] But in the end, the voters who turned out to provide Obama with a victory in the state likely helped propel Perdue over the victory line.

Not surprisingly, in 7 of the 11 gubernatorial contests, the party that won the governor's mansion also carried the state's presidential contest. But that figure obscures some interesting and important differences in the states. In five of the seven contests where a party claimed both the governor's mansion and an Electoral College victory, the party's gubernatorial candidate ran ahead—sometimes far ahead—of the party's presidential candidate.[94] In North Dakota, for example, GOP incumbent Governor John Hoeven ran 21 points ahead of Republican presidential candidate John McCain. Moreover, in the four states that supported gubernatorial and presidential candidates of *different* parties, incumbent governors—mostly popular and/or facing weak opposition—posted impressive showings. In West Virginia, for example, Democrat Joe Manchin racked up a 44-point margin over GOP challenger Russ Weeks despite Obama's 13-point loss to McCain in the state; in Montana, Democrat Brian Schweitzer's 33-point margin over Republican Ray Brown came despite McCain's (rather slim) victory in the state. On the GOP side, Republican incumbent Mitch Daniels handily defeated underfunded challenger Jill Thompson Long despite a McCain loss in Indiana, while in Vermont, Republican Jim Douglas defeated a hopelessly divided progressive opposition in the face of a 66.8 percent showing by Obama in the state. All told, the 2008 elections increased the number of Democratic governors by one (from 28 to 29), leaving Republicans with 21 governors.

Combined with changes in state legislative outcomes, the gubernatorial contests produced only a relatively small shift in party control of state governments. (See Table 6.) The GOP's loss of the governorship in Missouri and the Alaska State Senate (now a 10-to-10 tie) moved both states from unified GOP control to split control (though barely so in Alaska). Tennessee also moved into the split control category (though from unified Democratic control) after Republicans won both houses of the Tennessee state legislature.[95] Meanwhile, newly won Democratic majorities in the Delaware House, the New York State Senate, and the Wisconsin Assembly moved these states from split control to unified Democratic control. Shifts in party control of state legislatures—but which didn't yield a change in overall party control of state government—include a Democratic takeover of the Ohio House and the Nevada Senate and a GOP takeover of the Oklahoma and Montana State Senates.[96]

**Table 6. Party Control of State Governments, Pre- and Post 2008 Elections**

|  | Party Control of State Government | | Party Control of Governrships | | Party Control of State Legislatures | |
| --- | --- | --- | --- | --- | --- | --- |
|  | Pre-2008 | 2008 | Pre-2008 | 2008 | Pre-2008 | 2008 |
| Democrat | 16 | 17 | 28 | 29 | 23 | 27 |
| Republican | 10 | 8 | 22 | 21 | 14 | 14 |
| Divided | 23 | 24 | — | — | 12 | 8 |
| Nonpartisan | 1 | 1 | — | — | 1 | 1 |

Source: National Conference of State Legislatures. Party control of the Montana state government was uncertain as of this writing.

The importance of changes in the composition of state governments hardly needs to be stated. From a policy perspective, the partisan composition of state governments will obviously inform how states deal with the mounting fiscal problems they will inevitably confront over the coming years. Moreover, from a political perspective, the 2008 election outcomes (combined with the results in 2010) will play a critical role in determining which party gains the upper hand in the upcoming decennial redistricting process.

## CONCLUSION

The 2008 elections left Democrats with the presidency, 21 additional U.S. House seats, seven more U.S. Senate seats, one additional governor, and control of four additional state governments. While Senate Democrats will not have a filibuster-proof (60 seat) majority, they will be close. By wisely keeping renegade Joe Lieberman in the party—Lieberman received only a mild sanction for campaigning against Democratic presidential-elect Barack Obama[97]—Democrats may be able to shut down at least some GOP filibusters if they can enlist the support of the few remaining GOP moderates such as Maine Republicans Susan Collins and Olympia Snowe.

What Democrats accomplish with their new-found power obviously impacts how they will fare in the 2010 elections. But the magnitude of the problems facing the nation means that establishing a favorable party reputation won't be easy. Bringing the war in Iraq to a sensible close, providing security in Afghanistan, and rescuing the economy from a potentially deep and long-lasting recession are only the most immediate problems confronting the nation. Indeed, addressing these matters alone would be a sufficient challenge for any party. But the public also expects Democrats to find solutions to the nation's longer-term problems, including fixing Social Security and Medicare, devising a long-term plan for energy and climate change, paying down the nation's mountainous debt, and reigning in skyrocketing healthcare costs. What's more, items such as healthcare reform will be difficult to pass in light of the fiscal constraints facing the nation. Finally, and obviously, the public expects the government to keep the nation safe from terrorist threats.

In theory, unified control of the national government should help Democrats push through legislation that works to address the nation's needs. But practice is never so tidy. As political scientist David Mayhew has shown, unified government is not always a panacea for government gridlock, and this is especially true for a big, diverse party such as the Democrats.[98] In fact, the last time Democrats enjoyed unified control of the national government— the first two years of the Clinton administration (1993–1995)—is not a period

Democrats recall fondly. While the 103rd Congress and Clinton had some legislative accomplishments—though many, such as NAFTA, were not supported by a majority of Democrats—there were several notable policy failures.[99] The starkest, of course, was the Clinton healthcare bill, no version of which could garner sufficient support among the various factions of the House Democratic Party. Democrats' governing incompetence led directly to the Republican revolution of 1994, a midterm election which turned over control of both houses of Congress to Republicans. The 1994 House results were especially stunning. Winning 53 seats, Republicans took control of that chamber for the first time in 40 years.

Democrats will obviously work hard to avoid a repeat of the 103rd Congress—and of the 1994 midterms. But it will take skillful leadership. Inevitably, the larger the congressional Democratic Party becomes, the more ideologically diverse, and thus difficult to hold together, it becomes. If Democrats in the 111th Congress are to avoid the same fate as Democrats in the 103rd, the party's House and Senate leaders will need to identify common ground and, when need be, enforce discipline within the diverse Democratic caucus. The House Democratic Party especially needs to avoid being perceived as too liberal. Democratic leaders insist that they will govern from the center.[100] But the rapid ouster of moderate Energy and Commerce Committee chair John Dingell (D-MI) by liberal environmentalist Henry Waxman (D-CA) surely concerned some Democratic moderates.[101] (The close 137-to-122 vote on the Dingell-Waxman contest highlights the fault line within the House Democratic Party.) Finally, giving Republicans a greater role in the legislative process—if they want it—might buy some strategic breathing space for Democrats. After all, when minority parties are shut out of the legislative process, as they have been for the past few decades, they have little else to do but crank up the campaign machinery and attack the majority.

For their part, congressional Republicans will need to decide whether to fight Democrats at every turn or try to work with them where possible. There are few recent precedents for the accommodation model, and several of the newly elected House GOP leaders have hinted that they want to steer the party toward its conservative base.[102] Whichever course of action Republicans choose, the GOP needs to be very mindful that the party tent doesn't shrink further. In the 2006 and 2008 elections, Republicans lost a sizable number of seats in regions of the nation put off by the GOP's ultra-conservative base—in the 111th Congress, New York's 29-member House delegation will include only three Republicans. But in the United States' two-party system, any party that loses the ability to win across several different regions is deservedly destined to sit on the sidelines of power. As defeat-ed Representative Phil English (PA-3) noted after the election, "I think there are some in our party who don't understand the dynamics that it takes to compete in the some areas of the country. We cannot be a majority party unless we can be competitive in New England, in the upper Midwest, and in the mid-Atlantic."[103] Certainly, comments made by some Republicans about who is a "real American" and who is not have not helped the GOP expand its size, and in this regard, the GOP should have learned lessons from George Allen's 2006 defeat in Virginia.[104] Republicans, then, need to find a way—and quickly—to appeal to the increasingly diverse and large groups of Americans that populate growing areas such as Northern Virginia. These Americans will be an integral part of the American narrative for the twenty-first century, and any party that cares about winning elections needs to appeal to them. Actually, besides being smart politics, bringing new groups of voters into the fold is American representative democracy at its best.

Working in the GOP's favor is the historically reliable trend of the pres-ident's party losing seats, especially in the House, in midterm elections. Since 1862, the president's party in Congress has avoided this fate only four times, the most recent of which are 1998 and 2002. Combined with Democratic "exposure"—a party with *more* seats has more *vulnerable* seats—the 2010 midterm elections have the potential to reduce the size of the House and Senate Democratic caucuses. But historical trends don't occur automatically. To capitalize on the vulnerability that typically confronts members of the president's party during midterms, Republicans will need to recruit effective, pragmatic candidates who appeal to voters in the areas in which they are competing. In the Senate, moreover, the GOP will once again be defending more seats (19) than Democrats (16), and as of this writing, four GOP incum-bent senators have already announced they will not seek reelection in 2010, creating open-seat headaches for Republicans.[105]

The outcomes of 2008 gubernatorial elections, which brought more con-tinuity than change, are enormously important as well. Clearly, the nation's deepening recession will place many states in fiscal peril.[106] States will require innovative leadership with a common-sense approach if they are to weather the storm. Governors, along with state legislatures, will also help shape national politics through their influential role in the upcoming decennial redistricting process. The 2008 elections, which handed political control of state governments to Democrats in four additional states, leaves the Democratic Party well positioned to exercise considerable influence over those processes. But the story doesn't end with 2008. The 2010 elections will afford Republicans the opportunity to erase some of those Democratic gains.

Elections are the means to representative government. And Americans are no doubt hoping that the candidates they elected on November 6, 2008, will quickly get down to the hard work of governing the United States in a deliberate and intelligent fashion that advances the nation's fortunes. Elected officials, it is clear, have not always met that standard. In the end, we can only hope that the nation's voters, exercising their oversight in the electoral process, have the intelligence to defeat elected officials who have set the nation behind and reelect those who have moved the nation forward.

## NOTES

[1] I would like to thank Alice Carter for her editing and revision suggestions; as always her suggestions greatly improved the chapter. I would also like to thank Lily Larson for her patience and exemplary behavior while I wrote this chapter. It's a good bet that no seven-year old in the United States knows more about the U.S. Congress than does Lily.

[2] The Dow dropped 777 points, its largest single-day drop since the so-called "Black Friday" of 1987. Carl Hulse and David Herszenhorn, "Bailout Fails; Stocks Plunge: Dow Loses 777 Points After Vote House Rejects Bailout Package, 228–205." Accessed at www.nytimes.com., September 29 2008.

[3] At the time of this writing, the U.S. Senate contest in Minnesota is locked in a recount and remains undecided.

[4] As political scientist Gary Jacobson writes, "The more seats a party holds, the more of its seats are vulnerable to the opposition." Gary Jacobson, *The Politics of Congressional Elections*, 7th edition (New York: Pearson Longman), p. 158.

[5] Greg Giroux, "Democrats Add Two to House Roster," *CQ Weekly*, March 17, 2008, p.732. Accessed online on November 19, 2008 at http://library.cqpress.com/cqweekly/document. php?id=weeklyreport110-000002877948&type

[6] Greg Giroux, "Cazayoux, Scalise Win Louisiana Seats," *CQ Weekly*, May 12, 2008, p. 1268. Accessed online on November 21, 2008, at http://library.cqpress.com/cqweekly/

[7] Rachel Kapochunas, "Democrats Pick Up Third Seat This Year," *CQ Weekly*, May 19, 2008, p. 1363. Accessed online on October 15, 2008, at http://library.cqpress.com/cqweekly/ document.php?id=weeklyreport110-000002877948&type=toc&num=122&. Davis retired in 2008, and Democrats won his seat.

[8] In a November 2007 Pew poll, 32 percent of respondents listed Iraq as the most important issue facing the nation, while 15 percent listed the economy. By contrast, in an April 2008 Pew poll, 44 percent of respondents listed the economy as the most important issue, while 24 percent said Iraq. Pew Research Center for People and the Press, April 2008. Accessed online on November 21, 2008, at http://people-press.org/reports/questionnaires/436.pd. Most other poll results were showing the same trends. See, for example, Megan Thee, "More Poll Findings: The Economy Trumps the War, by Far," *New York Times*, July 16, 2008. Accessed online on November 21, 2008 at http://thecaucus.blogs.nytimes.com/2008/07/16/more-poll-findings-the-economy-trumps-the-war-by-far/

[9] "The End of the Affair: America's Return to Thrift Presages a Long and Deep Recession," The *Economist*, November 22, 2008, pp. 39–40.

[10] Les Christie, "August Foreclosures Hit Another High," *CNN Money*, September 18, 2008. Accessed online on September 18, 2008 at http://money.cnn.com/2008/09/12/real_estate/ foreclosures/index.htm.

[11]Benton Ives, "Attitude Shift at Fed Shows in Big Bailout," CQ *Weekly*, March 24, 2008. Accessed online on November 21, 2008, at http://library.cqpress.com/cqweekly.

[12]Energy Information Administration. Accessed online on November 22, 2008, at http://www.eia.doe.gov/

[13]Kathleen Hunter, "Two More Weeks of Energy Protests, Boehner Says," CQ *Today Online News*, August 7, 2008. Accessed on December 1, 2008, at http://www.cqpolitics.com/wmspage. cfm?docID=news-000002936001 Steven T. Dennis, "Gingrich to Join Protest," *Roll Call*, August 5, 2008. Accessed online on August 10, 2008, at http://www.rollcall.com.

[14]David M. Herszenhorn, "Word Reaches Congress: As the Market Goes, So Goes the Electorate," *New York Times*, October 2, 2008. Accessed online at http://www.nytimes.com on October 2, 2008. Altmire voted against the bailout legislation twice and won reelection.

[15]My own analysis of the September 29 vote on HR 3997 shows that four variables explained a member's position: district median household income (the higher a district's income, the more likely a member was to vote yes), ideology (both very liberal and very conservative members were less likely to vote yes), electoral security (the more secure a member was, the more likely he or she was to vote yes), and retirement (members who were leaving the House were more likely to vote yes).

[16]David M. Herszenhorn, "Word Reaches Congress: As the Market Goes, So Goes the Electorate," *New York Times*, October 2, 2008. Accessed online at www.nytimes.com on October 2, 2008.

[17]The bill was H.R. 1424. 77 percent of senators not up for reelection supported the measure, whereas 67 percent of senators up for reelection supported it.

[18]Tory Newmeyer and Steven K. Dennis, "Bailout Supporters Scramble for Votes," *Roll Call*, October 3, 2008. Accessed online at www.rollcall.com on October 3, 2008

[19]Representative Jim McDermott (D-Wash) was the only House member to change his vote from support on HR3997 to opposition on HR1424.

[20]Accessed online on November 21, 2008 at http://msnbcmedia.msn.com/i/msnbc/sections/news/081103_NBC-WSJ_Poll.pdf

[21]Jeffrey M. Jones, "Bush Approval Rating Doldrums Continue: Average 29.4% Approval Rating for Most Recent Quarter One of All-time Worst," *Gallup*, October 20, 2008. Accessed online November 21 at http://www.gallup.com/poll/111280/Bush-Approval-Rating-Doldrums-Continue.aspx.

[22]The generic ballot question is as follows: "If the elections for U.S. Congress were being held today, would you vote for the Republican Party's candidate or the Democratic Party's candidate for Congress in your district?" Indeed, in the final five national polls asking the generic ballot question (as reported by RealClearPolitics), Democrats were ahead by an average of 9 percentage points. Accessed online on November 5, 2008, at http://www.realclearpolitics.com/epolls/other/generic_congressional_vote-901.html#polls

[23]Jennifer Yachnin and Paul Singer, "Scandalized Lawmakers Face Voters," *Roll Call*, November 4, 2008. Accessed online on November 4, 2008, at www.rollcall.com.

[24]In 2004, Bush won an average of 54.5 percent of the vote in the 13 districts. Kerry won Shays' district (CT-4) with a slim 49.3 percent of the vote in 2004.

[25]Larry Sabato's *Crystal Ball*, "Update," July 21, 2008. Accessed online on November 26, 2008, at http://www.centerforpolitics.org/crystalball/2008/house/?state=OH

[26]In a campaign ad, Feeney apologized to voters for his involvement with Abramoff, which he characterized as a "rookie mistake." Election Preview, *Roll Call*, "A Year When Everybody's Vulnerable, October 7, 2008, p. 10. Accessed online on October 10, 2008 at http://www.rollcall.com.

[27]David Nather, "Will the 'Real America' Please Stand Up?," CQ *Weekly*, October 27, 2008, p. 2861. Accessed online on November 30, 2008, at http://library.cqpress.com/cqweekly/document.php?id=weeklyreport110-000002979085&type=toc&num=131&&action=print&time=1228051035782& .

John Ramsey, "Hayes Regrets Rally Remarks," *Fayetteville Observer*, October 22, 2008. Accessed online on November 30, 2008. at http://www.fayobserver.com/article?id=308127. CQ Politics, *Midday Update*, October 22, 2008. Accessed online on November 30, 2008 at http://www.cqpolitics.com/wmspage.cfm?docID=cqmidday-000002977862

[28]"Political Clippings," CQ *Today Midday Update*, October 24, 2008. Accessed online on December 1, 2008, at http://www.cqpolitics.com/wmspage.cfm?docID=cqmidday-000002978917. Jackie Koszczuk and Martha Angle, *CQ's Politics In America 2008: The 110th Congress* (Washington, DC: Congressional Quarterly Press), p. 757

[29]As with GOP presidential candidate John McCain, Shays didn't help his case by proclaiming—a month before the October financial meltdown— that "our economy is fundamentally sound." Carl Hulse and David Herszenhorn, "GOP Facing Tougher Battle for Congress," *New York Times*, October 9, 2008. Accessed online on October 9, 2008 at http://www.nytimes.com. David Halbfinger, "'Bullheaded' and a Rhodes Scholar, and Now Headed to Capitol Hill," *New York Times*, November 10, 2008. Accessed online on November 10, 2008, at http://www.nytimes.com.

[30]Tim Storey and Edward Smith, "Election 2008: History Making," *State Legislatures*, December 2008, p. 16.

[31]Additionally, the median-vote share for GOP incumbent winners (64 percent) was 9.5 percentage points lower than the median-vote share for Democratic incumbent victors (73.5 percent).

[32]Election Preview, *Roll Call*, "A Year When Everybody's Vulnerable, October 7, 2008, p. 10. Accessed online on October 10, 2008 at http://www.rollcall.com.

[33]Larry Sabato's *Crystal Ball*, accessed online on November 26, 2008, at http://www.centerforpolitics.org/crystalball/2008/house/?state=MN See also "Blaming the Messenger?" *The Hotline*, Wednesday, October 22, 2008. Accessed online on November 1, 2008, at http://www.nationaljournal.com/hotline/php?ID=hr_20081022_1894. Additionally, Bachmann noted that "I wish the American media would take a great look at the views of the people in Congress and find out: Are they pro-America or anti-America?" http://www.nationaljournal.com/hotline/print_friendly.php?ID=hr_20081022_1894.

[34]"St. Cloud TV Will Never Be The Same," *The Hotline*, Oct. 21, 2008. Accessed online on November 1, 2008, at http://www.nationaljournal.com/hotline/print_friendly.php?ID=hr_20081021_9883

[35]Greg Giroux, "Virginia GOP Rep Goode Seeks Recount After State Certifies Democratic Prick Up," CQ *Today Online News*, November 24, 2008. Accessed online on November 24, 2008 at http://www.cqpolitics.com.

[36]John McCardle, "Virginia: Name-Calling NRCC Ad Hits 'N.Y. Lawyer'," *Roll Call*, October 30, 2008. Accessed online on November 1, 2008, at http://www.rollcall.com.

[37]Jackie Koszczuk and Martha Angle, *CQ's Politics In America 2008: The 110th Congress* (Washington, DC: Congressional Quarterly Press), p. 1048.

[38]Molly K. Hooper, "Rep. Mahoney, Accused of Paying Ex-Mistress, Says He Broke No Laws," CQ *Today Online News*, October 14, 2008. Accessed online on November 25, 2008 at http://www.cqpolitics.com/wmspage.cfm?docID=news-000002974513.

[39]Greg Giroux, "Indicted Louisiana Rep. Jefferson Upset in 2008's Last House Election Day," CQ *Today Online News* December 7, 2008. Accessed online on December 8, 2008, at http://www.cqpolitics.com/wmspage.cfm?docID=news-000002994117.

[40]Jonathan Allen, "Pennsylvania's Murtha, in a Tight Race, Still Wield$ Power," *CQ Today Online News*, November 1, 2008. Accessed online on December 1, 2008 at http://www.cqpolitics.com/wmspage.cfm?docID=news-000002981958.

[41]See, for example, Bruce Larson, "The 2004 Congressional Elections." In *Divided States of America: The Slash and Burn Politics of the 2004 Presidential Election*, edited by Larry J. Sabato (New York: Longman, 2005).

[42]Gary Jacobson, *The Politics of Congressional Elections*, 7th edition (New York: Pearson Longman), p. 209.

[43]Roger Wicker was appointed when GOP Senator Trent Lott resigned; John Barrasso was appointed when Senator Craig Thomas died.

[44]The most recent tallies had Coleman slightly extending his razor-thin edge. See Emily Cadei, "Coleman Edges into Plus Territory in Minnesota Senate Recount," *CQ Politics*, November 27, 2008. Accessed online at http://www.cqpolitics.com on November 28, 2008.

[45]The reelection rate for GOP incumbents excludes the contest in Minnesota, undecided as of this writing, from both the numerator and denominator.

[46]Interestingly, many polls showed Begich with a big lead in the days leading up to the race. See http://www.realclearpolitics.com/epolls/2008/senate/ak/alaska_senate-562.html. Perhaps survey respondents were reluctant to tell interviewers they were supporting a convicted felon.

[47]John Stanton, "Reid Says Stevens Cannot Serve," *Roll Call*, November 2, 2008. Accessed online on November 2 at http://www.rollcall.com.

[48]David Herszenhorn, "Rematch in Senate Race Finds a New Climate," *New York Times*, August 4, 2008. Accessed online on August 4, 2008 at http://www.nytimes.com/2008/08/04/us/politics/04sununu.html.

[49]Obama improved on Kerry's 2004 Maine showing by nearly 4 percentage points as well. On Sununu's voting record, see Jackie Koszczuk and Martha Angle, *CQ's Politics In America 2008: The 110th Congress* (Washington, DC: Congressional Quarterly Press), p. 630. For Collins' voting record, see the same publication, p. 461.

[50]William Yardley, "An Oregon Republican Reaches for Coattails—Obama's,"*New York Times*, October 15, 2008. Accessed online on October 15, 2008, at http://www.nytimes.com.

[51]William Yardley, "An Oregon Republican Reaches for Coattails—Obama's,"*New York Times*, October 15, 2008. Accessed online on October 15, 2008, at http://www.nytimes.com.

[52]Rob Christensen, "Hagan puts Dole in Unfamiliar Bind," *Charlotte Observer.com*, September 07, 2008. Accessed online on November 28, 2008 at http://www.charlotteobserver.com/local/story/177392.html

[53]Marie Horrigan, "North Carolina's Dole Playing Defense in Race Now Rated as Tossup," *CQ Today Online News*, September 16, 2008. Accessed online on November 29, 2008 at http://cqpolitics.com. "Senate Sensabilities: The October 2008 Update." Larry Sabato's *Crystal Ball*, October 1, 2008. Accessed online on October 1, 2008, at http://www.centerforpolitics.org/crystalball/

[54]Election Preview, *Roll Call*, "A Year When Everybody's Vulnerable," October 7, 2008, p. 27. Accessed online on October 10, 2008 at http://www.rollcall.com. The Campaign Finance Institute, "A First Look at Money in the House and Senate Elections," November 6, 2008. Accessed online on November 10, 2008 at http://www.cfinst.org/pr/prRelease.aspx?ReleaseID=215

[55]Marie Horrigan, "Race Rating Change: Dole in Jeopardy of Losing Senate Seat." *CQ Today Online News*, October 31, 2008. Accessed online on November 29, 2008 at http://cqpolitics.com.

[56]"Now that I've Won, It's No Big Deal," *The Hotline*, November 14, 2008. Accessed online on November 29, 2008 at http://www.nationaljournal.com/hotline/ID=hl_20081114_8482

[57]The increased turnout among African American voters enthusiastic about Obama's candidacy may have also helped Hagan. Jonathan Allen, "African American Turnout for Obama Could Pad Democratic Majorities in Congress," *CQ Today Online News*, October 17, 2008. Accessed online on November 29, 2008 at http://cqpolitics.com.

[58]Shira Toeplitz, "Coleman to Pull All Negative Ads Through Election Day," *Roll Call*, October 10, 2008. Accessed online on October 10, 2008, at http:// www.rollcall.com. Carl Hulse, "Republicans Scrambling to Save Seats in Congress," *New York Times*, November 3, 2008. Accessed online on November 4, 2008 at http://www.nytimes.com

[59]Emily Cadel, "Franken Opens Three-Front Offensive in Minn. Senate Dispute." *CQ Politics*, January 12, 2009. Accessed online on January 13 at http://www.cqpolitics.com.

[60]Larry Sabato, "U.S. Senate Update," *Crystal Ball*, October 22, 2008. Accessed online on October 16, 2008 at http://www.centerforpolitics.org/crystalball/

[61]John Stanton, "Chambliss is First Senator to Explain Bailout Vote in TV Ad," *Roll Call*, October 7, 2008. Accessed online on October 7, 2008 at http://www.rollcall.com.

[62]Alex Knott, "Money Increases the Focus on Georgia Senate Race," *CQ Today Online News*, November 21, 2008. Accessed online on November 29, 2008 at http://cqpolitics.com. Shaila Dewan, "A Senate Runoff in Georgia Tries to Rouse Voters After an Intense Election." *New York Times*, November 14, 2008. Accessed online on November 14, 2008 at http://www.nytimes.com.

[63]Robbie Brown and Carle Hulse, "Republican Wins Runoff for Senator in Georgia," *New York Times*, December 3, 2008, accessed online on December 3, 2008, at http://www.nytimes.com. Shaila Dewan, "A Senate Runoff in Georgia Tries to Rouse Voters After an Intense Election." *New York Times*, November 14, 2008. Accessed online on November 14, 2008 at http://www.nytimes.com.

[64]See http://www.realclearpolitics.com/epolls/2008/senate/ky/kentucky_senate-917.html. Lunsford's campaign released a poll in very late October showing the race to be tied. John McCardle, "Lunsford Pulls Even with McConnell in New Democratic Poll," *Roll Call*, October 30, 2008. Accessed online on November 3, 2008 at http://www.rollcall.com/news/29671-1.html

[65]David Herszenhorn, "Senate Races Hang in Balance; Democrats Gain," *New York Times*, November 5, 2008.

[66]David Drucker, "NRSC, Vitter Deny Report that Senator Influenced Committee's Decision on Louisiana Expenditures," *Roll Call*, October 19, 2008. Accessed online on October 20, 2008, art http://rollcall.com.

[67]"Senate Sensabilities: The October 2008 Update." Larry Sabato's *Crystal Ball*, October 1, 2008. Accessed online on October 1, 2008, at http://www.centerforpolitics.org/crystalball/

[68]In this regard, the GOP may have been better off nominating New Mexico's third House member, centrist Heather Wilson, who also threw her hat into the nomination ring. "Senate Sensabilities: The October 2008 Update." Larry Sabato's *Crystal Ball*, October 1, 2008. Accessed online on October 1, 2008, at http://www.centerforpolitics.org/crystalball/

[69]The governorships were won by Warner in 2001 and Tim Kaine in 2005; Jim Webb won the U.S. Senate seat in 2006.

[70]Gary Jacobson, *The Politics of Congressional Elections*, 7th edition (New York: Pearson Longman), p. 207.

[71]The Campaign Finance Institute, "A First Look at Money in the House and Senate Elections," November 6, 2008. Accessed online on November 10, 2008 at http://www.cfinst.org/pr/prRelease.aspx?ReleaseID=215 According to the CFI report, In the

contests in which House Republican incumbents won with 55% or less of the vote, Democratic challengers raised, on average, only about half the sum ($882,374) raised by Democratic challengers who toppled GOP incumbents.

[72]The Campaign Finance Institute, "A First Look at Money in the House and Senate Elections," November 6, 2008. Accessed online on November 10, 2008 at http://www.cfinst.org/pr/prRelease.aspx?ReleaseID=215

[73]The fundraising figures for Senate contests come from the Center for Responsive Politics, accessed online on November 25, 2008, at http://www.opensecrets.org.

[74]These figures do not include the Minnesota Senate races, which was undecided as of this writing. They also do not include funds spent in Georgia after November 6 for the December 2 runoff between Saxby Chambliss and Jim Martin.

[75]The Campaign Finance Institute, "A First Look at Money in the House and Senate Elections," November 6, 2008. Accessed online on November 10, 2008 at http://www.cfinst.org/pr/prRelease.aspx?ReleaseID=215

[76]On this trend, see Diana Dwyre, Eric Heberlig, Robin Kolodny, and Bruce Larson, "Committees and Candidates: National Party Finance after BCRA." In *The State of the Parties: The Changing Role of Contemporary Parties*, edited by John Green and Daniel Coffey (Boulder, CO: Rowman & Littlefield, 2006).

[77]Federal Election Commission, "FEC Summarizes Party Financial Activity," August 15, 2008. Accessed online on September 20, 2008, at http://www.fec.gov.

[78]Jonathan Allen and Greg Giroux, "Incoming Freshmen Share the Wealth," CQ Weekly, November 10, 2008, p. 2956. Accessed online on November 30, 2008 at http://library.cqpress.com/cqweekly/document.php?id=weeklyreport110-000002984465&type=toc&num=37&

[79]Diana Dwyre, Eric Heberlig, Robin Kolodny, and Bruce Larson, "Committees and Candidates: National Party Finance after BCRA." In *The State of the Parties: The Changing Role of Contemporary Parties*, edited by John Green and Daniel Coffey (Boulder, CO: Rowman & Littlefield, 2006).

[80]By June 30, at least three Senate Democrats (Baucus-MT, Feinstein-CA, and Kennedy-MA) had already made donations of $500,000 or more to the DSCC. On the GOP side, the biggest member donors to the NRSC were NRSC Chair John Ensign (NV-$300,000), Lindsay Graham (NC-$260,000), and Orrin Hatch (UT-$200,000). Senators also help out their congressional parties by sponsoring joint fundraising committees with them.

[81]Greg Giroux, "Dems' Success in Drawing Members' Money a Growing GOP Sore Spot," CQ Politics, August 24, 2008. Accessed on November 24, 2008, at http://www.cqpolitics.com/wmspage.cfm?docID=news-000002940459

[82]Josh Kurtz, "Ensign Predicts Dire Consequences as Schumer Seeks More Cash," Roll Call, November 3, 2008. Accessed online on November 4, 2008 at http://www.rollcall.com

[83]These data come from the Center for Responsive Politics, accessed online on November 24, 2008 at http://www.opensecrets.org/overview/cand2cand.php?cycle=2008.

[84]Eric Heberlig, "Congressional Parties, Fundraising, and Committee Ambition," *Political Research Quarterly* 56 (2003), pp. 151–162. Eric Heberlig, Marc J. Hetherington, Bruce A. Larson, "The Price of Leadership: Campaign Money and the Polarization of Congressional Parties," *Journal of Politics* 68 (2006), pp. 992–1005. Elizabeth Newlin Carney, "In the Money," *National Journal*, July 10, 2004, p. 2173. Larry J. Sabato and Bruce A. Larson, *The Party's Just Begun: Shaping*

[85]Gary W Cox and Eric Magar, "How Much Is Majority Status in the U.S. Congress Worth?," *American Political Science Review* 93 (1999), pp. 299–309.

[86]Center for Responsive Politics, accessed online on November 24, 2008 at http://www.opensecrets.org/overview/index.php?cycle=2008&Display=T&Type=G See also Alex Knot, "PACs put House Democrats on Top for First Time Since 1994," CQ Politics, November 18, 2008. Accessed online on November 20, 2008 at http://www.cqpolitics.com/wmspage.cfm?parm1=5&docID=news-000002987563

[87]The 2002 Bipartisan Campaign Reform Act's very clear definition of electioneering communications was considerably narrowed (and muddied) by the Supreme Court in FEC v. Wisconsin Right to Life (2007). In that case, the Court held that a candidate (express advocacy) ad is "an ad susceptible of no reasonable interpretation other than as an appeal to vote for or against a specific candidate."

[88]While Manchin was never directly implicated, the scandal led WVU faculty to force WVU president Mike Garrison to resign. Ian Urbina, "University Head Resigns After Degree Dispute, New York Times, June 7, 2008. Accessed on November 17, 2008 at http://www.nytimes.com/2008/06/07/education/07west.html?_r=1&scp=5&sq=joe+manchin&st=nyt

[89]For a description of the vitriol, see "Gubernatorial Races: No Time for a Novice," The Economist, November 8, 2008, pp. 46–47.

[90]"Governor Outlook for 2008," Larry J. Sabato's Crystal Ball '08, October 4, 2008. Accessed on October 15, 2008, at http://www.centerforpolitics.org/crystalball/2008/governor/

[91]Obama garnered 49.2 percent of Missouri's vote in 2008 compared to 46 percent for Kerry in 2004.

[92]For a sampling of the poll results for this contests, see http://www.realclearpolitics.com/epolls/2008/governor/nc/north_carolina_governor-582.html#polls

[93]Mark Johnson and Benjamin Niolet, "Race for Governor Remains Close: McCrory, Perdue are Campaigning Across North Carolina in the Final Days Before the Election," The Raleigh News and Observer, November 2, 2008. Accessed on November 8, 2008 at http://www.newsobserver.com/politics/story/1278609.html

[94]The five states are Delaware, New Hampshire, Missouri, North Dakota, and Utah. Obama ran ahead of Democratic incumbent governor Christine Gregoire in Washington and nearly even with Beverly Perdue in North Carolina.

[95]Prior the 2008 elections, Democrats held a 53-to-46 advantage in the Tennessee State House, while Democrats and Republicans each had 16 seats in the Tennessee Senate. Tennessee still has a Democratic governor.

[96]For a good review of the 2008 state legislative election results, see Tim Storey and Edward Smith, "Election 2008: History Making," State Legislatures, December 2008.

[97]Carl Hulse and David Stout, "Democrats Let Lieberman Keep Chairmanship," New York Times, November 19, 2008. Accessed online on November 19, 2008, at http://www.nytimes.com

[98]David Mayhew, Divided We Govern: Party Control, Lawmaking, and Investigation, 1946–1990 (New Haven, CT: Yale University Press, 1991).

[99]David Mayhew, Parties and Policies: How the American Government Works (New Haven, CT: Yale University Press, 2008), p. 112.

[100]Alan, K. Ota, "Leadership Battles Break Out in the House," CQ Weekly, November 10, 2008. Accessed online on November 10, 2008, at http://library.cqpress.com/cqweekly/.

[101]"Waxman Topples Dingell, Claims Gavel at House Energy and Commerce," CQ Today Midday Update," November 20, 2008. Accessed online on November 30, 2008 at http://www.cqpolitics.com/wmspage.cfm?docID=cqmidday-000002989094

[102]Steven Dennis and Tory Newmeyer, "House GOP Turning Right," *Roll Call*, October 23, 2008. Accessed online on October 24, 2008 at http://www.rollcall.com

[103]David Nather, "The Big Tent Collapses," *CQ Weekly*, November 17, 2008. Accessed online on November 29, 2008, at http://library.cqpress.com/cqweekly/document.php?id=weeklyreport110-000002986583&

[104]David Nather, "Will the 'Real America' Please Stand Up?," *CQ Weekly*, October 27, 2008, p. 2861. Accessed online on November 30, 2008, at http://library.cqpress.com/cqweekly/document.php?id=weeklyreport110-000002979085&type=toc&num=131&&action=print&time=1228051035782&

[105]"Ohio's Voinovich Fourth GOP Senator To Announce Retirement Plans," *CQ Today Midday Update*, Jan. 12, 2009. Accessed online on January 14, 2009, at http://www.cqpolitics.com.

[106]Humberto Sanchez, "Lawmakers, Governors, Stress Urgent Fiscal Relief," *CongressDailyPM*, November 17, 2008. Accessed online on November 30, 2008 at http://www.nationaljournal.com/congressdaily/cdp_20081117_7733.php.

# Chapter 6

# The Impact of Federal Election Laws on the 2008 Presidential Election

## Michael E. Toner[1]

Senator Barack Obama's victory in the 2008 presidential election was historic on many political and cultural levels, and the impact of Obama's campaign on the federal election laws was certainly no exception.

In 2008, Senator Obama became the first presidential candidate since Richard Nixon in 1972 to turn down public funds for both the primary campaign and the general-election campaign. In so doing, Obama raised an unprecedented $750 million for his campaign, which was more than twice what George W. Bush raised in 2004 and more than seven times what Bush raised in 2000, which were both record-breaking amounts at the time. Obama's decision to become the first presidential candidate since 1972 to decline public funds for his entire campaign will likely transform the fundraising strategies of presidential candidates from both major parties in the future. It could also be the death knell of the presidential public financing system, absent major congressional action to overhaul the system in time for the 2012 presidential election.

We witnessed a number of significant campaign finance and election law trends during the historic 2008 presidential campaign. But first we turn to Senator Obama's pivotal decision to turn down public funding for his general-election and primary campaigns, which helped ignite the extraordinary campaign-finance arms race that took place in 2008.

## 2008 WAS THE FIRST BILLION-DOLLAR PRESIDENTIAL ELECTION, AS OBAMA AND McCAIN RAISED RECORD AMOUNTS OF MONEY

Campaign finance observers predicted in the early days of the 2008 election cycle that the first billion-dollar presidential race was in the offing, and they certainly were not disappointed. Senator Obama's decision to privately finance his entire presidential campaign, and turn down public funds for the general election as well as for the primaries, paved the way for Obama to raise approximately $750 million for his campaign, including $414 million for the primaries alone. With Senator McCain raising $221 million for the primaries and spending another $85 million of public funds for the general election, the Obama and McCain campaigns combined spent a record-breaking $1 billion on the 2008 presidential race.

Under the presidential public financing system, presidential candidates have the option of accepting public funds for their primary election or general election campaigns, or both. For the primaries, presidential candidates can receive matching funds from the government of up to $250 for each individual contribution they receive. To be eligible to receive matching funds, candidates must raise at least $5,000 in 20 or more states from individuals in amounts of $250 or less. For the 2008 primaries, each presidential candidate could receive a maximum of approximately $25 million in matching funds. However, candidates electing to receive matching funds were subject to a nationwide spending limit during the primaries of approximately $50 million, as well as state-by-state spending limits based on the population of each state.[2] Under the federal election laws, the primary season runs from the time a person legally becomes a candidate for the presidency through the national nominating conventions, which can last 18 months or longer. The national and state-by-state spending limits apply throughout this period of time. By contrast, candidates who decline to take matching funds are not subject to any spending limits for the primaries and are free to raise as much money as they can, subject to the contribution limits.[3] For the general election, presidential candidates have the option of accepting public funds to finance all of their political activities[4] and be subject to a nationwide spending limit, or candidates can turn down public funds and raise private contributions subject to the contribution limits and operate free of spending limits. The public grant for the general election in 2008 was approximately $85 million as was the corresponding national spending limit for candidates who accepted public funds.[5]

Apart from John Edwards, all of the top-tier candidates from both major parties turned down matching funds for the primaries in 2008 so they could be free of spending limits and raise as much funds as they could, subject to the contribution limits. The Democratic and Republican candidates collectively raised a record-breaking $1.22 billion for their primary campaigns, which was 81 percent more than the presidential candidates raised collectively in 2004.[6] Obama and the other Democratic candidates collectively raised far more funds for the primaries than did McCain and the other Republican candidates by a margin of $787 million to $477 million.[7] Table 1 summarizes the fundraising totals for the top-tier candidates of both major parties during the 2008 primary season.

**Table 1. Fundraising Totals for Top-Tier
Presidential Candidates During the 2008 Primary**

| Candidate | Total Amount Raised | Compared to Spending Limit |
|---|---|---|
| Obama | $414 million | 8x |
| Clinton | $224 million | 4x |
| Edwards | $53 million | 1x |
| Richardson | $23 million | .5x |
| Dodd | $17 million | .3x |
| McCain | $221 million | 4x |
| Romney | $110 million | 2x |
| Giuliani | $60 million | 1x |
| Paul | $35 million | .7x |
| Thompson, F. | $24 million | .5x |
| Huckabee | $16 million | .3x |

Source: Federal Election Commission

The decision of the top-tier candidates apart from Edwards to turn down public funds for the primaries made strategic sense given that most of the candidates raised and spent far more funds than the approximately $50 million they would have been legally permitted to spend had they accepted matching funds. Specifically, Obama raised eight times more than the spending limit, Clinton and McCain four times more, and Romney two times more.[8]

However, from a fundraising perspective, what made the 2008 presidential race unprecedented was Senator Obama's bold decision to also decline public funds for the general election and collect as many private contributions as he could for the fall campaign. Since the advent of the presidential public financing system in 1976 following the Watergate scandal, no major-party candidate had ever turned down public funds for the general election, which had ensured that the Democratic and Republican nominee each had the same amount of campaign funds for the fall campaign.[9] All of this changed in 2008, when Obama raised approximately $336 million for the general election, on top of the more than $400 million he had previously raised during the primaries, for a fundraising total of approximately $750 million. McCain, by contrast, accepted the $85 million public grant for the general election, which turned out to be only one-fourth of the amount of money that Obama amassed for the general election.

Table 2 summarizes the fundraising totals for the major party nominees for the 2000, 2004, and 2008 elections.

**Table 2. Summary of the Fundraising Totals for the Major Party Nominees During 2000, 2004, and 2008 Elections**

| Candidate | Primary Fundraising Total | General Fundraising Total | Total Campaign Funds |
|---|---|---|---|
| **2000** | | | |
| Bush | $100 million | $75 million[a] | $175 million |
| Gore | $50 million | $75 million[a] | $125 million |
| **2004** | | | |
| Bush | $270 million | $80 million[a] | $350 million |
| Kerry | $235 million | $80 million[a] | $315 million |
| **2008** | | | |
| Obama | $414 million | $336 million | $750 million |
| McCain | $221 million | $85 million[a] | $306 million |

[a]Candidate Accepted Public Grant

Source: Federal Election Commission

Table 2 reveals the substantial financial advantage that Obama enjoyed over McCain, which exceeded $400 million and included a nearly 4-to-1 advantage during the general election campaign. Obama's broad financial advantage was even more pronounced in the final weeks before Election Day. In September alone Obama raised over $150 million, and between October 15 and November 24 the Obama campaign raised another $104 million and spent an additional $136 million.[10] To put these fundraising and spending figures in perspective, McCain received only $85 million in public funds to finance his entire general-election campaign.

Numerous commentators have analyzed Obama's fundraising performance during the 2008 campaign and have produced dizzying statistics. However, two simple statistics perhaps illustrate best the remarkable Obama fundraising performance in 2008: 1) The Obama campaign raised more money than all of the private contributions raised by *all* of the Democratic and Republican presidential candidates *combined*; and 2) The Obama campaign raised more money than the Republican National Committee (RNC) and the Democratic National Committee (DNC) raised *combined*. Needless to say, since the adoption of the Federal Election Campaign Act in the 1970s, no presidential campaign had ever come close to either achievement, and we may never see it happen again.

A key component of Obama's record-setting fundraising performance in 2008 was the half a billion dollars that he collected online. The Obama campaign reported receiving $500 million of Internet contributions from three million online donors, with an average online contribution of $80.[11] As remarkable as the total amount of money that Obama collected online was, the hundreds of thousands of donors who made multiple contributions, often in monthly increments of $100, $50, or even $25 was even more impressive. Specifically, through Federal Election Commission (FEC) disclosure reports for the period ending on August 31, 2008, over 200,000 Obama donors started off giving contributions of $200 or less and then made repeat contributions; 93,000 individuals ended up contributing up to $400 to the campaign and another 106,000 ended up contributing between $401 and $999.[12] Interestingly, although Obama received a record number of contributions in amounts of $200 or less, due to a large number of repeat contributors, the proportion of funds that Obama received from donors whose contributions aggregated $200 or less was actually not significantly greater than what past presidential candidates had achieved, with Obama's figure at 26 percent, compared with 25 percent for George W. Bush in 2004, 21 percent for John McCain in 2008, and 20 percent for John Kerry in 2004.[13]

A number of academics have analyzed how online fundraising by presidential candidates has been associated with a high degree of public interest in the campaigns and a highly polarized and competitive political environment—starting with John McCain's online surge after winning the New Hampshire primary in 2000 and Howard Dean's strong online fundraising performance in 2004. However, more academic work needs to be done in analyzing the role of the Internet in facilitating political contributions by making it easier for individuals to contribute to the candidates of their choice. A decade ago, if someone was impressed with what a candidate said at a debate or rally and wished to make a contribution, he or she needed to find their checkbook, figure out the payee, determine where to send the check, and get the check in the mail. Today, if someone likes what a candidate says, he or she can make an online contribution on their iPhone in a matter of minutes. Moreover, presidential campaign Web sites today provide donors with the option of making recurring monthly contributions on their credit cards in $25, $15, or even $5 amounts. Through this technology, individuals who may not be willing or able to afford a single contribution of $300 may cumulatively make the same contribution over a year's time in monthly $25 installments. In this way, the Internet facilitates the making of political contributions separate and apart from public interest in presidential races, which may partially account for the record-breaking amounts of money that presidential candidates have raised in recent years. At the very least, this phenomenon deserves further study.

There is no question that the Obama campaign capitalized on its financial advantage over the McCain campaign in numerous ways. The Obama campaign reportedly spent approximately $250 million on television advertising, which exceeded McCain's television advertising efforts by approximately $100 million, and which surpassed the $188 million that the Bush-Cheney campaign spent in 2004.[14] Obama spent $77 million on television advertising in the first two weeks of October alone, which reportedly was more than McDonald's Corporation typically spends on television advertising in a month.[15] Obama's advertising budget was so extensive that he became the first presidential candidate to air a national network television commercial since Ross Perot in 1992, spending approximately $5 million to broadcast a 30-minute infomercial on several networks during the final days of the campaign.[16] Obama's advertising advantage over McCain was particularly striking in a number of battleground states. For example, according to published reports, Obama outspent McCain on television advertising by 4 to1 in Florida, 3 to1 in Virginia and North Carolina, and 2 to1 in New Hampshire.[17] Perhaps not coincidentally, Obama won all of those states, becoming the first Democratic presidential candidate to carry Virginia since 1964.

Obama's spending advantage was no less impressive in terms of field operations and get-out-the-vote activities. The Obama campaign and the Democratic Party reportedly operated at least 770 offices nationwide, as compared with only 370 offices for the McCain campaign and the Republican Party.[18] The Obama campaign and the Democrats also reportedly hired 5–10 times more field staff than did the McCain campaign and the Republican Party, and between June 1 and October 15, Obama and the Democrats spent a total of $56 million on staff expenditures as compared with only $22 million by McCain and the GOP.[19] In many ways, in light of these stark resource disparities, it is somewhat surprising that Obama's winning margin on Election Day was not even greater.

## THE REPUBLICAN NATIONAL COMMITTEE RAISED RECORD SUMS OF MONEY FOR THE 2008 ELECTION AND BOTH PARTIES CONTINUED TO FARE WELL UNDER THE MCCAIN-FEINGOLD LAW

The RNC raised unprecedented sums of money for the 2008 election, continuing the upward fundraising trend it began during the 2004 and 2000 presidential election cycles. For the 2008 presidential election, the RNC raised a record-breaking $417 million, which was a 26 percent increase over what the

RNC raised during the 2004 election cycle and a 136 percent increase from 2000.[20] These record-breaking figures are all the more impressive given that all of the funds raised by the RNC for 2008 and 2004 were hard dollars raised subject to the limitation and prohibitions of the federal election laws, whereas for the 2000 presidential election cycle the national parties were permitted to raise soft money in the form of unlimited corporate, union, and individual contributions. The DNC raised $255 million for the 2008 presidential election, which was 15 percent less than what the DNC raised during the 2004 election cycle but 145 percent more than it had collected for the 2000 election.[21]

The 2004 presidential election was the first conducted under the McCain-Feingold campaign finance law, which made the most significant changes to the federal election laws in a generation. The cornerstone of the McCain-Feingold law was a prohibition against the national political parties from raising or spending soft money for any purpose.[22] In addition to barring the national political parties from raising and spending soft money, McCain-Feingold increased the individual contribution limits to the parties from $20,000 per year to $25,000 per year and indexed the limits for inflation. For the 2008 presidential election cycle, individuals could contribute up to $28,500 per year to the RNC and DNC, and that limit will likely approach $30,000 per year for the 2010 election cycle.

Table 3 details the fundraising totals for the RNC and DNC during the 2008, 2004 and 2000 election cycles.

**Table 3. Summary of the Fundraising Totals for the RNC and DNC During 2008, 2004 and 2000 Election Cycles**

|      | 2008          | 2004          | 2000          |
| ---- | ------------- | ------------- | ------------- |
| RNC  | $417 million  | $330 million  | $316 million  |
| DNC  | $255 million  | $299 million  | $210 million  |

Source: Federal Election Commission, "FEC Releases Summary of National Party Financial Activity," FEC Press Release, October 29, 2008 and RNC and DNC FEC Post Election Reports filed on Dec. 4, 2008.

As Table 3 indicates, although the Obama campaign raised vastly more than the McCain campaign during the 2008 presidential race, the RNC was able to maintain its historical fundraising edge over the DNC, which helped reduce the resource advantage that Obama enjoyed over McCain. Specifically, the RNC out-raised the DNC by $162 million, which reduced the Obama campaign's net resource advantage over the McCain campaign from approximately $444 million to $282 million. With Obama now in the

White House, it will be interesting to see if the DNC will be able to match the RNC's fundraising prowess in the years ahead.

One innovation that helped fuel the RNC and DNC's fundraising tallies in 2008 was extensive use of joint fundraising committees between the presidential campaigns, the national parties, and selected state parties. Under FEC regulations, candidates and political parties may simultaneously raise hard-money funds through joint fundraising committees (JFCs) which permit them to combine the per-recipient contribution limits and solicit greater amounts of money from donors at any one time.[23]

JFCs had been used extensively during the last decade by congressional candidates and national and state political parties, but they had not been used on a broad scale by presidential candidates until 2008. Once Senator McCain clinched the Republican nomination in the spring, the McCain campaign and the RNC created a number of JFCs which included several groups of state parties from battleground states. Because the Republican nominating contest ended months before the Democratic nominating race, McCain and his GOP allies had the JFCs to themselves for several months before Senator Obama and the DNC began joint fundraising activities in the early summer. All told, the McCain campaign and Republican Party committees raised approximately $221 million through ten separate JFCs.[24] Although Obama and Democratic Party entities got a late start using JFCs, they ended up surpassing the Republicans by raising approximately $228 million through three JFCs.[25] Published reports indicate that House, Senate, and presidential candidates, along with their political parties, raised more than $415 million through JFCs during the 2008 election cycle, which shattered the previous record of $111 million that was set during the 2004 presidential campaign.[26]

Given the great fundraising success both major parties enjoyed with JFCs during the 2008 election, joint fundraising activities will likely remain a key part of presidential fundraising in the future. There is no question that the ability of candidates and political parties to combine applicable contribution limits makes it easier for donors to make larger hard-money contributions to the participating entities. The extraordinary growth of JFCs in the 2008 presidential race is yet another example of parties and candidates successfully adapting to the new campaign finance law.

## THIRD-PARTY GROUPS HAD AN APPRECIABLE IMPACT ON THE 2008 PRESIDENTIAL RACE BUT WERE LESS INFLUENTIAL THAN IN 2004

As was outlined above, under the McCain-Feingold law the national political parties are prohibited from raising and spending soft money for any purpose.

Prior to the enactment of McCain-Feingold, the RNC and DNC spent hundreds of millions of dollars of soft money each election cycle on issue advertisements—attacking and promoting presidential candidates—as well as on ticket-wide get-out-the-vote operations in the battleground states.[27] With the national political parties subject to the soft-money ban for the first time in the 2004 presidential race, soft-money spending migrated from the national parties to a number of prominent Section 527 organizations. Section 527 organizations get their name from the section of the federal tax code under which they operate.[28] All told, 527 groups reportedly raised and spent approximately $409 million on activities designed to influence the 2004 presidential race.[29] Of this amount in 2004, Democratic-oriented 527s reportedly spent $266 million, or 65 percent of the total, and Republican groups spent $144 million, or 35 percent of the total.[30] Although Democrats in 2004 were the first to make major use of 527 groups as soft-money vehicles, Republicans quickly followed suit, and the Republican-oriented Swift Boat Veterans for Truth became perhaps the most influential outside group during that election cycle.

However, following the 2004 election the FEC found that a number of 527 organizations had broken the law by failing to register with the FEC as political committees and by failing to adhere to hard-dollar contribution limits. As a result, as the 2008 presidential campaign began, it was unclear whether 527 organizations would be as active in raising and spending soft-money funds as they had been four years earlier. By Election Day 2008, it was clear that federally oriented 527 groups had spent significantly less than they had during the 2004 election, but it was also clear that greater amounts of soft-money had been spent by various 501(c) organizations,[31] including an innovative group called the American Issues Project.

The CFI reported that through October 15 federally oriented 527 organizations had raised and spent approximately $185 million in connection with the 2008 presidential race and likely would end up spending a total of $200 million by Election Day.[32] The biggest Democratic-oriented 527s were reportedly operated by the American Federation of State, County and Municipal Employees (AFSCME) with $28 million raised, Service Employees International Union (SEIU) with $24 million, America Votes ($16 million), and Emily's List ($13 million).[33] The leading Republican-oriented 527 groups included American Solutions for Winning the Future ($19 million raised), RightChange.com ($7 million), College Republicans ($6 million), and Club for Growth ($4 million).[34] CFI also estimated that federally oriented 501(c) groups would likely raise and spend an additional $200 million on activities related to the 2008 presidential election, for a total of $400 million spent collectively by 527 and 501(c) groups.[35]

One particularly aggressive outside organization in 2008 was the American Issues Project (AIP), which spent approximately $3 million to air negative television advertisements linking Senator Obama to former Weather Underground radical Bill Ayres.[36] AIP operated as a 501(c)(4) social-welfare organization and, as such, was not required to disclose its donors. However, AIP also operated as a Qualified Nonprofit Corporation (QNC) under FEC regulations.[37] By operating as a QNC, AIP, unlike other incorporated 501(c) and 527 organizations, was free to air hard-hitting advertisements attacking Obama that contained full-blown express advocacy and which generated considerable press attention for the group.

AIP's innovative use of QNC status could be a harbinger of future outside group advertising strategies in connection with presidential elections. The FEC has adopted a broader interpretation of express advocacy in recent years, which has resulted in a greater possibility that the FEC will find hard-hitting candidate advertisements aired by outside organizations unlawful. The great advantage of an outside group operating as a QNC, assuming that the fundraising and other operating restrictions of QNC status can be met, is the flexibility to air aggressive candidate-oriented advertisements regardless of content, even if they contain express advocacy. That key feature may prove to be very appealing to political consultants as they develop outside group advertising strategies for the 2010 midterm election and beyond.

## ONLINE POLITICAL ACTIVITY CONTINUED TO GROW IN IMPORTANCE IN 2008 AND REMAINED LARGELY UNREGULATED BY THE FEC

While the 2004 presidential election was the first election in which online politics played an important role in campaign strategy, we witnessed the full flowering of the Internet in the 2008 presidential campaign. There is no question that the Obama campaign developed an unprecedented Web-based strategy and involved millions of Americans in the campaign through sophisticated and cutting-edge Internet technologies. The Obama campaign's Web strategy in 2008 will likely be studied in the future as rival campaigns seek to narrow the competitive online advantage Obama enjoyed.

One only has to study the raw numbers to appreciate the depth and breadth of the Obama campaign's online advantage. Table 4 compares the Obama and McCain campaign's Internet activities in several key areas.

**Table 4.** Comparison of Obama Campaign and
McCain Campaign Internet Presence

|  | Obama | McCain |
|---|---|---|
| Number of Facebook friends on Election Day | 2,397,253 | 622,860 |
| Change in the number of Facebook friends since Election Day (as of Nov. 8) | +472,535 | −2,732 |
| Number of unique visitors to the campaign Web site for the week ending Nov. 1 | 4,851,069 | 1,464,544 |
| Number of online videos mentioning the candidate uploaded across 200 platforms | 104,454 | 64,092 |
| Number of views of those videos | 889 million | 554 million |
| Number of campaign-made videos posted on YouTube | 1,822 | 330 |
| Total amount of time people spent watching each campaign's videos, as of Oct. 23 | 14.6 million hours | 488,000 hours |
| Cost of equivalent purchase of 30-second TV ads | $46.9 million | $1.5 million |
| Number of Twitter followers | 125,639 | 5,319 |
| Number of references to the campaign's voter contact operation on Google | 479,000 | 325 |
| Number of direct links to the campaign's voter contact tool | 475 | 18 |

Source: Andrew Rasiehj and Micah Sifry, "The Web: 2008's Winning Ticket," *Politico*, November 12, 2008, p. 24.

As Table 4 indicates, the Obama campaign far outpaced the McCain campaign in a wide variety of online indicators, particularly in the volume of Obama political activity that took place on popular social networking Web sites such as Facebook, MySpace, YouTube and Twitter. The Obama campaign reportedly consulted with Facebook cofounder Chris Hughes to develop and launch its own social networking site called MyBarackObama.com.[38] The MyBarackObama.com Web site reportedly "recruited more than eight million volunteers, attracted more than 500,000 accounts and helped organize more than 30,000 supporter-created campaign events in all 50 states."[39] In the final weeks before Election Day, the Obama campaign launched an application for the Apple iPhone called "Obama '08," which enabled supporters to receive information about local campaign events and volunteer opportunities in their areas directly on their iPhones, complete with GPS maps and driving instructions. In addition, the Obama campaign made some of its biggest announcements via the Internet, including Obama's selection of Senator Joseph Biden to be his running mate, which was unveiled in an e-mail that was sent to millions of Obama supporters. By Election Day the Obama campaign had amassed approximately 13 million e-mail addresses, which far surpassed the number of e-mail addresses collected by previous presidential campaigns.[40]

One key factor that has contributed to the rapid growth of the Internet in presidential politics has been the FEC's deregulatory approach to online activities. In 2006, the FEC adopted regulations, which remain in place today, concerning use of the Internet in federal elections. The FEC's regulations exempt the Internet from the various prohibitions and restrictions of the McCain-Feingold law with only one exception: paid advertising placed on another person's Web site.[41] The practical effect of the FEC's regulations has been that individuals, volunteers, and anyone else with access to a computer can conduct a wide range of Internet activities on behalf of presidential candidates and other federal candidates—such as setting up and maintaining Web sites, blogging, e-mailing, linking, and posting videos on YouTube—without fear that the FEC will monitor or restrict their activities. Although it is difficult to measure or gauge precisely, undoubtedly the FEC's hands-off regulatory approach to online political activities has helped the Internet play a growing and vital role in presidential politics.

## THE SIGNIFICANT GROWTH OF EARLY VOTING IN 2008 HAD A MAJOR IMPACT ON CAMPAIGN STRATEGY

The number of Americans voting prior to Election Day grew steadily during the 1990s and the early part of this decade, reaching 16 percent of voters in 2000 and 22 percent of voters in 2004.[42] However, analysts estimate that up to one-third of all Americans cast their ballots prior to Election Day in 2008, which far surpassed the number of early voters in previous presidential elections. Strikingly, some states began early voting more than a month before Election Day and even before the three presidential debates concluded. As a result, presidential campaigns no longer tailor their advertising and get-out-the-vote efforts to culminate on Election Day, but rather, must sustain their efforts for many weeks in most states. In many ways, we no longer have a single Election Day in America, but rather an election window that lasts for a month or even longer in some states.

For many years, voters who expected to be absent from their home communities on Election Day could apply for an absentee ballot and could cast an absentee ballot prior to the election. However, in order to obtain an absentee ballot, many jurisdictions required voters to show cause or otherwise explain why they were not able to vote on Election Day in their local precincts, which reduced the number of people who voted absentee.[43] However, in 1978 California amended its laws to permit voters to cast ballots before Election Day without providing any excuse or showing any cause, and today 32 states have similar laws in effect.[44] The early voting states provide voters with locations to vote early in-person or by mail.[45] Early voting has historically been most prevalent in a number of western states, including Colorado, Nevada and New Mexico.[46]

The early voting that took place in 2008 was remarkable not only for the number of people who cast their ballots before Election Day, but also for how early they began voting. In Iowa, which was considered a battleground state for much of the campaign, voters began casting their ballots on September 23, which was less than three weeks after the Republican National Convention adjourned in Minneapolis-St. Paul. In Ohio, which proved to be decisive in the 2004 presidential election and was strongly contested in 2008, early voting began on September 30, which was prior to the second and third presidential debates between Obama and McCain and before the vice-presidential debate took place.

The rise in early voting has affected the strategy and tactics of presidential campaigns in the twenty-first century. For many years, the last 72 hours before the election were the primary focus for get-out-the-vote efforts, but now those operations have expanded to last a month or even longer in certain jurisdictions. Mike DuHaime, the McCain campaign's political director, observed that early voting "fundamentally changes two things: timing and budgets. You need to close the deal earlier for some voters, and Election Day can be spread out over weeks. That means your get-out-the-vote costs are more than ever."[47] With some analysts projecting that up to half the electorate may vote early by 2012, there is no question that future presidential campaigns will continue to refine their get-out-the-vote and voter contact strategies to reflect the modern election-window electoral environment.

## LOOKING AHEAD TO 2012

Barack Obama's momentous decision to turn down public funds in 2008, not only for his primary campaign but for his general-election campaign as well, has the potential to transform the fundraising strategies of presidential candidates from both major parties in 2012 and beyond. Obama's refusal of public funds laid the groundwork for his campaign to raise approximately $750 million for his 2008 candidacy, including over $400 million for the primaries alone. If Obama runs for reelection, and Congress does not take decisive legislative action to overhaul the presidential public financing system, all of the top-tier Republican candidates in 2012 will likely plan to join Obama in turning down public funds for the primary and general elections. However, any Republican who wishes to run in 2012 must seriously weigh whether he or she is capable of raising the $700 million or more that likely will be needed to compete financially with Obama. In that sense, the entry price for the White House has never been greater. The stage is set for the 2012 presidential race to be the most expensive in history.

## NOTES

[1]Michael Toner is former chairman of the Federal Election Commission and currently heads the Election Law and Government Ethics practice group at Bryan Cave LLP in Washington, D.C. Mr. Toner would like to thank Rebekah Miller for her outstanding research assistance in preparing this chapter.

[2]The state spending limits in some of the most important early primary and caucus states were very low. For example, the spending limit in New Hampshire in 2008 was only $841,000, which was the same spending allotment as existed in American Samoa. Similarly, the spending limit for the Iowa caucuses was only $1,532,000. See the Federal Election Commission brochure, "Public Funding of Presidential Elections," http://www.fec.gov/pages/brochures/ pubfund_limits_2008.shtml, February, 2008. The primary spending limits are adjusted for inflation each election year.

[3]Individuals could contribute up to $2,300 per election to presidential candidates for the 2008 election and federal multi-candidate PACs could contribute up to $5,000 per election, with the primary and general elections considered separate elections. The individual contribution limits are adjusted for inflation each election cycle.

[4]The only exception is that publicly financed general-election presidential candidates are permitted to raise private contributions for legal and accounting costs incurred in complying with the federal election laws. These funds, which are known as general election legal and accounting compliance funds (GELAC funds), may accept individual and PAC contributions subject to the federal limits.

[5]The general-election public grant and corresponding spending limit are adjusted for inflation each election cycle.

[6]Campaign Finance Institute, "After Holding Financial Advantage in the Primaries, Obama Likely to Achieve Only Parity with McCain in General Election," http://www.cfinst.org, September 26, 2008.

[7]Campaign Finance Institute, "After Holding Financial Advantage in the Primaries, Obama Likely to Achieve Only Parity with McCain in General Election," http://www.cfinst.org, September 26, 2008.

[8]It should be noted that of the $110 million Mitt Romney reported raising for the primaries, $45 million stemmed from contributions that Romney made to his campaign. The Center for Responsive Politics, "Summary Data for Mitt Romney" at: http://www.opensecrets.com,

(December 12, 2008).

[9]In 2000, George W. Bush became the first candidate to win the presidency after turning down public funds for the primaries, and he repeated that feat in 2004. However, he accepted public funds for the general election in both 2000 and 2004.

[10]Jim Kuhnhenn and Jim Drinkard, "Obama Raised $104 million Towards Election's Close," Associated Press, December 5, 2008.

[11]"Obama's Internet Haul: Half a Billion Online," *Washington Post*, November 21, 2008, page A4.

[12]Campaign Finance Institute, "Reality Check: Obama Received About the Same Percentage from Small Donors in 2008 as Bush in 2004," htpp://www.cfinst.org, November 24, 2008. Under the federal election laws, individuals whose contributions aggregate $200 or less per election cycle to a presidential campaign are not required to be disclosed by name on FEC disclosure reports. This is known as the donor itemization threshold.

[13]Campaign Finance Institute, "Reality Check: Obama Received About the Same Percentage from Small Donors in 2008 as Bush in 2004," htpp://www.cfinst.org, November 24, 2008 (analyzing contribution data through August 31, 2008).

[14]Greg Gordon, "Obama Spent $250 Million on TV Ads in General Election," *Miami Herald*, November 6, 2008; Tahman Bradley, "Obama's Money Was Three Times as Much as McCain in General Election," http://www.abcnews.com, December 5, 2008.

[15]Jim Kuhnhenn, "Money Makes the Political World Go Around," Associated Press, November 3, 2008.

[16]Tahman Bradley, "Obama's Money Was Three Times as Much as McCain in General Election," http://www.abcnews.com, December 5, 2008. Obama also spent considerable funds on niche advertising that targeted specific audiences. For example, the Obama campaign advertised on video games such as "Guitar Hero" and "Madden NFL 09." Jim Kuhnhenn, "Money Makes the Political World Go Around," Associated Press, November 3, 2008.

[17]Tahman Bradley, "Obama's Money Was Three Times as Much as McCain in General Election," http://www.abcnews.com, December 5, 2008. Obama reportedly held net television adverting margins of $8.9 million in Miami, $7 million in Tampa, $2.6 million in Charlotte, and $1.6 million in Denver. Ibid.

[18]T.W. Farnam and Brad Haynes, "Democrats Far Outspend Republicans on Field Operations, Staff Expenditures," *Wall Street Journal*, November 3, 2008.

[19]Ibid.

[20]RNC and DNC 2008 FEC Post-Election Reports; "FEC Releases Summary of National Party Financial Activity," FEC Press Release (October 29, 2008).

[21]Ibid.

[22]"Soft money" is defined as funds raised and spent outside of the prohibitions and limitations of federal law. Soft money includes corporate and labor union general treasury funds and individual donations in excess of federal limits. Funds raised in accordance with federal law come from individuals and federally registered PACs, and have historically been harder to raise; hence, these funds are referred to as "hard money."

[23]For example, if a JFC included a presidential campaign, a national party, and two state parties, donors could contribute up to a maximum of $53,100 to the JFC—up to $4,600 to the presidential campaign ($2,300 for the primary and $2,300 for the general election), $28,500 to the national party, and $10,000 each to the two state parties. Any prior contributions that donors made to any participating entities would count against what could be contributed to the JFC. In addition, publicly financed presidential candidates such as Senator McCain may include their GELAC funds in JFCs that operate during the general election.

[24]Center for Responsive Politics, "Joint Fundraising Committees," http://www.opensecrets.org, December 9, 2008.

[25]Ibid.

[26]Alex Knott, "Joint Fundraising Soars in '08," CQ Today Online News, http://www.cqpolitics.com, November 17, 2008 (analyzing fundraising data through October 15, 2008).

[27]"Issue advertisements" are public communications that frequently attack or promote federal candidates and their records, but which refrain from expressly advocating the election or defeat of any clearly identified federal candidate, which is referred to as "express advocacy." "Vote for McCain" and "Vote Against Obama" are examples of express advocacy. The Supreme Court established the express advocacy standard in *Buckley v. Valeo*, 424 U.S. 1 (1976).

[28]Under the tax code, groups may organize under Section 527—and therefore shield many of their activities from taxation—if their exempt function is "influencing or attempting to influence the selection, nomination, election, or appointment of any individual to any Federal, State, or local public office or office in a political organization, or the election of Presidential or Vice-Presidential electors." 26 U.S.C. § 527(e)(2). Thus, 527 entities are partisan political organizations as a matter of law.

[29]Eliza Newlin Carney, "Rules of the Game: The 527 Phenomenon: Big Bucks for the Upstarts," NationalJournal.com, December 13, 2004.

[30]Ibid.

[31]501(c) organizations refers to entities that are organized and operate under Section 501(c) of the Internal Revenue Code. They include 501(c)(4) entities (social welfare organizations) and 501(c)(6) entities (business leagues including trade associations). 501(c)(4) and 501(c)(6) organizations are permitted to engage in partisan political activities, provided such activities are not their primary purpose. By contrast, the activities of 527 organizations may be entirely partisan. 527 organizations are legally required to disclose their donors; 501(c) organizations are not.

[32]Campaign Finance Institute, "Outside Soft Money Groups Approaching $400 Million in Targeted Spending in 2008 Election," http://www.cfinst.org, October 31, 2008.

[33]Ibid. (analyzing contribution data through October 15, 2008).

[34]Ibid. (analyzing contribution data through October 15, 2008).

[35]Ibid.

[36]Kenneth Doyle, "Anti-Obama Group's Future Plans Unclear; Others Spending on Issue Ads for Hill Races," BNA *Money & Politics Report*, September 9, 2008; Jim Kuhnhenn, "Obama Seeks to Silence Ad Tying Him to 60s Radical, Associated Press, August 25, 2008.

[37]QNCs are narrowly defined ideological nonprofit corporations that were first recognized by the Supreme Court in *FEC v. Massachusetts Citizens for Life*, 479 U.S. 238 (1986) The key characteristics of QNCs are that they exist to promote political ideas, do not engage in business activities, have no shareholders, and do not accept contributions from for-profit corporations. See 11 C.F.R. § 114.10. The Supreme Court ruled in *Massachusetts Citizens for Life* that it was unconstitutional to prohibit such nonprofit corporations, unlike other corporations, from expressly advocating the election or defeat of federal candidates.

[38]"Barack Obama's Cutting-Edge campaign," APCO *Worldwide*, November 19, 2008, p. 3.

[39]Ibid.

[40]Jonathan Salant, "Obama's Army of E-Mail Backers Gives Him Clout to Sway Congress," *Bloomberg News*, December 1, 2008.

[41]For example, if an individual spends money to take out an advertisement for a presidential candidate that appears on the home page of Yahoo.com or CNN.com, the transaction will be subject to regulation in a fashion similar to television, radio, and other mass-media advertising. However, messages that individuals create on their own Web sites or post without charge on other Web sites, such as YouTube, are not subject to FEC regulation.

[42]Stephen Ohlemacher and Julie Pace," "A Third of Electorate Could Vote Before Nov. 4," Associated Press, September 22, 2008.

[43]For example, scholars estimate that only about five percent of the nation's voters cast absentee ballots in 1980. June Krunholz, "Forget Election Day—Early Voting for President Has Started," *Wall Street Journal*, September 23, 2008.

[44]Domenico Montanaro, "Can Early Voting Ease Election Day Drama?" http://www.msnbc.com, September 24, 2008. By contrast, in 1996 only 11 states provided for early voting; by 2004, the number had climbed to 26. Ibid.

[45]In Oregon voting is done entirely by mail and there are no physical precincts.

[46]In the 2004 presidential election, 53 percent of the ballots were cast early in Nevada, with 51 percent in New Mexico, 47 percent in Colorado, and 36 percent in Florida. June Krunholz, "Forget Election Day—Early Voting for President Has Started," *Wall Street Journal*, September 23, 2008

[47]Adam Nagourney, "campaigns Adjust Their Pace to Meet Short Season," *New York Times*, October 1, 2008.

# Chapter 7

## Media in the 2008 Election

### 21st Century Campaign, Same Old Story

**Diana Owen**

The 2008 presidential election was a media extravaganza unparalleled in American history. Old and new media provided nonstop coverage to a public that was unusually eager for campaign information. The election dominated mainstream press coverage for more than two years, and inspired a barrage of new media activity that had the potential to transform campaign communication in the modern era.

In some ways, media in 2008 was, as *Politico* founder Jim Vernde Hei observed, "like walking into a different century" (Stelter and Perez-Pena, 2008: 2). The campaign prompted the development of groundbreaking political applications employing a host of innovative communication platforms, including social networking and video-sharing sites. Older online media platforms, including Web sites, blogs, and discussion boards, were an integral part of the communication landscape. The mainstream media were able to move somewhat beyond established protocols and adapt to evolving technological trends. In other ways, however, it was the same old media story. While new media were a focal point of the nominating campaign, the general election media scenario largely resembled that of past campaigns. Some of the platforms were novel, but the content was all too familiar. The press inordinately employed the tired reporting frames of the horserace and campaign strategy. Issues received relatively little coverage, and sensational story lines were overplayed.

This chapter will examine the ways in which the media in the 2008 presidential election were both pathbreaking and predictable. The media's presence in this contest was ubiquitous—more so than in any recent presidential campaign. The mainstream press started its coverage long before any serious candidates had declared their intentions to run. Saturation coverage was sustained throughout a drawn-out nominating campaign that challenged the endurance of even the most die-hard political junkies. The media continued in overdrive during the general election, with the campaign overshadowing other news stories even as the country's financial crisis loomed large. Entertainment media came to play a significant role in the campaign. Comedy

**167**

programs drew record audiences, and candidate parodies were popular with the press and public. Voters had an unprecedented number of options for campaign information, and online media attracted record election audiences.

## THE MEDIA CAMPAIGN

Media coverage of the 2008 election cycle began long before a single candidate had officially decided to run for the presidency. The press began speculating about possible candidates in early 2005, more than a year before the first nominating contests. While the public paid little attention, this "exhibition stage" of media coverage was important for candidates seeking to demonstrate their viability to donors and volunteers. The media spotlight focused heavily on a small number of "rock star" prospects who provided interesting stories lines. Democrats, especially Hillary Clinton, who became a candidate, and Al Gore, who did not, received more coverage than any Republican hopeful. The possibility of Clinton becoming the first female major party presidential candidate earned her the largest share of media coverage. Barak Obama also was a subject of media speculation as an African American and rising star in the Democratic Party who was considered a long shot for winning the nomination. Well before the Iowa caucuses, the media effectively had ruled out many of the eight Democrats and nine Republicans who eventually entered the race, simply by ignoring them. Republicans Rudy Giuliani and Mitt Romney garnered more early media attention than the future nominee, John McCain. Fred Thompson, a latecomer to the campaign, received considerable coverage due to his recurring role on the popular television series, *Law and Order*. Of the eventual Democratic candidates, Clinton and Obama were mentioned in the most stories (Hoyt, 2007). John Edwards, who ended his bid for the nomination on January 31, received more media attention for his alleged affair with Rielle Hunter, a woman hired to make a documentary video of his campaign, than for his candidacy.

The nominating phase of the campaign extended from January, when the competitive candidates officially announced their candidacies, to early June, when the last primaries were held. The media environment encompassed a complex mix of old and new platforms, which seemed to signal the emergence of a new era in campaign media. The use of new media was a big part of the election story. The traditional press—print newspapers and news magazines, television network news programs, and radio news shows—was overshadowed by the buzz surrounding the latest communications innovations. The situation was exacerbated by the financial cutbacks faced by traditional news organizations whose pool of journalists and budgets for covering the campaign shrunk (Steinberg, 2008). Media organizations publicized their own techno-logically-driven developments in campaign reporting. With fewer profession-al journalists on the political beat, the mainstream media engaged an array of new techniques for covering the campaign. The Web sites of major media organizations, such as Washingtonpost.com, CNN.com, and MSNBC.com, enhanced their video-sharing and interactive capacities, arranged for audi-ence members to receive text message alerts about key campaign happenings, and hosted election-related reports from average citizens.

Press reports highlighted campaign communication tactics that creative-ly employed information technologies to reach voters and appeal to the media. The Internet, digital platforms, and cell phones were used to encour-age participation and to solicit record donations. In addition to convention-al television advertising, campaigns posted videos online that were distributed virally by e-mail, podcasts, and social networking sites (Brownstein, 2008). Candidates, especially those facing an uphill battle, used new media to tap constituencies that are traditionally difficult to reach, like young people and ethnic/racial group members. Obama's campaign was par-ticularly adept at employing cutting-edge strategies for voter outreach. The campaign took microtargeting techniques to a new level by not only tailoring messages to appeal to particular audience segments based on consumer data, but also customizing the delivery system. A young, Latina, first-time voter who worked in a major city and frequented Starbucks might have received a cell phone call from a peer encouraging her to vote and emphasizing the importance of "change" for their generation.

The media also drew attention to citizens' efforts to engage new commu-nication platforms. Voters used innovative Web 2.0 strategies that facilitate interconnectivity and group cooperation to disseminate campaign messages. They produced campaign videos and posted them to sites like YouTube, organized volunteers and events through social networking sites, including Facebook and MySpace, and developed independent election Web sites with advanced features for sharing information. Young voters, who typically are portrayed as being disinterested in elections, were lauded as pioneers in elec-tion media. Acting outside of official committees, they organized what amounted to digital grassroots campaign organizations. In addition, citizen journalism proliferated as individuals with no professional credentials pub-lished eyewitness accounts of campaign events, issue analysis, commentary, and rumor on blogs and independent news Web sites like the Huffington Post, Daily Kos, Town Hall, and Scoop08.

The lengthy nominating phase provided an opportunity for the media, campaigns, and citizens to experiment with novel approaches to communication. During the general election, however, the mainstream media took on a more prominent role that was reminiscent of past campaigns. The compressed timetable allowed the established media to dedicate significant resources to campaign coverage. The press readily fell into traditional patterns of coverage, focusing on the horserace, campaign strategies, conflict, and candidate character. As political journalist John McQuaid observed, "Because of tradition, inertia and command of the largest, most diverse audiences, the mainstream media still drive the campaign bus with the same old road map" (2008: 44).

This is not to say that new media disappeared or were not a factor. Rather, the new media story took a back seat to old-style coverage. Public enthusiasm over new media dissipated somewhat over the course of the long primary period and general election. Individuals were less likely to create and post original videos on YouTube during the general election than they were during the nominating campaign. Candidates still employed new media to rally voters, but they concentrated on using traditional media to mobilize their base.

In keeping with convention, the media focused on pseudo-scandals and churned sensational story lines that they felt would hold the public's interest. Barak Obama's associations with Reverend Jeremiah Wright, his outspoken pastor of twenty years, and William Ayers, a former member of the 1960s radical Weather Underground Organization, drove endless reports and debates. These ersatz controversies were fed by Sarah Palin's rhetoric on the stump accusing Obama of "palling around with terrorists who would target their own country." The Obama campaign shot back by resurrecting John McCain's involvement in the 1989 "Keating Five" scandal, where McCain and four other Senators were accused of attempting to influence federal regulators who were investigating a failed savings and loan. McCain's wife, Cindy, also was chided by the press for her involvement in the Keating Five scandal, as well as for allegedly stealing drugs from her nonprofit organization to satisfy her addiction to painkillers (Kantor and Halbfinger, 2008). During the final debate, McCain introduced the country to Samuel J. Wurzelbacher, "Joe the Plumber," to illustrate how Obama's tax plan would hurt working people. The press quickly discovered that Wurzelbacher was not a licensed plumber, he owed back taxes, and he had a lien on his house. Further, analysts revealed that Joe would likely benefit from Obama's tax plan. Sixty-four percent of the public heard a lot about Joe the Plumber during the final weeks of the campaign as he gave interviews and joined the Republican candidates on the campaign trail, making his story the fourth most publicized of the election (Pew Research Center for the People & the Press, 2008b).

### Election Media Blitz

The amount of press attention to the 2008 campaign far exceeded coverage of past presidential contests in the modern era. Journalists in 1996 and 2000 had complained openly that the campaigns were boring, and that they lacked the requisite drama and tension to warrant extensive coverage (Jamieson, 2001). The candidates in the 2004 campaign generated little press enthusiasm. In contrast, the 2008 election was full of uncertainty and excitement, and featured a cast of colorful characters. Voters perceived that they had the opportunity to make a decision that actually could result in the change that the candidates were hawking. In addition, the public had a lot to learn about the presidential candidates, especially Barak Obama who had spent little time in the national spotlight. John McCain, a war hero who had clashed with his own party's leadership, sparked story lines replete with patriotism and conflict. Sarah Palin, an Alaska governor who seemed to come out of nowhere to join the Republican ticket, generated a series of media firestorms over her qualifications, as well as family-related matters. The pregnancy of Palin's unwed daughter, Bristol, was the second most popularized campaign event, with 69 percent of the public reporting that they had heard a lot about it (Pew Research Center for the People & the Press, 2008b). The press dogged Palin about her involvement in "Troopergate." (She allegedly forced the resignation of the Alaska public safety commissioner because he refused to fire her former brother-in-law, an Alaska state trooper, who was in a custody dispute with her sister.)

The election dominated the news media agenda from early January 2008 until Election Day on November 4. The Project for Excellence in Journalism (PEJ) conducted a weekly analysis of election news coverage during this period that included major newspapers, network television news programs, cable news programs, radio news, and online sites associated with prominent news organizations. For all but four of the forty-four weeks of the primary/caucus period and the general election, the campaign commanded more attention than any other single news story. As Figure 1 demonstrates, the percentage of the mainstream news hole devoted to election coverage varied widely from week to week. The Democratic National Convention and the announcement of Sarah Palin as the Republican vice-presidential candidate during the last week in August resulted in the highest level of coverage, with 69 percent of the news hole devoted to the election. This figure was matched during the week of the presidential election itself. The presidential and vice-presidential debates also sparked significant coverage; the press and the public had the opportunity to evaluate the candidates as they faced off. While still the biggest story, election coverage waned during the summer in the period between the nominating campaigns and the conventions, falling to a low of 21 percent of the news hole in early August. There was a slight surge in election news in July when Obama took a trip to Europe and the Middle East which invigorated coverage in the U.S. and abroad.

Figure 1 compares trends in coverage of the election and the economy. Until early September, when the failures of mortgage companies Fannie Mae and Freddy Mac and investment firm Lehman Brothers signaled the start of a financial crisis, the economy received very little press attention. In the weeks leading up to the election, public interest in the economy grew, yet only 7 percent of the mainstream media news hole was devoted to coverage of the crisis compared to 40 percent for the presidential election (Pew Research Center for the People & the Press, 2008c). For only three weeks in September did coverage of the economic crisis surpass election reports. Mainstream media coverage of the worsening crisis decreased precipitously during the last five weeks of the campaign while election coverage soared.

**Figure 1. Percentage of News Hole**
**Devoted to the Campaign and the Economy**
**January 6–November 9, 2008**

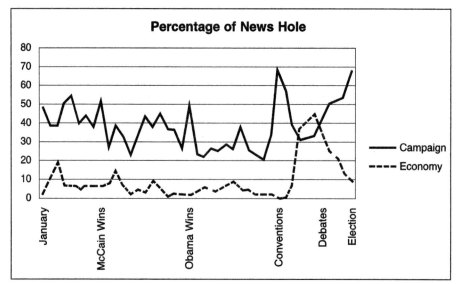

Source: Compiled from PEJ Campaign News Coverage Indexes (journalism.org)

The quantity of media coverage of the candidates was conspicuously imbalanced. The Democratic candidates received significantly more coverage during the nominating campaign than did the Republicans. John

McCain virtually fell off the media radar screen in the weeks after he won the Republican nomination in early March. The press focused heavily on the dramatic battle between Hillary Clinton and Barak Obama for the Democratic nomination, which was not resolved until June. During the general election, McCain and Obama received approximately the same amount of coverage. Democratic vice-presidential candidate Joe Biden commanded very little press attention, especially compared to Sarah Palin, who at times eclipsed John McCain in terms of coverage. Biden was covered following his debate with Palin and when he committed campaign trail gaffes. When discussing the economic crisis, Biden mentioned that Franklin Delano Roosevelt "got on the television" to address the matter. FDR was not president in 1929 when the stock market crashed and television would not become a household appliance for two decades. Biden gave the press and the opposition a bonus when he stated that Obama would be tested like John F. Kennedy—he would face an international crisis within six months of taking office.

## *The Horserace Dominates—As Usual*

The omnipresent coverage of the campaign was in many ways a positive development. Election information was difficult for voters to avoid, and audience members could obtain news from a wide range of sources. However, more media coverage did not necessarily translate into better information. Despite the availability of quality news, especially detailed reporting from elite newspapers and newsmagazines, journalists defaulted to the horserace frame that has typified election coverage in the mass media era. Stories focused heavily on who was leading and trailing in the polls and the strategic maneuvers of campaigns as they jockeyed to gain a favorable position (Patterson, 1993). A study conducted by the PEJ revealed that over half of the coverage from January to October 2008 dealt with the horserace, a figure that climbed to almost two-thirds in the last three weeks of the campaign. An additional 10 percent of stories concentrated primarily on candidates' advertising and fundraising strategies, and 5 percent focused on their personal lives. Only a quarter of the stories considered issues (20 percent) and the candidates' public record (5 percent) (Project for Excellence in Journalism, 2008b). (See Table 1.) The vast majority of stories were primarily relevant to political insiders and strategists; a mere 12 percent of coverage was useful to voters' decision making (Seelye, 2008b). Stories often were framed to emphasize how the candidates were managing their issues stances in order to gain campaign momentum rather than presenting comprehensive information about their positions.

Table 1. Topic of Campaign Stories
January–October 2008

| Topic | Percentage of Stories |
|---|---|
| Horserace | 53% |
| Policy | 20% |
| Advertising/Fundraising | 10% |
| Candidates' Personal Lives | 5% |
| Candidates' Public Record | 5% |

Source: Project for Excellence in Journalism, 2008b

Instead of providing greater substance, the media employed new techno-logical gimmicks for reporting on the horserace. CNN's Multi-Touch Collaborative Wall, more commonly referred to as the Magic Wall, used iPhone technology to enable a color-coded map to depict the latest state-based predictions. By touching the map, political correspondent John King could display statistics, move battleground states in and out of candidates' camps, and compare campaigns' movements across the country. King's performance with the map, where he was seen "poking, touching and waving at the screen like an over-caffeinated traffic cop" (Farhi, 2008), eclipsed the barrage of sta-tistics that overwhelmed some viewers. (The Magic Wall, or "journalistic super-weapon," received comedic treatment on Comedy Central's *The Daily Show with John Stewart* and NBC's *Saturday Night Live*.) CNN was not the only broadcast network to use this technology. Fox News and NBC used virtual reality studios where they could manipulate images, data, and maps.

Horserace coverage influenced the amount of favorable press the presi-dential candidates received, especially during the general election. The can-didate who led in the polls received more positive media evaluations than those who trailed. Obama had an advantage over McCain in the horserace throughout most of the campaign, a trend that was reflected in the tone of mainstream media accounts. Stories about Obama were more positive (36 percent) than negative (29 percent); 35 percent of stories were neutral. In contrast, coverage of McCain was highly unfavorable, as 57 percent of reports were negative, 14 percent were positive, and 29 percent were neutral.

This trend did not hold for the vice-presidential candidates, who often were charged with being the attack dogs for their ticket. Coverage of Sarah Palin, who attracted three times more press attention than Joe Biden, began on a positive note and became increasingly negative as her lack of political experience became apparent in a series of high profile interviews with CBS's Katie Couric, ABC's Charlie Gibson, NBC's Matt Lauer, and Fox News's

Greta Van Susteren, who also spoke with her husband, Todd. In the end, 39 percent of Palin's mainstream media coverage was negative, 28 percent was positive, and 33 percent neutral. Biden received the most disapproving coverage of all four candidates. Forty-eight percent of Biden stories were negative, 17 percent were positive, and 35 percent were neutral (Project for Excellence in Journalism, 2008j).

Issue coverage, especially in the most readily accessible mainstream television media, fell short of public expectations in an election considered to be of momentous importance. The economy garnered significantly more media attention than any other issue, yet still occupied only between 20 percent and 12 percent of the weekly election news hole. The war in Iraq and healthcare, the next most prominent issues, averaged 2 percent of the news hole during the general election (Project for Excellence in Journalism, 2008d). Despite the dearth of coverage, the media's emphasis on issues dovetailed the voters' priorities. National surveys by the Pew Research Center, the National Election Pool Exit Polls, and CNN identifying the public's issue concerns had consistent results. As Table 2 indicates, a solid majority of the public considered the economy to be the most important issue followed distantly by the war in Iraq, healthcare, terrorism, energy, and immigration.

**Table 2. Public's Most Important Issue in General Election**

|  | Pew | Exit Polls | CNN |
|---|---|---|---|
| **Economy** | 58% | 63% | 57% |
| **War in Iraq** | 10% | 10% | 13% |
| **Healthcare** | 8% | 9% | 13% |
| **Terrorism** | 8% | 9% | 10% |
| **Energy** | 6% | 7% | — |
| **Immigration** | — | — | 5% |
| **Race** | — | 2% | — |

Sources: Pew Research Center for the People & the Press, 2008d; National Election Pool Exit Polls; CNN Issue Tracker, October 30–November 1, 2008

Despite Obama's history-making candidacy, press reports generally treated the issue of race with ambiguity. The "race issue" or "post-racial politics" were terms employed regularly by the media, but only occasionally were they defined or discussed in detail. Pundits raised the possibility that a racially motivated "Bradley Effect" might work against Obama. The phenomenon occurs when white voters claim to pollsters that they are undecided when they actually favor the white candidate. It is named for Tom Bradley, an

African American gubernatorial candidate in California who led his opponent in the polls in 1982 and then lost the election. However, the "Bradley Effect" was seldom discussed within the context of race. Instead, it was considered in relation to the horserace, as speculation focused on how many points ahead in the polls were needed for Obama to win a particular state, or what tactics his campaign might employ to overcome this perceived disadvantage. The subject of race was more likely to be raised in conjunction with a sensationalized campaign story than as a topic for serious deliberation. *The Washington Post's* Issue Coverage Tracker, which tallied issue mentions across a wide range of information Web sites, found only five mentions of civil rights in over 10,000 pieces relating to Barak Obama and six mentions for John McCain. Yet, a media frenzy erupted over inflammatory statements by Obama's longtime pastor, Reverend Jeremiah Wright, associating the United States with terrorism. Wright also denounced the country for its treatment of blacks. The remarks prompted Obama to give an inspired speech on race in March, in which he drew upon his personal story and stressed unity among Americans. Obama acknowledged that the issue of race had "bubbled to the surface" on occasion, but that it had taken a divisive turn at that point in the campaign. According to national exit polls, 80 percent of voters reported that the candidates' race had no impact on their decision, while 2 percent considered it to be the most important issue in the campaign.

Similarly, the press mostly avoided reporting on the substantive significance of Hillary Clinton as a female presidential aspirant and Sarah Palin as the first Republican woman vice-presidential candidate. Instead, coverage focused on their clothing, appearance, and personal mannerisms, as is traditionally the case for female candidates (Carroll, 2003). Hillary Clinton's penchant for pant suits and Sarah Palin's $150,000 wardrobe commanded lengthy discussions. Tabloid-style revelations about Clinton becoming teary-eyed at an event the day before the New Hampshire primary and Palin's returning to work shortly after giving birth to a baby with Down Syndrome had strong gender-based undercurrents.

The 2008 campaign showcased the best and worst of press reporting and behavior. The findings of the studies presented in this chapter highlight the failure of the press in general to report on meaningfully on issues. It is, however, important to note that there was extraordinary coverage in virtually all media, which is masked by aggregate research. The *New York Times*, for example, provided balanced coverage of the Democratic and Republican candidates during the primary campaign, with each party receiving 44 percent of front-page election stories. While PEJ found that only 10 percent of newspapers' front-page stories dealt with issues, the figure was 46 percent for the *New*

*York Times*. The paper's Web site, like other online resources, contained the full text of candidates' speeches, transcripts and complete videos of debates, detailed issue platforms, and a blog featuring analysis by noted journalists that welcomed comments (Hoyt, 2007).

## ENTERTAINMENT MEDIA

The role of entertainment media in the electoral process has become more central since the 1992 presidential election. In an effort to wrest control of the campaign media agenda from the mainstream press, candidates used alternative avenues for getting their messages out to voters. Bill Clinton famously played his saxophone on the *Arsenio Hall Show* and answered a query about whether he preferred boxers or briefs on MTV. Popular magazines featured stories about the personal lives of candidates, and the tabloid press broke scandalous accounts of candidates' indiscretions, such as Clinton's affair with Gennifer Flowers, which the mainstream media were compelled to cover (Davis and Owen, 1999).

Entertainment media can be influential in campaigns, especially as mainstream news programs increasingly emulate their sensational, gossip-laden style of reporting. They reach audiences that are not attuned to news and politics, and can shape individuals' views of candidates (Moy, Xenos, and Hess, 2006). Comedy programs, such as *The Daily Show with John Stewart* and *The Colbert Report*, have become sources of political information for young people, in particular. In addition, exposure to election content in entertainment media can stimulate interest in a campaign, and lead people to seek information from traditional news sources (Feldman and Young, 2008). During the height of the 2008 election, the fake news programs on Comedy Central attracted more viewers than some network programs, with the *Daily Show* drawing an audience of upwards of two million. Late-night programs, such as *The Tonight Show with Jay Leno, The late Show with David Letterman*, and *Late Night with Conan O'Brien*, also exceeded their typical audience numbers (Carter, 2008b).

In 2008, the celebrity-style appeal of the candidates, especially Barak Obama and Sarah Palin, made the election a particularly compelling topic for entertainment magazines, television programs, and Web sites. The candidates became a staple of nightly celebrity television programs. Obama was criticized for using his two daughters to advance his candidacy after they appeared in a four-part interview on *Access Hollywood* in July. In responding to the public disapproval during an interview with Matt Lauer on *Today*, Obama stated, "We wouldn't do it again, and we won't be doing it again" (Celizic, 2008). The candidate vowed to protect his family from the media spotlight, a promise that proved difficult to keep.

Entertainment magazines, including *US Weekly, OK!*, and *Essence*, devoted considerable space to the candidates both in their print editions and on their Web sites. *People* is generally considered to be the most successful magazine in the country, with 3.7 million weekly subscribers and another 1.45 million in newsstand and supermarket sales (Seelye, 2006). The magazine's audience increased over the course of the campaign due to its featured coverage of the candidates, which was mostly positive in tone. The magazine produced what prove to be a highly popular series of covers profiling the presidential and vice-presidential candidates and their families. The accompanying articles gave the public informal glimpses of the candidates at home and at work. The Obama family appeared on the cover twice during the campaign and again the week following the election. The September 12 edition featured a rare photo and piece about the entire McCain family entitled, "Meet the McCains: An intimate look at the trials and triumphs of a big, blended, not-so-typical family." *People* also scored the first interview with Sarah Palin at the Republican National Convention. The Alaska governor, John McCain, and their families were questioned about Palin's qualifications for the job of vice president as well as how she would balance a high-profile position with caring for her five children.

For the past 34 years, *Saturday Night Live* has gained recognition for its sketches poking fun at politicians. *SNL* was able to boost its flagging ratings during the nominating season with a series of skits depicting Hillary Clinton facing a hostile press while Barak Obama was treated with adoration. The program was criticized for taking a pro-Clinton stance, and was even credited with contributing to her victories in Ohio and Texas. A PEJ study indicated that Obama's press coverage soured considerably in the wake of the publicity generated by *SNL* (Carter, 2008a; Seelye, 2008b). The most high-profile of the election entertainment offerings was comedienne Tina Fey's spot-on impression of Sarah Palin on *SNL*, which premiered in September and continued until the final days the campaign. Fey's caricature of the candidate was so convincing and replays of the sketches so widespread that people erroneously attributed certain lines of dialogue to Palin. Twenty-six percent of the public believed that Palin had stated on the campaign trail, "I can see Russia from my house," which was a line from a sketch. While Fey's characterization was widely praised for its comedic value, it was also criticized for being sexist, especially as it poked fun at Palin's beauty pageant past. Palin, in an attempt to capitalize on the publicity and to show that she was a good sport, appeared on *SNL* in a highly anticipated cameo while Fey performed in character. The presidential candidates also made guest appearances during the election cycle. *SNL's* ratings skyrocketed, as over ten million viewers tuned in to the late-night program, an increase of 50 percent from the previous season (Carter, 2008b). A national survey conducted by FirstView 2008 found evidence of an "*SNL* effect." Sixty-seven percent of voters had seen *SNL's* campaign-related skits. Ten percent of all voters and 16 percent of those who had seen the skits reported that the sketches had influenced their vote. Ten percent of viewers become less likely to vote for McCain and 6 percent were less likely to cast their ballot for Obama. *SNL* viewers leaned heavily Democratic, with 59 percent voting for Obama and 39 percent for McCain. When asked to choose between Sarah Palin and Tina Fey for vice president, the sample was evenly split (FirstView, 2008).

Video-sharing sites contributed to the entertainment side of the campaign. Comedic videos created by professionals and amateurs populated the Internet, including jibjab.com's "Time for Some Campaignin'" and "Obama Girl" Amber Lee Etinger's take on Sarah Palin on YouTube. The top videos of 2008 featured Fey as Palin on *SNL* being interviewed by cast member Amy Poehler as Katie Couric, campaigning with Poehler as Hillary Clinton, and participating in the vice-presidential debate. In fact, more people viewed the video on NBC.com and Hulu.com than on television (Coyle, 2008). Over 200 video clips related to the *SNL* skits were posted on YouTube alone. The real Sarah Palin was the second most popular subject of online videos, as almost every move she made on the campaign trail was documented. Entertainment personalities, such as Matt Damon, John Cleese, and Betty White, weighed in on Palin via video. Palin continued to be a popular online video subject after the election, as a clip of her pardoning a Thanksgiving turkey while another bird met its demise in the background received millions of views.

The imbalance in the tone of coverage of particular candidates was evidenced in entertainment media as well as hard news. McCain did not fare as well as Obama on the morning show, talk show, and late night television circuit. Both Barak and Michelle Obama made light-hearted appearances on *the Ellen DeGeneres Show*, and their dance moves with the host earned rave reviews from Hollywood reporters. In contrast, John McCain was subject to a grilling by DeGeneres about his opposition to gay marriage (Kurtz, 2008). During the final two months of the campaign, the Republican ticket was the butt of 475 jokes by Letterman and Leno compared to 69 jokes about the Democratic slate (Center for Media and Public Affairs, 2008).

## THE ELECTION MEDIA AUDIENCE

The 2008 campaign witnessed some marked shifts in audience media preferences. As is the case with media coverage, however, these shifts were only partially transformative. While a sizable portion of the electorate consulted new media sources, the majority relied primarily on established television network and cable news for their campaign information. The most important development was the age-related differences in media use, leading to speculation that a dual media system may be developing in response to the preferences of younger and older audiences. In addition, audience appetite for political news was fleeting, and dropped off immediately following the campaign.

## High Interest Election, Media Boon

The American public was more interested in the 2008 campaign than in any other in over 20 years, and attention to news reached new heights. Sixty percent of registered voters reported that they followed campaign news very closely the week before the election, compared to 52 percent in 2004 and 39 percent in 2000 (Pew Research Center for the People & the Press, 2008b). An estimated 71.474 million people watched the election returns on fourteen television networks (Nielson, 2008; Weprin, 2008), while countless others followed online. The collective sense that the result of this campaign would be momentous for the nation, the openness of a race that did not include an incumbent president or vice president, and a dramatic story line compelled people to engage. Democrats were more interested in following campaign news than Republicans (Pew Research Center for the People & the Press, 2008a). The Democratic nominating process was more dramatic and drawn out than the Republican contest. In addition, Democrats were less familiar with Obama, who was a relatively new face on the political scene, than Republicans were with McCain, a war hero and national political figure who had sought the nomination before.

There was intense interest in the campaign in other countries, as well. People were captivated by Barak Obama's candidacy and fascinated by the spectacle of the American electoral process. Foreign journalists worked overtime to follow the race, as news organizations stepped up coverage of the election. The Voice of America broadcast election night coverage in 44 languages to a record 134 million people worldwide (McGuire, 2008).

The high levels of interest in the campaign translated into a windfall for most, but not all, media. Audience members in past elections were primarily drawn to a particular medium for most of their news. In 2008, an increasingly number of people relied on a variety of media for information, and checked on election news throughout the day.

As Table 3 indicates, television is still the main source of election information for a majority of people despite the proliferation of options. However, the popularity of television news has declined significantly since the 2004 election. The percentage of those naming television as their main source dropped from 76 percent to 68 percent. A somewhat higher percentage of people reported relying heavily on cable news for election information in 2008 (44 percent) than in 2004 (40 percent) (Pew Research Center for the People & the Press, 2008d). Cable channels which adopted a thinly veiled partisan approach to coverage fared well. MSNBC's ratings climbed 158 percent over the previous year, as the channel played the role of ardent opponent of the Bush administration. Conservative Fox News's ratings increased 101 percent as it continued to represent the Republican perspective. CNN, whose espoused approach was to provide news without an overt ideological spin, experienced a ratings boost of 124 percent in the final three months of the campaign. Even fake cable news programs benefitted from the election. *The Daily Show with John Stewart* had a record audience of 3.6 million for its program featuring an interview with Barak Obama in late October (Carter, 2008).

The story was vastly different for network television news. Evening newscasts, which have seen their audiences dwindle over the past 20 years, continued their downward ratings trend, averaging 23.7 million viewers per night combined compared to 36.7 million viewers in 1991. As shown in Table 3, only 18 percent of the public said that network news was their main source of election information in 2008, compared to 29 percent in 2004 (Pew Research Center for the People & the Press, 2008d). ABC's *World News with Charles Gibson* lost 2 percent of its audience and CBS's *Evening News with Katie Couric* viewership declined 3 percent. NBC's *Nightly News with Brian Williams* was the only one of the "Big Three" networks to experience a slight increase (Meyers, 2008). Industry experts noted that the drop in viewership, particularly over the summer months, likely would have been greater if it were not for the election (Stelter and Perez-Pena, 2008). For the first time, more Americans got their daily news from cable (40 percent) than network programs (34 percent) (Gallup, 2008).

Similarly, print newspapers continued to lose readers even as the election reached its pinnacle. As Table 3 demonstrates, the decline in the percentage of people identifying print newspapers as their primary source of information was more precipitous than for any other medium, falling from 46 percent in 2004 to 33 percent in 2008 (Pew Research Center for the People & the Press, 2008d). Hard-copy newspapers have been forced to raise prices while, at the same time, they are losing readers and advertising revenue to online media. The 507 American daily newspapers averaged a 4.6 percent drop in Sunday and 3.5 percent decline in weekday paid subscriptions in the year leading up to October 2008 (Rosenthal, 2008). Circulation increased for a small number of papers, including *USA Today*, a national newspaper, the *Wall Street Journal*, whose extensive coverage of economic issues drove readership as the country experienced a financial downturn, and a handful of papers specializing in local community news (MacMillan, 2008). Print magazine and radio audiences also fell off in the four years between presidential elections.

Online media had the biggest election-related audience gains. Fifty-six percent of the public reported that they had gotten at least some news online, an increase of 15 percentage points over 2004. As depicted in Table 3, 36 percent of the public named the Internet as their main source of election news (Pew Research Center for the People & the Press, 2008d). Cable news Web sites associated with established news organizations as well as independent news sites experienced significant bumps in the number of users they attracted. In the month prior to the election, MSNBC.com attracted 40.9 million unique visitors. Many people were drawn to the unique video features of the online news sites. Users spent an average of 42 minutes per live stream session on news sites watching the candidates give speeches and interviews (Market Watch, 2008). *Politico*, then a two-year-old start-up aimed at Washington insiders and political junkies, saw the circulation of its print paper rise to 26,000. Over 2.5 million people per day accessed its Web site, Politico.com, pulling in a national audience (Stelter and Perez-Pena, 2008).

**Table 3. Main Source of Election Information**

|                 | 2008 | 2004 |
|-----------------|------|------|
| Television      | 68%  | 76%  |
| Cable TV        | 44%  | 40%  |
| Network TV      | 18%  | 29%  |
| Print Newspaper | 33%  | 46%  |
| Radio           | 16%  | 22%  |
| Magazine        | 3%   | 6%   |
| Internet        | 36%  | 21%  |

Source: Pew Research Center for the People & the Press, 2008d

### The Generational Media Divide

The 2008 election solidified the media preference gap between younger and older voters. For almost a decade, young people have been abandoning traditional news media, especially network television broadcasts and print newspapers (Wattenberg, 2008). While over 70 percent of older Americans read a daily newspaper, only 20 percent of young people do so (Mindich, 2008). The decline of news media use among young people was not accompanied by a shift to alternative news sources until the 2008 campaign. As Table 4 indicates, large percentages of younger people consulted news sites. Fifty-nine percent of 18- to 29-year-olds got campaign information from campaign news sites compared to only 12 percent of those over age 65 (Pew Research Center for the People & the Press, 2008e). It may be the case for at least some young people that the practice of consulting online news media established during the campaign will be become an enduring habit.

In addition to news Web sites, young people were drawn to dynamic and populist media formats, such as blogs, candidate Web sites, social networking sites, and video-sharing platforms (Winograd and Hais, 2008). These sites typically employ interactive features, and give young people the opportunity to engage in the campaign more directly (Owen, 2008). Again, the age difference among users for these online information sources is substantial. As Table 4 shows, 42 percent of people under age 30 read campaign blogs in contrast to 9 percent of those over 65. Similarly, 38 percent of young people visited candidate Web sites, compared to only 7 percent of senior citizens. Perhaps the biggest difference was for viewing videos online, as 65 percent of young voters viewed a campaign-related video online versus 17 percent of older people. More than a quarter of 18- to 29-year-olds learned about the campaign from social networking sites; the percentage of people age 30 and older using these sites was miniscule (Pew Research Center for the People & the Press, 2008e).

**Table 4.** Age Difference in Online Media Use

|  | News Sites | Blogs | Candidate Sites | Online Videos | Social Network Sites |
|---|---|---|---|---|---|
| **18–29** | 59% | 42% | 38% | 65% | 28% |
| **30–49** | 42% | 30% | 26% | 41% | 6% |
| **50–64** | 33% | 24% | 21% | 34% | 3% |
| **65+** | 12% | 9% | 7% | 17% | 1% |

Source: Pew Research Center for the People & the Press, 2008e

### Post-Election Retreat

The record audiences for election media dissipated almost immediately after Election Day, when they had reached their peak. Even an engaged electorate became weary of blanket election coverage, as 82 percent of Americans stated that they would not miss following campaign news (Pew Research Center for the People & the Press, 2008c). While news organizations attempted to build upon audiences' perceived appetites for political information with coverage of Obama's transition to power, the story had limited appeal.

News Web sites, which had gained a tremendous following during the campaign, saw the biggest drop in traffic. On election night, 8.572 million individuals per minute visited the online news sites for CNN, MSNBC, Reuters, and BBC, besting a record set during the final game of the World Cup soccer match in 2006 and the NCAA basketball championship in 2007 (Schonfeld, 2008). MSNBC.com, the site which attracted the most eyeballs during the campaign, experienced a 25 percent decline in audience share, falling from 25.1 million unique visitors during the week of the election to 18.7 million the following week. CNN.com lost one-third of its traffic, while Fox News and Yahoo News each experienced declines of over 20 percent (Fahri, 2008b). Only network evening newscasts maintained their election campaign audience share, which consists largely of committed viewers who tune in out of habit.

## CONCLUSION

The 2008 election was clearly a watershed for political media. There were significant developments that provided new options for the press, candidates, and citizens for disseminating and receiving information. The nominating phase of the campaign, in particular, was important for the evolution of political media. It brought to light the simultaneous tension and cooperation among the growing communications corps as well as the emergent hybridization of campaign media in the twenty-first century. The integration of old and new media became routine. For example, when Colin Powell endorsed Barak Obama in October during the taping of NBC's *Meet the Press*, the network rushed the video onto MSNBC.com hours before the television broadcast in order to capitalize on the scoop (Carr and Stelter, 2008).

Still, the election stopped short of being truly game-changing. The most dramatic transformations involved communication technology, and not media content. Old-style narratives, especially the horserace, were repurposed to suit newer platforms. As former CBS News president Andrew Heyward observed, "We should be careful of these zero-sum games where the new media drives out the old. I think what we see is growing sophistication about making the channels work together effectively" (Carr and Stelter, 2008). In the end, it was largely a case of old stories in new packages for campaign media.

## REFERENCES

Carr, David, and Brian Stelter. 2008. "Campaigns in a web 2.0 world," nytimes.com. November 3. http://www.nytimes.com/2008/11/03/business/media/03media.html?_r=1&scp=8&sq=Comedy%20Central%202008%20election&st=cse (accessed 3 2008, December).

Carroll, Susan J., ed. 2008. *Women and American Politics* (New York: Oxford University Press, 2003).

Carter, Will. "Pro-Clinton: 'SNL' says you're joking," 2008a. nytimes.com. March 13. http://www.nytimes.com/2008/03/13/arts/television/13snl.html?_r=1 (accessed November 20, 2008).
———. 2008b. "No need for recount here: Political comedy is winning, big time," nytimes.com. October 9. http://query.nytimes.com/gst/fullpage. html?res=9C00E4D6143DF93AA35753C1A96E9C8B63 (accessed December 2, 2008).
———. 2008c. "Election's over, so what's next for the cable news channels?" nytimes.com. November 15. http://www.nytimes.com/2008/11/15/arts/television/15netw.html (accessed November 20, 2008).
Celizic, Mike. 2008. "Obama calls 'Access Hollywood' interview a mistake," msnbc.msn.com. July 9, 2008. http://www.msnbc.msn.com/id/25600445/ (accessed November 22, 2008).
Center for Media and Public Affairs. 2008. "Obama's coverage was historic, too," cmpa.com. December 2. http://www.cmpa.com/media_room_press_12_2_08.htm (accessed December 4, 2008).
Coyle, Jake. 2008. "Fey, Christian the lion, top viral videos of 2008," msnbc.msn.com. December 11. http://www.msnbc.msn.com/id/28177464/ (accessed December 11, 2008).
Davis, Richard, and Diana Owen. 1999. *New media and American politics* (New York: Oxford University Press, 1999).
Fahri, Paul. 2008. "Post-election, the audience drifts away," *Washington Post*, November 21, 2008, p. C01.
Feldman, Lauren, and Dannagal Goldthwaite Young. 2008. "Late-night comedy as a gateway to traditional news: An analysis of time trends in news attention among late-night comedy viewers during the 2004 presidential primaries," *Political Communication* 25, no. 4: 401–422.
FirstView. 2008. "FirstView 2008 National Post Election Topline Results," firstviewsurvey.com. November 11. http://www.firstviewsurvey.com/assets/topline-results.pdf (accessed December 2, 2008).
Gallup. 2008. "Poll: Internet, cable news up. Others stable or down," mediabistro.com. December 15. http://www.mediabistro.com/tvnewser/web newser/poll_internet_cable_news_up_others_stable_or_down_103396.asp (accessed December 20, 2008).
Hoyt, Clark. 2007. "The campaign and the horse race," nytimes.com. November 18. http://www.nytimes.com/2007/11/18/opinion/18pubed.html (accessed November 22, 2008).
Jamieson, Kathleen Hall, *Everything You Think You Know About Politics . . . and why you are wrong* (New York: Basic Books, 2001).
Kantor, Jodi, and David M. Halbfinger. 2008. "Behind McCain, outsider in capitol wanting back in," nytimes.com. October 17. http://www.nytimes.com/2008/10/18/us/politics/18cindy.html?_r=1 (accessed December 5, 2008).
Kurtz, Howard. 2008. "Obama's talk show advantage is no idle chatter," *Washington Post*, November 3, p. C01.
MacMillan, Robert. 2008. "U.S. newspaper circulation declines accelerate," reuters.com. October 27. http://www.reuters.com/article/companyNews/idUKN2731531120081027?symbol=MEG.N (accessed November 20, 2008).
Market Watch. 2008. "MSNBC.com wins November election coverage by a landslide," marketwatch.com. November 13. http://www.marketwatch.com/news/story/Msnbccom-Wins-November-Election-Coverage/story.aspx?guid=%7B74CDA95B-6C98-41EB-B3D9-0332737CB3D6%7D (accessed November 20, 2008).
McGuire, Stryker. 2008. "The world hopes for its first president," newsweek.com. November 10. http://www.newsweek.com/id/166910 (accessed November 22, 2008).
Meyers, Jim. 2008. "Despite election, network news audience shrinks," newsmax.com. November 21. http://www.newsmax.com/insidecover/tv_news_shrinks/2008/11/21/153902.html (accessed November 22, 2008).
Mindich, David T. Z., *Tuned out*. 2005 (New York: Oxford University Press, 2005).
Moy, Patricia, Michael A. Xenos, and V.K. Hess. 2006. "Priming effects of late-night comedy." *International Journal of Public Opinion Research* 18: 198–210.

Nielson. 2008. "National tv audience estimates for election night 2008," nielson.com. November 5. http://blog.nielsen.com/nielsenwire/wp-content/uploads/2008/11/mediaalert_revised.pdf (accessed November 20, 2008).

Owen, Diana. 2008. "Election media and youth political engagement," sowi.net. October. sowi.net/owen (accessed November 25, 2008).

Patterson, Thomas. 1993. *Out of order* (New York: Alfred A. Knopf, 1993).

Pew Research Center for the People & the Press. 2008a. "Dems led in campaign news interest, too," pewresearch.org. December 8. http://pewresearch.org/pubs/1049/some-final-thoughts-on-campaign-08 (accessed December 11, 2008).

———. 2008b. "Election weekend news interest hits 20 year high," pewresearch.org. November 6. http://pewresearch.org/pubs/1025/election-news-interest (accessed November 22, 2008).

———. 2008c. "Few will miss campaign news." pewresearch.org. November 12. http://people-press.org/report/470/favorite-campaign-journalists (accessed November 19, 2008).

———. 2008d. "High marks for campaign; High bar for Obama," pewresearch.org. November 13. http://people-press.org/report/?pageid=1429 (accessed November 20, 2008).

———. 2008e. "Internet's broader role in campaign 2008," people-press.org. January 11, 2008a. http://people-press.org/report/384/internets-broader-role-in-campaign-2008 (accessed November 20, 2008).

Project for Excellence in Journalism. 2008a. "The invisible primary—Invisible no longer," *journalism.org*. October 27. HYPERLINK "http://www.journalism.org/node/8187" http://www.journalism.org/node/8187 (accessed November 19, 2008).

———. 2008b."Winning the media campaign," journalism.org. October 22, 2008b. http://www.journalism.org/node/13307 (accessed November 19, 2008).

Rosenthal, Phil. 2008. "New newspaper paid-circulation figures out," chicagotribune.com. October 27. http://newsblogs.chicagotribune.com/towerticker/2008/10/new-newspaper-p.html (accessed November 20, 2008).

San Miguel, Renay. 2008. "Election night tv 2008: Technology for technology's sake," technewsworld.com. November 7. http://www.technewsworld.com/rsstory/65073.html (accessed November 20, 2008).

Schonfeld, Eric. 2008. "News sites attract record audience on election night," techcrunch.com. November 5. http://www.techcrunch.com/2008/11/05/news-sites-attract-record-audience-on-election-night/ (accessed November 22, 2008).

Seelye, Katharine Q. 2006."Celebrity appeal keeps magazine circulation mostly higher," nytimes.com. February 21. http://www.nytimes.com/2006/02/21/business/media/21circ.html (accessed November 22, 2008).

———. 2008a. "News coverage changes, and so does tone of the campaign," nytimes.com. March 5. http://www.nytimes.com/2008/03/05/us/politics/05press.html?scp=1&sq=New%20coverage%20changes,%20and%20so%20does%20tone%20of%20the%20campaign&st=cse (accessed November 24, 2008).

———. 2008b. "2008 coverage focuses on the horse race," nytimes.com. October 29. http://thecaucus.blogs.nytimes.com/2007/10/29/2008-coverage-focuses-on-the-horse-race/ (accessed December 2, 2008).

Steinberg, Jacques. 2008. "The buzz on the bus: pinched, press steps off," nytimes.com. March 26. http://www.nytimes.com/2008/03/26/us/politics/26bus.html?hp (accessed November 1, 2008).

Stelter, Brian, and Richard Perez-Pena. 2008. "Media outlets are seeking a campaign bounce of their own," nutimes.com. August 4. http://www.nytimes.com/2008/08/04/business/media/04ratings.html?_r=2&oref=login&pagewanted=print (accessed November 20, 2008).

Wattenberg, Martin P. 2008. *Is voting for young people?* (New York: Pearson Longman, 2008).

Weprin, Alex. 2008. "71.5 million tuned in for election coverage," broadcastingcable.com. November 5. http://www.broadcastingcable.com/article/CA6611690.html (accessed November 20, 2008).

Winograd, Morely, and Michael D. Hais. 2008. *Millennial makeover* (New Brunswick, NJ: Rutgers University Press, 2008).

# Chapter 8

## No Laughing Matter: The Role of New Media in the 2008 Election

### Girish J. Gulati

In a democratic society, one of the most fundamental responsibilities of the news media is to provide the public the necessary information to make sound decisions on whom to elect to office and assess the performance of those already serving. The media performs this function by gathering information about the candidates, their positions on the issues, and their campaign activities, selecting the most newsworthy information, and then organizing and presenting that information to the public in an intelligible way.[1] The candidates have a significant stake in what gets reported about them—and their opponents—and, thus, are actively trying to shape the coverage to their advantage.

While the role of the media and the goals of the candidates did not change in 2008, the media environment in which both voters and candidates navigate did go through a significant transformation. Not only did the Internet become fully institutionalized as a media platform, but also the range of online applications expanded. In addition to candidate Web sites and discussion blogs, voters turned to video-sharing sites and online social networks to learn about the 2008 campaign. On television, voters saw soft news programs and late-night comedy shows as viable alternatives for learning about elections, governance, and public affairs. By expanding the range of choices for voters on how they learn about campaigns, this new media environment provides candidates with a combination of new opportunities and greater challenges in getting their message out to the public.

## NEW VOTERS LEAD THE WAY: CITIZENS AND THE NEW LEARNING

While advances in technology guarantee that every set of elections will be contested in a "new" media environment, only rarely do terms such as "revolutionary" or "transformative" apply to the changes in the campaign process and how voters learn about candidates. One of these revolutionary moments was during the 1964 presidential campaign, when television and the nightly newscasts of ABC, CBS, and NBC supplanted newspapers as the primary way Americans get their news. In every election cycle since then, the gap between television and newspapers has grown.[2] The 2008 election seems to be another of these transformative events, as the Internet became a major source of campaign news for the American public. According to preelection survey data gathered from the Pew Research Center for the People & the Press, 33 percent of Americans claimed that the Internet was a major source for news about the 2008 campaigns. In 2004, only 10 percent of American made that claim. Also remarkable about this past election cycle was that the Internet surpassed newspapers as the second most popular source for following the campaigns, trailing only television, which was mentioned by 72 percent of all Americans as a primary source. Only 28 percent cited newspapers as a primary source in 2008. Even fewer cited radio (15 percent ) and news magazines (2 percent).[3]

Further evidence that 2008 will be viewed as a transformative election year comes from the substantial generational gap in news consumption habits. Among younger Americans, those between the ages of 18 and 29, 61 percent cited television as a main source of election news, 49 percent cited the Internet, and only 17 percent cited newspapers. Among Americans 65 and older, however, 82 percent cited television, 45 percent cited newspapers, and only 12 percent cited the Internet as a main source of election news.[4] As today's younger generation become the leading trendsetters of tomorrow and more households gain access to high-speed Internet service, it is not inconceivable that the Internet will be the number one source for campaign news in 2012.

The public's growing disenchantment and declining confidence in traditional media, examined in this chapter, is at least partly responsible for contributing to the growing popularity of the Internet. Yet the Internet has certain characteristics that make it a popular medium for following news in its own right, independent of the troubles at the networks or in print media. The Internet allows people quicker access to breaking news, continuous updating and follow-up, and the ability to access news on demand. The World Wide Web in particular gives users more control and allows them to have a more interactive experience when reading the news. It also is capable of combining the best of what television and newspapers have to offer, including visual images of news events through video, photos, and graphic links. At the same time, however, there is an opportunity to learn more about a story through archived articles, online databases, and links to external sites. Furthermore, the vast array of choices for news available on the Web, varying in topics, tone, perspective, and comprehensiveness, provides users with a way of reading news to fit their own needs and interests. The Internet even allows them to participate in the news-making process by including their comments, observations, and photographs on the Web site.

The unique combination of features offered on the Internet explains the medium's increasing popularity for following campaigns. Pew's surveys conducted just a few weeks before Election Day found that 59 percent of voters had gone online to seek out election content or communicate with others about the campaign. The most popular activity was watching videos: 39 percent of voters said that they had watched some type of campaign-related video online. More specifically, 28 percent said that they had gone online to watch a candidate's speech, 27 percent said they had seen an interview, 23 percent said they had seen one or more of the candidate debates, and 21 percent said they had seen a campaign commercial. About one-fourth of the electorate read a political blog (27 percent ) or visited one of the presidential candidates' Web sites (23 percent ). Many of these sites, moreover, included videos directly embedded throughout their sites. Although social networking sites such as Facebook and MySpace have received considerable media attention in the past two years for their potential in online campaigning, only 8 percent of voters said that they had visited a social networking site to learn about the 2008 campaigns.[5]

Young voters were even more likely to use the Internet for campaign-related activity. An overwhelming majority (65 percent ) of voters between the ages of 18 and 29 said they had watched some kind of campaign–related video online, and 59 percent said they had read a political blog, visited a candidate's Web site or used a social networking site as a source of campaign information in 2008. Among voters between 30 and 64, however, 38 percent said they had watched a campaign video online, and 38 percent said they had visited a blog, Web site, or social networking site. Only 17 percent of voters 65 and older had seen an online video and only 12 percent had visited a blog or other campaign Web site.[6]

Another interesting difference that emerged in 2008 was that Democrats were more likely than Republicans or Independents to use the Web for obtaining campaign information. Among Democrats registered to vote, 43 percent said that they had seen an online video and 12 percent had visited a blog or other campaign Web site. As the Internet expands its reach in both news delivery and content creation, and the partisan loyalties of younger voters—those who favored Obama over McCain for president by a 66-percent to 32-percent margin—become hardened, the Democrats could be in line to significantly affect the policy agenda and the way that issue debates and policy alternatives are framed.[7]

While the rapid growth of the Internet signifies an exciting new direction in the way Americans follow campaigns, the 2008 campaign brought a transformation in the way they were learning about politics on television. Local newscasts continue to rank as the most popular news programs on television—capturing 52 percent of the viewing public on a regular basis in 2008 (but have experienced a steady decline since 2002). Since 2002, the three major cable networks (CNN, FOX, and MSNBC) have claimed the second spot and were watched regularly by 35 percent of the public in 2008. Only 29 percent of the American public relied on the nightly network newscasts (ABC, CBS, and NBC) to get their campaign news, representing a decline for the fourth consecutive election cycle.[8]

An even more significant change in television viewing habits is that more Americans increasingly are turning to late-night comedy shows to follow campaigns and current events. While *Saturday Night Live* (*SNL*) and other late-night comedy programs, like those hosted by Jay Leno and David Letterman, have mocked politicians and the news for years, more recent programs like *The Daily Show with John Stewart* and Stephen Colbert's *Colbert Report* dedicate their entire program to satirizing world leaders and current issues. The Pew Research Center's "2008 Biennial News Consumption Survey" revealed that 23 percent of adults said they sometimes or regularly watched *The Daily Show* and 19 percent said the same about *The Colbert Report*. Younger audiences are even more drawn to these two shows. Among those between 18 and 29, 43 percent at least sometimes watched *The Colbert Report* and 42 percent watched *The Daily Show*. Also popular with the public of all ages are "soft news" programs such as *The O'Reilly Factor*, *Larry King Live*, Rush Limbaugh's radio show and *Hardball with Chris Matthews*, which offer audiences a personality driven presentation of current events with content that emphasizes sensation and drama rather than factual reporting.[9]

Although Americans seem to be abandoning traditional media sources such as newspapers and the networks' nightly newscasts while turning increasingly to comedy shows and other forms of soft media, this does not necessarily mean that people are tuning out of politics. To the contrary, a study conducted by the Annenberg Public Policy Center of the University of Pennsylvania revealed that regular viewers of *The Daily Show* were found to know more about world events than nonviewers, even when education, party identification, watching cable news, and other factors were taken into consideration.[10] And a recent Pew study found that voters who regularly watch late-night comedy shows are more knowledgeable of current affairs than the average voter.[11] This phenomenon does not suggest that soft news makes citizens more informed and engaged, but that these programs tend to draw well-educated audiences and those already following politics. Well-informed young voters in particular gravitate to newer media to learn about politics. The candidates that fail to recognize these major transformations in news consumption and are not equipped to navigate this new environment will miss an opportunity to connect with a significant segment of the population.

## FOLLOW THE VOTERS: CANDIDATES AND NEW WAYS TO CONNECT

Every election cycle requires candidates to devise a communication strategy that builds on conventional practices, while seeking out ways to distinguish themselves from their opponents and adapt to current electoral conditions. In 1992, when the concept of a 24-hour cable news network was still considered the "new" media, presidential candidates began the practice of appearing on live television talk shows as a way to avoid tough questioning from the traditional news media and speaking more directly to the voters. In February of that year, Ross Perot announced his intention to launch an independent bid for the presidency in an appearance on CNN's *Larry King Live* and then appeared the following year on the same program to debate future Vice President Al Gore on the merits of the North American Free Trade Agreement. Since that time, few serious candidates for the presidency have not sat down at least once to be interviewed by King and take questions from viewers across the country. CNN and the other two cable news networks, moreover, have expanded their offerings of primetime interview programs hosted mostly by gregarious personalities such as Bill O'Reilly, Sean Hannity, Chris Matthews, and Keith Olberman and frequently include interviews with presidential candidates and others aspiring for national office. While most of these hosts have vast experience in politics or professional broadcasting, their format is geared more towards entertainment and drama rather than an in-depth examination of the issues, which allows the candidates to stay on message.

For the most part, primetime interview shows are watched by those who closely follow politics and are unlikely to alter their preferences and points of view based on the conversations and shouting matches they see on television.[12] Daytime interview programs that focus on the latest celebrity gossip, homemaking tips, and self-help advice, however, tend to attract an audience less attentive to politics. In addition, these shows tend to be popular with married women with children who have vacillated between parties in recent elections and, therefore, have drawn the interest of many of the presidential candidates.[13] In September 2000, both Al Gore and George W. Bush sat down for interviews with Oprah Winfrey on her syndicated television show. During the 2008 campaign, interestingly, Oprah interviewed only

Barack Obama, whom she endorsed and campaigned for. Obama also appeared live on *The Ellen Degeneres Show*, *The Tyra Banks Show*, and *The View*. John McCain was less active on daytime television, but did make an appearance with his wife on *The View*. Surprisingly, McCain received some tough questioning about his campaign tactics from three of the four hosts, including veteran broadcast journalist Barbara Walters. But, for the most part, the hosts rarely press the candidates to explain their issue positions or to defend charges they made on the campaign trail. Rather, these light-hearted, nonconfrontational interviews allow the predominantly female audience to gain some insights into the more personal side of the candidate, on the candidate's terms.[14]

Another way candidates have taken advantage of the opportunities afforded by the new media and further avoided traditional journalists has been to appear as guests on late-night interview and comedy programs. During the 1992 presidential campaign, candidate Bill Clinton inaugurated this practice by appearing on *The Arsenio Hall Show*. Donning a pair of sunglasses, Clinton closed the interview by playing "Heartbreak Hotel" on the saxophone before the live studio audience. The 2000 elections brought both major party candidates to *The Tonight Show with Jay Leno*, *The Late Show with David Letterman*, and *Saturday Night Live*. On separate occasions in 2004, Jon Stewart interviewed Democratic candidates John Kerry and John Edwards on *The Daily Show*. Even candidates who eventually campaigned for the 2008 nominations—Senator John McCain (R-AZ), Senator Joe Biden (D-DE), and Governor Bill Richardson (D-NM)—tried to jump start their campaigns by appearing with Stewart at their respective party's 2004 national convention.

Candidate appearances on the comedy show circuit skyrocketed during the 2008 cycle, as it become almost a rite of passage and an invitation that no one could refuse. Former Senator Fred Thompson (and at the time, a star of NBC's *Law & Order*) announced his candidacy for the 2008 Republican nomination during an interview with Jay Leno on *The Tonight Show*. On the eve of the Iowa caucuses, former Arkansas Governor Mike Huckabee appeared on Leno and played his electric bass guitar rather than campaign in the state.

John McCain was the most frequent guest on the late night circuit in 2007 and 2008, making four live appearances on *The Tonight Show*, three on *The Late Show*, three on *The Daily Show*, and one on *Saturday Night Live*. Barak Obama appeared live four times on *The Late Show*, three on *The Daily Show*, and one on *Saturday Night Live* during the same period. Hillary Clinton appeared once on all four of these shows as well as once on *The Colbert Report*.

Although she made only one appearance on the comedy circuit during campaign, McCain's running mate, Alaska Governor Sarah Palin, was by far the star of the season. Palin opened the show by appearing as herself in a skit with Alec Baldwin and Tina Fey, ending with her shout of, "Live from New York, It's Saturday Night!" She also appeared on the show's "Weekend Update" segment. That night's program was watched by over 15 million television viewers, the most to see a *SNL* episode in 14 years.

Although audience interest is somewhat limited, administration officials and sitting members of Congress also have tried to get in on the act. Jon Stewart and Steven Colbert frequently conduct interviews with individuals with various roles in the policy-making process, both in the United States and other parts of the world. Since 2005, *The Colbert Report* has included a regular segment to highlight the work of members of Congress and describe the constituencies they represent. Through 2008, 43 members of Congress have sat down with Colbert for an interview as part of the "Better Know a District" segment. Five congressional challengers also have appeared as guests after the incumbent whom they were challenging refused to be interviewed by Colbert. Also appearing have been the nonvoting members from American Samoa, the District of Columbia, Guam and the Virgin Islands, and also South Carolina Governor Mark Sanford. Although the very first interview in the series was with Georgia Republican Jack Kingston, 36 of the 43 members of Congress appearing in the segment have been Democrats.[15]

As with daytime interview programs, appearances on the late-night comedy shows allow candidates to connect with a particularly important group of voters. Many of these viewers are especially susceptible to persuasion, either because they are not regularly attentive to politics or because they are young and have not yet formed a strong identification with either party. Still, the candidates must contend with an interviewer whose main objective is to entertain the audience, possibly by throwing the candidate off message. Today, the World Wide Web is the single best medium for allowing candidates to communicate directly, without any filter, to a multitude of constituencies simultaneously while maintaining a great deal of control over their own message.

Although the Internet's potential was available to all in 2008, it was the Democratic candidates who were more willing to experiment online and integrate the Web applications into their larger communication strategy. Senator Hillary Clinton was the first of the 2008 presidential candidates to make the foray online by producing a Web-only video announcing her intention to seek the Democratic nomination, uploaded onto her Web site and YouTube.

This was followed by a series of live Web chats where she answered questions from the online community and then made recordings of those chats available online.[16] Later in the summer, Senator Clinton's team continued their online outreach by conducting a Web poll to help chose a theme song for the campaign. To promote the contest, Senator Clinton and former President Bill Clinton appeared in another Web-only ad that spoofed the final scene from the series finale of *The Sopranos*.[17]

A number of analysts were impressed with the innovativeness and production value of these videos and praised the campaign for attempting to connect with younger voters and the online community. At the same time, the Clinton campaign's experience also illustrated the hazards of the new media environment, where the multitude of participants makes it harder to influence the media's agenda and control their own message. For example, the song chosen by her online supporters was "You and I," performed by Celine Dion, a legendary performer but also a Canadian citizen. During the primaries and caucuses, Hillary Clinton's gaffes and her husband's tirades were broadcast repeatedly over YouTube and captured a significant share of the media discourse throughout the campaign. These experiences and the realization that their candidate was no longer the inevitable nominee forced the campaign to abandon many of its online activities and rely on a more traditional form of communicating their message for the remainder of the campaign.[18]

The Obama campaign was much more successful at using the Web to communicate their message and shape the media discourse. It helped that that they were able to completely dwarf the online communication efforts of every other campaign. Whereas Senator Clinton posted only 76 videos on her YouTube channel before dropping out of the race, Senator Obama had posted 944 videos by the same date and a total of 1,820 videos over the course of the entire campaign. Moreover, the objective of their online strategy was somewhat different than that of any of their rivals, as it was an attempt to demonstrate the participatory and community aspects of the campaign to both supporters and observers.[19] Many of the videos depicted the excitement present at campaign rallies with behind-the-scenes footage of supporters working enthusiastically for the candidate. Registered users to Obama's in-house social networking site, MyBarackObama.com, were not simply exposed to the usual talking points and materials that preached to the choir, but given the information, tools, and training to assist in contacting their neighbors and host events on behalf of the campaign. In a nutshell, Obama's online strategy was about selling the concept of the Obama campaign itself rather than promoting the candidate's ambition.

While the Obama campaign experienced fewer difficulties than Senator Clinton's, there were a few causes for concern. For example, the group BarelyPolitical.com produced a racy music video, "I Got a Crush . . . on Obama," in which an attractive, scantily clad woman expressed her love for the candidate and his message. The video has received over 11 million views since its release and, fortunately for the campaign, generated mostly laughs.[20] Also potentially embarrassing was the revelation that an Obama supporter produced a Web-only attack ad on Senator Clinton, spoofing Apple's 1984 commercial that introduced the new Mac computer.[21] Another supporter was pressured by the campaign to close the pro-Obama MySpace profile he had created in 2004, which had amassed a friend list of over 160,000 users, so as not to interfere with Senator Obama's own official MySpace page.[22]

While it is unlikely that any of these examples, even collectively, would have distorted the campaign's message or overall communication strategy, all three illustrate possible ways that overzealous supporters can alter the candidate's message and image that he or she is trying to convey. More of a concern, however, is the ability of opponents to use the very same platform and applications as the candidate, and to do so with only a small amount of resources. Throughout the nomination contests and the general election, the Obama campaign had to contend with video clips spreading over the Internet, exposing inflammatory comments made by his former pastor, Reverend Jeremiah Wright, and Wright's further exposure on traditional media outlets.[23] This story dominated the headlines for roughly a month and did not subside until the media, both new and old, turned their attention back to Senator Clinton's misrecollection of her visit to Bosnia as first lady.[24]

The Republican presidential candidates were relatively absent on the Web. Former Massachusetts Governor Mitt Romney experimented extensively with Web-only ads during the primaries. John McCain's campaign also produced a few ads for the Web, including a humorous, satirical ad in July— "The One"—that ridiculed Senator Obama's worldwide celebrity status by suggesting that he thought of himself as sort of a messiah figure.[25] But for the most part, the McCain team dedicated little time and few resources to the Web for their campaign.[26]

An examination of the traffic to the presidential candidates' YouTube channels and social networking sites illustrates more clearly the greater emphasis the Democrats placed on online communication than the Republicans. As indicated in Table 1, videos stored on Barack Obama's official YouTube channel received over 11.5 million views, the most of any candidate still in the race on the day of the Iowa caucuses. Hillary Clinton trailed far behind with only 1.2 million views, but this number was still higher than any of the major GOP candidates. Ron Paul, a former Libertarian Party presidential candidate with an independent Internet constituency, was the leader among Republicans, with his videos seen over six million times through January 3.

**Table 1. YouTube Activity in the**
**2008 Presidential Campaign, January 3, 2008**

| Democratic Candidates | Channel Subscribers | Video Views |
|---|---|---|
| Barack Obama | 14,307 | 11,518,246 |
| Hillary Clinton | 7,446 | 1,175,047 |
| Dennis Kucinich | 5,331 | 643,996 |
| John Edwards | 4,866 | 741,035 |
| Mike Gravel | 3,853 | 817,118 |
| Joe Biden | 1,799 | 422,493 |
| Bill Richardson | 1,715 | 595,042 |
| Christopher Dodd | 852 | 471,005 |
| Republican Candidates | Channel Subscribers | Video Views |
| Ron Paul | 42,692 | 6,547,547 |
| Mitt Romney | 3,826 | 28,671 |
| Rudi Giuliani | 3,001 | 800,492 |
| John McCain | 2,001 | 556,668 |
| Duncan Hunter | 883 | 422,141 |
| Mike Huckabee | no channel | 387,715 |
| Fred Thompson | no channel | 75,006 |

Source: Personal Democracy Forum, techPresident.com

Table 2 shows that there was a similar pattern on Facebook. Senator Obama had almost 183,000 Facebook members identify themselves as supporters by January 4, making him the leader among all presidential candidates at that point. Representative Paul again ranked second and was first among the GOP field. Senator Clinton had over 57,000 supporters, more than twice as many as Governors Huckabee and Romney and three times as many as Senator McCain. It was not until he became the presumptive nominee after his sweep of five primaries on March 4 that McCain was able to also have the most supporters among the group of Republican candidates. Obama maintained the top spot throughout the campaign, however, and amassed a network of 2,397,253 supporters by Election Day. McCain managed to build a network of only 622,860 supporters during the same period.

Table 2. Facebook Support in the 2008 Presidential Campaign
January 4, 2008–November 4, 2008

| Democratic Candidates | 4–Jan | 5–Feb | 4–Mar | 3–Jun | 4–Nov |
|---|---|---|---|---|---|
| Barack Obama | 182,898 | 364,207 | 665,187 | 875,286 | 2,397,253 |
| Hillary Clinton | 57,150 | 89,300 | 127,350 | 159,277 | |
| John Edwards | 28,867 | | | | |
| Dennis Kucinich | 20,595 | | | | |
| Joe Biden | 9,248 | | | | |
| Bill Richardson | 7,883 | | | | |
| Mike Gravel | 7,521 | | | | |
| Christopher Dodd | 2,457 | | | | |
| Republican Candidates | 4–Jan | 5–Feb | 4–Mar | 3–Jun | 4–Nov |
| Ron Paul | 61,670 | 82,134 | 84,558 | 88,176 | |
| Mike Huckabee | 26,381 | 47,676 | 57,558 | | |
| Mitt Romney | 23,710 | 41,479 | | | |
| Fred Thompson | 17,770 | | | | |
| John McCain | 17,001 | 42,671 | 79,695 | 134,417 | 622,860 |
| Rudi Giuliani | 14,914 | | | | |
| Duncan Hunter | 1,487 | | | | |

The Democrats' ability to better harness the potential of the Internet was also apparent in congressional races. While there was no significant difference between Democrats and Republicans in the percentage of candidates who created their own "channel" on YouTube, the Democrats were significantly more successful in attracting subscribers and having people view their videos and browse through their channels. Among Senate candidates, the 23 Democrats with channels had an average of 91 subscribers, posted an average of 37 videos on their channels, and received an average of 5,452 channel views over the course of the campaign (see Table 3). In contrast, the 24 Republican candidates with channels had an average of only 43 subscribers, posted an average of only 25 videos on their channels, and received an average of only 3,848 channel views during the same period. The gap between Democratic and Republican House candidates told a similar story.

## Table 3. YouTube Activity in the 2008 Congressional Campaigns

| Senate | Democrats | Republicans | All |
|---|---|---|---|
| Candidates w/own channel (%) | 70.6 | 72.7 | 71.6 |
| N | 35 | 34 | 69 |
| | | | |
| Channel subscribers (average per candidate) | 91.0 | 42.5 | 66.8 |
| Channel views (average per candidate) | 5,451.7 | 3,848.3 | 4,798.9 |
| Videos uploaded (average per candidate) | 36.6 | 25.0 | 30.4 |
| N | 23 | 24 | 48 |
| House | Democrats | Republicans | All |
| Candidates w/own channel (%) | 30.8 | 25.5 | 28.2 |
| N | 422.0 | 396.0 | 818.0 |
| | | | |
| Channel subscribers (average per candidate) | 29.4 | 25.8 | 27.8 |
| Channel views (average per candidate) | 1,881.8 | 1,517.6 | 1,722.7 |
| Videos uploaded (average per candidate) | 26.7 | 16.6 | 22.3 |
| N | 129 | 100 | 229 |

Note: Averages do not include data for incumbents who all ran for president or vice president: Joe Biden, Dennis Kucinich, and Ron Paul.

Source: Data collected by the author.

There also was no significant difference between the percentage of Democratic and Republican candidates who activated their official page on Facebook. Table 4 also shows that Democratic candidates for both the House and the Senate attracted a substantially greater number of supporters than their Republicans counterparts. Among Senate candidates, the average number of supporters claimed by Democrats was 1,853 compared to an average of 572 supporters claimed by Republicans. House Democratic candidates amassed an average of 417 supporters, while Republicans amassed only an average of 261 supporters.

The Democrats clearly were more adept at navigating the 2008 version of the new media environment than the Republicans.[27] Democrats not only were more comfortable with the latest communications technology, but also were able to hold their own on television and its expanding notion of public affairs programming. Republicans seemed to have trouble adjusting to the new environment for several reasons. First, it is common for the party in power to rely on communication and mobilization strategies that they have pursued and successfully implemented in the past. When the Republicans took control of

**Table 4. Facebook Activity in the 2008 Congressional Campaigns**

| Senate | Democrats | Republicans | All |
|---|---|---|---|
| Activated Facebook account (%) | 85.3 | 90.9 | 87.9 |
| N | 34 | 33 | 67 |
| Number of supporters (average per candidate) | 1,853.2 | 571.9 | 1,212.6 |
| N | 33 | 33 | 66 |
| **House** | **Democrats** | **Republicans** | **All** |
| Activated Facebook account (%) | 69.9 | 67.3 | 68.8 |
| N | 333 | 260 | 593 |
| Number of supporters (average per candidate) | 416.7 | 260.8 | 348.4 |
| N | 332 | 259 | 591 |

Note: Averages do not include data for incumbents who all ran for president or vice president: Joe Biden, Dennis Kucinich, and Ron Paul.

Source: Data collected by the author.

Congress in 1994 and retook the White House in 2000, analysts and their Democratic opponents heaped considerable praise on Republican strategists for their success at using the new media (i.e., talk radio and FOX News Channel) to energize core constituencies and taking advantage of traditional media sources such as the Sunday morning interview programs and the editorial pages of major newspapers to influence the policy agenda and public opinion. Second, Republican strategists and activists are used to working within a top-down organizational structure and find the unruly nature of the Internet foreign and unpredictable.[28] Third, the financial difficulties felt by the McCain campaign in 2007 prevented the Republican nominee from investing early in the infrastructure and staff needed for an extensive online effort. McCain, in fact, was one of the pioneers of online campaigning and may have been able to break new ground in 2000 if that campaign had been better planned and managed in its initial stage. Following his surprise blowout win in the New Hampshire primary over George W. Bush, McCain's finance team raised over $2 million through his campaign Web site in four days, a milestone in the short history of online campaigning.[29]

A diverse group of Republican Internet activists already have come together to try to convince their fellow Republicans to build a permanent, independent grassroots volunteer infrastructure fueled by Internet technologies and to recruit more candidates who understand the value of technology.[30]

The key for the Democrats during the next eight years is to avoid becoming complacent and believing that they have discovered an unbeatable formula for winning elections. Not only will the Republicans soon be able to replicate the Democrats' online techniques, but the media environment will continue to evolve and require new strategies to successfully navigate the new means of communication.

## CONCLUSIONS: TRADITIONAL MEDIA AND NEW MEDIA COLLIDE

The 2008 elections provided voters with many more options for learning about the candidates and seeing the campaigns unfold. In addition to obtaining news and information from traditional outlets such as newspapers, radio, and television, over a third of the public regularly uses the Internet for the same purpose. While almost all of the established media organizations have their own Web sites and are the most viewed news sites on the Web, Americans are increasingly turning to alternative sources such as discussion blogs, social networking sites, and content produced by the candidates themselves. Maybe the most surprising development in Americans' changing media habits is that late-night comedy shows are now considered a legitimate way to follow public affairs. All the major presidential candidates seemed eager to take every opportunity to appear on the late night shows and show a different side of themselves to the American public.

A media environment where the candidates, political operatives, and entertainers assume a major responsibility in helping voters hold their leaders accountable and selecting candidates is a troubling phenomenon. Clearly, the candidates cannot be expected to provide the public with objective information about themselves and their opponents. Instead, the candidates and their online supporters have their own responsibilities to carry out in the democratic process. The goal for most of the television personalities serving as today's journalists, many of whom have no professional training or substantive expertise, is to facilitate the most entertaining exchange with their guests as possible rather than uncover hard information, probe deeper into a subject, and place the news in its larger context. Studies have shown, moreover, that citizens who rely extensively on comedy shows become more cynical about politics and have less trust in government's effectiveness to address important problems.[31]

A significant portion of the blame for this deterioration in the gatekeeper function of the news media may rest with the media themselves. There has been a growing public disenchantment with the press and, specifically, the more established forms of media. Recent Pew Research Center surveys have revealed that only 42 percent of the public say that they have confidence in the press. In 1985, three in every four Americans expressed this confidence. In that same year, 56 percent believed that news organizations got the facts straight most of the time and only 55 percent believed that they tried to cover up their mistakes. In 2007, only 39 percent believed that the media tend to be factually accurate and 63 percent believed that they conceal their mistakes. A majority of Americans (55 percent) now see the press as politically biased, two-thirds (66 percent) perceive the press as favoring a particular side, and almost three-fourths (70 percent) believe that the news media are influenced by powerful people and organizations. Furthermore, a growing number of people see the press as unfair to candidates and lacking compassion for the people whom they cover.[32]

An analysis of the media's performance in the 2008 presidential election further reveals why the alternative media has become more popular. As in past years,[33] horserace reporting rather than an examination of the issues or candidate characteristics comprised a majority of coverage (53 percent), while issues and policy matters only comprised 20 percent of the coverage. On most occasions, moreover, the reporting consisted mainly of either simple descriptive accounts of the candidates' speeches and itinerary or an accounting of misstatements and gaffes by the candidates and their surrogates.[34] Thus, rather than compete in the new media environment by offering higher quality reporting, journalists and media organizations have continued the practices that have caused the public to lose confidence in them in the first place. And when they have tried to adapt, it has been to focus on the more sensational aspects and trivial aspects of the campaign.

For better or for worse, the new forms of media that came of age in the 2008 elections are here to stay. The youngest generation of voters is the most attached to the Internet and soft news sources for learning about campaigns and are unlikely to abandon them in favor of the media of yesterday. As these traditional forms of media have declined, citizen engagement and voter turnout have been on the rise. For the third consecutive presidential election, voter turnout was higher than in the previous election. For everyone concerned about strengthening the democratic process, the key phenomenon to monitor in 2010 and 2012 is whether this increased participation is accompanied by a greater ability for Americans to hold their government accountable for its performance. For traditional media, the key question is whether they want to be leaders in that process, or continue to cede these responsibilities to someone else.

# NOTES

[1]See James Curran, "What Democracy Requires of the Media," in Geneva Overholser and Kathleen Hall Jamieson, eds., *The Press*, (New York: Oxford University Press, 2005), pp. 120–40.

[2]Stephen Ansolabehere, Roy Behr, and Shanto Iyengar, *The Media Game: American Politics in the Television Age* (Boston: Allyn and Bacon, 1993), p. 43.

[3]Pew Research Center for the People & the Press, "Internet Now Major Source of Campaign News: Continuing Partisan Divide in Cable TV News Audiences," October 31, 2008. <http://pewresearch.org/pubs/1017/internet-now-major-source-of-campaign-news>

[4]*Ibid.*

[5]Pew Research Center for the People & the Press, "Liberal Dems Top Conservative Reps in Donations, Activism: More Than a Quarter of Voters Read Political Blogs," October 23, 2008. <http://people-press.org/reports/pdf/464.pdf>

[6]*Ibid.*

[7]*Ibid.*

[8]The Pew Research Center for the People & the Press, "Internet News Audience Highly Critical of News Organizations—Views of Press Values and Performance: 1985–2007," August 9, 2007. http://people-press.org/reports/pdf/444.pdf

[9]*Ibid.*

[10]Annenberg National Election Survey, "The Daily Show Viewers Knowledgably about Presidential Campaign," September 21, 2004. http://www.annenbergpublicpolicycenter.org/Downloads/Political_Communication/naes/2004_03_late-night-knowledge-2_9-21_pr.pdf. Also see Patricia Moy, "The Political Effects of Late Night Comedy and Talk Shows," in Jody C. Baumgartner and Jonathan S. Morris, eds., *Laughing Matters: Humor and American Politics in the Media Age*, (New York: Routledge, 2008), pp. 295–314.

[11]The Pew Research Center for the People & the Press, "What Americans Know: 1989–2007," April 15, 2007.

[12]The Pew Research Center, "Internet News Audience Highly Critical of News Organizations," August 9, 2007. http://people-press.org/reports/pdf/444.pdf

[13]Matthew A. Baum, *Soft News Goes to War*, (Princeton, NJ: Princeton University Press, 2003) and Matthew A. Baum, "Talking the Vote: Why Presidential Candidates Hit the Talk Show Circuit," *American Journal of Political Science* 49 (2005): 213–34.

[14]A complete list of every candidate's appearances on any television program can be found searching contents of The Internet Movie Database. Video clips of almost all of these appearances can be accessed either directly from the program's own Web site or on YouTube. For example, Sarah Palin's October 18, 2008 appearance on Saturday Night Live is listed at http://www.imdb.com/title/tt1294054/ and can be accessed at http://www.nbc.com/Saturday_Night_Live/video/clips/gov-palin-cold-open/773761/.

[15]http://www.colbertnation.com/video/tag/Better+Know+a+District

[16]See her announcement at http://www.youtube.com/watch?v=SJuRQZ2ZGTs and web chats at http://www.youtube.com/watch?v=jzxfVPeepGE.

[17]See http://www.youtube.com/watch?v=shKJk3Rph0E.

[18]Joe Garofoli, "How New Media Affected Clinton Campaign," *San Francisco Chronicle*, June 6, 2008, p. A14.

[19]For example, see Jose Antonio Vargas, "Obama's Wide Web," *The Washington Post*, August 20, 2008, p. C1+.

[20]See http://barelypolitical.com/video/link/1/.

[21]See http://www.youtube.com/watch?v=6h3G-lMZxjo and Lynn Sweet, "Big Sister Unmasked: Hillary Ad Traced to Staffer of Firm Hired by Obama," *Chicago Sun Times*, March 22, 2007, pg. 26.

[22]See Micah L. Sifry, "The Battle to Control Obama's Myspace," *Personal Democracy Forum: techPresident*, May 1, 2007, http://www.techpresident.com/node/301 and Michael Kranish, "Internet and Politics an Uneasy Fit: Campaigns Strain to Control Message," May 10, 2007, p. A1.

[23]See http://www.youtube.com/watch?v=hAYe7MT5BxM for the clip broadcast on the FOX News Channel.

[24]See the CBS News story in which a correspondent who was at the same airport as Mrs. Clinton aired footage of the event and Clinton's version of the event at http://www.youtube.com/watch?v=8BfNqhV5hg4.

[25]See http://www.youtube.com/watch?v=mopkn0lPzM8.

[26]See Jose Antonio Vargas, "On the Web, Supporters of McCain Wage and Uphill Battle," *The Washington Post*, June 26, 2008, p. C1.

[27]Michael Scherer and Jay Newton-Small, "Why Democrats Rule the Web," *Time*, April 28, 2008, p.34.

[28]Kalee Thompson, "Election 2008: Measuring the Power of 'Netroots'," Popular Science, January 3, 2008. http://www.popsci.com/scitech/article/2008-01/election-2008-measuring-power-netroots

[29]Richard Rapaport, "Net Vs. Norm," Forbes, May, 29, 2000 <http://www.forbes.com/asap/2000/0529/053_print.html>.

[30]Marc Ambinder, "Young Republicans Push Internet Organizing Priority," *The Atlantic*, November 6, 2008. http://marcambinder.theatlantic.com; see www.rebuildtheparty.com to learn the more about these online Republican activists.

[31]See Jody Baumgartner and Jonathan S. Morris, "The Daily Show Effect: Evaluations, Efficacy, and American Youth," *American Politics Research* 34 (2006): 341–367 and Jonathan S. Morris and Jody C. Baumgartner, "The Daily Show and Attitudes Towards the New Media," in *Laughing Matters*, pp. 315–32.

[32]Robert Ruby, "Public Attitudes," The State of the News Media 2008: An Annual Report on American Journalism," Project for Excellence in Journalism, March 17, 2008. http://www.stateofthenewsmedia.com/2008/narrative_special_attitudes.php?cat=1&media=13

[33]See Girish Gulati, Marion Just, and Ann Crigler, "News Coverage of Political Campaigns," in Lynda Kaid, ed., The Handbook of Political Communication Research, (New York: Lawrence Erlbaum Associates, Inc., 2004), pp. 237–56.

[34]Project for the Excellence in Journalism, "Winning the Media Campaign," October 22, 2008. http://www.journalism.org/files/WINNING%20THE%20MEDIA%20CAMPAIGN%20FINAL.pdf

# Chapter 9

## Game-Changers

### New Technology and the 2008 Presidential Election

#### Michael Cornfield

Change was the byword of the 2008 presidential election. It was the sur-name for Barack Obama's family of slogans and titles, of course: "Vote for Change," "Change We Can Believe In," "Change for America," "Unite for Change," "We are the change we've been waiting for." John McCain played off "change" for a while too, sometimes mockingly ("*That's* not change we can believe in!"), sometimes in an effort to co-opt it. Pundits talked often about the latest campaign occurrences as potential "game-changers." With this ver-bal hacky sack they kicked around the idea of whether the day's news would affect the outcome of the nomination and election. Sometimes, too, they ventured into academic territory and mulled whether the political process—the combined rules, norms, strategies, and tactics of the game—was being altered for elections to come.

Changes keyed to emergent information and communication technology, principally computers, the Internet, and mobile devices, were among the most palpable changes people experienced during the two-year campaign cycle. The "wired" portion of the American populace could check out an innovation as soon as they heard about it.[1] Others got wind of the latest in Web videos, online fundraising, social networking sites, citizen journalism, the blogosphere, voter data, and text messages via television, print media, and word of mouth. These changes were vivid enough to make following the campaigns experientially different than in 2004, or even the 2006 midterm elections. But we can all think of things that struck us as important when they happened, but turned out to be trivial. So it is worth asking, in retro-spect, how consequential these technologically related "game-changers" real-ly were for the outcomes of the primary and general elections, and for civic and political life, and even the very structure of the game. To change the game, and not just make an impression, new uses of technology would have to affect campaign strategies, public perceptions and discussions, and the turnout of volunteers and voters.

This chapter focuses on two big changes: Web video and social network sites.

# WEB VIDEO AND THE SUBSUMING OF POLITICAL TELEVISION

## A New Platform for Presidentiality

Like the citizens of many nations, Americans form an emotional bond with their heads of state. But there may be nothing on earth that compares with the protracted audition presidential candidates must undergo—a series of tests in the performing arts in which policy positions and coalitional strategies often take a backseat to the capacity of an aspiring president to connect with the electorate on the basis of the personality he or she projects. For generations, the principal conduit of this emotional dynamic has been a mass medium: radio, and then television. And the epitome of presidentiality has been Franklin D. Roosevelt's blend of buoyant optimism and constant action.

The model can be seen in microcosm in the three great performances that opened FDR's first term. His March 4, 1933 Inaugural Address, constructed and delivered as a traditional speech, set a tone of radiant aggressiveness. It was a dramatic departure from recent presidencies, one whose main precedent reposed in the still photographs, print accounts, and voter memories of his fifth cousin, former President Theodore Roosevelt. In FDR's first press conference, held on March 8, he allowed direct questioning from reporters and selectively permitted quotation. This began a series of 998 sessions that raised the profile and influence of Washington correspondents and simultaneously advanced FDR's control of the national dialogue vis-à-vis Congress and influential publishers. Then the first Fireside Chat, a radio broadcast on March 12, brought the president into close quarters with the American people as a fatherly explainer and protector.

Ever since, aspirants to the Oval Office have had to demonstrate a worthy personality in the company of media stars and the context of media formats. As media power grew, the party nominating conventions metamorphosed from decision-making institutions into infomercials. Presidential debates became star-making competitions. Candidates sought guest spots on entertainment programs, including interview slots on talk shows. News conferences were engineered for photo opportunities and sound bites. Consultants created radio and television ads and purchased advertising air time for existing programs to reach their audiences. A few candidates found mass media pathways around industry filters and standards. Ronald Reagan, a professional actor and, more importantly, a television show host for decades before he was a governor and president, had an established media persona and audience relationship, which opponents sought in vain to reframe. Candidate Pat Robertson presided over his own cable television show. Presidential hopeful Ross Perot purchased a half hour of network time for a personal broadcast.

The 2008 presidential campaign was the first to occur with the existence of an online media platform that offered the would-be presidents the reach of a mass medium, but with a markedly different architecture and aesthetics than radio and television. YouTube and similar portals for Web video with smaller shares of the online viewership are not broadcast media. They are multicast, in so far as they enable individuals to download, upload, and share content, an activity greatly aided by access to gargantuan and superbly indexed archives. Web videos do not fill the viewer's screen, at least not in the default setting; instead, they are embroidered with interactive options, for example, "rate/comment on this video," and hyperlinks to and from the rest of the Web.

These new controls and capacities made Web videos hugely popular in an astoundingly short time. YouTube began operations in February 2005. By 2008, its parent company Google reported that net users were adding ten hours of new video every minute of the day. In November 2007, according to the Web metrics firm comScore, 74.5 million people viewed 2.9 billion videos on YouTube alone (that works out to 39 videos per viewer, more than one a day); Google sites hosted 31 percent of all Web video viewings. By the end of 2007, one in four Americans had watched a political video online; by mid-2008, that percentage had risen to 35 percent.[2]

Before YouTube *et al.*, Web video was a sideshow. The hit video of the 2004 presidential campaign was the Jib-Jab parody of George W. Bush and John Kerry slinging insults at each other set to Woody Guthrie's tune, "This Land is Your Land." In 2006, with YouTube a fast-growing phenomenon, the loose coalition of activists and partisans on the left known as the "netroots" used Web video to carry out political sting operations against incumbents they wished to unseat, entangling Senators George Allen, Conrad Burns, Joe Lieberman, among others, in unflattering situations.[3] In 2008, Web video humorists and insurgents were joined by journalists (both professional and amateur, or "citizen journalists"), supporters, and the campaigns themselves in depicting the candidates. By this time, e-mail had been a direct line from candidates to supporters for more than a decade; in the 2008 cycle, in tacit tribute to the power of moving pictures and sound, campaign e-mails frequently contained little more than a synopsis and request to watch their embedded videos.

So here was a game-changer: Campaigns competing to promote their candidates' presidentiality through a channel where television and radio formats could be replicated, but where other forms were popular as well—and where viewers were in the practice of responding with remixes and original videos of their own. On January 20, 2007, two years to the day before the inauguration of the forty-fourth president, Senator Hillary Rodham Clinton announced her candidacy via a 1:43-long video with two featured sound bites: "I'm in it to win it." and "Let the conversation begin." Clinton was one of seven 2008 presidential hopefuls to announce their candidacies by Web video.

The conversation began, all right. On March 20, 2007, a video entitled "Vote Different" surfaced. Its creator, "ParkRidge47" (Hillary Clinton was born in 1947 and was raised in Park Ridge, Illinois) grafted video clips of Clinton into a 1984 television ad for Apple Computer. She was recast as Big Brother, the evil dictator in George Orwell's novel, *1984*. In the original Apple ad, Big Brother is propagandizing on a giant screen, and a rebel wearing an outfit emblazoned with the Apple icon hurls a javelin, shattering the screen. The "Vote Different" video replaces the Apple icon with the Obama campaign logo. The creator of the video turned out to be a political consultant named Phil De Vellis, acting on his own authority.

"Vote Different" set politicos buzzing. In response to criticisms that she was too uptight and controlling to be a good president, and a figure of the past instead of the future, her campaign devised an online contest to pick her campaign's theme song. On June 20 (something about the 20th!), to promote the winning selection and drive people to her Web site, the campaign released a Web video mimicking the finale of the television series, *The Sopranos*. Set in a diner, the ad included the following bit of scripted dialogue between the candidate and her husband, the forty-second president of the United States:

> SHE: "I ordered for the table."
> HE: "No onion rings?" (Reluctantly takes a carrot stick from the bowl on the table between them.)
> SHE: "I'm looking out for you."

The video was a hit. But it confirmed opinions of Clinton's critics as well as her supporters.

The advent of Web video appeared to expand the relevance of humor and music to public assessments of presidentiality. Jib-Jab garnered attention but had no political points to make. It lost the top jester's cap to an outfit called Barely Political, whose "I Got a Crush on Obama—Obama Girl" did not have much to say, either, beyond calling attention to Obama's sex appeal. Yet other videos used humor and music to advance arguments. Antiwar activists rallied around a clip of John McCain singing "Bomb, bomb, bomb; bomb, bomb Iran," set to the Beach Boys song, "Barbara Ann" (Obama would cite this in one of the fall debates). John Edwards reached what might have seemed at the time like the nadir of public humiliation as he combed his hair to a dubbed soundtrack of "I Feel Pretty." By mid-July 2007, a Pew poll found that 44 percent of the public had heard of at least one of these four videos ("Obama Girl," "Bomb Iran," "I Feel Pretty," and the Clintons' parody of the *Sopranos* final episode) and 27 percent had seen at least one.[4] The larger number attested to the fact that Web videos were regarded as news. They qualified as news because sufficient numbers within the news business, the political insider community, and the net user populations believed that Web video now mattered in the making of a president. YouTube was an accepted venue for the presidentiality competition.

Throughout the cycle, candidates, correspondents, and celebrities put forth videos to be viewed on demand and, ideally, shared. Clinton was not the only candidate to turn to contests as an enticement. Mitt Romney's campaign supplied a packet of video clips and stills and staged a competition for Web users to construct the best ad. In May 2008, the Republican National Committee (RNC) and the McCain campaign announced, via a video featuring then-McCain campaign manager Rick Davis, a contest pivoting off McCain's persona: Entrants were to record a tribute to someone they knew who deserved honor for serving a cause greater than themselves.

Now that we have YouTube and other platforms to access videos on demand by keyword, broadcast television is becoming the sideshow, especially for the tens of millions of political "attentives" who dominate participation until the very end of a campaign. It is likely that more people watched Katie Couric's subtly withering interview of Sarah Palin online than on television. The same goes for Tina Fey's broader, but equally deadly parodies of the Republican vice-presidential nominee, which lived in video from one *Saturday Night Live* to the next and beyond. Governor Palin's star debut at the Republican Convention in early September, as much a cultural as a political event, was seriously tarnished by the online exposure and discussion. (The Obama campaign was mute during this extreme makeover, which has not always been the case in similar situations: Vice President Hubert Humphrey publicly made fun of his opponent, v.p. hopeful Spiro Agnew, and v.p candidate Lloyd Bentsen humiliated v.p. candidate Dan Quayle, both on losing campaigns.)

Popular culture is smoothing the public migration from television to Web video. Just as early television shows consisted of vaudeville and radio acts, so early Web video relies on genres of contemporary television. However, there is more to political Web video than popular culture. In 2008, uses of the new platform for moving pictures emerged that incorporated elements of civic forums. The platform being what it is, these elements drew from town hall meetings and cutting-edge technologies as well as broadcast debates.

## *The CNN/YouTube Debates: A Big Step Forward in Campaign Dialogue*

Numerous Web ventures constructed venues for video-based dialogues between citizens and campaigns in 2008. YouTube was the most successful. It began in December 2006 by rolling out a section of the portal, or channel, dedicated to the election, entitled CitizenTube. It invited the presidential candidates to submit "call-out" videos which it lodged in its "YouChoose08 Spotlight," a featured collection or "playlist" on CitizenTube. Fourteen candidates posted videos, each of which attracted views in the hundreds of thousands, as well as a few dozen response videos. Each candidate received a channel to fill with content. Seven candidates for the Democratic and Republican nominations (along with former Speaker of the House Newt Gingrich, political activist Ralph Nader, and Speaker of the House Nancy Pelosi) agreed to answer questions from citizens submitted in video form on CitizenTube. The ten-minute compilations received tens of thousands of views.

The top achievement resulted from a collaboration between YouTube and CNN: a television/Web hybrid debate format presented twice, for Democratic candidates on July 23, 2007, and Republicans on November 28, 2007. These events turned out to be a rare instance of authentic corporate synergy, in that the debates exceeded in civic generativity what could have been accomplished through either medium alone.[5] Within the category of televised debates—which is to say, debates with enough press and public attention to make an impression on the electorate—the CNN/YouTube debates set a new standard for democratic participation by staging an open competition for questions. One did not have to be an undecided voter from the city where the debate occurred to win the prize of posing a question to a presidential candidate on live television, as was the case with the Commission on Presidential Debates' "town hall style" segments held in the fall of election years since 1992.

Entrants had one month to submit 30-second videos that would be evaluated on the criteria of originality and personal perspective. For the Democratic debate, 39 out of 2,989 qualified submissions became part of the two-hour telecast; for the Republican debate, held closer to the onset of the primaries and building on the success of the first event, 34 of 4,927 video questions made the cut. Unlike some other Web-based campaign dialogues, the CNN/YouTube debates stopped short of determining the winners according to which proposals received the greatest online approbation. Instead, the organizations chose the winners themselves. The judges selected some offbeat questions, notably one voiced by an animated snowman in the Democratic debate. But the questions (including the snowman's) were for the most part substantive, surprising, interesting, and occasionally followed up by either the moderator or the questioner.

One query came from an Alzheimer's caregiver—they appeared together in the camera frame, and another from a refugee camp in Darfur. Another person changed the game by asking Obama if he would meet directly with foreign dictators in his first year as president. Obama's affirmative answer launched a long and prominent colloquy that probably has not yet ended. In the Republican debate, Mike Huckabee's wit ("Jesus would never run for public office") contributed to his rise as a candidate. Meanwhile, candidates with less air time could do more than grumble offstage—they could (and did) take advantage of the Web to upload post-debate videos, which YouTube housed within view of the well-organized debate archive (which is still available as of this writing).

The best aspect of the CNN/YouTube debates consisted of the civic example they set. As Joe Garafoli of the *San Francisco Chronicle* noted after the Democratic event, "It might have been the first debate in which the questions…were more important than the answers."[6] It was exemplary to see individuals in charge of much of their own presentations, citizens given the chance to think, compose, and ask a question of powerful politicians before the entire world. Even when the videomakers resorted to whimsy or bizarreness, they took their civic responsibilities seriously. Their distance from the live event may have emboldened them; they could overcome any stage fright and improve their delivery through retaping.

In contrast to the citizen contributions, most of the candidate videos screened during the CNN/YouTube debates were stiff stabs at humor, or television ads that looked stale in the innovative format. But as the campaign cycle wore on, the candidates got better at it—particulary Barack Obama.

### Obama and Web Video: Preaching To (and Conversing With) the Self-Assembled

The 2008 election pivoted on judgments about Barack Obama's character. The question of whether the nation should continue in the direction and manner of the Bush administration had been settled in the negative by the 2006 elections; with a large majority preference for change being a given, the question for 2008 resolved into who best would lead the departure. Obama's chief rivals, Hillary Clinton and John McCain, were well known at the start of the cycle. They were famous for where they had been (the White House, a P.O.W. camp) and what they had done in politics. Obama's fame, on the other hand, rested almost entirely on his displays of eloquence in books and on stage. In negative ads, Clinton and then McCain hit Obama hard for inexperience and insubstantiality. He was, as one ad put it, the political equivalent of a Paris Hilton, a celebrity who could not, as another ad put it, be relied upon to do the right thing in a crisis. The ads resonated with many voters. Obama was of unfamiliar and, to some, controversial heritage: a mixed-race newcomer to elective office who had grown up partly in a Muslim-dominated nation.

Obama needed to inspire respect and trust in voters while seeming ordinary enough to be likeable to them. He needed to depict his opponents as denizens of official Washington (Bush-led, partisan-riven, special-interest dominated) while minimizing his own junior membership in that insiders' club, and keeping true to his self-definition as a politician who did not "descend" to attacking his opponents. To accomplish these goals, Obama relied heavily on a corporate-style branding campaign that systematically blended his persona with the sights, sounds, and ideas of change, youth, hope, and Abraham Lincoln. (America and the American people were part of the brand, too, of course, but those were not differentiating characteristics, or unique selling propositions.) As it turned out, there was a branding bonus for adopting this approach; the Obama campaign's very embrace of business marketing techniques for its message development and propagation achieved the purpose of distinguishing its candidate from everyone else in the contest, including, ironically, the corporate veteran Mitt Romney, who advanced a more traditionalist brand in traditional campaign ways.

The new platform for presidentiality suited his style of speaking, writing, dressing, and moving. Obama's smile, his family, his cool demeanor, his spectacular logo, and his palette of blue colors were ubiquitous staples in the content his campaign put forth. He dressed conservatively—including, after initial criticism for its absence, an American flag pin in his lapel. But he also appropriated gestures from the hippest reaches of youth culture (a shoulder flick here, a fist-bump, or "dap," there). A popular video of his entrance as a guest on the *Ellen DeGeneris Show* demonstrated that, as host Ellen DeGeneris exclaimed, "You are the best dancer of the presidential candidates we've seen so far." Obama was quick with a dry retort: "That's a low bar."

Through the Web, Obama's formal, meticulous, smoothly modulated remarks could come across intact, especially for those net users who opted to pause and replay videos and read transcripts. Such consideration played into Obama's rhetorical strengths. A commanding speaker, equally and extraordinarily adept at conversational exchange as well as oratorical call-and-response, Obama nevertheless typically communicates in the careful, sometimes dense, expository style of a professor. His rolling eloquence is appreciated best by the paragraph instead of the sentence or phrase; in a paragraph, one can appreciate his crisply formed observations and, most importantly, his calibrating of divergent positions so as to suggest, if not declare, that a compromise or consensus can be formed. One can lift sound bites from the quintessential paragraph of the speech that made him a star, the fourth from the last in the Keynote Address at the 2004 Democratic Convention: "There's not a liberal America and a conservative America, there's the United States of America"; "We coach Little League in the blue states and have gay friends in the red states." But the excerpts diminish, as do paraphrases, summaries, and exegeses. On the Web, the full Obama effect, spoken and written, is conveniently available for consumption, as it is not through radio, television, print, or live broadcast.

Since Obama's "back catalog" of speeches and writings are always accessible to everyone on the Web, corporate discipline in brand fidelity was a crucial asset as opinion leaders and voters made their presidentiality assessments. The satire of *The Daily Show with John Stewart* has schooled political attentives in how artfully rearranged clips from the Web archive can make a politician look vacillating, repetitive, hypocritical, contradictory, and so on. A day seemingly won by a campaign in news coverage can come undone at 11:00 p.m., after Jon Stewart and company have processed it. So, visual and political continuity in content and style are more valuable than in the era of "drive-by" television and radio, where remarks and images were publicly consumed in a single sequence. Obama and his campaign possessed the discipline to keep his persona consistent, particularly in comparison to Clinton's, whose campaign was riven by faction, or McCain's, a guerrilla campaigner at heart, devoted to improvisation, surprise and above all breaking away from a pack. Where George W. Bush was "misunderestimated," Barack Obama was unjuxtaposable.

The Obama campaign, like others, hired a videography team. Arun Chaudhary, a film professor at New York University, took leave to follow the candidate, along with two assistants.[7] For more than a year, the team recorded Obama in semispontaneous scenes evocative of postelection documentaries (hand-held camera, odd angles, sudden edits). The candidate was "unobtrusively" observed rallying his troops in his Chicago headquarters, scrimmaging with the University of North Carolina men's basketball team, mingling with the regulars at a barbershop in South Carolina, helping out with a phone bank in Colorado. Videos of these campaign mementos are interspersed on the Obama channel with his talk show cameos and speeches. Wherever one clicks, the same political themes and graceful movements surface.

The videos were part and parcel of the vaunted campaign fundraising operation. For example, an online $5 raffle to have dinner with him became "Dinner with Obama." Glasses clink and silverware rattles while the professor and host gently quizzes the four guests about their lives. He responds to their answers with sympathy and detailed knowledge about the programs that affect their lives, from veteran's benefits to student loans. In the second half of the ten-minute feature, the guests get to ask the candidate about his life, and he reflects on the privations of being caricatured in the media and away from his family. The video sells the next contest. Who wouldn't want to attend one of these events? It also shows off Obama's concern and common touch, attributes made explicit in the accompanying texts on the campaign site: "While a typical political dinner these days consists of officials being wined and dined by Washington lobbyists and bigwigs from special interest PACs, Barack will be sitting down with four regular people from across the country who will share their stories and discuss the issues that matter most to them."

The Obama campaign not only posted videos, it screened them at rallies and e-mailed them to voters who could not attend. Videos became part of the campaign's rapid responses, and a presence on the personal pages of social network users. The results were definitive. YouTube registered channels for 110 political candidates in the 2008 cycle, which attracted 220 million views. Half of those views went to the Obama channel, which contained, by Election Day, more than 1,800 videos, with 100 uploaded in the last week of the campaign.[8] That total does not include views for videos contributed from those outside the campaign. Indeed, the largest viewership for a political Web video in the 2008 cycle was garnered by "Yes We Can," a celebrity tribute to Obama put together by hip-hop star Will.i.am of the Black Eyed Peas.

The most notable sequence of videos involving Obama served a crucial function in the campaign's management of the March 2008 controversy over Reverend Jeremiah Wright—the pastor who presided over the Obama's wedding and who had coined the phrase Obama used to entitle his second book, *The Audacity of Hope*. Videotapes of Wright sermons, including a 2003 sermon with the repeated phrase "God damn America," were aired on ABC News on March 13.[9] Like all news these days, the videos continued to affect Obama's reputation (brand) through a protracted life on television and the Web. Remarkably, within a week, half the nation had seen parts of the videos.[10] (It is just as remarkable that until then, no one in public life had bothered to review them. Wright's relationship with Obama was well known, and the tapes were available for purchase at the church.)

Half the nation also saw parts of Obama's most memorable response, a 37-minute speech at Independence Hall in Philadelphia on March 18. It was viewed by more than ten million people in its entirety on the Web, without commercial interruption or journalistic intervention, and often with links to the Obama campaign Web site. Part of the viewership for Obama's response was stimulated by the campaign, which urged supporters via e-mail to watch and/or read the speech, and then forward it to friends. By the end of March, 2008, one in ten Americans had seen a version of the speech online. Obama's poll standing held steady.

The video measurement firm, Divinity Metrics, examined more than 200 video archive sites over a 400-day period spanning the second half of the 2008 cycle. In that period, 104,454 videos about Obama were viewed 889 million times, while 64,092 videos about McCain were viewed 554 million times.[11] After his victory, Obama modified the practice begun by President Reagan of broadcasting a message to the nation on Saturday mornings. He continued to use radio, and added YouTube.

### Conclusion

Web video did not supplant television as a political force in 2008, not by a long shot. Television's reach to voters who do not go online, and who go online but do not seek out political information, remains invaluable to campaigners. Yet Web videos have altered the shape, sensibility, and impact of television by chunking its programs and ads into small pieces, making them available on demand, and housing them as videos along with countless counterparts uploaded by what NYU press scholar Jay Rosen has dubbed "the people formerly known as the audience,"—a category that includes campaigns as well as voters. Videos gain further political value through their proximity to action tools, such as donating, volunteering, commenting, and sharing. They have additional salience by being available through mobile devices; the daily commute, once the province of radio and print media, has become another opportunity to view videos.

The Web videos of the 2008 presidential campaign are now historical documents, but they are not squirreled away in a library, awaiting declassification and rediscovery. Instead, as part of the Web, they will be recontextualized for use during the Obama presidency—by opponents, satirists, and the Obama team itself.

## INTERLUDE: A FEW WORDS ABOUT ALL THAT MONEY

For several decades, presidential candidates raised money to get to the point where they could accept public financing. Some used the onset of primary voting as their point of transfer from private to public monies. Even master fundraiser George W. Bush, who amassed $270 million for the 2004 primaries, accepted $75 million from the government for the fall campaign, on the conditions that his fundraising would cease (except for a couple of loophole functions) and that he would not spend more than that amount to win the general election. But in June 2008, Barack Obama became the first nominee to decline public money, after saying he would take it if McCain did. He risked public disapproval for going back on a commitment, and the chance that his donations would shrivel up, leaving him with less than the $85 million guaranteed to him under the public financing system. In announcing his decision, Obama said that the system was broken, that the Republicans routinely "gamed" it, and would expend "millions and millions of dollars in unlimited donations" to defeat him.[12]

The results of Obama's decision were stunning: So much money poured into the campaign that the Republicans' historical advantage in spending was shifted to the Democrats. From the conventions until the general election, Obama and the DNC spent twice as much as McCain and the RNC, $380 to $195 million. (Under the rules, national parties could raise up to $28,500 per person, as compared with $2,300 for a candidate in that period.) Analysis of television buys disclosed Obama advantages in the swing states of as much as 5 to 1.[13] Obama raised $150 million in September 2008 alone, and ended the 2008 cycle having raised more than $750 million.

The changes promoted and perceived in these bottom lines may prove extremely consequential for the future of campaign finance. Many commentators, not just Obama, have declared the existing system broken. A new system may be enacted and implemented by the time the 2012 or 2016 presidential election cycles commence. As that policy debate begins in earnest, however, it is important to recognize that the epically grand totals the Obama campaign achieved in its fundraising were more a matter of proficiency and excitement (hard to replicate) than approach and innovation (easy). He out-raised and outspent his rivals mainly through the same techniques that campaigns in both parties have relied upon: dividing prospective donors into three tiers of expected giving, high, middle and low, and then extending a different mixture of candidate access and appeals at each level. Like its predecessors and competitors, the Obama campaign publicized its low-tier contributions, amassed through mail, phone, and Internet, in order to demonstrate the extent of the candidate's popularity and his independence from special interests. High-tier events and meetings were pushed to the background.

Obama was a charismatic and disciplined candidate in a long, close, dramatic race, and money flowed into his campaign for those reasons quite apart from any new technological adaptations. But there were some. The Obama campaign counted the merchandise and event tickets it sold as contributions.[14] It developed "widgets," a vernacular term for readily portable packets of software code, that made it easier for supporters to set up their own fundraising pages, goals, progress indicators (e.g., a thermometer), events, and lists.[15]

For a winning campaign, it also attracted a remarkable percentage of its funding, 48 percent, in amounts of $200 or less. More than three million people would wind up giving money to the Obama campaign, and its leadership relied on this extraordinary number—as many people as gave to all candidates for president in 2004—to reinforce the theme that small donors were big deals for the future of American politics, proof positive that they were indeed changing the game for the better.

This claim has substance behind it, although much remains to be seen. A large number of donors and a high degree of diversity has the potential to act as a salutary check on the domination of policymaking by the wealthy. The Obama presidency may well put this view to its greatest empirical test. At the individual level, small donors are also regarded as good for democracy because they are not just "checkbook citizens," but campaign "investors" who become volunteers and spokespersons. At this writing the jury is out on whether the Obama campaign exacted and inspired more participation than usual from its donors. Small donors may also become repeat donors of small amounts, which is why the term "small donor" is somewhat misleading. As Michael Malbin of the Campaign Finance Institute points out, not all small donations derive from small donors. Individuals who gave more than once to a campaign sometimes graduated into a higher category. Strictly speaking, Obama's small donors whose cumulative donations remained beneath the $200 threshold accounted for 26 percent of his total givers, virtually the same as the 25 percent who donated to George W. Bush in 2004. McCain's technical small donors accounted for 21 percent and Clinton's, 13 percent.[16]

Vermont governor and presidential candidate Howard Dean's "people-powered campaign" depended on small donors for 38 percent of his total funders in 2004. Dean's campaign put the word "contribute," instead of "donate" or "give," in the action box on its home page because it wanted to foster other modes of activism from those who opened their wallets.[17] The idea that a connection between giving money and giving time and effort could be solidified through the Internet was not newsworthy four years later. But there were new routes for such connections, through social networking sites. And there were new methods to nudge people along those routes, on the strength of community organizing principles and traditions familiar in advocacy but not electoral politics. By stirring these two elements into the mix of motivations and activities, the Obama campaign was an authentic changer of the game.

## SIGNED, SEALED, DELIVERED: SMART NETWORKS
## AND THE MOBILIZATION OF VOLUNTEERS AND VOTERS

### Lincoln Would Have Loved Microtargeting

The purpose of the campaign field operation, or "ground game," is to move people deemed likely to support the candidate from their social circles into the voting booth at the appropriate time. The essentials of field operations have not changed since Abraham Lincoln summarized them in a circular he and four colleagues wrote while working on behalf of William Henry Harrison's presidential bid in 1840: Gather as many active supporters as possible. Assign them to geographic districts. "[K]eep a *constant watch* on the *doubtful voters*, and from time to time have them *talked to* by those *in whom they have the most confidence.*"[18] The durability of this two-stage model of mobilization—campaign to volunteers, volunteers to voters—attests to its superiority. But knowing that this is the best way to get out the vote does not make it any easier. Supporters must be identified, contacted, motivated, registered, reminded, and sometimes physically escorted to the polls. The volunteers carrying out these duties must be trained, assigned, monitored, coordinated, and rewarded. Both phases must be executed largely without resort to the two great enforcement tools of organizational life: financial compensation and the threat of being demoted or fired.

Advances in information and communication technology have been incorporated into the ground game in recent years, changing it on the margins, and making a difference in close elections. In 2004, the RNC and the Bush campaign parlayed a huge database of voter and consumer information, computerized modeling of likely voters, a Web interface for organizing volunteers, thousands of local group meetings, and extensive person-to-person campaigning into a "72 Hour Task Force" for voter turnout. The "72 Hours" refers to the last phase of the turnout drive, just before the first Tuesday after the first Monday in November. But the Task Force also focused on ancillary activities such as registration and early voting. Continuous intelligence was an important feature. The ground game became "smarter" by having volunteers update data as they worked. Seven million volunteers, including two million "supervolunteers" charged with additional responsibilities, added three million new voters to President Bush's totals. The impact was generally regarded to have been decisive, particularly in the battleground state of Ohio.[19]

Microtargeting is a prominent and expensive element of a cutting-edge ground game. The term refers to the capacity of a campaign to pinpoint individuals for voter contact according to what can be learned about them through consumer as well as voter and survey data. The hallmark of microtargeting lies in discovering—through customized appeals that bring up issues and identifications known to be especially important to them—population segments consisting of individuals who can be persuaded to vote for a candidate when they might not otherwise. Microtargeting profiles and models draw upon hundreds of data categories, or fields, and yield dozens of segments of an electorate.

Every time a campaign with a good intelligence system reaches out to voters, it receives data about how well the message initiative has worked. The better the feedback—that is, the more precise, accurate, frequent, and voluminous are the reports on how targets responded to contacts—the better the campaign's voter profiles, message contents, and delivery methods in the next round. (This intelligence-through-iterative-optimizing principle applies to the "air game" of media content as well.) For several years, campaigns from the RNC to Rock the Vote have conducted clinical studies in which responses from two similar groups of targets are compared, with one group receiving a "treatment" of a particular initiative and the other not. As a result of this intelligence, for example, when volunteers meet voters through door-to-door canvassing, they benefit from empirically grounded analysis that informs a campaign as to what sort of person to send to talk to a segment of prospects, what that person should say and not say, ask and not ask, what information the volunteer should include in reporting back to headquarters, and what the realistic rates of contact are for a particular precinct (e.g., 20 doors an hour per team of two).

Alex Gage, the microtargeting impresario of the 2004 GOP presidential campaign, worked for Mitt Romney in the 2008 race. Under his direction in early 2007, the Romney campaign purchased the names and e-mail addresses of 1.3 million people around the country who subscribed to or Web-registered with the conservative magazine *NewsMax*.[20] (Other campaigns did, as well.) Knowing who was reading *NewsMax* and how to reach them by e-mail enabled a campaign to craft messages to be sent to them right after a news article on a particular subject appeared. Depending on the extent of data obtained, it might also be possible to target readers of a specific columnist, respondents to ads and fundraising appeals, and so forth.

Democratic Party professionals were keenly aware that the John Kerry presidential campaign in 2004 met and exceeded its turnout goals in Ohio, yet still lost there. DNC Chairman Howard Dean plowed party resources into the development of a voter database comparable to that of the Republicans, and, more controversially, into building up local parties in all 50 states. So the 2008 candidates for the Democratic nomination could import microtargeting data from VoteBuilder.com, a party resource for field organizers. They could also turn to Catalist, a private company run by and for progressives, which licenses access to data drawn from commercial as well as political files.

Catalist has an electronic dossier on just about every eligible and registered voter in the United States. Its models predict the likelihood of someone being a Democratic donor and voter.

The Obama campaign went further in search of data and analytics. It contracted with another firm, Strategic Telemetry, for additional models of likely voters keyed to a variety of geographic, demographic, and issue-by-issue factors.[21] It also looked to social networking Web sites as a promising venue for recruiting volunteers, contacting voters, extracting data, and applying a fresh method to the analysis of the state of the ground game. With Facebook, in particular, the Obama campaign struck pay dirt. And it refined that ore through a social networking apparatus of its own: MyBarackObama.com, or "MyBO." But the apparatus was only half the innovation.

### Online Social Networks and Community Organizing

The newest large social networking sites (MySpace, Facebook, LinkedIn, BlackPlanet) received considerable attention from political observers in the 2008 cycle. These sites are homes for a new kind of social activity which one marketing consultancy has dubbed "communitainment": the production and consumption of content for social purposes.[22] Communitainment includes the posting of photos, random comments about life, links to content worth sharing, and updates on what one is doing at the moment (the standard Facebook prompt to an entry asks that very question). Social networking sites are virtual "third places" between work and home. They are inviting to those caught in the frenzy of contemporary capitalist life because one can come, hang out, and depart in a matter of seconds. Communitainment has cut into the time that people spend watching television, along with Web video and video games. By the summer of 2008, 65 percent of Americans ages 18 to 24 had a profile page on a social network site, the equivalent of a regular's seat in a pub. The percentage dropped off fast by age group: 45 percent for ages 25 to 29, 33 percent for 30 to 34, 15 percent for 35 to 49, and 7 percent for 50 to 64. Still, one in five Americans eligible to vote engaged in communitainment.[23] The sheer size of this subpopulation, along with the traditional role of young people as enthusiastic campaign volunteers, made social networking sites valuable territory to stake out in this cycle.

It was not a big conceptual leap for campaigns to seek support through social networks. Politicians have always made beelines to places where people eligible to vote frequently congregate. For 2008, many presidential campaigns put links to social networking sites on their home pages, a move that broke with the convention of the previous decade of campaign Web sites of not providing out-links to visitors. By May 2008, 14 percent of Americans between 18 and 30 had "friended" (linked to, essentially) a candidate on My Space or Facebook. One in four had sent e-mails about the campaign, and three in four had talked about the candidates with friends and family. However, this rising use of the Internet for campaign-related communication begged the question of what was being communicated.[24]

Extracting political support from social networking sites proved difficult. Voter apathy does not vanish in cyberspace. Nor does the ancillary challenge of coordinating unpaid volunteers bent on overcoming apathy. The Internet expanded the pool from which campaign volunteers emerge, making it feasible for supporters in Florida to contact voters in Iowa and New Hampshire without having to own a winter coat. This was a tremendous boon: Without the energy of volunteers, a campaign could not muster the enthusiasm to put together a good field operation. On the other hand, without the hierarchy of a structure that includes the power to hire, fire, or at least shift responsibilities away from underperformers, freelancers, and rebels, a field operation will lack focus, and be less capable of acquiring and dispersing resources well. In the space of a minute, a far-flung volunteer could do something productive—or destructive, or digressive. The Obama campaign appealed to antiwar and anticorporate activists skilled at being part of "smart mobs," protesters who mobilized on the fly. Young activists, in particular, were accustomed to political activity "often related to lifestyle concerns that seem outside the realm of government," according to political scientist Lance Bennett.[25]

How could a campaign find the balance between freedom and order? The Obama campaign's distinctive contribution to the answer was to draw on the progressive tradition of community organizing.

In any kind of organization, productive activities are divided according to roles, teams, districts, and other functional categories; activities are also measured according to quotas and deadlines. In any campaign, some people must fill the role of mediators between volunteers and staff; they must formulate and follow protocols for mediation, and there should be special procedures for the intense and high stakes periods of crises and mass mobilizations (rallies, votes). In tying this mediator role to community organizing, the Obama campaign sought to compensate for the absence of typical organizational enforcement mechanisms with the pressures of direct communication, both one-on-one and small group settings, and the inspirations of a sense of mission that was as much locally grounded as nationally (and to a degree, internationally) oriented. The core idea was that volunteers would agree to give of themselves and yet observe limits, in the hope that victory would improve their own lives as only community action can do.

Part of the community organizing tradition consists of resistance and confrontation against institutions viewed by participants as inflicting unjust policies on their lives. Another, equally idealistic but more consensual strand emphasizes the creation of "social capital": the forging of connections to share opportunities and resources (known as "networking" among business-oriented practitioners of the technique). Community organizers help local citizens define themselves and forge a shared identity through successful action, in both senses.

To meld community organizing with electoral politics, the Obama campaign staged an extensive series of training sessions for thousands of volunteers selected from an even larger pool of applicants. Temo Figueroa, a union organizer who served as national field director of the Obama campaign, described "Camp Obama" as follows:

> Attendees go through a vigorous two to four day program that includes training on setting up and running phone banks, planning and organizing a door-knocking program and role playing common scenarios from the campaign trail including the process of registering voters and speaking with voters about Obama's leadership on key issues. But the focus is also on building upon Barack Obama's vision for grassroots community organizing. We took some of the community organizing tactics—like relationship building and the ability to find common interests in people and employ them within this training. These trainings are about building local leaders in the communities and fostering long-term relationships to support our common values. We split people up into teams based on their congressional districts and they work in these teams from the moment they show up to the moment they leave. We create, in a way, mini-campaign offices with these groups—self-sufficient, interdependent teams that take responsibility for all aspects of a campaign within their congressional district.[26]

At Camp Obama sessions, recruits learned the drills of campaign field work, from voter registration to data entry, surrogate speaking to phone banking, while also learning how to detect potential leaders who could teach the same drills to others.[27] These "neighborhood team leaders" in the making were tested for commitment and competence, and then asked in one-on-one meetings to sign a contract stipulating their responsibilities. Deadlines and quotas were predicated on the relationships forged, as well as the data needs and strategic goals. Ryan Clay, an Ohio volunteer, came up with a precise and vivid metaphor for this process:

> Don't pass the baton to someone until you get someone else running at your speed. It's important for organizers and team leaders to find that point where a new leader is running at the same speed—mentally, physically, time-wise,

interest level, desire to win—all those things. You find that point, and then all of a sudden it hits you: they're running neck and neck with you and that's the time that you pass it off and move on to building the next new team.[28]

The basic elements of the smart network, then, might be represented in diagram form as a set of educational ladders for volunteers to climb; a hub-and-spoke map of the precincts and districts of the United States, with the Camp Obamas as hubs and the ladder ascendants traveling outward as field organizers imbued with a community building philosophy; inset maps with block-by-block routes for canvassers and voters to follow; and, at each point along the ladders, hubs, spokes, and travel routes, a corresponding swatch of arrayed data for headquarters to survey so that adjustments could be made. David Plouffe, the campaign's chief of staff, described the system thusly at Harvard's Institute of Politics on December 11, 2008:

> In our own campaign, polling was just one way we viewed how we were doing in a state in the general election. We had a lot of voter identification work. We had a lot of field data. So we'd put all that together and model out the election in those states every week. So we'd say, okay, if the election were held this week based on all our data, put it all in a blender, where are we? And obviously, with technology today, we could measure this very carefully. We don't have to wait for a state to report in how they did that night; we can look at it, down to the volunteer level, because we trusted our volunteers. We gave them the voter file, we said here are the people on your block, you go talk to 'em, you record the result of the conversation. We in Chicago could look at that . . .
>
> . . . It makes you enormously agile. You've got real-time data, and that makes you make scheduling decisions and resource-allocation decisions and where to send surrogates and you're adjusting those by the end multiple times a day. Not just down to the media market, but down to chunks of voters in those media markets. We're not doing as well as we need to here, so we've got to throw a lot of our resources in there. These guys are making a surge in a media market, we've got to go try and correct that.[29]

## Results

The Obama smart network experienced a few technical difficulties. For example, the campaign underwent an all-too-public dispute in May 2007 with Joe Anthony, an independent volunteer who had created a MySpace page for Obama supporters in 2004. Chicago HQ wanted to take over the page and the data about Anthony/Obama's 160,000 "friends." Anthony wanted financial compensation for the transfer. The results of the dispute remain fuzzy; it is not clear how many of those dossiers, and the people they described, made their way into the campaign, and at what levels of participation.

Joe Anthony did not get a position on the Obama campaign. But, as director of online organizing, Chris Hughes, the cofounder of Facebook, did. He started in early 2007.

The Obama campaign's ties to Facebook helped it reach young voters and volunteers, many of whom rely on it instead of e-mail, much as they prefer mobile to landline telephones. Facebook also gave the campaign a leg up on making use of social networks revolving around school ties. Much as the Bush campaign leveraged corporate and congregational clusters of people, so the Obama campaign would take advantage of existing networks of current students and alumni. A third benefit flowed from the Facebook practice of notifying group members when any of them agreed to take part in an event—automated peer pressure, as it were.

A smart network routinizes sequences of alerts and protocols found effective. For example, when someone joined an Obama-related group on Facebook, a campaign volunteer would connect with them online and ask for their phone number. The caller would draw on information in the person's Facebook profile to establish a social bond before asking him or her to attend, and perhaps help run, an upcoming campaign event.[30] Another example: Volunteers interested in joining the phone bank could access a list of 20 microtargeted phone numbers on MyBarackObama, and follow a series of prompts to execute the task. In Ohio, MyBO held a phone-banking contest, and the top ten callmakers won—what else?—a meeting with Obama.[31] In September 2008, Joe Rospars and the campaign's online technology team unveiled an application for use via the hot consumer device iPhone. The application enabled volunteers to organize their phone directory so that those residing in battleground states appeared at the top of the list. Like the device itself, the application became a bestseller, albeit offered for free as a download on iTunes.[32]

This application and similar mobile phone razzle-dazzle was effective because the Obama campaign collected mobile phone numbers. (The McCain campaign had no such data.)    Sound bites from Obama speeches were "mashed up" into ring tones. Among Spanish-language mobilization sequences, there appeared a mariachi music video and a ring tone with a reggaeton option, as well as full translations of the phone bank prompts.

Mobile phone users who indicated interest by texting the word "hope" to the campaign code number (62262) received follow-up messages seeking their zip code, so they assisted, however unwittingly, in the microtargeting process. Idaho was one of numerous caucus states where texters and others touched by the smart network were asked to participate in mock caucuses so they would be familiar with the often labyrinthine process before the day of reckoning. Since the training was so good that independents and Republicans often joined in, the Idaho activists ran people through their paces by having them support Superman, Batman, and Wonder Woman.[33] The announcement of Joe Biden as Obama's vice-presidential selection was text messaged in the middle of the night as an enlistment gambit.

The Obama campaign's field organization was most visible to the public during its huge rallies. Rallies were shows of electoral strength, of course, but they were also occasions to recruit, and reward those who recruited. When, for example, Oprah Winfrey appeared in a South Carolina football stadium in late 2007, blocks of tickets were given to precinct captains to disperse, while other tickets went to individuals who pledged four hours of volunteer time. Attendees were asked to text-in contact information, and to make calls to four registered voters whose names and numbers had been printed on flyers. After they did this, a representative from the Guinness Book of World Records showed up to certify "the largest phone bank" in history. By May 2008 the Obama campaign had staged and benefited from voter registration rallies in 110 cities.[34]

The *piece de resistance* was the nominee's acceptance speech at Invesco Field in Denver. The more than 75,000 in attendance were to be put to work (while they stood in line to pass through the security equipment, and while awaiting the start of the program) using their mobile phones to contact some of the 55 million unregistered potential Obama voters in the campaign data base. The campaign was especially keen to reach 8 million unregistered yet eligible blacks, another 8 million unregistered Hispanics and nearly 7.5 million unregistered people between the ages of 18 and 24. It also targeted potential voters on fixed incomes and those who had moved across state lines in recent years.[35] Approximately 30,000 phones wound up being used for outreach that night.

During the Republican Convention the following week, both Rudy Giuliani and Sarah Palin derided community organizing. Obama's campaign promptly received its largest single-day influx of donations, more than $10 million. By the end of the campaign cycle, one million people had signed up for Obama's text-messaging program. The e-mail databank had entries for more than 13 million people, who had received over 1 billion messages from the campaign, with more than 7,000 different messages. On MyBarackObama.com, supporters created 2 million profiles, planned 200,000 offline events, posted 400,000 blog entries, and started more than 35,000 volunteer groups. Approximately 3 million calls were made in the final four days of the campaign using MyBO's virtual phone-banking platform. On

Facebook, campaign supporters numbered 3.2 million, and 5.4 million clicked on an "I Voted" button to let their friends know they had performed their civic duty.[36]

One of the standard songs played at Obama rallies was Stevie Wonder's "Signed, Sealed, Delivered." Its chorus runs: "Here I am baby, Oh you got the future in your hand, signed, sealed, delivered I'm yours." It was an exemplary choice for a recessional, an infectious tune whose words were emblematic of the process newcomers embraced and enacted by the millions.

## CONCLUSION

Did the Obama campaign's use of the Internet and mobile phones change the outcome of the 2008 election? It is hard to see how he could have won without it. Yet it is equally hard to conclude that the technology alone—the Web videos, online fundraising, smart mobilization network, and (not discussed in this chapter) his rapid news detection and response system—would have sufficed. The Obama campaign's greatest achievement in connection with information and communication technology consisted of harnessing it to strategic purposes. Absent strategies to win the primary and general elections, and the discipline to stick to them, there would have been no focus to the technological applications. Focus was all the more important given the superabundance of options online technology makes feasible. Which links mattered most? How many versions of a message should be developed, and where should they be placed?

The strategies were plain to see. The Obama campaign's path to the nomination sought to take advantage of the proportional allocation of delegates. Defeating John McCain in the fall hinged on expanding both the electorate (as with the targets of the Denver phone bank, the main categories were young people, African Americans, and Hispanics) and the roster of battleground states. To implement these strategies, the Obama campaign integrated new media and old media to a degree without peer in the cycle. Other candidates matched the Obama campaign in several aspects of communication, but none matched it across the board of functionalities and media channels.

If something did not serve the campaign in its strategic judgment, such as having the candidate confer regularly with bloggers, participate in a series of shared-stage town hall meetings, and, above all, accepting public financing, it was accorded less of a priority or shunned altogether. MyBO did not create an API, or Application Programming Interface, to permit techies to build microsites and specialized functions as they saw fit. Instead, networkers used what was provided, under the coding strictures and protocols established by the campaign. Similarly, while community organizing and feeling was solicited, it was also filtered and regulated. Said Joe Rospars of the campaign, "We published content that reflected well on the community, that embodied the theme of community, that helped us tell a story about our campaigners that we could show back to them."[37]

The Obama operation was also proprietary in key respects. For example, there were larger e-mail lists out there than the 13 million on Obama's. One of them, compiled in connection with the 2004 film, *The Passion of the Christ*, had more than 71 million entries when its proprietor, Randy Brinson, an Alabama physician who inherited it from the filmmaker, allowed Mike Huckabee to use it. The data helped Huckabee immensely, furnishing contact information for 414,000 people in Iowa alone likely to be sympathetic to his message, information that fed the impressive "Huck's Army." [38] But Obama's list contains information about people who by and large had already demonstrated an interest in him. The specific nature of the interest was part of the database. So was the record of activity that followed. One Californian told Marc Ambinder of *The Atlantic* that when he donated money to the Obama campaign, he supplied his work contact information, yet they left a message for him on his unlisted home number to invite him to a meeting two blocks away from his unlisted home address.[39]

If something did advance the campaign, it was embraced and replicated and worked to the hilt. Message was knitted in along with strategy and technology. For instance, it was impressive when the Mitt Romney campaign ran a "make your own ad" contest enabling net users to put together clips and captions and voiceovers. However, the messages generated were all over the map. The Hillary Clinton "choose a theme song" contest was similarly engaging and novel enough to win some press. And there was an important boost for McCain and the Republicans when a Newt Gingrich message, "Drill Here, Drill Now," caught fire online as a response to high gas prices.[40] Yet contrast these sporadic successes with the "Dinner with Obama" contests: In a sustained series, the campaign asked not for ingenuity or slogans, but contributions, and the prize as visualized echoed the longstanding campaign theme of Obama as a man at one with people desirous of change. Hillary announced the winner of her contest; Obama was seen talking with and listening to the winners of his. And those dinners were connected to the same database being fed by grassroots canvassers. Within the smart network, organizers spread good ideas quickly for replication, as when one noticed in the summer of 2008 that canvassing at gas stations was working well with drivers irate about rising prices.[41]

The Obama campaign welcomed dialogue and dissent but (like CNN and YouTube) did not put things up to a vote. The most notable example occurred when the Obama campaign acknowledged a protest of his announcement in June 2008 that he now favored a bill permitting government wiretapping. While the campaign posted more than 15,000 unfavorable comments, it did not change back to its original policy.

Voting patterns attest to the success of the technology inflected, but not technology driven strategy. In the Texas two-step of March 4, 2008, Senator Clinton won the popular vote contest but Obama won the caucus through superior field organizing, and he netted five delegates. In the fall, Obama's Texas-based network organized bus trips to battleground states, since McCain was certain to win the Lone Star State. In North Carolina, where the Obama campaign maintained 45 field offices, Democratic registration rose 7 points between March and October, while Republican rose only 1 point. The state went Democratic. And if there is something to the notion that the young embraced Obama in part because of his embrace of the net, then there is one more number to credit: the remarkable 2-to-1 margin (66 to 32 to be precise) among voters ages 18 to 29, a 13-point difference from the total, and the first time since 18-year-olds were eligible to vote for president (1972) that the cohort was more than 6 points apart from the total.

Are the trends outlined in this chapter positive for American politics regardless of which party or candidate one favors? I think the answer is an unqualified "yes." We will be a better democracy with video subsuming television, because it promotes citizen activity over passivity. The same applies to the rise of donors who do more than just donate, regardless of how much they donate and whether the aggregation curbs the power of big money. And it applies as well to the development of smart networks in which social capital can be accumulated without having to resort to exclusionary motivations and institutional restrictions.

There are downsides, to be sure. Some argue the new technology amplifies an echo chamber effect in which likes only listen to likes, at the expense of fruitful community dialogue. The evidence of that effect remains undemonstrated online (as opposed to on cable television, talk radio, and small group meetings). Others worry about the speed and force with which rumors, distortions, smears, and outright lies circulate online. Yet such misinformation is more visible and combatable now that society-wide editing follows media publication, and "Google" as a verb means to vet, fact-check, and consult before acting.

Sometimes, change is good. That seems to be the impact on the game as a process after the campaigns of 2008.

# NOTES

[1] Nearly three-quarters of the U.S. adult population has access to the Internet, but daily usage is a better indicator of technological adoption, and that stood at about half the population in 2007–2008. Karen Mossberger, Caroline J. Tolbert, and Ramona S. McNeal, *Digital Citizenship: The Internet, Society, and Participation*, MIT Press, 2007. Available at http://mitpress.mit.edu/catalog/item/default.asp?ttype=2&tid=11334.

[2] General statistics from http://www.comscore.com/press/release.asp?press=2002; political video data from Pew Research Reports, "Internet's Broader Role in Campaign '08," January 11, 2008 and "The Internet & the 2008 Election," June 15, 2008.

[3] Michael Cornfield, "The Netroots Break Through: On-Line Campaigning in the 2006 Midterm Elections," in Larry J. Sabato, ed. *The Sixth Year Itch: The Rise and Fall of the George W. Bush Presidency*, (New York: Pearson Longman), pp. 167–190.

[4] Pew Research Center, "Campaign Internet Videos: 'Sopranos' Spoof vs. 'Obama Girl,'" July 12, 2007.

[5] An ABC/Facebook debate enjoyed large participation, but one had to be a member of the social network, and the end result was mostly noise, with more than 114,000 comments streaming by concurrently with the debate, and no search function or even a tag cloud to make sense of the commentary afterward. More coherent, but lacking in impact were the MySpace/MTV-sponsored chats with the candidates, featuring a moderator, audience, and streamed questions. The same fate met a Yahoo!/HuffingtonPost/Slate "build your own" debate, a collection of clips that users could assemble from candidates' answers to 15 minutes of user-submitted questions posed by Charlie Rose of PBS and featuring questions posed by comedian Bill Maher. None of these hybrid debates contained a live interactive element among candidates. The CNN/YouTube debates did, largely because its organizers procured the imprimatur of the DNC. After the Democratic candidate debate triumphed in public, the RNC had little choice but to follow suit.

[6] "YouTube Steals the Dem Debate," July 24, 2007. At http://www.sfgate.com/cgi-bin/article. cgi?file=/c/a/2007/07/24/YOUDEBATE.TMP

[7] Aswini Anburajan, "Obama's Auteur," *National Journal*, April 19, 2008.

[8] YouTube statistics from Steve Grove, Political Director, YouTube, public remarks at George Washington University, December 8, 2008.

[9] Brian Ross and Rehab El-Buri, "Obama's Pastor: God Damn America, U.S. To Blame for 9/11," ABC News, March 13, 2008. Available at http://abcnews.go.com/Blotter/DemocraticDebate/story?id=4443788&page=1

[10] Pew Research Center, "Obama Weathers the Wright Storm, Clinton Faces Credibility Problem," survey released March 27, 2008.

[11] Fred Aun, "Over Long Campaign, Obama Videos Drew Nearly a Billion Views," ClickZNews, www.clickz.com, November 7, 2008.

[12] Michael Luo and Jeff Zeleny, "Obama, In Shift, Says He'll Reject Public Financing," *New York Times*, June 20, 2008.

[13] Alec MacGillis and Sarah Cohen, "Final Fundraising Tally for Obama Exceeded $750 Million," *Washington Post*, December 6, 2008.

[14] David D. Kirkpatrick, Mike McIntire, and Jeff Zeleny, "Obama's Camp Cultivates Crop in Small Donors," *New York Times*, July 17, 2007.

[15] Joshua Green, "The Amazing Money Machine," *The Atlantic*, June, 2008.

[15] "Reality Check: Obama Received About the Same Percentage from Small Donors in 2008 as Bush in 2004," Campaign Finance Institute news release, November 24, 2008.

[17]Nicco Mele, "A Web Activist Finds Dean," in Zephyr Teachout and Thomas Streeter, et al., *Mousepads, Shoe Leather, and Hope: Lessons from the Howard Dean Campaign for the Future of Internet Politics* (Boulder, CO: Paradigm Publishers, 2008), p. 187.

[18]Circular as cited and described in Doris Kearns Goodwin, *Team of Rivals: The Political Genius of Abraham Lincoln* (New York: Simon and Schuster, 2005), p. 89.

[19]Republican National Committee, "72 Hour Task Force –A National Effort," undated public statement, accessed November 20 2008. At www.72hour.org/72Hour.pdf.

[20]Scott Helman, "Candidates Spend Heavily on Voter Lists," *Boston Globe*, July 19, 2007.

[21]Marc Ambinder, "How To Tell Your VoteBuilders From Your MyBOs, Your Catalists From Your VANs," *TheAtlantic.com*, November 14, 2008.

[22]Safa Rashtchy, "The User Revolution: The New Advertising Ecosystem and the Rise of the Internet as a Mass Medium," research report from Piper Jaffray Companies, February 2007. www.piperjaffray.com/1col.aspx?id=287&releaseid=966627

[23]Pew Research Center, "Key News Audiences Now Blend Online and Traditional Sources: Audience Segments in a Changing News Environment," survey report, August 17, 2008.

[24]Democracy Corps, "The My Space Election," May 5, 2008 public memo posted at www.democracycorps.com .

[25]W.L. Bennett, "Changing Citizenship in the Digital Age," essay posted at www.oecd.org/dataoecd/0/8/38360794.pdf .

[26]Memo posted on barackobama.com August 29, 2007. Also see Zack Exley, "Obama Organizers Plot A Miracle," www.huffingtonpost.com, August 27, 2007.

[27]Peter Slevin, "Obama Volunteers Share the Power of Personal Stories," *Washington Post*, July 26, 2008.

[28]Zack Exley, "The New Organizers," blog post at www.oxdown.firedoglake.com/diary/546 .

[29]Colin Delany, blog post, Dec. 23, 2008. At www.epolitics.com.

[30]Joe Garofoli, "Appetite for change finally draws young voters to the polls," *San Francisco Chronicle*, January 6, 2008.

[31]Brian C. Mooney, "Technology aids Obama's outreach drive; Volunteers answer call on social networking site," *Boston Globe*, February 24, 2008.

[32]Ari Melber, "Obama's Web-Savvy Voter Plan," *The Nation*, October 27, 2008.

[33]Aaron Rutkoff, "Texting for Votes In Unusual Radio Ads, Obama Asks Listeners To Send Text Messages," *Wall Street Journal Online*, February 5, 2008.

[34]Marc Ambinder, "Obama's Massive Voter Registration Kickoff," blog post, *TheAtlantic.com*, May 9, 2008.

[35]Nedra Pickler, "Obama's Convention Crowd: Biggest Phone Bank Ever," Associated Press, July 30, 2008.

[36]Jose Antonio Vargas, "Obama Raised Half a Billion Online," *WashingtonPost.com*, November 20, 2008.

[37]Comments at Google/National Journal conference, June 11, 2008, Washington, D.C.

[38]Chris Cilazza and Shailagh Murray, "The Man Who Helped Start Huckabee's Roll," *Washington Post*, December 2, 2007.

[39]Ambinder *op cit.*, May 9, 2008.

[40]Avi Zenilman, "Drill Now as the Conservative MoveOn?" *Politico*, July 1, 2008.

[41]Peter Slevin *op cit.*, July 26, 2008.

# Chapter 10

# The Nominating Process in 2008: A Look Inside the Rube Goldberg

## Alexander George Theodoridis[1]

## DID THE RULES DECIDE?[2]

The party and state rules governing the nominating process achieved greater salience in 2008 than they have in recent election cycles. On the Democratic side, in particular, these often quite complex rules played a visible role in shaping a closely contested race between Barack Obama and Hillary Clinton. Just as the Election 2000 aftermath in Florida taught many voters, scholars, political operatives, and journalists about the varieties of chad and types of voting machines, the drawn-out contest between Clinton and Obama served as a pedagogic instrument when it came to topics such as "superdelegates," proportional allocation, odd- and even-number districts, the sanctions for states jumping ahead of their assigned "window" in the calendar, and the various incarnations of primaries and caucuses.

Scholarship and conventional wisdom have tended to characterize nominating contests in the post-McGovern-Fraser world, less in terms of delegate count and more in terms of momentum built through media depictions of the horserace,[3] or the power of elites as expressed through endorsements and financial backing during an "invisible primary" preceding the state-by-state primaries and caucuses.[4] (The McGovern-Fraser Commission is discussed in this chapter.) And, in fact, recent presidential nominating battles have not appeared to be waged primarily over delegates. The front-runner was established either by lining up endorsements and contributions before the voting started or by performing well in the early contests. Then, most of the delegates needed for the nomination were racked up after most or all of the serious contenders had dropped out. After this front-runner established his grip on the nomination, most of the remaining contests, at best, took on the air of a coronation or, at worst, held no significance at all. Of course, even in a race like the one just described, the rules do matter. In particular, the structure of the nominating calendar is important, especially when momentum is the key force. And, presumably, other structural features of the process are important via backward induction even when the nomination is effectively decided by endorsements and contributions.

In 2008, however, the impact of the rules was far more direct and overt, even if for no other reason than the fact that the race was so closely contested on the Democratic side. Observers have suggested that the failure of the Clinton campaign to anticipate the importance of amassing pledged delegates was central to the early front-runner's failure to win the Democratic nomination.[5] Obama's campaign, on the other hand, is credited with pursuing a strategy that recognized the importance of securing pledged delegate support, despite the aforementioned conventional wisdom suggesting that modern presidential nominations are won either before or during the first few contests. Whether they were thrust to the forefront by the near-even split of the Democratic Party or by the strategies pursued by the two campaigns, the rules played a prominent role in 2008.

This chapter examines some of these rules and their impact on this historic nominating contest. Special attention is paid here to the Democratic Party, for a variety of reasons. For starters, even a quick glance at the evolution of the nominating process rules over the last few decades reveals that much of the action has been on the Democratic side, with the Republican process being transformed by some very significant spillover effects. This means that the rules are considerably more consistent among the Democratic contests and can thus be expected to have greater across-the-board impact. The more important reasons, however, for the focus in this chapter have to do with the specific dynamics of the 2008 election. Given the pro-Democratic tide this year, one could argue that the Democratic nominating contest was where much of the real "selection" took place in this presidential election. It is certainly where most of the suspense resided. Therefore, for the sake of documenting and assessing the importance of the rules in this presidential contest, the Democratic side of things is far more noteworthy. Lastly, the Republican contest this year was neither as close nor as protracted as the Democratic one. Thus, it is more difficult to examine the marginal effects of certain rules and procedures in that race. That is not to say that the rules governing the GOP nominating process were not important. In fact, I will argue that they were just as important. They will, however, be discussed primarily as a point of comparison with the Democratic rules, thus highlighting contrasts that helped create vastly different dynamics in the two parties.

The chapter begins by providing some historical context interspersed with discussion of some theory related to the nominating process. We will then go on to examine various aspects of the rules and the ways in which the Clinton and Obama campaigns navigated the process. The nominating cal-

endar is discussed with special attention paid to Florida and Michigan's decisions to break with party rules in scheduling their contests. These decisions
were consistent with the quickly resolved, momentum-centered nominating
contests in recent cycles (and even this year, on the Republican side), but
turned out to be problematic given the importance of the delegate count in
the 2008 Democratic race. Also addressed is the role of "superdelegates"
(party leaders and elected officials, or PLEOs) in the Democratic Party
process. This class of delegate exists partly as a check on the influence of the
mass electorate and an effort to appease party elites, but has not played a
noticeable role in the recent past. As this year's nominating process proceed-
ed, the PLEOs became central to any Clinton strategy for victory and therefore began to garner critical attention.[6] However, as suggested above, the
bulk of this chapter will be focused on the rules governing the allocation of
pledged delegates, both to jurisdictions and then to candidates, especially on
the Democratic side. The history of these rules will be assessed, especially
the ways in which they have accumulated over recent decades. I compare
the results under the current allocation paradigm with what they would have
been under alternative approaches.

## HISTORY

It is a peculiarity of American government that after more than 200 years no
fixed system exists for selecting the president of the United States. Almost every
nomination contest brings with it a different arrangement for the schedule of primaries, the allocation of delegates, and the regulation of campaign finance. No
one can get used to the system before it has changed again . . . To invoke the
wooden terminology of political science, the presidential nomination system has
not achieved full "institutionalization."

James W. Ceaser[7]

The nominating process is, indeed, a peculiar "institution" in American
politics. It is notable that such a key feature of our political system is not guid-
ed by our Constitution. Many of the founders, after all, were wary of the role
that "factions" might play. Thus, our founding document did not mention parties, let alone contain provisions for the selection of nominees by those parties
for the nation's highest office. The entirety of today's presidential selection
process is starkly different from what the Constitution outlines. The Electoral
College is still the official locus of selection, but even the meeting of that body
has taken on a character far from what the founders anticipated. The emergence of a party based system is largely responsible for the deviation.[8]

Desirable or not, parties have been part of American politics and the presidential selection process since just about the very beginning. After George Washington's two terms, the next two decades saw party presidential candidates selected by partisan congressional caucuses. After tumultuous elections in 1824 and 1828, the job of selecting party nominees fell to national conventions for the rest of the nineteenth century. During this period, control over the selection process was limited to a small number of elites.

The nomination process after 1908, but before the 1970s, is referred to as a "mixed system." Party organizations and bosses were still largely decisive during this period, but public opinion did have some new outlets for expression as the process unfolded.[9]

Consideration of the relative influence of elites and the mass public has motivated analysis of the nominating process over the last hundred years.[10] It is under the mixed system that some uncertainty begins to emerge. This period, especially after World War II, is largely characterized by nominating contests playing an advisory role in the selection of the party nominees. Delegates would choose the nominee, but most delegates were controlled by the state party organizations. It could be said that voters would weigh in during the primaries and then party leaders would select whomever they preferred at the convention. Victory for a candidate in "beauty contest" primaries did not always translate into securing even the delegates from that state. And, many delegates were still selected by way of closed, and unpublicized, caucuses. There is some debate as to the extent to which party insiders lost or retained control of the process under the mixed system, especially after 1950. Some scholars argued that candidate appeal to the mass public and mass media mattered more in the nominating process of that era (between 1950 and 1970) than it had before, suggesting that the mass electorate may be beginning to substantially influence the parties and the process. Others have suggested that the process still remained fundamentally controlled by the parties. As Cohen et al. put it: "The two parties . . . kept candidates, pollsters, journalists—the so-called forces of mass democracy—at bay throughout the final years of the old system. They faced strong challenges, but they responded effectively."[11]

While I will not weigh in regarding the relative importance of mass and elite opinion in the 1950s and 1960s,[12] it is useful to highlight the extent to which the system of that era differs substantially from today's process. It is difficult to imagine, for instance, a candidate today dominating the primaries but losing the nomination at the convention. This is precisely what happened in 1952, though. Tennessee Senator Estes Kefauver won 12 of 15 primaries, but lost the nomination to Illinois Governor Adlai Stevenson. It was quite common for candidates to forego campaigning, even failing to place their names on the ballot, in many state contests. And, even candidates who effectively used the primaries sometimes did so by picking a few contests to display their electoral prowess and popular appeal for the purpose of swaying state party leaders around the country. John F. Kennedy, for instance, famously used the West Virginia primary to prove that he could win among non-Catholics.

The nominating process history most directly relevant to this chapter begins with the 1968 Democratic race, a contest that again showcased the power of party insiders. It was an especially tumultuous time for the nation as a whole, and the Democratic Party would serve as a worthy microcosm that year. Minnesota Senator Eugene McCarthy, who vocally opposed the war in Vietnam, challenged incumbent President Lyndon Johnson for the nomination. After McCarthy exceeded expectations by coming within 7 percentage points of Johnson in the New Hampshire primary, New York Senator and former Attorney General Robert Kennedy decided to enter the race. Johnson, surprisingly, opted to not seek the nomination and vowed he would not accept it if offered. When Johnson exited the race, Vice President Hubert Humphrey entered it, but did not campaign in any primaries, instead focusing on garnering support from party elites and delegates in states where no primaries were held. McCarthy and Kennedy, meanwhile, battled for popular votes in several states, including the June 4 California primary, which was billed as decisive in the race between the two senators. Kennedy won that primary, but he was assassinated just minutes after making his victory speech.[13]

This set the stage for the infamous 1968 Democratic National Convention in Chicago, a gathering etched deeply into the American political consciousness. Clashes raged between anti-Vietnam protesters and police in the streets of the Windy City, and the tumult even made its way onto the convention floor. Reporters, such as Dan Rather, were memorably seen being bounced around in the mayhem. The "Chicago Eight" (later, when defendant Bobby Seale has his trial severed, the "Chicago Seven" ) would gain national prominence and draw indictments. The machinations of Chicago Mayor Richard J. Daley became even more legendary. And, amid the chaos, the Convention chose Humphrey as the party standard bearer. The choice of Humphrey, on the first ballot no less, was viewed as incongruous with the fact that the vast majority of primary votes had been cast in favor of explicitly antiwar candidates. The disenchantment and division within the party was only heightened by Humphrey's loss to Richard Nixon in the general election.[14]

McCarthy supporters had come to the convention in Chicago demanding reform of the nominating process and the gathering's outcome only heightened the strength of this call. Humphrey granted the request and the convention created the Commission on Party Structure and Delegate Selection. This would come to be called the McGovern-Fraser Commission, for South Dakota Senator George McGovern and Minnesota Congressman Donald Fraser, and would fundamentally change the nominating process.

To begin with, the reforms put forward by the McGovern-Fraser Commission and adopted by the Democratic National Committee (DNC) created national rules, usurping the power of the state parties. The state parties would have to comply with these national rules if they wished their delegates to be seated at the Democratic National Convention. These reforms served to take control of delegate allocation away from state party central committees, which would now be allowed to select no more than ten percent of the delegates. Party meetings for the purpose of delegate selection had to be well publicized. And, although it was not the Commission's intention, these reforms led to a proliferation of primaries, which now dominate the process. In 1968, 17 jurisdictions held Democratic primaries for presidential selection. In 2008, that number was 41.[15]

After McGovern, demonstrating mastery of the rules he had helped draft, won the Democratic nomination in 1972 and went on to lose badly to Richard Nixon, the Democratic National Committee created the Mikulski Commission to examine the nominating process. The most notable legacy of this commission, named for then Baltimore city councilwoman and current Maryland Senator Barbara Mikulski, is the requirement that delegates be allocated proportionally to all candidates with at least 15 percent of the vote. In 1976, the Winograd Commission, named for Michigan Democrat Morley Winograd, contributed the notion of a "window" for the completion of the nominating process. Primaries would need to be scheduled within a three-month window, an innovation some believe was designed to protect incumbents.[16]

In 1980, the Democratic Party was, once again, divided, with Senator Edward Kennedy taking his challenge of incumbent President Jimmy Carter all the way to the convention. After this contentious battle for the nomination, the Hunt Commission, named for North Carolina Governor James Hunt, was created. The Hunt Commission's primary impact was to reassert the role of party elites, most notably by creating a new class of delegates. The Hunt Commission recommended adding a slate of uncommitted party leaders and elected officials (PLEOs) to the convention delegates. This new automatic category of delegates, commonly referred to as superdelegates, would receive special attention during the 2008 Democratic contest. In 1984, the DNC created the Fairness Commission, which was chaired by South Carolina Democrat Donald Fowler. This commission contributed relatively modest reforms, primarily increasing the percentage of PLEOs.

Reforms of the Republican process have been far less substantial and not mandated to the same extent by the national party. In fact, much of the change that has occurred on the Republican side during the same period has come about because the Democratic Party reforms forced changes at the state level that have impacted the Republican nominating process.

Examinations of the nominating process in the post-McGovern-Fraser era initially tended to express great concern that the power of the party leadership and state parties had been forfeited to the masses.[17] "Once upon a time, presidential nominations were won by candidates who courted the support of party leaders from the several states," write Polsby, Wildavsky and Hopkins. "These leaders appeared at the national conventions as representatives of their state parties. That system is history. Now, nominations are won by accumulating pledged delegates in a state-by-state march through primary elections and delegate-selection caucuses—a time-consuming, complicated, and costly process."[18] In this new system, according to Larry Bartels, momentum gained from media accounts of the horse race became central to a candidate's success.[19] More recently, Cohen et al. have argued that party leaders, albeit a larger group than occupied the "smoke-filled rooms" of the past, have recovered some control over the process. Those leaders, it is suggested, have effectively employed an "invisible primary," which precedes the state contests, as a means of preventing the selection by voters of a candidate unacceptable to party elites.[20]

The nominating process rules, especially those governing delegate allocation, seem to have received less scholarly attention in recent years as compared to previous decades.[21] This may be because the 1970s and 1980s saw more fundamental change in this area. Relatedly, it may be that the fundamental questions surrounding this topic had been largely addressed. It is also possible, however, that the nature of recent contests had not suggested the importance of these rules. In 2008, though, there is little doubt that the rules played an important role in a very close race between Senators Hillary Clinton and Barack Obama.

## STRATEGY

The suggestion that the rules featured prominently in a given nominating process should not be interpreted as an assertion that the process was arbitrary. It certainly does not imply that the winning campaign is less deserving of credit, or the winning candidate of less esteem. Quite the opposite: The rules are especially important when one campaign develops a strategy that fully recognizes their implications and/or a campaign pursues a strategy that fails to do so. Both were arguably the case in 2008. Obama proved a remarkable candidate in terms of his ability to inspire passion among his followers. His campaign was unprecedented in terms of fundraising, especially on the Internet and among smaller donors, and organization—particularly on the ground. For these reasons and others, the Obama campaign for the Democratic nomination will likely be remembered as one of the great strategic successes in the history of modern American electoral politics. A comprehension of the "rules of the game" was part of that success.

Fair or not, the Clinton campaign will be regarded as fundamentally outmatched in this area. Clinton entered the race as the frontrunner as far as conventional wisdom was concerned and as early poll numbers and support from PLEOs indicated. Her failure to win the nomination, inevitably, has prompted substantial second-guessing, much of which has centered on the perception that the Clinton campaign failed to appreciate the ways in which the rules would shape the contest. Before Clinton's campaign was even complete, Karen Tumulty of *Time* had already enumerated "The Five Mistakes Clinton Made."[22] Item number two on the list was "She didn't master the rules." Specifically, Tumulty suggests that some of Clinton's top aides were not sufficiently versed in the delegate allocation procedures. She relates insider accounts of a now famous campaign meeting in which chief strategist Mark Penn reportedly claimed that a Clinton win in California would be decisive because that state allocated its delegates in a winner-take-all fashion. By Tumulty's telling, Penn's apparent ignorance of the fact that all pledged delegates were assigned proportionally aroused shock from Clinton supporter and DNC Rules and Bylaws Committee member Harold Ickes.[23]

Mid-campaign finger pointing and infighting, and the stunning suggestion that the campaign's chief strategist may not have recognized a fairly fundamental tenet of the DNC rules do not reflect well on the Clinton campaign. More damning, though, is the fact that Penn cannot simply point to their campaign strategy as proof he actually knew that delegates in all states were assigned proportionally as mandated by the Democratic National Committee. If anything, the manner in which the Clinton team allocated resources might lead one to believe Tumulty's account. If we give Penn the benefit of the doubt, however, and assume that the campaign strategy was not based upon ignorance of the rules, we are left to conclude that it was based upon the expectation that this campaign would go the way other recent ones had gone. Early endorsements would set the stage for early wins, which would set the stage for later wins. The eventual winner would hinge less on the delegate count than on the perception of momentum built up through wins, especially wins in large states. In such a campaign, it is less important to win in lots of little states and more important to pick up wins in fewer big states, even if those wins are by smaller margins. In fact, prior to this year's contest, this seemed like a fairly reasonable approach. It is difficult to fault the Clinton campaign for imagining things would play out in this manner. However, it is not so difficult to critique the failure to adequately account for other possibilities. This failure is especially evident in the Clinton campaign's woeful showing in caucuses.

### Primaries versus Caucuses

Item number three on Tumulty's list of Clinton mistakes: "She underestimated the caucus states."[24] Tumulty points out that the Clinton team paid little attention to even relatively large caucus states and argues that this approach was based upon the belief within the campaign that Clinton "core supporters—women, the elderly, those with blue-collar jobs—were less likely to be able to commit an evening"[25] to participate in a caucus meeting. The result according to Tumulty: "unilateral disarmament" by the Clinton campaign in caucus states.[26]

Obama's success in caucuses was staggering. His average margin of victory in those contests was 34 percent. He won almost twice as many pledged delegates in caucuses as did Clinton. Nearly 20 percent of Obama's pledged delegates came from caucuses, while these jurisdictions accounted for just over 10 percent of Clinton's total. Were there fundamental advantages for Obama in caucus states (which accounted for more than one in eight pledged delegates)? Almost certainly—this is where his ground organization helped the most, and the passion of supporters is tested the most. So, yes, it is possible that Clinton faced an uphill battle in the caucus states. Jay Cost, in his analysis of the process highlights the difficulties Clinton faced in caucuses. In particular, he points to the four states that held both caucuses and primaries as evidence.

> Interestingly, the type of contest might have had a causal effect on Obama's performance. That is, if the contests had been primaries rather than caucuses, Obama's vote share might have declined. Washington state, Nebraska, and Idaho allocated their delegates by the results of their caucuses. At some point afterwards, each held nonbinding primaries, or beauty contests. In the caucuses, Obama defeated Clinton in Washington and Nebraska by 2 to 1, and by 4 to1 in Idaho. In the nonbinding beauty contests, Obama's margins fell to just five points in Washington, two points in Nebraska, and 18 points in Idaho. Meanwhile, Texas was the only state to allocate delegates by pri-

mary and caucus. Both contests were held on the same day. Clinton won the Texas primary by four points. However, Obama bested Clinton in the caucuses by 12 points. That's a 16-point swing on the same day.[27]

While the "design" behind these "natural experiments" does not fully support causal inference, these anecdotes are very interesting and do highlight the extent to which Clinton's performance varied in relation to the type of contest. The reason for this discrepancy remains unclear. In offering his expert assessment in the *New York Times*, ("What Went Wrong?") Penn suggests that money was the major challenge.

> Are there a lot of other things the campaign could have done differently? Of course. We should have taken on Mr. Obama more directly and much earlier, and we needed a different kind of operation to win caucuses and to retain the support of super delegates. From more aggressively courting young people earlier to mobilizing the full power of women, there are things that could have been done differently. While everyone loves to talk about the message, campaigns are equally about money and organization. Having raised more than 100 million in 2007, the Clinton campaign found itself without adequate money at the beginning of 2008, and without organizations in a lot of states as a result. Given her successes in high-turnout primary elections and defeats in low-turnout caucuses, that simple fact may just have had a lot more to do with who won than anyone imagines.[28]

Undoubtedly, Clinton did not have the financial resources at her disposal that Obama did. Nobody else ever has. As the contest wore on, she was consistently and significantly outraised and outspent. It is not clear exactly how much it would have cost for Clinton to become competitive, or at least minimize the hemorrhaging when it comes to pledged delegates, in the caucus states. What is clear, however, is that even a modest improvement in her performance in caucuses could have drastically changed the shape of this close overall contest. It is also likely that dollars spent mobilizing voters in smaller caucus states would have produced more substantial marginal effects than dollars spent in paid media-focused campaigns in larger states.

## THE CALENDAR

Almost certainly, the scheduling of contests is the aspect of the nominating process rules that has attracted the most attention in recent years. The nominating calendar seems to become more and more frontloaded each cycle. The role of Iowa and New Hampshire is a constant sore point for many, but the challenges to the monopoly these states have established have been no match for their grip on first-in-the-nation status.[29]

After its 2004 national convention, the Democratic Party established the Commission on Presidential Nomination Timing and Scheduling, "charged with the responsibility of studying the timing of presidential primaries and caucuses and developing appropriate recommendations to the Democratic National Committee for the nominating process beginning in 2008."[30] That commission produced some minor changes to the nominating calendar, but the general trend toward frontloading was not altered. The 2008 nominating process featured the earliest kickoff ever, with Iowa holding its caucuses on January 3.[31] More than the frontloaded calendar, though, it was the effort on the part of Florida and Michigan to hold nominating contests before their allotted "window" in the calendar that had the greatest impact on the process.

### Florida and Michigan

The party rules designate appropriate windows within which states may hold their nominating contests. In 2008, Florida and Michigan chose to move ahead of their allotted slot on the calendar. The goal was to increase the relative importance of the state's primary by moving ahead of other large states. On the Democratic side, it did not quite work out this way: The DNC's Rules and Bylaws Committee voted to strip Florida and Michigan of all of their delegates (including unpledged delegates and PLEOs), and the candidates agreed to refrain from campaigning in those states. This was, as one might imagine, the harshest possible penalty. And, despite the severity of the sanction, some state officials anticipated that their state would still figure prominently in the process. From the *Washington Post* just after the decision regarding Florida:

> Florida's state party chair, Karen L. Thurman, showed no signs of backing down yesterday. The former congresswoman said she will consult with state Democrats but added that she expects all the presidential candidates to ignore the national party's edict and campaign vigorously in advance of the Sunshine State's primary. "Whether you get a delegate or don't get a delegate, a vote is a vote," a defiant Thurman said. "That is what Floridians are going to say is important."[32]

As it turned out, though, the Democratic contests in Florida and Michigan garnered relatively little attention when they occurred. Later, the fate of the delegates from these two states became a prominent theme in the bickering between Clinton and Obama supporters. This was undoubtedly not the way in which leaders from the two states imagined that they would make their contests central to determining the nominee.

However, before suggesting that the strategy completely backfired, one must remember that Florida *was* pivotal in the GOP race in a way it could not have been later on. First, because of one of the more unfortunate (albeit perhaps unavoidable) strategies in recent presidential campaigning, the Sunshine State was Rudy Giuliani's first and last stand. And, despite the fact that the state had its delegate total docked by 50 percent for jumping ahead in the calendar, the 57 winner-take-all delegates made the GOP race John McCain's to lose.

On the Democratic side, the importance of Florida and Michigan came less in the ultimate allocation of delegates. As things turned out, when the contest had ended, the full set of delegates from these two states were seated. And, even if, when they convened to discuss this matter toward the end of the nominating process, the DNC Rules and Bylaws Committee had seated all of the delegates from these two states and allocated them exactly as the Clinton campaign had hoped, Barack Obama still would have maintained a lead in the pledged delegate count. These facts do not mean that the rules did not significantly impact the process in this case. We must remember that the importance of the delegate totals in this race does not mean that momentum was irrelevant. It is in this sense that Florida and Michigan may have represented the first strategic misstep or oversight by the Clinton campaign. Obama campaign manager David Plouffe, looking back on the race, notes that they were keenly aware of the importance of Florida, in particular.

> I think the big question is, if Florida and Michigan had been valid contests, how would that have altered the calendar? The Clinton folks controlled the Rules Committee. They had a majority and we were very surprised back in the summer of '07 that the Rules Committee unanimously [sic] voted to fully sanction Florida and Michigan. Now, that was our viewpoint. We did what we could to help that along, but we did not control that process. And, so my view was, if you had an ability to choose your preferred calendar, it was your obligation to do so . . . February 5th for us: 22 primaries, huge states, we weren't going to have a lot of time to campaign there, we weren't going to have weeks of advertising. We were terribly frightened of February 5th, and Hillary Clinton was, even a month out, ahead in all of those states, including the caucus states. So, the only way that we could survive February 5th

was to go into that with maximum velocity, and South Carolina gave us the opportunity potentially to have a big win as the last contest before February 5th. Now, we thought if Michigan actually counted on January 15th, we could probably do pretty well there. Whether we win or not, I don't know, but close. Florida was concerning to us. And if that Florida primary, coming three days after South Carolina, had happened, it might have mitigated all the momentum out of South Carolina. In fact, we might not be the nominee . . . And then we all took a vow to not campaign in those two states. It was codified. And when they agreed to do it, the Clinton campaign, you know I was very surprised, because we then had the calendar that we preferred. And, so, by the time we get into redos in Florida and Michigan and what was going to happen to the delegates, it was clear it was not going to alter the delegate race to a great degree. And so it was more coming in for a soft landing and we were able to do that at that Rules Committee meeting. But, really the whole Florida-Michigan story is one I think that is very, very important, because if we hadn't had that moment of velocity coming out of South Carolina, particularly having lost the New Hampshire primary, I don't know if we could have survived February 5th. And, in fact, on that day, which we thought was really going to be our toughest challenge, that we won more states and more delegates, it was really about 3:00 a.m. on February 6th that I thought, all things being equal, we're going to be the Democratic nominee, 'cause we just survived the greatest threat to our candidacy, until Jeremiah Wright.[33]

Plouffe's assessment makes a great deal of sense. Florida, in particular, could have impacted the race substantially, even with a diminished delegate allocation (as was the case in the Republican race). Based upon composition, Florida was almost certain to end up as a victory for Clinton. The mood heading into February 5 could have been altered dramatically by such a win. This possibility begs the following question: Why did Clinton supporters on the Rules and Bylaws Committee vote for this full sanction?

[Clinton strategist Harold Ickes] voted in August to strip Florida and Michigan of their delegates as a sitting member of the Rules and Bylaws Commission. "There's been no change," Ickes said, adding that he was then acting as a member of the Rules and Bylaws Committee "not acting as an agent of Sen. Clinton. We had promulgated rules—if Florida and Michigan violated those rules" they'd be stripped of their delegates.[34]

Perhaps it is the case that his vote and those of the other Clinton supporters on the Rules and Bylaws Committee were rooted in conviction and that they were able to compartmentalize their roles as supporters of Clinton and agents of the DNC. If so, this is a sense of conviction and separation that waned for some as each delegate became more precious. It is also possible, though, that the implications of this decision for the campaign were not as clearly contemplated on the Clinton side as Plouffe suggests they were on the Obama side.

## DELEGATE ALLOCATION TO STATES AND DISTRICTS

The allocation of base delegates on the Democratic side was based upon an allocation factor generated by the following formula:

$$Allocation\ Factor = \frac{1}{2}\left(\frac{SDV\ 1996 + SDV\ 2000 + SDV\ 2004}{TDV\ 1996 + TDV\ 2000 + TDV\ 2004} + \frac{SEV}{538}\right)$$

in which SDV = State Democratic Vote for the year identified, SEV = State Electoral Vote, and TDV = Total Democratic Vote in the nation for the year listed.

The number of base votes assigned to a state is the allocation factor multiplied by the total number of base votes to be divided between the 50 states: 3,000. Figure 1 illustrates the relative size of each state based upon population and Democratic delegate allocation. Seventy-Five percent of each state's pledged delegates are to be allocated proportionally at the congressional district level. The remaining 25 percent must be allocated in proportion to the statewide vote. Candidates receiving less than 15 percent in the nominating contest do not receive delegates, and proportions for the other candidates are calculated based upon the percentage received of the vote shared among delegate-eligible candidates. The manners by which states must allocate delegates to congressional districts are prescribed by the DNC such that delegates are allocated based upon a district's support for previous Democratic candidates.[35]

As Cost points out, the allocation factor itself leads to two consistent, but relatively small, biases.[36] Both result from the inclusion of the Electoral College in the formula. For starters, this imports the small-state bias present in the Electoral College. But, more interesting is the fact that the allocation factor, by equally weighting proportion of the Electoral College vote and proportion of the overall Democratic vote, actually biases allocation slightly in favor of Democrats in Republican states.

> What kind of effect did the small-state and Republican-state biases have on the Democratic nomination? Combined, they created a modest, pro-Obama

## Figure 1. Cartograms

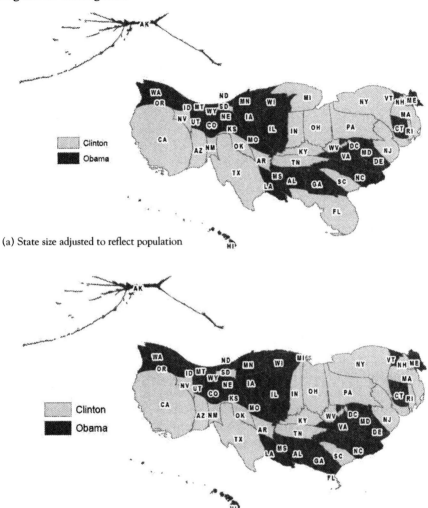

(a) State size adjusted to reflect population

(b) State size adjusted to reflect Democratic Party
pledged delegates assigned during state nominating contest

These cartograms adjust the relative size of each state and the District of Columbia based, instead of geographic area, upon population (Figure 1(a)) and number of pledged delegates allocated by the Democratic Party during the nominating campaign (Figure 1(b)). The shapes are altered using the diffusion-based method developed by Michael T. Gastner and M. E. J. Newman (Gastner, 2004) as operationalized in the open-source Java application ScapeToad, developed by Dominique Andrieu, Christian Kaiser and André Ourednik. State population figures are based upon United States Census estimates (United States Census Bureau, 2008). State pledged delegate allocations used in generating this image assign no delegates to Florida and Michigan, as this was the number assigned to those states at the time of their nominating contests.

movement in delegate allocation. If we "correct" for these biases by allocating delegates strictly according to each state's share of the Democratic vote, we would find that Obama's lead in pledged delegates would have decreased by about 25 percent, from 106 to 80. This should not come as a surprise. Obama tended to win smaller states, while Clinton won larger states. What is more . . . Obama had an enormous advantage in the Republican states.[37]

On the Republican side, allocation was also based upon both a state's relative representation in constitutional offices and upon the extent of that state's support for Republicans. The process for determining those things, however, is quite different. They begin by allocating delegates to states (five for each U.S. senator) and congressional districts (three for each). Then, bonus delegates are assigned for: 1) states casting their electoral votes for George W. Bush in 2004 (proportional to the size of the Electoral College delegation); 2) each Republican senator elected from 2002 to January 1, 2008; 3) the election of a Republican governor between 2004 and 2007; 4) election of Republicans to 50-percent or more of the state's U.S. House seats between 2004 and 2007; 5) a Republican majority in one chamber of the state legislature; and 6) a Republican majority in all chambers of the state legislature.[38]

## PLEDGED DELEGATE ALLOCATION TO CANDIDATES

By revealed preference, the Democratic Party can be said to have taken the position that proportional allocation is a more suitable way to assign pledged delegates. Proportionality is centrally mandated and the procedures for that allocation are largely prescribed by the DNC.[39] The GOP rules are more agnostic, and this is manifested in the variety of approaches taken in the Republican contests.[40] As Figure 2(a) indicates, Republican contests take a variety of forms in the various states and jurisdictions. A few states even use "advisory" and "loophole" primaries, methods reminiscent of the early and mid-twentieth century.[41]

Before discussing this topic further, there is some value in stepping back and considering the rules from a more theoretical perspective. Normative and empirical work in political science suggest that the question of which allocation rules are more "democratic" lacks a straightforward answer.[42] This is largely because the values of representativeness (also called proportionality) and responsiveness are in more or less direct conflict with each other. Representativeness, in the extreme, demands that votes and delegates be

## Figure 2. Types of Nominating Contests in the Democratic and Republican Races

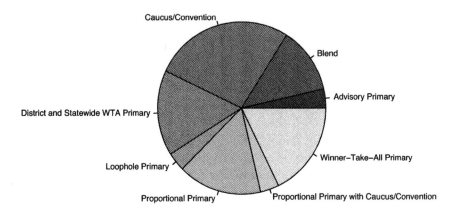

(a) Republican nominating contests

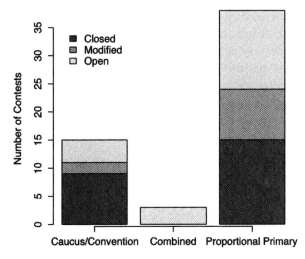

(b) Democratic nominating contests

These charts illustrate the number of contests in each party being held under each set of rules. The Republican nominating contests took an astonishing number of forms. The "blend" category includes a number of different variations, with some of these states having different rules at the district and state levels and some allocating delegates on a winner-take-all basis if a majority winner emerged and a proportional basis otherwise. On the Democratic side, while there was variety, it was far more limited by DNC rules. This figure presents data from *TheGreenPapers.com* and from various state government Web sites and documents.

allocated in the same proportion by an electoral system. Responsiveness, on the other hand, refers to the ability of a system to reflect small changes in opinion. Figure 3 illustrates the difference between these two competing norms in a two-candidate election. Put more simply, someone advocating representativeness would dislike winner-take-all approaches and argue that it makes no sense for one candidate to receive all the delegates in a state from which he or she did not win *all* the votes. An individual desiring responsiveness would point out that it seems unfair for two candidates to split a slate of ten delegates evenly when one received 51 percent of the vote and the other received 49 percent.

As it pertains to the nominating process, winner-take-all contests are quite responsive at the 50-percent point in a two-candidate race. But, they generally do a poor job of representing the range of popular views, especially in a race with multiple viable candidates, such as was the case on the Republican side in 2008. Proportional representation contests, like the ones mandated by the Democratic Party, do well when it comes to making sure that any sizeable (in this case, larger than 15 percent) voting bloc is represented by delegates. However, they are not especially responsive to small variations in public opinion. Take, for example, a congressional district in the Democratic race with four pledged delegates (this was the number of delegates in over one-fifth of the districts in 2008). In order to avoid splitting the delegates evenly, the winning candidate needs to receive just over 61 percent of the vote. In other words, a 20-percentage-point win in such a district could yield no delegate advantage.

This section examines the course of the Democratic and Republican races as they transpired, and attempts to explore the ways in which the race might have differed under alternative delegate allocation rules (especially on the Democratic side). Of course, true counterfactuals cannot be obtained, as changes in the rules would have generated myriad other changes in strategy, media coverage, and voter behavior. However, this *ceteris paribus* analysis should still be meaningful and interesting. On the Democratic side, the effects of the methods by which pledged delegates were awarded to candidates had obvious effects, especially given how tight the Democratic race ended up. The focus here is on pledged delegates. This is because, despite the fact that neither Obama nor Clinton could cross the necessary threshold based upon just pledged delegates, this still was the tally that mattered most. Also, it is the only type of delegate for which systematic analysis of this sort is possible. The idiosyncratic nature of individual, unpledged delegates precludes such an examination. On the Democratic side, the breakdown of pledged delegates was roughly: 65 percent district-level delegates, 22 percent at-large delegates

**Figure 3.** Responsive Versus Representative

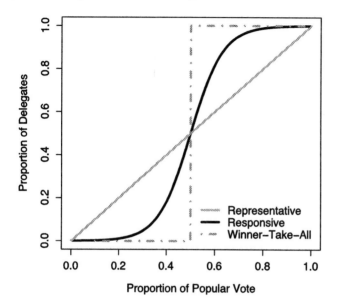

The lines in this figure illustrate the difference, in a two-candidate contest, between hypothetical delegate allocation under a system that is purely representative as opposed to one that is more responsive and one that is winner-take-all. Figure replicates "Figure 1" in Ansolabehere & King (1990).

assigned to each state, and 13 percent pledged PLEOs. The superdelegates (PLEOs) made up over 90 percent of the unpledged delegates, with the rest being unpledged add-ons. It should be noted that the calculations discussed in this section are estimates. Furthermore, the estimates in this section do not include delegates from Florida and Michigan, as I believe this should be treated as an independent issue.

### Statewide Winner-Take-All

As Figure 4(b) illustrates, the Democratic race would have played out very differently under winner-take-all allocation at the state level. Holding everything else constant, Clinton would have taken a 332 pledged-delegate lead after February 5. She would relinquish that lead by February 19, but end the contest with an advantage of 231 pledged delegates. Again, this is a purely academic exercise. The two campaign strategies would have differed greatly under such fundamentally different rules. And, voters did not cast their ballots independent of previous outcomes and the delegate tally. Furthermore, we can expect that media coverage would have taken on an entirely different character.

There are also reasons, however, to think that this particular analysis has some value. The state-level contests demonstrated a certain degree of predictability. As the contest wore on, it became clear that Obama had his core supporters and Clinton had hers. The composition of each state's electorate generally offered prognosticators useful clues regarding the eventual outcome of that contest. So, while the campaigns clearly would have allocated resources differently and altered their messages under a statewide winner-take-all system, it is likely that many of the statewide outcomes would not have changed. The campaign for California's pledged delegates certainly would have taken on added significance and would have attracted more attention from both campaigns. Would Obama have been able to overcome the 8 percentage points by which Clinton won in that state? It is difficult to imagine Clinton competing successfully in Illinois and it is unlikely that Obama could have contested New York. Clinton won the primaries in Ohio and Pennsylvania by roughly 9 percentage points. And, the vast majority of Obama's wins were landslides. Under this scenario, Obama accrues nearly 90 percent of his pledged delegates in contests he wins by 10 percentage points or more (many of them closer to 30 percentage points). Clinton wins less than 50 percent of her delegates in contests decided by 10 or more percentage points. However, that percentage jumps to nearly 90 when one includes delegates won in contests decided by 8 percent or more. The most contestable delegate-rich states would have been Texas, where Clinton won the primary by 3.5 percent, Indiana and New Mexico, both of which Clinton won by 1 percent, Missouri, where Obama won by 1 percent, and Connecticut, where Obama won by 4 percent. Clinton supporters would argue that she could have more readily overcome large percentage point leads by Obama in low-turnout caucus states. While this is true, it is also hard to see why the Clinton campaign would have paid more attention to the caucus states under a scenario in which they could win without them, when they failed to do so under the actual scenario in which they evidently could not.

It is almost certainly the case that the overall dynamics of the race would have changed substantially under such winner-take-all allocation at the statewide level. These changes would have likely favored Clinton. For starters, the "inevitability" argument put forward by her supporters might have held more water had she actually overtaken Obama on February 5. At the very least, she would have spent less time explaining why she was remaining in the race. Furthermore, the shift in super delegate support toward Obama might not have been so overwhelming.

**Figure 4**
**Cumulative Pledged Delegates Over Time in the Democratic Race Under Actual and Alternative Allocation Rules**

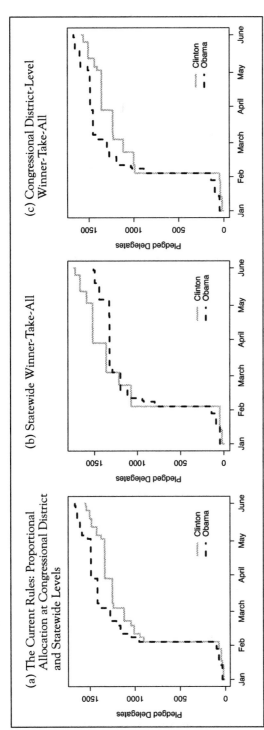

(a) The Current Rules: Proportional Allocation at Congressional District and Statewide Levels

(b) Statewide Winner-Take-All

(c) Congressional District-Level Winner-Take-All

These figures present estimates of cumulative delegate allocation over time in the race between Hillary Clinton and Barack Obama. Figure 4(a) illustrates the race as it transpired. Figure 4(b) shows what the race might have looked like under winner-take-all allocation at the statewide level. Figure 4(c) shows delegate totals over time if district-level pledged delegates were allocated on a winner-take-all basis within each congressional district. In this case, the roughly 25 percent of pledged delegates allocated to the entire state are awarded on a winner-take-all basis in each state. Delegates from Florida and Michigan are not included in these estimates. These figures incorporate electoral data from various sources, including TheGreenPapers.com, "Dave Leip's Atlas of U.S. Presidential Elections," and from various state government Web sites and documents.

This alternative scenario highlights one feature of the Democratic rules that substantially impacted this race. Clinton did quite well toward the end of the contest, especially considering the fact that her chances of winning had already greatly diminished, that party leaders were flocking to Obama, and that she faced constant calls for her withdrawal from the race. Much of this is surely a result of the compositions of the states holding their primaries in March, April, May, and June. It is also possible, and widely asserted, that the Clinton campaign had righted its ship at this point and was more effectively competing in these states. It is difficult to know how much of this effect, if any, came out of any possible "buyer's remorse" felt by some Democrats as Obama took on the status of front-runner, or if voters were impacted by the substantial attention paid to issues surrounding Reverend Jeremiah Wright. Empirically, though, it is clear that Clinton closed out the nominating campaign on a strong note. The proportional allocation of delegates at both the statewide and congressional district levels made it exceedingly difficult for either candidate to quickly overcome a delegate deficit or expand substantially upon a built-up lead. In other words, the pursuit of proportionality or representativeness created a Democratic nominating process that lacked responsiveness.

### Congressional District Winner-Take-All

As Figure 4(c) illustrates, the final outcome of the contest is not changed by the allocation of pledged delegates to the candidates in a winner-take-all manner at the congressional district level (with statewide delegates being allocated, winner-take-all at the state level). Here too, though, the race might have been quite different. This is because, unlike the actual contest, this race has Clinton taking the lead in pledged delegates after February 5. She relinquishes that lead by mid-February. However, that period of advantage could have altered the contest in some of the ways discussed above.

### The GOP Race

The impact of the rules on the Republican selection process is not apparent in the consistent manner seen in the Democratic contest. However, though certainly the subject of far less discussion, the rules on the Republican side were at least as influential. The GOP's blend of winner-take-all (at both the state and district levels) and proportional allocation served to establish a winner long before the Democratic rules did. This is despite the fact that the

Republican base was more segmented and did not appear as likely to converge on one or two leading candidates. Under the Republican Party rules, McCain benefitted from windfalls in several winner-take-all states. In Florida, for instance, McCain received 36 percent of the vote, edging Romney by 5 percentage points. But, that gave McCain all of the Sunshine State's 57 delegates. In Missouri, the vote was nearly evenly split between McCain (32.95 percent), Huckabee (31.53 percent), and Romney (29.27 percent), but all of the Show-Me State's 58 delegates would be pledged to McCain. The effect was often the same in the cases where the delegates were assigned on a winner-take-all-basis at the congressional district level. In Oklahoma, for instance, it was McCain with 36.64 percent, Huckabee with 33.40 percent, and Romney with 24.78 percent. That gave roughly 78 percent of the state's delegates to McCain. In California, McCain won 42.25 percent of the vote to Romney's 34.56 percent, which was good enough to garner nearly 90 percent of the state's delegates (155 for McCain as compared to 15 for Romney).

These facts concur with recent findings by authors David Karol and Jack Citrin, who apply various delegate allocation rules to the GOP nomination process and demonstrate that McCain benefited immensely from winner-take-all allocation in a number of states. They conclude that he might still have been nominated, but that the process would likely not have played out so smoothly.[43] We do not get to observe the counterfactuals and, since the GOP race did not go the distance, we cannot as easily estimate outcomes under alternative delegate allocation scenarios. But, there is some evidence in the results we do have to suggest that, had the Republican process been as consistently "proportional" as the Democratic process, the GOP might have risked a brokered convention.

## SUPERDELEGATES

As things turned out, the superdelegates (PLEOs) did not appear poised to overturn the pledged delegate count. But, this class of delegates certainly garnered a tremendous amount of attention in 2008. Many suggested that the PLEOs ought not contradict the electoral outcome or pledged delegate count. This begged the question of whether such an adherence to electoral results should apply at the overall level or at the level of the particular PLEO's constituency (in the case of those with constituencies). Of course, the suggestion that PLEOs should simply serve as a rubber stamp for the pledged delegate count calls into question the very rationale for their existence, unless it is simply to secure automatic DNC credentials for party leaders.

The history behind the PLEOs comes with an interesting bit of irony. In 1981, the initial plan was to set the relative weight of this group of delegates at 30 percent. This was decreased to 15 percent, largely in response to the protests of Senator Edward "Ted" Kennedy's supporters. One of those supporters, lawyer and feminist activist Susan Estrich (who would go on to run Michael Dukakis's presidential campaign in 1988 and who supported Clinton in 2008), submitted a memo, titled "Unintended Consequences," arguing that the PLEOs would be predominantly white males, thus running afoul of the DNC mandate (which had emerged from the McGovern-Fraser Commission) for equal representation on gender and a delegate slate that reflected the composition of the party.[44] (Estrich is also credited with coining the term "superdelegates" in an effort to mock the concept in testimony before the Hunt Commission.) She later admitted that her arguments regarding race and gender were at least partly born out of something akin to motivated reasoning. The Kennedy supporters were concerned that the PLEOs would align primarily with Walter Mondale, former vice president under Jimmy Carter, whom they expected to be the primary obstacle to Kennedy's pursuit of the nomination in 1984. "Mondale was the establishment candidate and Kennedy was the insurgent," writes Estrich, "and so my marching orders from on high, or from Harold Ickes anyway, were to oppose the effort to create a category of superdelegates allowed to come to the convention unpledged, without having to run for a delegate spot and not bound by the results of their state's contests."[45] The importance of gender and racial representation would be the "principled argument" Estrich and others would advance. As things turned out, the PLEOs did tend to support Mondale, but his opponents were Reverend Jesse Jackson and Senator Gary Hart, rather than Ted Kennedy.

In 2008, the PLEOs accounted for 19 percent of the total delegates, having expanded beyond the initial 15 percent. One can never know, but it is certainly possible to argue that the dynamics of the race might have been altered in Clinton's favor had the PLEOs accounted for 30 percent of the total. Because she was more successful at securing PLEO support early on, her lead before the first state contests and during the first few weeks of the race might have been larger. This could have played into the perception of her as "inevitable." And, as the nominating calendar drew to a close, it might have been less likely that Obama would have crossed the critical threshold for total delegates (which he did on the day of the final contests), leaving open the possibility of the nomination being decided at the convention. Perhaps the first serious female contender for the White House found herself wishing that the "feminist" arguments against the PLEOs had not been presented quite so effectively in the early 1980s.

## LOOKING TOWARD THE FUTURE

An overwhelming call for reform has not emerged in either party. On the Democratic side, this is despite the close split between Clinton and Obama, and the potential existence, therefore, of an aggrieved faction. However, the process picked a winning candidate and victory can prove an excellent salve when it comes to these sorts of wounds. Furthermore, despite initial fears, there is anecdotal evidence that the drawn-out contest may have helped Obama by generating organizations and building up a ground game in states like North Carolina and Indiana. And, his general election wins in those states and Virginia took the edge off any of the arguments made by Clinton supporters that Obama's nominating contest victories were disproportionately in "red states." When it comes to the roles of Iowa and New Hampshire, there is reason to believe the case against first-in-the-nation status for those states took a major blow when Iowa supported Obama. One of the major objections, especially in the Democratic Party, has been that those states are lacking in diversity. The basic demographics have not changed, but the fact that Iowa played an important role in nominating what turned out to be the first African American president in the nation's history certainly takes some of the rhetorical bite out of arguments regarding the composition of those states. After the 2008 convention, the DNC did create the Democratic Change Commission to examine the nominating process. Nonetheless, there is little reason to expect the Democratic Party to be especially inclined to seek "change" when it comes to its nominating process. The Republicans, on the other hand, have plenty of other places to look for explanations of their party's failings in 2008. There is no narrative readily available suggesting that one of the other contenders would have fared much better in November and was specifically disadvantaged by the rules.

## REFERENCES

*www.TheGreenPages.com*

Aldrich, J.H. *Why Parties?: The Origin and Transformation of Political Parties in America.* (Chicago: University of Chicago Press, 1995).

Ansolabehere, S.D. and G. King, "Measuring the Consequences of Delegate Selection Rules in Presidential Nominations," *Journal of Politics* 52, no.2 (1990), pp. 609–621.

Bartels, L.M. *Presidential Primaries and the Dynamics of Public Choice,* (Princeton, NJ: Princeton University Press,1988).

Brady, H.E. and S.D. Ansolabehere, "The Nature of Utility Functions in Mass Publics," *American Political Science Review* 83, no. 1 (1989), pp. 143–163.

Ceaser, J.W., *Presidential Selection: Theory and Development,* (Princeton NJ: Princeton University Press, 1979).

Ceaser, J.W., "The Presidential Nomination Mess," The Claremont Institute, November 5, 2008, http://www.claremont.org/publications/crb/id.1571/article_detail.asp

Center, J.A. "1972 Democratic Convention Reforms and Party Democracy," *Political Science Quarterly* 89, no. 2 (1974 ), pp. 325–350.

Cohen, M., D. Karol, H. Noel, and J. Zaller, *The Party Decides: Presidential Nominations Before and After Reform*. (Chicago: University of Chicago Press. 1988).

Republican National Committee. November 9, 2007. "Call for the 2008 Republican National Convention."

Cost, J., "How Obama Won The Nomination," *Policy Review* (August and September, 2008).

Downs, A., *An Economic Theory of Democracy* (Boston: Addison-Wesley, 1957) (Paperback, 1997).

Estrich, S., "Beware What You Wish For," *www.RealClearPolitics.com*, February 13, 2008.

Gastner, T.M. and M.E.J. Newman, "Diffusion-based method for producing density-equalizing maps," *PNAS* 101, no. 20 (2004), pp. 7499–7540.

Geer, J.G. 1986. "Rules Governing Presidential Primaries," *The Journal of Politics* 48, no.4,(1986), pp. 1006–1025.

Hammond, T.H., "Another Look at the Role of 'The Rules' in the 1972 Democratic Presidential Primaries," *The Western Political Quarterly* 33, no. 1, (1980), pp. 50–72.

Kamarck, E.C., 1990 "Structure as Strategy: Presidential Nominating Politics in the Post-Reform Era." *The Parties Respond: Changes in the American Party System*, pp. 160–186.

Kamarck, E.C. 2008 (Summer). "A History of 'Super-Delegates' in the Democratic Party," John F. Kennedy School of Government, Cambridge, Mass.

Karol, D. and J. Citrin, "Introduction" in *Evolution and Revolution in the Presidential Nominations Process: 2008 and Beyond*. J. Citrin and D. Karol, eds. (Rowman & Littlefield, 2009).

Kaufmann, K.M., J. G. Gimpel, and A.H. Hoffman, "A Promise Fulfilled? Open Primaries and Representation," *Journal of Politics* 65, no. 2,(2003), pp. 457–476.

Leip, D. *Dave Leip's Atlas of U.S. Presidential Elections*. 2008, http://uselectionatlas.org/

Lengle, J.I. and B. Shafer, "Primary Rules, Political Power, and Social Change," *The American Political Science Review* 70, no. 1, (1976), pp. 25–40.

Lengle, J.I. *Representation and Presidential Primaries: The Democratic Party in the Post Reform Era*. (Greenwood Publishing Group,1981).

Levin, C., T. McAuliffe, and D. Dingell, "Resolution Establishing a Commission on Presidential Nomination Timing and Scheduling," July, 2004, available at http://a9.g.akamai.net/7/9/8082/v001/democratic1.download.akamai.com/8082/pdfs/200 51215_commissionfinal.pdf

Maisel, L.S., *Parties and Elections in America: The Electoral Process*. (Rowman & Littlefield Publishers, 2002).

Mayer, W.G. and A.E. Busch, *The Front-Loading Problem in Presidential Nominations*. (Brookings Institution Press, 2003).

Meinke, S.R., J.K. Staton, and S.T. Wuhs, "State Delegate Selection Rules for Presidential Nominations, 1972–2000," *Journal of Politics* 68, no.1 (2006), pp. 180–193.

Montanaro, Domenico "Clinton camp: All the way to convention," February 16, 2008, at www.MSNBC.com.

Norrander, B., "Presidential Nomination Politics in the Post-Reform Era," *Political Research Quarterly* 49, no. 4, (1996), p.875.

Norrander, B., "The End Game in Post-Reform Presidential Nominations," *Journal of Politics* 62, no. 4, (2006), pp. 999–1013.

Democratic Party of the United States, "Delegate Selection Rules for the 2008," Democratic National Convention.

Democratic Party of the United States, "Call for the 2008 Democratic National Convention," as Adopted by the Democratic National Committee, February 2, 2007.

Penn, M. "The Problem Wasn't the Message—It Was the Money," *New York Times*, June 8, 2008.

Plouffe, D. "War Stories: Inside Campaign 2008," Institute of Politics at the Harvard Kennedy School, December 11, 2008.

Polsby, N.W., *Consequences of Party Reform*. (New York: Oxford University Press, 1983).

Polsby, N.W., A. Wildavsky, and D.A. Hopkins, *Presidential Elections: Strategies and Structures of American Politics*. (Rowman & Littleffeld Publishers, 2007).

Pomper, G.M., "New Rules and New Games in Presidential Nominations," *Journal of Politics* 41, no. 3, (1979), pp. 784–805.

Ranney, A., *The Doctrine of Responsible Party Government: Its Origins and Present State*. (University of Illinois Press, 1962).

Ranney, A., "Turnout and Representation in Presidential Primary Elections." *Political Opinion and Behavior: Essays and Studies*. (1976.)

Sabato, L.J., and B.A. Larson, *The Party's Just Begun: Shaping Political Parties for America's Future*. (New York: Longman, 2002).

Schattschneider, E.E., *Party Government*. (New York, Rinehart, 1942).

Schattschneider, E.E., *The Semisovereign People: A Realist's View of Democracy in America*. (Holt, Rinehart and Winston, 1960).

Schwartz, T. "Why Parties?" Unpublished, 1989.

Shear, M.D., "DNC Strips Florida Of 2008 Delegates: No Convention Slots Unless Later Primary Is Set," *Washington Post*, Sunday, August 26, 2007, Page A01.

Southwell, P.L.,"Rules as 'Unseen Participants': The Democratic Presidential Nomination Process," *American Politics Research* 20, no. 1, (1992), pp. 54–68.

Tufte, E.R., "The Relationship between Seats and Votes in Two-Party Systems," *American Political Science Review* 67, no 2 (1973), pp. 540–554.

Tumulty, K., "The Five Mistakes Clinton Made," *Time*, May 8, 2008.

United States Census Bureau, Population Division. Annual Estimates of the Resident Population for the United States, Regions, States, and Puerto Rico: April 1, 2000 to July 1, 2008 (NST-EST2008-01), December 22, 2008.

University of Virginia Center for Politics, *Presidential Selection: A Guide to Reform*, 2001, http://www.centerforpolitics.org/reform/report_electoral.htm.

Wilson, J.Q., *The Amateur Democrat*. (Chicago: University of Chicago Press, 1966).

# NOTES

[1] The author owes a great debt of gratitude to a number of individuals. Richard E. Berg-Andersson and Tony Roza of *TheGreenPapers.com* have not only compiled one of the best online resources for examination of data and original documents pertaining to the nominating process, but were very generous in sharing their raw data, which were used in several of the analyses presented herein. Data compiled by David Leip are also used extensively. This chapter benefitted from the patience and careful eye of Larry J. Sabato, Daniel Keyserling, and Isaac Wood of the University of Virginia Center for Politics. Jasjeet Sekhon provided some essential methodological guidance. David Karol, in particular, was extraordinarily generous with his time and his encyclopedic knowledge of the nominating process. Additionally, the author is grateful for the support of Berkeley's Integrative Graduate Education and Research Traineeship (IGERT) program in Politics, Economics, Psychology and Public Policy, which is funded by the National Science Foundation (Award Number 0504642) and the principal investigators for which are Henry Brady and Steven Raphael.

[2] The title references *The Party Decides: Presidential Nominations Before and After Reform* by Marty Cohen, David Karol, Hans Noel and John Zaller, a book only recently published but which, in its manuscript form, has already greatly impacted scholarly thinking regarding a potential resurgence of influence by party elites on the nominating process.

[3]Bartels, 1988

[4]Cohen et al., 2008

[5]Tumulty, 2008

[6]It is also true that Obama needed the PLEOs to cross the threshold necessary for victory.

[7]Ceaser, 2008

[8]Theories of parties in political science seem to suggest their inevitability. When leaders seek control of government, the formation of coalitions or parties is the logical strategic conclusion (Aldrich 1995, Schwartz 1989). And, despite the initial concerns of the Founders, many scholars have come to see parties (and, often, two parties specifically) as essential to the functioning of American republican government. Political scientists have tended to espouse this view. E.E. Schattschnieder, along with many others, argued for the desirability of Westminster-style, strong, differentiated, "responsible" parties. "The political parties created democracy," he wrote, "and modern democracy is unthinkable save in terms of the parties" (Schattschneider, 1942).

[9]For what remains the authoritative treatment of the pre-1980 history of the nominating process and an outstanding examination of its theoretical foundations, see Ceaser (1979). Also see Polsby (1983).

[10]One of the most important questions to answer about a party is: Who is in control? James Q. Wilson famously explored this question by examining the relative influence of "professionals" as opposed to "amateurs" in his analysis of local Democratic politics (Wilson, 1966). Professionals were those involved in the party for the sake of the party and for the spoils that the party's success brought. Amateurs were motivated largely by policy objectives. Wilson saw a rise in the latter at the expense of the former.

[11]Cohen et al., 2008

[12]It is not important for the purposes of this chapter that we wade into this debate. Furthermore, it is difficult to empirically adjudicate between the competing claims. To begin with, even if one can define the parties and their insiders in a satisfactory way, it becomes difficult to quantify or even ascertain qualitatively what preferences those insiders would have had independent of anticipated popular support. And, of course, popular support is not independent of elite opinion. The public can take cues from elites and the two could be linked by intervening variables. Analysis of the limited number (a problem in and of itself) of nominating contests during this period is, thus, challenged by a potential observational equivalence problem.

[13]Whether Kennedy would have gone on to win the nomination remains an open question. While it appears many delegates at the time of the assassination intended to vote for Humphrey, there is no way of knowing how the post-primary/pre-convention period would have played out (Polsby, 1983).

[14]For more extensive discussions of the relevance of the 1968 Democratic nomination contest for the future of the nominating process, see Polsby (1983) and Cohen et al. (2008).

[15]For more discussion of the reforms emerging from the McGovern-Fraser Commission, see Polsby (1983) and Center (1974).

[16]Maisel, 2002

[17]See, for instance, Polsby, 1983.

[18]Polsby et al., 2007

[19]Bartels, 1988

[20]Cohen et al., 2008

[21]See, for instance, Ansolabehere and King 1990, Geer 1986, Hammond 1980, Lengle 1981, Lengle and Shafer 1976, Meinke et al. 2006, Norrander 2000, Norrander 1996, Pomper 1979, Southwell 1992.

[22]Tumulty, 2008

[23]Ibid.

[24]Ibid.

[25]Ibid.

[26]Ibid.

[27]Cost, 2008

[28]Penn, 2008

[29]For an overview of major reform proposals related to this topic, please see the chapter on the "Nominating Process" in *Presidential Selection: A Guide to Reform* published in 2001 by the University of Virginia Center for Politics, and available at www.CenterForPolitics.org. Or, for a more extensive treatment, see Mayer (2003).

[30]Levin, 2004

[31]There was even talk of New Hampshire moving its contest into 2007 in an effort to fend off attempts by other states to jump ahead.

[32]Shear, 2007

[33]Plouffe, 2008

[34]From *MSNBC.com*

[35]Democratic National Committee, 2007

[36]Cost, 2008

[37]Ibid.

[38]Republican National Committee, 2007

[39]Democratic National Committee, 2007

[40]Republican National Committee, 2007

[41]In a loophole primary, participants cast a vote indicating their party preference and can then vote for delegates. The former is advisory to those selected via the latter. The results of an advisory primary, also known as a "beauty contest," do not bear directly on the allocation of delegates.

[42]See, for instance, Ansolabehere and King (1990) and Ceaser (1979).

[43]Karol and Citrin, 2009

[44]Kamarck, 2008

[45]Estrich, 2008

# Conclusion

# Presidential Election 2008

## *An Amazing Race, So What's Next?*

### Susan A. MacManus

**(With the assistance of David J. Bonanza and Christopher J. Leddy, Jr., University of South Florida Honors College students)**

> *"Election '08, with its plot twists and vivid characters, topped any reality show the networks could cook up. . . . Now, after being embedded in our daily conversations and popular culture, the campaign is about to end . . . Let's admit it: When this amazing race ends, a part of us is going to miss it. And it's likely to be a long time before we see another one like it."*
>
> USA Today Editorial, November 4, 2008

Elections are often best understood when put in the context of the dominant pop culture of the day. After all, it's often the "casual" voter, rather than the staunch party activist, who is the most heavily sought after by the candidates, but the hardest to energize and win over.

In 2008, Americans were still hooked on television reality shows.[1] This popular format burst onto the stage with a bang in the early 2000s, with CBS's captivating show *Survivor*. Soon thereafter, over half of all of American TV shows (both on cable and broadcast networks)[2] were reality shows with "through-the-roof ratings."[3]

These rather addictive reality shows have been described as "raw, unscripted drama" showing "real life events unfolding in an often stressful and at times chaotic environment." The producers of such TV reality shows can greatly affect the outcome of the events "through editing strategies to manipulate the footage in such a way as to portray participants in a certain light; some as villains, others as heroes."[4] Likewise, these same "producers [can effectively] design scenarios, challenges, events and settings to encourage particular behaviors and conflicts."[5] And participants are often "coached by handlers off camera."[6] Viewers are encouraged to participate by interactively using other media (the Internet and wireless communication devices) to denote their favorites.

The parallels between widely-watched television reality shows and the most recent presidential election are striking. Descriptions of one could just as aptly be used to capture the essence of the other, the major difference being that in the world of politics, it is the campaign strategists and journalists—mainstream and from alternative media—who most often play the roles of handlers and producers.

The incredibly exciting, highly engaging, suspenseful 2008 presidential election had all the elements—and more—of a top-rated reality show. While some early projections were on target (e.g., the race being Democrats' to lose in light of an unpopular president, the long war in Iraq, and voter fatigue with one party occupying the White House for eight years), many others were dead wrong. Prognosticators and pundits alike (and even some of the candidates) erred in their predictions of how long the nomination process would last; who would be each party's nominee; which party would have the most competitive and protracted nomination fight; which candidate/party would raise the most money, how, and why; the level and effectiveness of spending by 527-type groups; the degree to which a third-party candidate would play a spoiler role; the issue that would be the major concern of voters by Election Day; the extent of "the Bradley Effect among white voters"; turnout rates, especially among young voters; and the likelihood of another election administration debacle in key states like Florida and Ohio, to name but a few errant expectations.

One major newspaper's Election Day editorial summarized the amazing 2008 race as follows: *"This past year has been an eternity. Surprise after surprise has shattered calculations. Today's election looks nothing like that...of a year ago.*[7]*"* [Back then], *"The Dow Jones Industrial average had broken 14,000. The war in Iraq seemed sure to dominate the presidential race. The big political guessing game was which Republican—Rudy Giuliani? Mitt Romney?—would face inevitable Democratic nominee Hillary Clinton in the general election. John McCain was all but out of funds and steam."*

In this chapter, we highlight some of the biggest surprises of the 2008 presidential election, pinpoint some "conventional wisdoms" that were affirmed, and end with some speculations about the election's lasting impacts.

## MANY SURPRISES ALONG THE WAY

Looking back, it is easy to see why the 2008 presidential election was truly a "raw, unscripted drama" that kept the electorate engaged throughout one of the longest, most contentious, costly, and unpredictable races in quite some time. Surprises kept popping up every step of the way. We highlight some of the most memorable below and discuss how they played out over the course of the campaign.

## The Candidates

- **A large number of contestants who were winnowed down over the course of two years; 8 Democrats, 11 Republicans.**
  Campaigns often start years in advance. In the case of the 2008 election, candidates formally announced their intention to seek the presidency much earlier than usual. Televised debates began in 2007.[8] At one point, it even looked like New Hampshire would move its primary to December 2007 to maintain its "first in the nation" status.[9] The larger-than-usual field of candidates was attributable to the fact that the presidency was, in essence, an open seat. No incumbent was in the race (although McCain was cast in that light by the Democratic contenders), nor was any vice president throwing a hat into the ring.

- **Fascinating pathbreaking candidates with the potential to overcome race, gender, age, and religion.**
  Americans love underdogs and they revere candidates who have the potential to make history by breaking down long-standing barriers. Among the crowded field in 2008 were many possible trailblazers: 1. Race/ethnicity: First African American (Obama), and first Hispanic (Richardson); 2. Gender: First woman (Clinton), and first woman Republican vice president (Palin); 3. Age: Oldest president at time of inauguration (McCain); 4. Religion: First Mormon (Romney), first ordained Baptist minister (Huckabee), first Evangelical (Palin), and first Black Liberation Theology (Obama).

  At the same time, trailblazers often threaten those wed to the status quo out of prejudice. The level of racial, gender, age, and religious "persecution" of the various potential pathbreakers evident in Campaign 2008 was somewhat unexpected.[10] Many saw it as somewhat ironic that at the very time that discriminatory stereotyping seemed to be at an all-time high, the educational level of Americans was on the upswing.[11]

## The Nominating Process

- **A topsy-turvy race, with the early front-runners either struggling or bowing out early, or losing over the long haul.** (See Table 1.)
  For many presidential hopefuls, their dreams are soon dashed. They make major gaffes from which they cannot recover, have insurmountable fundraising difficulties, or simply never catch fire with either the voters or the press. Those realities are commonplace in every election. What made the 2008 race so different was the media's early designation of New Yorkers Hillary Clinton (D) and Rudy Giuliani (R) as the presumptive nominees for their respective parties. Their front-runner status was fueled by the

results of widely publicized national horserace-type polls that began early in 2007.[12] The speed with which these "conventional wisdoms" were tossed aside created a suspenseful campaign early on, thereby enticing more voters to begin following the presidential contest much earlier than usual.[13]

- **Large and critical "rogue" states (Florida and Michigan) not adhering to the primary calendars adopted by the parties.**
  Crime? Punishment? What would happen to these two battleground states, each of which dared to buck party rules and schedule their presidential primary elections in advance of February 5, Super Tuesday? (These states argued they were more diverse and representative of the nation's electorate than Iowa or New Hampshire.) This "raw and unscripted" drama yielded months-on-end of highly contentious debates, particularly among Democrats, as to whether Florida and Michigan delegates would be seated at the national conventions and the consequences if not. Who would have predicted that the national Democratic Party would have to convene a two-day nationally televised "hearing" by the Rules and Bylaws Committee in late May to attempt to untangle what had become a giant mess with the potential to allow McCain to carry these two vital states?

  Many have speculated that Florida's defiant stance may ultimately have cost Hillary Clinton the Democratic nomination.[14] She easily won the Florida primary over Obama (Clinton 49.7 percent, Obama 33.0 percent).[15] Had the Florida Legislature voted to hold the state's primary on February 5 instead of January 29,[16] the results would likely have been the same. Then Clinton would have exited from Super Tuesday with her front-runner status secure, having carried three of the nation's four largest states (California, New York, Florida) and a passel of others. (See Table 2). She very likely would have gone on to secure the nomination.

- **An unexpectedly long, drawn out nomination process (Democrats) that allowed a higher proportion of Americans than ever to see a presidential candidate in their own state.**
  The extremely competitive race between Obama and Clinton meant that states with primaries or caucuses scheduled late into the nominating process (April, May, and June) actually mattered for a change. It kept the drama alive and Americans tuned in. Candidate visits and television ads saturated the airwaves, even in the smallest of states. More voters than ever participated in the nomination process because their vote really did make a difference. In retrospect, the protracted campaign confirmed some political truisms, namely that primary competition makes the winner a better

candidate in the general election portion of the campaign[17] and provides the candidate with media coverage vital to increasing visibility among the electorate at-large. McCain's early securing of the Republican nomination made it difficult for him to energize voters via free media.[18]

- **Fierce controversies over the fairness of caucuses versus primaries as a nominating mechanism.**
Decisions about whether to nominate via a caucus or a primary have generally been left up to individual states. Prior to 2008, there had been few battles over the relative superiority of each. That all changed in 2008 when it became evident that caucuses were aiding Obama, while primaries were boosting Clinton. (See Table 2.) The issue came to a head when the seating of the Florida delegates got elevated to the national level.[19] The national party had suggested Florida Democrats conduct caucuses (in effect, a revote) so that their delegates could be seated at the national convention. They refused. The chair of the Florida Democratic Party cited the unfairness of caucuses which disproportionately tamp down the participation rates of elderly, disabled, shift workers, and active-duty military personnel stationed outside their communities.

- **The number and length of debates during the long nominating process would keep Americans tuned in.**
Perhaps it was to accommodate the large number of candidates on the stage at the beginning of the formal debates or maybe it was to help cable networks fill time: Whatever the reason, there was considerably more interest and attentiveness to the debates than initially expected, especially in light of the fact that most lasted an hour and a half to two hours.[20] "Exit polls showed that a sizable portion of voters made up their mind who to vote for after watching debates in their home state."[21]

- **Controversies over the selection of and support from superdelegates (Democrats).**
So what exactly *is* a "superdelegate"? Most Americans had never heard of one before the 2008 election. Under Democratic Party rules enacted following the 1980 victory of Republican Ronald Reagan over Democrat Jimmy Carter, this special type of convention delegate was created. "Unlike standard delegates to the [Democratic] national convention, who are selected by voters in primaries and caucuses, the supers—simply because they hold key public or party offices—are entitled to cast a vote for the nominee of their choosing."[22] The 852[23] superdelegates quickly became the center of attention of both the Obama and Clinton campaigns when it

became evident that Clinton could only secure the nomination by winning a large share of their votes. Debates sprung up over whether they should vote like their state, county, or district voted or on their own intuition as to which candidate would be the best president.[24] But to many Americans, the whole discussion was terribly confusing, much like that perennially surfacing about the workings of the Electoral College.

### Media Coverage

- **Voters preferring to view candidate appearances and hear their speeches either firsthand or via the nontraditional media.**
  As the campaign unfolded, competition intensified, and candidate visits escalated, the crowds at rallies, town hall meetings, and debates swelled. Who would have thought that so many Americans would have stood in lines for hours to see a candidate in person? Record-level crowds were the norm, rather than the exception. Most recognized that they were watching history in the making, especially in the case of Obama, Clinton, and Palin, and they wanted to say "I was there." For others, it was an opportunity to take a firsthand look at the candidate, rather than rely on secondhand accounts from a media some found quite biased. And many created their own "media coverage," by posting personal photographs and accounts of the events on social networking sites and/or blogs.[25] For others not lucky enough to be there in person, they could still see these momentous events firsthand via online streaming or YouTube.

- **A growing sense of media bias, beginning with candidate refusals to debate on certain cable television outlets.**
  As the campaign unfolded, candidates in both parties, like viewers, perceived the cable networks as being segmented ideologically. The Democrats refused to debate on Fox News Channel even though the debate was cosponsored by the Congressional Black Caucus.[26] The Republicans initially refused to participate in a YouTube-cosponsored debate on CNN.[27] Over the course of the campaign, attitudes against the mainstream national media hardened. Polls gauging the public's grading of debates often were considerably at odds with those made by newspapers and television analysts. A Pew survey found that 70 percent believed the national media was trying to throw the election toward their favorite candidate. A stunning one-third believed that it was more effective for a candidate to have a reporter on their side than to have campaign funds.[28] The disparate treatment of Obama and McCain led one well-respected journalist to describe coverage as "...the most disgusting failure of people in our business since the Iraq War. It was extreme bias, extreme pro-Obama coverage."[29]

- **Women would be treated fairly by the media and as serious candidates.**
  With a popular former first lady as the initial front-runner for the nomination, many women's rights groups were hopeful that there would finally be equity in the press's treatment of female candidates. However, once it became evident that an African American candidate would have a real shot at capturing the Democrats' nod, an intense debate emerged among journalists, women's rights advocates, and minority advocates as to whether race or gender was the tougher barrier to break on the road to the White House.[30] For many journalists, the answer was race. But for many women voters (the majority of the electorate), it was gender. By campaign's end, many Democratic and Republican women were outraged over what they perceived to be the media's unfair, even crude coverage of Clinton and Palin, respectively. For many older women, it brought back bad memories of sexist treatment they had experienced as they broke into male-dominated fields. To them, it seemed as though no progress had been made in the fight for gender equality. For conservative women, it was particularly disappointing to see Palin "subjected to an atrocious and at times delusional level of defamation merely because she [had] the temerity to hold pro-life views."[31]

### The Party Conventions

- **National conventions drawing record numbers of viewers.**
  In the latter part of 2007 and well into 2008, many in the media were anticipating little-watched national party conventions, even thinking about scaling back coverage.[32] As it turned out, nothing could have been further from reality. Americans watched both conventions in record numbers. An analysis by Nielsen found that "nearly two-thirds of all U.S. households (64.5 percent, or 73.2 million homes) tuned in to at least one of the 2008 political conventions."[33] Obama's acceptance speech from Denver's Invesco Stadium, before more than 80,000 supporters on the forty-fifth anniversary of the Reverend Martin Luther King Jr.'s "I Have a Dream" speech, drew a television audience of over 38 million. John McCain's acceptance speech a week later drew over 40 million. And Palin's vice-presidential nomination acceptance speech drew the largest viewing audience in history (over 37 million) for a vice-presidential speech. This led one newspaper to conclude that the conventions combined were "the first smash hit of the new television season." The public's intense interest in them was attributed to the competitiveness of the race, the pathbreaking candidates, along with "drama, suspense and pageantry—the same elements that drew 32 million people for the finale of *American Idol*.[34]

- **Democratic Convention's failure to immediately heal wounds inflicted over the course of a long primary.**
  Democrats were hopeful that their national convention would bring the Obama and Clinton factions together, thereby creating a unified party heading into the general election phase of the campaign.[35] However, while Hillary Clinton's speech to the Democratic Convention "brought her supporters to tears...[and] allowed them to vent their frustration and anger at her failure to get the nomination,"[36] it did not erase their double disappointment when she was not selected as his vice-presidential running mate. It took a long time for her supporters to warm to Obama. Some never did. Consequently, from the convention to Election Day, media coverage constantly raised the issue of what proportion of Clinton's supporters would vote for Obama. The issue of whether Clinton and her husband Bill would actively campaign for Obama never died either, contributing to some of the lingering resistance to Obama from Clinton's fans.[37]

- **Democratic Party icons unexpectedly endorsing candidates, appearing at national conventions, and sparking talk of political family "feuds."**
  Prior to the convention, much had been written about the parallels between Barack and Michelle Obama and President John F. and Jackie Kennedy. The closeness of the families became quite evident when early on in the primary season, Senator Ted Kennedy endorsed Obama. Caroline Kennedy also made a high-profile endorsement, breaking with her past reticence to endorse candidates.[38] She then agreed to serve on Obama's vice-presidential selection committee. At the national party convention, she introduced her uncle, Senator Edward Kennedy, in a tribute to him. The appearance of both Kennedys on the stage together was a powerful, highly emotional, moment, perceived as an important element of restoring party unity. And, of course, Obama's deliverance of his acceptance speech at Invesco Stadium was the first time such a venue was used since JFK gave his at the Los Angeles Coliseum in 1960.[39] Yet another Kennedy-Obama connection was through JFK's speechwriter, Theodore Sorensen, who came out of retirement to help craft Obama's stirring speeches.[40] The strong Kennedy-Obama ties led some commentators to cast the Obama-Clinton primary battle as merely an extension of a long-standing tug of war between two powerful political Democratic families—the Kennedys versus the Clintons.[41]

- **Unusually heated debates over the selection of vice-presidential running mates as well as the timing of the announcement and the means of doing it.**
  It is typical for presidential nominees to be offered plenty of advice as to *who* they should select as their vice-presidential running mate, along with

the reasons *why*, and suggestions as to *when* to announce the decisions. But in 2008, they even got recommendations as how and where to announce their picks to maximize media coverage.

Early on, pundits were advising each nominee to pick someone who was strong in areas in which they were weak. For Obama, it was foreign policy experience; for McCain, domestic policy expertise.

Obama was cross-pressured by those who wanted him to select Hillary Clinton to quickly unify the party and others who wanted him to select someone with stronger foreign policy credentials. He ultimately went in the latter direction and chose Senator Joe Biden, chair of the Senate Foreign Relations Committee after an intense two-month search.[42] Perhaps more significant than the choice itself was how he announced it—via a text message to his supporters released at 3:00 a.m. on Saturday, August 23, just two days away from the opening of the convention.[43] The buildup to the announcement had dominated the airwaves for days.

McCain had the luxury of waiting to see who Obama tapped before announcing his own selection. It was widely speculated that he would either pick former Massachusetts Governor Mitt Romney, former Democratic vice-presidential nominee Senator Joseph Lieberman, or Minnesota Governor Tim Pawlenty. Romney, one of his most formidable opponents, was favored by those felt he would bring a much-needed conservative voice to the ticket to fire up the base and close the widening "enthusiasm gap" between McCain and Obama.[44] Pawlenty would bring youth, a governor's policy expertise, and the possibility of turning a blue state red in 2008. Lieberman supporters felt he would help underscore McCain's bipartisanship claims, underscoring his reputation for being able to work across the aisle with Democrats, a very different kind of Republican than George W. Bush.

There was tremendous pressure on McCain to announce his selection during the Democratic Convention to get some much-needed media coverage. He did the next best thing—he "astonished the political world" by selecting Alaska Governor Sarah Palin, on Friday, August 29 at a press conference held in Dayton, Ohio.[45] It was the day most Democratic conventioneers were departing Denver and heading back home after a tremendously energizing four days. The effect was to immediately take Obama's highly acclaimed acceptance speech off the front page, as McCain and Palin left on a bus tour across the battleground states of Ohio and Pennsylvania. The selection of Palin was intended to burnish McCain's maverick status, as Palin herself had just that sort of reputation in Alaska. It was also with the expectation that Palin would appeal to disgruntled Clinton supporters. It was a bold, yet controversial pick. In the end, Palin succeeded in energizing Republicans who, up to that point, had been rather lukewarm toward McCain, but she was unable to appeal to Independents and Democratic Clinton supporters. Many in the press misrepresented the extent of Republican support for Palin, repeatedly describing her appeal as limited to Evangelicals. But for many Republicans, especially women, she represented something much bigger—a chance for them to brag about diversity on the national GOP ticket for the first time ever.

- **A hurricane working to the *advantage* of Republicans.**
  Who would have ever guessed that a hurricane would give some welcome relief to Republicans? But Hurricane Gustaf did just that—three years after the Bush administration's inadequate response to Hurricane Katrina wreaked havoc on his popularity ratings. The impending Gustaf kept President Bush and Vice President Dick Cheney from appearing in person on the first day of the GOP convention as planned. (President Bush appeared via video the second night; Cheney never appeared.) In their places on evening number one were the more popular First Lady Laura Bush and potential First Lady Cindy McCain.[46] A great sense of relief flooded over the McCain campaign staff. By one account, "the McCain camp didn't want the reviled president to touch their convention with a bargepole" and was thrilled with the fact that Laura Bush's "gracious, good-humored performance was far better received than her husband's remarks . . ."[47]

## Post-Convention Debates

- **A church-sponsored debate format sets the standard.**
  When it was announced that Obama and McCain had each agreed to sit for back-to-back hour-long televised interviews with Saddleback Church's Pastor Rick Warren, few pundits believed the "debate" would have much of a draw, much less a significant impact on the overall direction of the campaign. Once again, conventional wisdom was proved wrong. The Civil Forum on the Presidency held in August at the California megachurch (the candidates' first joint appearance on national television[48]) attracted many viewers and was replayed multiple times over the course of the campaign.[49] By campaign's end, many citizens and political analysts judged this unusual sit down, one-on-one interview format with questions designed to reveal the more personal and spiritual side of the candidates, as much more informative than the series of debates sponsored by the Commission on Presidential Debates.[50]

  The Commission-sponsored debates still drew large viewing audiences. The final presidential debate between Senators John McCain and Barack Obama drew 56.5 million U.S. viewers. The TV audience for the senators' third meeting edged past that of their first debate at the end of September, which drew 52.4 million viewers, but was easily surpassed by the audience of 63.2 million that tuned in for the second presidential debate.[51]

- **The lone vice-presidential debate draws more viewers than the three presidential debates.**

The vice-presidential debate between Senator Joe Biden and Governor Sarah Palin attracted some 70 million viewers. It outdrew all of the presidential debates and ended up being the second most watched debate of all time. (The 1980[52] debate between Republican Ronald Reagan and Democrat Jimmy Carter still holds the debate viewership record— 80.6 million.) Given the questions raised about the Alaska governor's readiness and the widespread lampooning of her previous appearances in the media, "a larger-than-usual TV audience was expected for Palin and Biden going into their debate,"[53] but no one predicted the huge audience that this male-versus-female, old-versus-young, Washington-insider versus Alaska-hockey-mom face-off would generate. Predictable, however, was the scoring of the debate, which was almost entirely based on partisan leanings.

### Personalities: Family, "Friends," and Foes

- **Unexpected "disses" of Hillary Clinton by a former member of the Bill Clinton administration and an early supporter.**

Loyalty is a strong element of politics. When individuals turn their backs on "them what brung you to the dance," it captures a great deal of media attention. Such was the case when Governor Bill Richardson, a failed candidate for the Democratic nomination early in the process, came out with a strong endorsement of Barack Obama.[54] At the time, it "was a cruel blow for Hillary as [Richardson's] ascendancy in politics, and accumulation of executive responsibilities, owned much to the Clinton era where he was elevated to important positions"[55] (Under Bill Clinton, Richardson was U.S. trade ambassador, then energy secretary). This act of "disloyalty" infuriated former President Bill Clinton who labeled Richardson a "traitor."[56] The Clintons are seen as having won this skirmish. Obama tapped Hillary for secretary of state, a position Richardson was widely thought to want. Instead, he was offered the job of secretary of commerce in the Obama administration.

A bigger disappointment for Clinton was African American Georgia Congressman John Lewis's withdrawal of his initial endorsement of her made early on in the campaign. Like many other members of the Congressional Black Caucus who had endorsed her early, Lewis experienced great pressure from his constituents to switch his allegiance to Obama.[57] As reported in the

*Atlanta Journal Constitution*, "Lewis' announcement [October 2007] that he was backing Clinton, a longtime friend, over Obama, the nation's first truly viable African-American candidate for the presidency, angered many of Georgia's black constituents and numerous civil rights elders who had fought for black voting rights alongside Lewis."[58] He acknowledged that "It was a long, hard, difficult struggle" to make the decision, but that "Sometimes, you have to be on the right side of history." Clinton graciously said she understood, but it was undoubtedly painful for her nonetheless.

- **Highly untimely commentaries by spouses that were anything but helpful to the candidate.**
Anyone who is married understands that those you love the most may inadvertently hurt you at the worst of times. Such was the case in Election 2008. Michelle Obama created quite a stir with her comment, "For the first time in my adult lifetime, I'm really proud of my country. And not just because Barack has done well, but because I think people are hungry for change." The comment was immediately attacked by conservatives as being unpatriotic and out-of-sync with her husband's message of America as the land of opportunity.[59] Cindy McCain stepped into the fray by taking a shot at the comment at a rally in Wisconsin: "I am proud of my country. I don't know about you? If you heard those words earlier, I am very proud of my country."[60] Her husband brushed it off and the story died. However, the initial comment by Michelle had staying power and remained controversial over the course of the campaign.

The "pride" comment ultimately had far less of a negative impact than Bill Clinton's comments belittling Obama's primary victory in South Carolina. Clinton seemed to downplay the significance of the Obama's victory over Hillary by noting Jesse Jackson had also won South Carolina in 1984 and 1988, inferring that the only reason Obama won the state in 2008 was his race and the large African American electorate. The remark was offensive to some black leaders, most notably Congressman Jim Clyburn, who found it insulting and racist in tone because it tried to paint Obama as "the black candidate."[61] It ended up costing Hillary a lot of support among African Americans for the remainder of the primary battle.

- **The intensity of "guilt by association" charges stemming from candidates' friends/associates, from their past, mostly pastors and politicos.**
Campaigns have always tried to make much of the company a candidate keeps, especially if the acquaintance is less than wholesome. What was surpris-

ing in 2008 was the intensity with which the "guilt by association" tactic was utilized—made possible by more easily retrievable print, audio, and video clips from days gone by, and a news industry and electorate hungry for controversy. The tactic was "the preferred tool of attack, for the campaigns themselves, news outlets, pressure groups, and partisan magazines and Web sites."[62] Infamous events from 20, 30, even 40 years back were dredged up by opponents in efforts to tarnish both Obama and McCain.[63]

Obama's opponents tied him to his longtime, somewhat radical, pastor—the Reverend Jeremiah Wright, Jr.—and to another political radical—William Ayers, a cofounder of the 1960s-era Weather Underground, a violent, radical left organization that bombed the Pentagon to protest the Vietnam War.[64] (The Wright connection stuck in the minds of more voters than the Ayers link.)[65] McCain's opponents linked him with unsavory personas as well—right-wing preachers (John Hagee and Rod Parsley), lobbyists,[66] and a corrupt savings and loan owner and big campaign donor named Charles Keating.[67] Both Obama and McCain tried their best to distance themselves as much as possible from past associations with undesirables.[68] They were never completely successful; "guilt by association" attacks ebbed and flowed with the polls. When a candidate was down, the guilt by association attacks against his opponent escalated.

- **Celebrities played a bigger role than usual.**
No one doubts the fact that Oprah and Tina Fey were powerful factors in the election. They greatly added to the exciting "reality show" feel of the campaign whenever they appeared on camera or, in the case of Oprah, at Obama's rallies. They each created suspense, causing an anxious public to wonder, "What will they do next?" "Who will it offend?" and "Will it help or hurt the candidate?"

Without question, Oprah had a major impact on Obama's ascension to the top:

> "The most decisive moment in Hollywood's attempt to influence the election was Oprah Winfrey's introduction of Barack Obama on her daytime television show. This simply had never happened before… But Oprah not only introduced Obama, she vouched for him, she gave him what Joan Crawford once called "the big okay," her seal of approval. Almost instantly, Winfrey transformed Obama from an ambitious young politician into a cultural star. He suddenly rocketed beyond politics. He became larger than all that. And there he remained, all through the campaign and up to election day, a man who was as much culture as candidate."[69]

Still her strong endorsement was not without controversy. As her show's ratings fell, some analysts attributed the falloff to a drop in white female viewers who were offended that she endorsed Obama over Hillary Clinton.

More debatable was the impact of Tina Fey's wildly popular portrayals of Sarah Palin on *Saturday Night Live*. Palin herself had to decide whether to appear live on the show and when she did, the show drew record numbers of viewers. But many believe that Tina Fey greatly harmed Palin:

> "Tina Fey never 'did' Sarah Palin. She took certain traits of Palin's, even traits Palin was simply assumed to have, then exaggerated them. Because Palin wasn't that well known, Fey had close to a blank slate, a rare advantage in the world of impressionists. And because her impression was entertaining and funny, it drew us in. But the impression ridiculed Palin, and went far to define her in the public mind as someone not quite up to the job, a political airhead. It wasn't the only factor, of course, but it played an important role in sending Palin from her starring role at the Republican convention, crashing down to her later image as someone grasping for respect."[70]

Each celebrity episode was interpreted by many as just further proof of media bias and to others of gender being more of a barrier than race.

### Issues and Polls

- **Constantly shifting issue priorities (from the war in Iraq to spiking gas prices—Drill Here, Drill Now—to the Wall Street meltdown).**
It is said that in politics, like life, "timing is everything" while it is almost impossible to predict. So it was in '08. Initially, the dominant issue was the *war in Iraq*. The assumption of nearly everyone was that it would dominate all the way to Election Day. That prognostication, like so many others, turned out to be way off mark. When gas prices hit $4.00+, the war took a backseat to energy costs. McCain and his running mate from oil-rich Alaska were much better positioned on that issue than on the war. Their "Drill Here, Drill Now" message resonated with an irate public whose attitudes on off-shore oil drilling had virtually changed overnight. The race narrowed. McCain even took a brief lead.

Then the economy took a nosedive and suddenly there was no other issue: "[The] meltdown on Wall Street brought the economy roaring back…and the question for the final seven weeks of the general-election campaign [was] whether Barack Obama or John McCain [could] convince voters that he is capable of leading the country out of the morass."[71] It was a ready-made issue for Democrat Obama and a nightmare for Republican

McCain who had to live with an ill-timed comment made at Jacksonville, Florida rally right after the meltdown. After acknowledging that the economy was a serious problem, he said he still thought "the fundamentals of our economy are strong." The Obama campaign made hay of the issue, even cut some powerful ads using McCain's own words against him. While McCain rebounded somewhat by strengthening his strong antitax message using "Joe the Plumber" (real name: Joe Wurzelbacher) to put a real face on the issue, many pundits say the election was really lost when the economy became the issue rather than energy costs, national security, or terrorism. (McCain had briefly tried to shift the issue to terrorism when polls showed him doing better against Obama on that issue.)[72] In the end, 63 percent of all voters identified the economy as the most important issue in determining their vote. Of those, 53 percent voted for Obama, 44 percent for McCain. There hadn't been that much consensus on a single issue in a presidential election in years.

- **Early projections that moral issues would trump economic issues for conservatives and Evangelicals.**
Beginning with the Republican primary, the focus was whether moderate candidates like Giuliani and McCain could energize "the Republican base" which is often a code word for religious conservatives, or Evangelicals. In 2008, the underlying presumption was that these voters dominate the GOP and care more about moral issues (abortion, gay marriage) than the war in Iraq, national security, taxes, or the economy. When McCain ultimately won enough victories to force his last GOP opponent out of the race (Mike Huckabee, a Baptist minister), many presumed McCain would not have a chance against either Clinton or Obama with such a "moral rift" in the party. So when McCain selected Palin, a Pentecostal, as his running mate, many saw it as a choice designed to appeal to the party's Evangelicals (although he proclaimed it was because of her role as a maverick and her executive experience as governor). The bottom line is that she did help unify the party. Without her on the ticket, Republican McCain would not have even come close to beating Obama. "It's hard to imagine conservatives rallying to McCain—even to the relatively limited extent that they did— without Palin on the ticket. And without the base, McCain's loss could have been far worse."[73] But the truth is that white Evangelical and born-again voters made up just 26 percent of all voters. And for many of these voters, like others, the economy was more of an issue than moral values from the beginning.[74] Severe economic downturns dominate people's priorities when they are worried about making ends meet.

- The proliferation of "horserace" polls showing lead changes on an almost daily basis—nationally and in up-for-grabs battleground states. Competition enhances interest. The 2008 election saw a tremendous upswing in the number of competing polls and Web sites devoted to polling— RealClearPolitics.com, Pollster.com, and FiveThirtyEight.com being three of the most trafficked. RealClearPolitics.com had 140 million page views in September alone.[75] As of less than a week away from the election, there had been 728 national polls with head-to-head matchups of the candidates, 215 in October alone. In contrast, in 2004, there were just 239 matchup polls, with 67 in October.[76] And this total doesn't even count the hundreds of polls in key battleground states. While academics argued over the validity of various pollsters' sampling frames, survey wording, and question sequencing, politicians, the public, and the press were fascinated with them. They contributed to the "Amazing Race" imagery.

- Intense debates among pollsters over survey methodology in the cell phone era, particularly the accuracy of identifying likely young voters. The expected increase in the size of the youth vote raised the issue that had been debated for quite some time in the polling world, namely what to do about cell phones. "Should pollsters weight their voter samples by age? And if so, by how much?" The concern was that young adults, who rarely use landline telephones and thus were "out of reach of the standard telephone samples,"[77] were being underrepresented in samples. The Obama camp was particularly interested in this, knowing how solidly the youth vote was for Barack.

  Defining a "likely voter" has always been a challenge to pollsters because it affects the ultimate accuracy of their polls (verified on Election Day) which, in turn, impacts their professional reputations. The difficulties of accurately identifying persons who would ultimately vote, not just tell a pollster they would, increased in 2008 because of so many new registrants and a higher level of interest in the election than usual.[78] The Gallup Poll even went so far as to employ two different models in their 2008 polls—a traditional and an expanded version.[79]

  In the end, while various polls differed in the margin of victory for the Obama-Biden ticket, they all correctly predicted the winner in their last national polls before the election. Some were more accurate than others.[80] Ironically, exit polls showed the youth vote as a proportion of the electorate in 2008 was only slightly larger than in 2004 (18 percent versus 17 percent).

## Money, Microtargeting, and Get-Out-The-Vote Efforts

- **Fundraising battles under unexpected conditions and with unpredicted outcomes.**

  Who would have anticipated that Democrats would raise vastly more money than Republicans and that a Democratic presidential candidate would turn down public financing? Yes, it happened in 2008. Initially, both John McCain and Barack Obama pledged they would participate in the public financing system for their presidential campaigns if the other did. Ultimately, McCain did and Obama did not. On June 19, 2008, Obama announced he would decline public financing of his campaign.[81] Obama gave as his rationales: 1) that the system was broken and 2) it was the only way he could raise enough to combat money raised by McCain, the Republican National Committee, and sympathetic 527 groups "who will spend millions and millions of dollars in unlimited donations."[82] The Obama's eschewing of public financing was a shocker; it was the first time a candidate of a major party had declined public finance. But, given the circumstances, it should hardly have been an unexpected move: At that time, he was amassing record levels of contributions from a wide variety of donors—three times more than McCain. The money gap widened as the campaign progressed. By campaign's end, Obama shattered all records, raising $750 million, "eclipsing the total amount of money raised by all of the presidential candidates combined in 2004."[83] McCain ran behind in the fundraising game from the beginning, and it clearly hurt him.

- **527 independent groups anticipated as big players, last-minute players, but never seriously emerged.**

  In the 2004 election, 527s, like MoveOn.org and the Swift Boat Veterans for Truth, were extremely influential. Expectations were that 527s would be even bigger players in 2008, but that never happened. While more than $180 million was spent by 527 groups in 2008, it was far less than the $338 million such groups spent in 2004.[84]

  The economy took its toll on potential donors, many of whom were "busy trying to salvage their own financial portfolios."[85] The legal climate was also different in 2008. Following the 2004 election, the Federal Elections Commission assessed major fines against seven 527 groups which prompted lawyers advising 527s in 2008 to warn that "FEC fines could be a precursor to action by the U.S. Justice Department."[86]

- **Record numbers of ads/videos were run in very different kinds of places on the Web (YouTube, candidate websites).**
  YouTube effectively introduced a new form of campaign ad (videos) which became a very engaging and entertaining way to attempt to sway voters. By some accounts, videos posted on YouTube "turned the old model of television advertising—and political propaganda—upside down." Video postings came from both directions—top down from the political parties and candidates; bottom up from videos posted by individual voters.[87]

  Online ads were utilized by both the Obama and McCain campaigns, but more by Obama. From January to August, 2008, he spent around $5.5 million on online ads, $4.4 million of which went to Google. He bought both AdWords ads on Google and display ads seen through the AdSense network.[88] However, online advertising did not come near to what was spent on television advertising. It was less than 1 percent of what was spent on television and not as effective. "In the political sphere, television is viewed as the ultimate persuasion medium and the Web more akin to direct mail…"[89] The number run by both candidates increased in the final weeks of the campaign; they both went after specific audiences in key battleground states. Obama's aim was getting voters in states with early voting to the polls; McCain's were primarily persuasion ads featuring either Sarah Palin or Joe the Plumber.[90]

- **Negative ads turned out to be less effective.**
  There has long been a debate about the effectiveness of negative ads, although political consultants swear by them. And there were plenty of them run in Campaign '08. Both candidates used sharp, stinging, highly derogatory words to describe their opponent in their television ads and direct mail pieces.[91]

  This time, however, the negative ads may have been less effective. McCain ran more of them than Obama. Over a five-month period, 47 percent of McCain spots were negative compared to 39 percent of Obama's ads.[92] The further behind McCain got in the polls near the end of the election, the more negative ads he ran, which caused tensions even among his own campaign staff.[93] One GOP pollster had some rather strong words for the propensity of many in his party to point fingers at everything and everyone for McCain's loss, instead of at its negative ads: "The blame was placed on everyone and everything but the issue-less, relentlessly negative campaigns that party operatives have promoted for years…This year, the same players dragged out the same, tired negative campaign strategy and, not surprisingly, the party hit a brick wall."[94]

- **The Electoral College map of 2004 changed considerably.**
  At the beginning of the campaign, many analysts were projecting that the battleground states would be the same and that the candidates would both focus their time and money on these "purple" states. By September, Obama "was taking a fresh look at the electoral map," as his campaign caught fire and the contributions kept rolling in.[95] Specifically, he had his eye on red states in the South and West, many of which had experienced significant demographic shifts since 2004. In the three days before Election Day, he visited Colorado, Missouri, Nevada, Florida North, Carolina, and Virginia. It paid off.[96] He ended up turning nine red states blue—North Carolina, Virginia, Florida, Ohio, Indiana, Iowa, Colorado, New Mexico, and Nevada. (See Figure 1.) Money mattered tremendously: "The campaign's final days brought a reminder of how Mr. Obama's financial might had allowed him to redraw the political map."[97] What was perhaps the most stunning outcome was his cracking of the previously solid Republican South. These "New South" states have "lots of suburbs, transplants, and younger college graduates."[98]

- **New technologies were effective in attracting first-time (mostly young) voters, keeping them engaged, and turning them out.**
  In 2004, blogs were the rage on the Internet, not social networking sites or "YouTube." But in 2008, the latter two were highly successful in engaging Web-savvy young voters, and blogging became more refined via microblogging sites like Twitter.[99]

  All of the major candidates had support on Facebook and MySpace profiles.[100] The Obama campaign's social networking was miles ahead of McCain's, partially because the high-tech community favored Obama, but mostly it was due to his money edge over McCain. It certainly helped that the cofounder of Facebook was on Obama's team.[101] By late October, "more than 2 million Facebook users [had declared] their support for Obama by "friending" him, while 750,000 [had] done so on MySpace. McCain [had] almost 590,000 Facebook friends and 189,000 on MySpace."[102]

  Through the Internet, campaigns were able to keep in constant touch with their young supporters. Daily e-mails, personally addressed, kept them informed about rallies, events, debates, polls, fundraising benchmarks, and television appearances. Hillary Clinton even launched her presidential campaign via her Web site. These communiqués detailed the candidate's issue stances and solicited feedback from the recipients, who were constantly reminded that their support—and vote—was vital to the candidate's victory.

  Text messages were used to make major announcements (for example, Obama's vice-presidential running mate). E-mail addresses were often the "price of admission" to major concerts, town hall meetings, and rallies. Access to millions of e-mails also made it easier to mobilize supporters into action (the Obama Action Wire), to rebut negative news stories, to complain about attack ads, or to protest guests on talk shows.[103]

YouTube became a great place for candidates to launch ads and share videos. It was particularly effective for Obama who "drew more than 110 million viewers for his 1,800 campaign-related videos."[104] And Flickr was a political junkie's goldmine for campaign photographs.

- **Early voting popularity rendered Republicans' famed 2004 72-Hour Campaign Get-Out-The-Vote plan obsolete.**
Conventional wisdom says that the party that loses an election borrows the playbook of the winning team, then improves on it by the start of the next cycle. That is precisely what Democrats did in 2008 after losing the turnout battle in 2004. On the other hand, Republicans continued to believe their 2004 Get-Out-The-Vote (GOTV) plan was as good as ever. It wasn't. The unraveling of the GOP plan came with the spread of early voting across the states. The Obama camp aggressively sought to spike Democratic turnout before Election Day. (In the final two weeks of the campaign, Obama held every one of his events in early voting states.)[105] It was quite successful. Democrats turned out in disproportionately high numbers and got lots of press about it. It rendered the GOP 72-Hour Plan ineffective and, in the minds of some, tamped down turnout among "soft" GOP voters. Said one former McCain adviser, "The election was lost three weeks before Election Day. What an old, old election model that was completely obsolete."[106]

## VOTE PATTERNS

- **Unexpectedly strong African American–Hispanic coalition.**
Political scientists have long debated whether Hispanics are more likely to form voting coalitions with whites or blacks. Early on, that led some pundits to anticipate that in some of the nation's large multiracial metropolitan areas, where minorities often compete with each other for local political power, Hispanics might be reticent to vote for a black candidate. But then again, some Republicans leaders in Congress had engaged in rather strong anti-immigrant rhetoric in the debate about immigration reform, which created hard feelings among Latino voters who had "an underlying sense that the debate about immigration [was] a debate about Hispanics."[107] While McCain had coauthored a bipartisan bill that "would have legalized some undocumented immigrants, created guest-worker programs and beefed up U.S. border enforcement,"

he backed away from that during the campaign to bring back the GOP base.[108] But in the end, whether it was the backlash against the GOP's anti-immigrant stance or the economy, 67 percent of Latinos voted for Obama—and an 11-percent gain over their vote for Kerry in 2004. It helped Obama win Florida, Nevada, New Mexico, Colorado, Virginia, and North Carolina—all battleground states.[109] Certainly, Obama ran many Spanish-language ads on radio and television to reach these voters, even cutting one where he voiced the entire ad "en español." McCain spent on Spanish language media too—but did not have as much money to do so, or as effective a message.

- **Little evidence of an extensive "Bradley Effect."**
Race dominated media coverage in 2008 after the conventions. Multiple polls were conducted which suggested white prejudice might be pervasive enough to block Obama's bid to be the first African American president of the U.S. An AP-Yahoo News study released in September "concluded that white Democratic racism may cause 2.5 percent of voters to 'turn away from Obama because of his race,' roughly the margin of George W. Bush's victory over John F. Kerry in 2004."[110] This created quite a stir and launched intense discussions over whether the "Bradley Effect" might be felt in 2008. (The Bradley Effect refers to white voters' telling pollsters in preelection polls they will support a black candidate, but then not doing so in the privacy of a voting booth on Election Day. It is named for Tom Bradley, the former African American mayor of Los Angeles who lost the 1982 California governor's race, even though polls had predicted he would defeat his white Republican opponent.) And although a later Gallup Poll found that more voters said they were more likely to vote *for* Obama because of his race than against (9 percent versus 6 percent),[111] fears of racially polarized voting escalated as media coverage focused more on it the closer it got to Election Day.

Obama insiders were less worried about this possibility than others, having seen his successes in capturing white votes in his U.S. Senate race. "There is no room he walks into where he doesn't feel comfortable and make the people feel that way. It's both his personality and his background—one contributes to the other. There's no doubt that being biracial contributes to a sense that he doesn't compartmentalize people by race or ethnicity or background."[112] Their intuitions proved right on point. Postelection analyses have concluded, "There is no evidence that people were lying to pollsters...About one in five voters said that race was a factor in their vote. Among them, Obama led McCain by 8 points. Obama led by 5 points among the rest of the electorate. So, the Democrat's race turned out to be a net plus for him."[113] He benefitted most from support among highly educated whites.

- **Spoiler role by third party and independent candidates predicted but never got any traction.**

Congressman Ron Paul, a Republican candidate for president, but with a strong Libertarian streak, was a "phenom" in the primary. He was the Republicans' antiwar candidate who captured the attention of multitudes of young and independent voters and broke a single day record for online contributions. When he withdrew from the GOP nomination fight, many expected him to run as a third-party candidate (Libertarian). He didn't. Instead, former Georgia Republican Congressman Bob Barr ended up the Libertarian Party's presidential nominee. In addition to Barr, other well-known minor candidates were the perennial candidate Ralph Nader, running as an Independent, and Green Party nominee Cynthia McKinney, a former African American congresswoman from Georgia. A *Time*/CNN poll taken in late August concluded these candidates were attracting enough support to play the role of spoiler. The fear was that they might get enough votes to wreak havoc in battleground states, as happened in Florida in 2000. The polls showed Nader getting 6 percent, Barr, 5 percent, and McKinney, 3 percent.[114] Much was being made that neither major party candidate was reaching the "magic 50-percent" support level. In fact, even as Obama was pulling away from McCain in the waning days of the campaign, there was still considerable concern that Obama had not been polling consistently above 50 percent in a number of electoral vote-rich swing states, including Ohio and Florida"[115]

Nader's running mate, Matt Gonzalez, vehemently downplayed the spoiler role of these minor candidates. He insisted that "it's not about spoiling in one state or another. The real point of running is to highlight electoral reform. If we're going to fix the problems of the 2000 election, it's not just enough to say the person with the most votes wins…The candidate should need to get 50 percent. You can't spoil a contest that's decided by 50 percent."[116] In the end, there were no spoilers in 2008. These candidates "found themselves on the sidelines, with little traction on their issues and no impact on the outcome."[117]

## THE ELECTORAL PROCESS

- **Concerns about the potential for fraud in the registration process dominated election administration issues in 2008.**

In 2000 and 2004, election administration controversies focused on the possibility of fraud in the voting process—miscounting of votes, spoiled or missing ballots, voter intimidation, and malfunctioning equipment. In 2008, the most heated battles were over registration-related improprieties—fraudulent multiple registrations by the same person, unsavory tactics used to get individuals to vote, incomplete information on registration forms—some intentional "caging" (groups holding back registration forms for those registering with the "wrong" party), and discriminatory purging of voters from registration lists. At the center of the controversy were actions by the Association of Community Organizations for Reform Now (ACORN), an activist group with a history of questionable voter registration tactics. Several states filed lawsuits against the group for engaging in fraudulent registration activities; the FBI began investigations as well. The issue gained a lot of national attention when Nevada's Democratic secretary of state and attorney general raided the group's Las Vegas headquarters and seized the group's computers, voter registration cards, and employee information after ACORN submitted fraudulent names and addresses as part of its voter-registration drive. It shocked Americans to hear the secretary of state announce that among these fraudulent forms was "basically the starting lineup for the Dallas Cowboys" and that "Tony Romo is not registered to vote in Nevada."[118] And in Cleveland, Ohio, a 19-year-old man admitted to authorities that he was given cash and cigarettes by ACORN to register and had personally filled out 72 separate voter-registration cards over an 18-month period.[119] The controversies took on an added political dimension when it was reported that Obama had once worked as the executive director of ACORN's voter-registration arm, Project Vote, in 1992 and later represented the group as its lawyer.[120]

Another controversial issue was the potential purging of names from voter registration lists. This problem arose as a consequence of the Help America Vote Act passed by Congress following the 2000 election. It required "each state to create a single voter database, which could then be matched with other data, such as driver's licenses, to detect false registrations, dead people and those who have moved or become 'inactive.'"[121] The most intense battle over the match requirement occurred in the battleground state of Ohio. There, the GOP sued the Democratic secretary of state over her failure to provide local officials with names of thousands of newly registered voters whose voter records didn't match the driver's license or Social Security databases. The U.S. Sixth Circuit Court of Appeals ordered the secretary to provide the lists to help county officials verify eligibility of voters. She appealed the decision to the U.S. Supreme Court to prevent the disenfranchisement of voters. The high court ruled in her favor, accepting her argument that the prescreening process within such a short time frame would "severely disrupt the voting process."[122]

- **Dire predictions of equipment and process meltdowns in key battleground states like Florida and Ohio never happened.**
Many believed that Election 2008 would be thrown into chaos, much like the 2000 election, because of equipment failures (especially of touch-screen vot-

ing machines and some types of optical scan machines), voter suppression (particularly of voting rights of felons and the homeless), voter intimidation, and problems with provisional ballots, to name a few. Election group spokespersons warned the nation that "unprecedented stress on the nation's polling infrastructure…and a wave of provisional ballots being cast in battleground states" might well result in controversies that would not be resolved until long after Election Day. Ohio and Florida were singled out as the most likely places where chaos would reign.[123] Fortunately, things weren't nearly as dire as predicted. Most of the problems that surfaced were due to long lines and record turnout, not the "fraud or other chicanery that marred closely contested presidential elections in 2000 and 2004."[124] But the shortcomings of 2008 will undoubtedly be addressed by reform groups before the next election.

## A DYNAMIC CAMPAIGN CREATED A "FLUID" ELECTORATE

The entire "presidential season" was filled with unscripted, surprising turns of events and numerous flawed predictions by prognosticators and pundits. So much in 2008 was counter to conventional wisdom that it kept the electorate highly engaged until the very end; there were, in effect, few " reruns" to tamp down their interest.

An Associated Press-Yahoo News poll tracking some 2,000 voters throughout the campaign found that, contrary to conventional wisdom, "it can be pretty much taken for granted that most voters lean sharply left or right and commit to one candidate early on," there was "a lively churning beneath the surface as people shifted their loyalties—some more than once." (See Figure 1.) In fact, "few voters made unwavering, long-term commitments to either candidate."[125] Seventeen percent of those who ended up voting for Obama had expressed support for McCain at one time or another in the series of ten polls taken beginning in November 2007; similarly, 11 percent of McCain voters had expressed support for Obama at least momentarily.

## ELECTIONS HAVE CONSEQUENCES, SO WHAT'S NEXT?

No sooner was Election 2008 in the history books than Election 2012 began. That's the reality of presidential election campaigns. Each one seems to be more exciting than the last. Whether that will be true in 2012, compared to the path-breaking 2008 election is anybody's guess. But we do have some strong indications of some of the impacts the 2008 election will have on the next campaign.

The money chase will continue to be the most daunting task facing potential candidates. Front-runners in the money game during the nomination stage

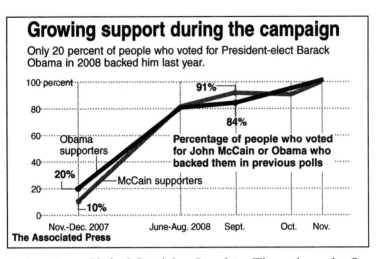

## Growing support during the campaign
Only 20 percent of people who voted for President-elect Barack Obama in 2008 backed him last year.

Figure 1. Americans Shifted Candidate Loyalties Throughout the Campaign
Source: Associated Press-Yahoo News Polls conducted November 2007–November 2008.

will undoubtedly reject public financing of their general election campaign. Taking the public financing route may even signal that a candidate may be experiencing even bigger problems—organizational difficulties, technological inadequacies—or suffering from a potentially fatal voter enthusiasm gap.

For those who would like to see the "failed public financing of campaigns" system markedly reformed, forget about it. The winning party is always reticent to change rules that have enabled it to capture control of the White House. And there is considerably less pressure to make changes when the same party controls both houses of Congress. Democrats will likely own Washington from 2008 to 2012.

Early money has become even more important. The 2008 campaign made it abundantly clear that it can give a candidate an insurmountable edge in registering voters by opening headquarters in key geographical locations and hiring staff whose initial responsibility is to register new voters.

During the nomination phase, candidates will not as easily fall into the trap of assuming the battle will be over quickly just because primaries and caucuses are being frontloaded. Candidates will be more hesitant to drop out early, having witnessed the unexpected turns campaigns can take and what, in retrospect, looked like the premature exiting of some candidates in 2008.

No longer will front-runners assume they will remain so. In fact, being tagged the front-runner for months, even years, on end may ultimately be a liability rather than an asset. Remember, voters like competition and intrigue and may even relish the thought of the front-runner being "voted off the island."

The importance of being ahead of the curve in utilizing the newest forms of communication in registering, informing, and mobilizing voters couldn't have been more striking than it was in 2008. Today's "alternative media" may very well be regarded as "mainstream media" by 2012. What will become the new alternative media is most likely to be considerably more interactive. The successes of the Obama campaign in building a massive voter e-mail-based network and the challenges of keeping it in place as he shifts from candidate to officeholder may prompt Congress to rewrite election-related laws to bring them up to speed in an increasingly high-tech society. It is less likely that Congress will tackle media bias or develop penalties for Internet-disseminated character assassinations, vulgarity, or hate speech. But it might very well reimpose the Fairness Doctrine.

In selecting key campaign staffers and advisers, much more attention will be paid to their social networking activities. The depth and effectiveness of guilt-by-association tactics in 2008 and the ease with which potentially damaging words, e-mails, photographs, etc. were retrieved and put on the Web made everyone around a campaign quite nervous. As even more refined technologies are developed that permit even easier invasions of individual privacy, it will become more imperative to screen staff, consultants, donors, volunteers, friends, and relatives.

Savvy candidates and their campaign staffs will focus on honing topnotch GOTV strategies for both primaries and caucuses—and they will be different. What the 2008 election made perfectly clear is that the likely participants differ by type of nominating election. Caucus participants are considerably younger and more educated than primary voters.

Staying on message has become the preeminent goal, especially when speaking before large crowds. The 2008 election saw candidates on the stump in the remotest of places relying on teleprompters. Giving scripted speeches has proven to be a less risky, more effective strategy than spontaneity. Scripted speeches also diminish the odds that a candidate will slip up and use regional or ethnic phrases that may play well in one part of the country but be fatal in another.

The 2008 campaign also proved the importance of demographic analysis and the payoffs from not being wedded to the Electoral College map from the previous election. This is an increasingly expensive part of campaign research, but one that a candidate minimizes at his or her own peril. Closely monitoring demographic shifts is a critical step to devising aggressive registration drives, especially those targeted at first-time voters.

Campaign timing and tactics have been forever changed by the spread and popularity of early voting. In 2008, high levels of GOTV and candidate visits in the early voting states proved to be a very effective campaign strategy for Democrats. But it also was possible because of their significant money edge. Early voting will likely spread to other states before 2012, the effect of which will be to require even more funds, and earlier, than in the past.

Table 1. The Long Winnowing Process

| Republican Candidate | Delegate Count | Campaign Status | |
|---|---|---|---|
| Jim Gilmore | 0 | Withdrew | 7/14/07 |
| Tommy Thompson | 0 | Withdrew | 8/13/07 |
| Sam Brownback | 0 | Withdrew | 10/19/07 |
| Tom Tancredo | 0 | Withdrew | 12/20/07 |
| Duncan Hunter | 0 | Withdrew | 1/19/08 |
| Fred Thompson | 0 | Withdrew | 1/22/08 |
| Rudy Giuliani | 0 | Withdrew | 1/30/08 |
| Mitt Romney | 271 | Suspended | 2/7/08 |
| Mike Huckabee | 278 | Withdrew | 3/4/08 |
| Ron Paul | 35 | Suspended | 6/12/08 |
| John McCain | 1,575 | Official Nominee 9/4/08* | |
| Democratic Candidate | Delegate Count | Campaign Status | |
| Joe Biden | 0 | Withdrew | 1/3/08 |
| Chris Dodd | 0 | Withdrew | 1/3/08 |
| Bill Richardson | 0 | Withdrew | 1/9/08 |
| Dennis Kucinich | 0 | Withdrew | 1/24/08 |
| John Edwards | 6 | Withdrew | 1/30/08 |
| Mike Gravel | 0 | Withdrew | 3/25/08 |
| Hillary Rodham Clinton | 1,896 | Withdrew | 6/3/08 |
| Barack Obama | 2,201 | Official Nominee 8/28/08* | |

Notes: *The dates given for McCain and Obama's nomination were the dates in which they gave their acceptance speeches. They had been the presumptive nominees since March (McCain) and June (Obama).

Sources:
   http://www.cnn.com/ELECTION/2008/primaries/
   http://projects.washingtonpost.com/2008-presidential-candidates/
   http://www.washingtonpost.com/wp-dyn/content/article/2007/08/12/
      AR2007081201451.html
   http://projects.washingtonpost.com/2008-presidential-candidates/tom-tancredo/
   http://www.gwu.edu/~action/2008/reps08.html

Addressing the issue of election fraud is likely to escalate, with even more attention to voter registration. There is a strong possibility of a push by Congress to further "nationalize" the election administration process. Already there is some discussion of a creating a national voter registration system. That is probably not imminent, but the fact that the issue is even being discussed signals a growing frustration with flaws in state databases.

But perhaps the most significant long-term impact that the pathbreaking presidential election of 2008 may have had is to make it difficult for any major party to run a ticket comprised of white males. The importance of Obama's and Palin's presence on their respective party tickets simply cannot be overstated.

Such a long campaign it was, with so many unexpected twists and turns, and so much excitement. And it ended with so many high hopes. It truly was an amazing race!

**Table 2. The Democrats: Primaries Best for Clinton; Caucuses for Obama**

| Date of Primary | States | Type of Primary | Democratic Winner |
|---|---|---|---|
| 3-Jan-08 | Iowa | Closed Caucus | Obama |
| 8-Jan-08 | New Hampshire | Semi-Open Primary | Clinton |
| 15-Jan-08 | Michigan | Open Primary | Clinton |
| 19-Jan-08 | Nevada | Closed Caucus | Clinton |
| 26-Jan-08 | South Carolina | Open Primary | Obama |
| 29-Jan-08 | Florida | Closed Primary | Clinton |
| 5-Feb-08 | Alabama | Open Primary | Obama |
| 5-Feb-08 | Alaska | Closed Caucus | Obama |
| 5-Feb-08 | Arizona | Closed Primary | Clinton |
| 5-Feb-08 | Arkansas | Open Primary | Clinton |
| 5-Feb-08 | California | Semi-Open Primary | Clinton |
| 5-Feb-08 | Colorado | Closed Caucus | Obama |
| 5-Feb-08 | Connecticut | Closed Primary | Obama |
| 5-Feb-08 | Delaware | Closed Primary | Obama |
| 5-Feb-08 | Georgia | Open Primary | Obama |
| 5-Feb-08 | Idaho | Open Caucus | Obama |
| 5-Feb-08 | Illinois | Open Primary | Obama |
| 5-Feb-08 | Kansas | Closed Caucus | Obama |
| 5-Feb-08 | Massachusetts | Semi-Open Primary | Clinton |
| 5-Feb-08 | Minnesota | Open Caucus | Obama |
| 5-Feb-08 | Missouri | Open Primary | Obama |
| 5-Feb-08 | New Jersey | Semi-Open Primary | Clinton |

**Table 2 continued**

| Date of Primary | States | Type of Primary | Democratic Winner |
|---|---|---|---|
| 5-Feb-08 | New Mexico | Closed Primary | Clinton |
| 5-Feb-08 | New York | Closed Primary | Clinton |
| 5-Feb-08 | North Dakota | Open Caucus | Obama |
| 5-Feb-08 | Oklahoma | Closed Primary | Clinton |
| 5-Feb-08 | Tennessee | Open Primary | Clinton |
| 5-Feb-08 | Utah | Semi-Open Primary | Obama |
| 9-Feb-08 | Louisiana | Closed Primary | Obama |
| 9-Feb-08/13-May-08 | Nebraska | Closed Caucus/Primary | Obama/Obama |
| 9-Feb-08/19-Feb-08 | Washington | Open Caucus/Primary | Obama |
| 10-Feb-08 | Maine | Closed Caucus | Obama |
| 12-Feb-08 | District of Columbia | Closed Primary | Obama |
| 12-Feb-08 | Maryland | Closed Primary | Obama |
| 12-Feb-08 | Virginia | Open Primary | Obama |
| 19-Feb-08 | Hawaii | Open Caucus | Obama |
| 19-Feb-08 | Wisconsin | Open Primary | Obama |
| 4-Mar-08 | Ohio | Open Primary | Clinton |
| 4-Mar-08 | Rhode Island | Semi-Open Primary | Clinton |
| 4-Mar-08 | Texas | Open Primary /Caucus | Clinton/Obama |
| 4-Mar-08 | Vermont | Open Primary | Obama |
| 8-Mar-08 | Wyoming | Open Caucus | Obama |
| 11-Mar-08 | Mississippi | Open Primary | Obama |
| 22-Apr-08 | Pennsylvania | Closed Primary | Clinton |
| 6-May-08 | Indiana | Open Primary | Clinton |
| 6-May-08 | North Carolina | Semi-Open Primary | Obama |
| 13-May-08 | West Virginia | Semi-Open Primary | Clinton |
| 20-May-08 | Kentucky | Closed Primary | Clinton |
| 20-May-08 | Oregon | Closed Primary | Obama |
| 3-Jun-08 | Montana | Open Primary | Obama |
| 3-Jun-08 | South Dakota | Closed Primary | Clinton |

Sources:
  http://www.cnn.com/ELECTION/2008/primaries/
  http://www.thegreenpapers.com/P08/events.phtml?s=c
  http://news.aol.com/elections/primary/main/democrats
  http://www.boston.com/news/politics/2008/primaries/

Table 2 continued

| Date of Primary | States | Type of Primary | Republican Winner |
|---|---|---|---|
| 3-Jan-08 | Iowa | Closed Caucus | Huckbee |
| 5-Jan-08 | Wyoming | Closed Caucus | Romney |
| 8-Jan-08 | New Hampshire | Semi-Open Primary | McCain |
| 15-Jan-08 | Michigan | Open Primary | Romney |
| 19-Jan-08 | Nevada | Closed Caucus | Romney |
| 19-Jan-08 | South Carolina | Open Primary | McCain |
| 29-Jan-08 | Florida | Closed Primary | McCain |
| 2-Feb-08 | Maine | Closed Caucus | Romney |
| 5-Feb-08 | Alabama | Open Primary | Huckbee |
| 5-Feb-08 | Alaska | Closed Caucus | Romney |
| 5-Feb-08 | Arizona | Closed Primary | McCain |
| 5-Feb-08 | Arkansas | Open Primary | Huckbee |
| 5-Feb-08 | California | Closed Primary | McCain |
| 5-Feb-08 | Colorado | Closed Caucus | Romney |
| 5-Feb-08 | Connecticut | Closed Primary | McCain |
| 5-Feb-08 | Delaware | Closed Primary | McCain |
| 5-Feb-08 | Georgia | Open Primary | Huckbee |
| 5-Feb-08 | Illinois | Open Primary | McCain |
| 5-Feb-08 | Massachusetts | Semi-Open Primary | Romney |
| 5-Feb-08 | Minnesota | Open Caucus | Romney |
| 5-Feb-08 | Missouri | Open Primary | McCain |
| 5-Feb-08 | Montana | Closed Caucus | Romney |
| 5-Feb-08 | New Jersey | Semi-Open Primary | McCain |
| 5-Feb-08 | New York | Closed Primary | McCain |
| 5-Feb-08 | North Dakota | Open Caucus | Romney |
| 5-Feb-08 | Oklahoma | Closed Primary | McCain |
| 5-Feb-08 | Tennessee | Open Primary | Huckbee |
| 5-Feb-08 | Utah | Closed Primary | Romney |
| 5-Feb-08 | West Virginia* | Closed Caucus | Huckbee |
| 9-Feb-08 | Kansas | Closed Caucus | Huckbee |
| 9-Feb-08 | Louisiana | Closed Primary | Huckbee |
| 9-Feb-08/19-Feb-08 | Washington | Open Caucus/Primary | McCain |
| 12-Feb-08 | District of Columbia | Closed Primary | McCain |
| 12-Feb-08 | Maryland | Closed Primary | McCain |
| 12-Feb-08 | Virginia | Open Primary | McCain |
| 18-May-08 | Hawaii | Convention | McCain |
| 19-Feb-08 | Wisconsin | Open Primary | McCain |
| 4-Mar-08 | Ohio | Open Primary | McCain |

**Table 2 continued**

| Date of Primary | States | Type of Primary | Republican Winner |
|---|---|---|---|
| 4-Mar-08 | Rhode Island | Semi-Open Primary | McCain |
| 4-Mar-08 | Texas | Open Primary | McCain |
| 4-Mar-08 | Vermont | Open Primary | McCain |
| 11-Mar-08 | Mississippi | Open Primary | McCain |
| 22-Apr-08 | Pennsylvania | Closed Primary | McCain |
| 6-May-08 | Indiana | Open Primary | McCain |
| 6-May-08 | North Carolina | Semi-Open Primary | McCain |
| 13-May-08 | Nebraska | Primary | McCain |
| 13-May-08 | West Virginia* | Closed Primary | McCain |
| 20-May-08 | Kentucky | Closed Primary | McCain |
| 20-May-08 | Oregon | Closed Primary | McCain |
| 27-May-08 | Idaho | Open Primary | McCain |
| 3-Jun-08 | New Mexico | Closed Primary | McCain |
| 3-Jun-08 | South Dakota | Closed Primary | McCain |

Note: *West Virginia had both a closed primary and a closed caucus; 18 delegates are tied to February 5 state convention; 9 are tied to May 13 primary; 3 unpledged RNC member delegates for a total of 30 delegates.

Sources:
http://www.cnn.com/ELECTION/2008/primaries/
http://www.thegreenpapers.com/P08/events.phtml?s=c
http://news.aol.com/elections/primary/main/republicans
http://www.boston.com/news/politics/2008/primaries/
http://www.cnn.com/ELECTION/2008/primaries/results/state/#WV

# NOTES

[1]For an interesting analysis of who watches such programs and why, see Steven Reiss and James Wiltz, "Why People Watch Reality TV," *Media Psychology*, 6 (2004), pp. 363–378.

[2]Statistic from Nielsen Media Research cited by Kelley Tiffany, "Reality Show Participants: Employees or Independent Contractors?" *Employee Relations Law Journal*, 32 (Summer 2006), pp. 15–38.

[3]Kelley Tiffany, "Reality Show Participants: Employees or Independent Contractors?" *Employee Relations Law Journal*, June 22, 2006.

[4]Tiffany, "Reality Show Participants."

[5]Op.cit.

[6]Tina Chadha, Darby Desmond, Diameshia Hill, Ashley Jones, and Courtney Shepard, "Teaching Genre Through Reality Television," at http://mediateacher.squarespace.com/tv-teaching-guides/ n.d.

[7]"Amazing Race of '08 Arrives at Finish Line," *USA Today*, op-ed, November 4, 2008.

[8]Huma Zaidi, "First Presidential Primary Debate In April," *MSNBC*, January 8, 2007.

[9]Joel Achenbach, "A December Primary in New Hampshire? It's His Call," *Washington Post*, October 12, 2007.

[10]Bonne Erbe, "Racism in the Presidential Race," *U.S. News & World Report*, May 14, 2008. Weisberg, Jacob, "If Obama Loses: Racism Is the Only Reason McCain Might Beat Him." *Slate*, August 23, 2008. CBS News, "CBS Poll: Gender Matters More Than Race," March 19, 2008. Andrew Kohut, "In November, Will Age Matter?" Pew Research Center, February 25, 2008 *Business Wire*. "Ageism May be a Bigger Barrier in Presidential Election than Racism (or Sexism)," *MarketWatch*, September 24, 2008.

[11]CNN Exit Polls: percent college graduates in 2000—42 percent, in 2004—42 percent, and in 2008—44 percent.

[12]Jeffrey M. Jones, "Hillary Clinton, Giuliani Early Favorites for 2008," *Gallup News Service*, November 16, 2004;. Fred Barnes, "The Two-Man Race: Only Rudy and Mitt have credible scenarios," *The Weekly Standard*, November 5, 2007. Pew Research Center, "Poll: Hillary Clinton Seen As Leader Of Democratic Party; Bush A Drag On Republican MidTerm Prospects," February 13, 2008.

[13]The Pew Research Center for the People & the Press, "Likely Rise in Voter Turnout Bodes Well for Democrats," July 10, 2008.

[14]CNN.com, "If allowed, Florida, Michigan could tip nomination," at http://www.cnn.com/2008/POLITICS/03/06/dems.delegates/index.html March 6, 2008.

[15]RealClearPolitics, "Florida Democratic Primary," January 29, 2008.

[16]Much has been made about this being a Republican tactic. But Democratic and Republican legislators alike voted to move the primary date forward and several Democratic leaders made public statements about the importance of Florida going earlier in the process. That said, the calendar change was part of a larger election reform bill which included getting rid of touch screen voting machines—a very high priority for Democratic legislators. See "Governor Crist Signs Legislation Creating Paper Trail for Florida Votes," http://www.flgov.com/release/9011.

[17]Todd Beeton, "The Benefits Of The Extended Primary," *MyDirectDemocracy*, November 23, 2008.

[18]McCain needed the free media coverage, especially in light of his difficulties in raising money vis-à-vis the Democrats and his acceptance of public financing.

[19]Susan Davis, "Obama's Caucus-State Magic," *The Wall Street Journal*, February 6, 2008.

[20]CBSnews.com, "Poll: Obama Leads; Interest In Debate High," September 25, 2008.

[21]CNN Exit Poll for Ohio (D)—73 percent of respondents answered yes to: "Were Debates Important to Your Vote?"

[22]Mark Halperin: 10 Things That Never Happened in a Campaign Before," *Time*, November 5, 2008.

[23]http://democratic-candidates.org/index-dem-convention.php/ accessed December 4, 2008.

[24]Jeffrey M. Jones, "Democrats Divided Over How Superdelegates Should Vote," Gallup, March 11, 2008. "Do superdelegates vote the same as their constituents?" February 7, 2008 at http://www.demconwatchblog.com/2008/02/do-superdelegates-vote-same-as-their.html

[25]PBS.org, "Social Websites Emerge as Way to Generate Supporters, Funds," July 17, 2007. Aaron Smith and Lee Rainie, "The Internet and the 2008 election," Pew Internet and American Life Project, June 15, 2008. Linnie Rawlinson. CNN.com, "Will the 2008 USA election be won on Facebook?" accessed December 4, 2008. Matthew Fraser and Dutta Soumitra, "Barack Obama and the Facebook Election," *U.S. News & World Report*, November 19, 2008.

[26]Matthew Felling, "Democrats Dismiss FOX News Debate," *CBS News*, May 31, 2007.

[27]Austin Modine, "Republican CNN/YouTube Debate is Back on," *The Register*, August 14, 2007.

[28]Pew Research Center, "Most Voters Say News Media Wants Obama to Win," October 22, 2008.

[29]Alexander Burns, "Halperin at Politico/USF Conf.: 'Extreme Pro-Obama Press Bias,'" *Politico*, November 23, 2008.

[30]CBSnews.com, "CBS Poll: Gender Matters More Than Race," March 19, 2008. Alternet.org, "Pitting Race Against Gender in Election '08," January 12, 2008.

[31]Camille Paglia, "Obama Surfs Through," Salon.com, November 12, 2008.

[32]Karen Tumulty, "The Conventions: Why Bother?" www.time-blog/swampland/2008/08/the_conventions_why_bother.html, August 17, 2008.

[33]Andrew Malcolm, "Geez, Did We All Watch Those Conventions! McCain, Palin, Obama, and the Delaware Guy," latimesblogs.latimes.com/Washington/2008/09/rnc-dnc-tv.html, accessed September 20, 2008.

[34]Jim Rutenberg and Brian Stelter, "Conventions, Anything But Dull, Are a TV Hit," *New York Times*, September 6, 2008.

[35]Billy House, "Democrats Aim For United Front at Convention," *Tampa Tribune*, August 24, 2008.

[36]Gerald F. Seib and Bob Davis, "Anxiety Over the Economy Tops Obama's Agenda," *Wall Street Journal*, August 30, 2008.

[37]Susan Page and Andrew Seaman, "Clinton ends '08 campaign, endorses Obama," *USA Today*, June 7, 2008. Huffington Post, "Bill Clinton To Campaign With Obama For First Time," October 25, 2008. Frank Newport, "If McCain vs. Obama, 28% of Clinton Backers Go for McCain," *Gallup*, March 26, 2008.

[38]Caroline Kennedy, "A President Like My Father," *New York Times*, January 27, 2008.. Shailagh Murray, "Caroline Kennedy Endorses Obama," *Washington Post*, January 26, 2008.

[39]David Lightman, "Convention Tribute a Last Hurrah for Kennedy Generation," McClatchy Washington Bureau, August 23, 2008.

[40]Doug G. Ware, "JFK's Speechwriter Now Putting Words Into Obama Campaign," *Four Points Media Group LLC*, February 9, 2008. Susan D. James, "Passing the Torch: Kennedy's Touch on Obama's Words," ABC News, February 8, 2008. Reese Schonfeld, "Advice to Barack Obama: Be Modest in All Things," Huffington Post, November 11, 2008.

[41]Carrie Dann, "Bill and Ted's Excellent Adventures," MSNBC, February 1, 2008. RaymondPronk.WordPress.org "The Kennedy Clinton Democratic Party Civil War Over Obama–Happy Days Are Here Again!" January 30, 2008.

[42]Adam Nagourney and Jeff Zeleny, "Obama Chooses Biden as Running Mate," *New York Times*, August 24, 2008.

[43]The text message read: "Barack has chosen Senator Joe Biden to be our VP nominee. Watch the first Obama-Biden rally live at 3pm ET on www.BarackObama.com. Spread the word!"

[44]Roger Simon, "Is There a McCain Enthusiasm Gap?" *Politico*, September 1, 2008.

[45]Michael Cooper and Elisabeth Bumiller, "Alaskan Is McCain's Choice; First Woman on G.O.P. Ticket," *New York Times*, August 30, 2008.

[46]David Espo, "Republican National Convention Opens: Cindy McCain, Laura Bush, Governors Focus On Gustav," Huffington Post, September 1, 2008.

[47]Lionel Shriver, "Why Americans Love Laura Bush," Telepraph.co.uk, November 16, 2008.

[48]The candidates appeared together on stage with Pastor Warren at the conclusion of the two-hour program.

[49]A joint study conducted by the Pew Research Center's Project or Excellence in Journalism and the Pew Forum on Religion & Public Life found that the August 16 Saddleback Civil Forum on the Presidency accounted for fully 11 percent of all religion-related election coverage. Catholic News Agency, "Pew Study Finds Election Coverage of Religion was Shallow," catholicnewsagency.com, accessed December 2, 2008.

[50]Idol Chatter Religion and Pop Culture Blog, "Election P.S.: Don't Quit Campaigning," November 7, 2008.

[51]Nielsen Wire, "56.5 Million Watched McCain And Obama's Final Debate," October 16, 2008.

[52]Nielsen Wire, "Highest Rated Presidential Debates: 1960 To Present," October 6, 2008.

[53]Steve Gorman, "Palin-Biden Debate Sets TV Ratings Record," Reuters, October 3, 2008.

[54]Zeleny, Jeff, "Richardson Endorses Obama," *New York Times*, March 21, 2008.

[55]"The Obama Administration: The Buzz is With Hillary," www.domain-b.com/economy/Govt/20081115_obama.html, November 15, 2008.

[56]Susan Davis, "Clinton Aide Says Richardson's Endorsement Is Insignificant," *Wall Street Journal*, March 21, 2008.

[57]Erica Werner and Ben Evans, "Black Caucus Says No Special Relationship to Obama," Associated Press, November 20, 2008.

[58]Bob Kemper, "Lewis Says He's Supporting Obama," *Atlanta Journal Constitution*, February 27, 2008.

[59]FOXNews.com, "Michelle Obama takes Heat for Saying She's 'Proud of My Country for the First Time,'" Feburary 19, 2008. Robin Abcarian, "Michelle Obama in Spotlight's Glare," *Los Angeles Times*, February 21, 2008.

[60]Mosheh Oinounou, "Spousal Spat: Cindy McCain Responds to Michelle Obama 'Proud' Comments," embeds.blogs.foxnews.com/2008/02/19/cindy-mccain-responds-to-michelle-obama-proud-comments," February 19, 2008.

[61]Kate Snow, "Bill Clinton Has Regrets on Campaign for Wife," ABC News, August 4, 2008. "Bubba: Obama Is Just Like Jesse Jackson," blogs.abcnews.com/politicalpunch2008/01/bubba-obama-is.html, January 26, 2008.

[62]S.A. Miller, "Candidates Attack Political Associations," *Washington Times*, October 31, 2008.

[63]Charles Babington, "Old Events Fuel New Presidential Campaign Attacks," Associated Press, October 6, 2008.

[64]Jill Lawrence, "Obama's Link to '60s Radical Fuels New Attacks," USA *Today*, October 5, 2008. Scott Shane, "Obama and '60s Bomber: A Look Into Crossed Paths," *New York Times*, October 4, 2008. Elisabeth Bumiller and Patrick Healy, "McCain Joins Attacks on Obama Over Radical," *New York Times*, October 10, 2008.

[65]Matthew Dallek, "'60s Radical? Today's Voters Don't Care," *Politico*, October 27, 2008.

[66]Matthew Mosk and David S. Hilzenrath, "Lobbyists Hired by Freddie Mac to Work on McCain Is Now Senator's Aide," *Washington Post*, October 3, 2008.

[67]Mike Allen, "Exclusive: Obama to Hit McCain on Keating Five," *Politico*, October 6, 2008.

[68]S.A. Miller, "Candidates Attack Political Associations," *Washington Times*, October 31, 2008; Laura Meckler, "'Attack by Association' Viewed as Fair Game by McCain Camp," Wall Street Journal blog, September 19, 2008.

[69]William Katz, "Tina Fey, Kingmaker," Power Line Blog, www.powerlineblog.com, December 1, 2008.

[70]Ibid.

[71]Dan Balz and Robert Barnes, "Economy Becomes New Proving Ground For McCain, Obama," *Washington Post*, September 16, 2008.

[72]Lydia Saad, "Obama Wins on the Economy, McCain on Terrorism," Gallup Poll, October 14, 2008. Also see Laura Meckler and Christopher Cooper, "McCain Tries to Shift Focus to Security," *Wall Street Journal*, October 30, 2008.

[73]Chris Cillizza, "5 Myths About an Election of Mythic Proportions," *Washington Post*, November 16, 2008.

[74]Dan Gilgoff, "Beliefnet Poll: Evangelicals Still Conservative, But Defy Issue Stereotypes," at beliefnet.com, n.d.

[75]Bernie Becker, "Political Polling Sites Are in a Race of Their Own," *New York Times*, October 28, 2008.

[76]Karl Rove, "Don't Let the Polls Affect Your Vote," *Wall Street Journal*, October 30, 2008.

[77]Mark Blumenthal, "Blumenthal: Is Youth Being Served in Polls," *National Journal*, October 1, 2008.

Andrew Malcolm, "Pew Poll: Voter interest high, but media tougher on GOP, especially Sarah Palin," *Los Angeles Times*, accessed December 4, 2008.

Gallup, "How Do Gallup's Likely Voter Models Work?" www.gallup.com/poll/111268, accessed December 4, 2008. Also see RealClearPolitics, "On Gallup's Two Likely Voter Models," October 13, 2008.

[78]Costas Panagopoulos, "Poll Accuracy in the 2008 Presidential Election," Initial report, November 5, 2008. Department of Political Science, Fordham University, cpanagopoulo@fordham.edu.

[79]Bonnie Erbe, "Obama's Public Finance Flip-Flop," *U.S. News and World Report*, December 4, 2008.

[80]Adam Nagourney and Jeff Zeleny, "Obama Forgoes Public Funds in First for Major Candidate," *New York Times*, June 20, 2008.

[81]Tahman Bradley, "Final Fundraising Figure: Obama's $750M," ABC News.com, December 5, 2008.

[82]Blake Dvorak, "527 Groups Spent Less," realclearpolitics.blogs.time.com/2008/11/04.

[83]Matthew Mosk, "Economic Downturn Sidelines Donors to '527' Groups," *Washington Post*, October 19, 2008.

[84]Ibid.

[85]Caitrona Palmer, "The First YouTube Election," Independent.it,

[86]Kate Kaye, "Web Ads Mattered More Than Ever in '08 Election," www.clickz.com, November 4, 2008.

[87]Ibid.

[88]Kate Kaye, "McCain and Obama Used Web to Persuade in Final Weeks," www.clicz.com, December 1, 2008.

[89]Mark Silva, "Campaign Ads Going Negative," *Chicago Tribune*, October 10, 2008. Eli Saslow, "Mailed Ads Have Become Mostly Negative, Experts Say," *Washington Post*, October 26, 2008.

[90]Dennis Chaptman, "Wisconsin Advertising Project Analyzes Tone of Ads in White House Race," Wisconsin Advertising Project at the University of Wisconsin-Madison, October 16, 2008.

[91]Monica Langley and Elizabeth Holmes, "McCain Campaign is at Odds Over Negative Attacks' Scope," *Wall Street Journal*, October 10, 2008.

[92]David Winston, "A Modern Agenda Would Lead the GOP Out of the Wilderness," *Roll Call*, December 1, 2008.

[93]Rhodes Cook, "Obama's New Look At The Map," Larry J. Sabato's Crystal Ball '08, September 11, 2008.

[94]"Face Time Turned Red States Blue," *National Journal*, November 12, 2008.

[95]Adam Nagourney of the New York Times quoted by Rick Klein, ABC News, *The Note: Red (State) November*, November 2, 2008.

[96]Charlie Cook, "Learn or Languish," *National Journal*, November 15, 2008.

[97]Andrew Rasiej and Micah L. Sifry, "With New Media, Obama Camp Takes Stage," *Politico*, September 10, 2008.

[98]Linnie Rawlinson, "Will the 2008 USA Election Be Won on Facebook?" CNN.com/2007/TECH/05/01/election.facebook/index.html.

[99]Alexander Burns, "McCain Camp Lacked in High-Tech," *Politico*, November 22, 2008.

[100]Mary Gilbert, "Campaigns Work to Turn 'Friends' Into Voters," *National Journal*, October 22, 2008.

[101]John McCormick, "Obama Mobilizes Rapid Response on the Web," *Chicago Tribune*, September 17, 2008.

[102]Frank Greve, "Obama Will Use YouTube to Reach Out Directly to Voters," McClatchy Newspapers, November 14, 2008.

[103]Ben Smith, "Big Crowds For Obama's 'Red-State Tour,'" *Politico*, October 27, 2008.

[104]Alexander Burns, "McCain Camp Lacked in High-Tech," *Politico*, November 22, 2008.

[105]Jack Chang, "Economy, Anti-Immigrant Rhetoric Drove Latinos to Obama," McClatchy Newspapers, November 7, 2008.

[106]Ibid.

[107]Sam Youngman, "Post-Mortem by Hispanic Conservatives," The Hill.com, November 17, 2008. David Saltonstall, "Latinos Helped Elect Barack Obama and Hope He Won't Forget Them," *New York Daily News*, November 15, 2008. Mark Hugo Lopez, "How Hispanics Voted in the 2008 Election," Pew Research Center, November 5, 2008.

[108]David Paul Kuhn, "Prejudice Among Dems May Cost Obama," *Politico*, September 20, 2008.

[109]Frank Newport, "Obama's race May Be as Much a Plus as a Minus," Gallup.com, October 9, 2008.

[110]David Remnick, "The Joshua Generation: Race and the Campaign of Barack Obama," *The New Yorker*, November 17, 2008.

[111]William Schneider, "Reality Check," *National Journal*, November 15, 2008. Also see Alan Fram, "No Hidden White Bias Seen in Presidential Race," Associated Press, November 7, 2008. Peter Wallsten, "White Americans Play Major Role in Electing The First Black President," *Los Angeles Times*, November 5, 2008. John Harwood, "Level of White Support for Obama a Surprise," *New York Times*, November 3, 2008. Adam Nagourney, "Obama Elected President as Racial Barrier Falls," *New York Times*, November 5, 2008.

[112]Wally Edge, "Nader, Barr Could Play Spoiler Role in NV," Politickernv.com, August 27, 2008.

[113]Bill Greener, "Why Obama Has to Stay Above 50 Percent," salon.com, October 27, 2008.

[114]Nathan Thornburgh, "Could Third-Party Candidates Be Spoilers?" *Time*, time.com, November 3, 2008.

[115]Maria Recio, "No Spoiler Role for Third-Party Candidates in 08." McClatchy Newspapers, November 4, 2008.

[116]Flynn, Daniel J., "Obama: The Oak Grown From Acorn," cityjournal.org, October 16, 2008.

[117]MacIntosh, Jeane, *New York Post*, October 10, 2008.

[118]"Is ACORN Stealing the Election?" *Investor's Business Daily* Editorial, October 8, 2008.

[119]Michael Scherer, "1. The Database Dilemma," Time.com, October 23, 2008.

[120]Amy Merrick, "Registration Discrepancies Complicate Ohio Vote," *Wall Street Journal*, October 17, 2008.

[121]Matthew Murray, "Experts, Lawyers Prepare for Election Day Woes," *Roll Call*, October 21, 2008.

[122]Andrew Zajac, and John Crewdson, "Few Voting Problems Seen Amid Big Turnout," *Chicago Tribune*, November 5, 2008. Also see Pauline Vu, "Election Day Mostly Smooth," stateline.org, November 6, 2008.

[123]Alan Fram, "AP Poll: Few Obama, McCain Backers Were Unwavering," Associated Press, November 26, 2008.